PEACE
FOR OUR
TIME

Also available from Brassey's

Baynes
SOLDIERS OF SCOTLAND

Danchev
VERY SPECIAL RELATIONSHIP

Hartcup
THE WAR OF INVENTION: Scientific Developments 1914–18

James
IMPERIAL REARGUARD: Wars of Empire 1919–85

Laffin
WAR ANNUAL 3: A Guide to Contemporary Wars and Conflicts

Laffin
BRASSEY'S BATTLES

Levchenko
ON THE WRONG SIDE: My Life in the KGB

Liddle
GALLIPOLI 1915

Messenger
HITLER'S GLADIATOR: The Life and Times of
SS-Oberstgruppenführer and General der Waffen-SS Sepp Dietrich

Perkins
A FORTUNATE SOLDIER

Chronology

1917	7 November	Bolshevik Revolution in Petrograd and then in Moscow
	2 December	Germano-Russian Armistice
1918	11 November	Armistice on the Western Front. Formation of Workers Councils in Germany
1919	January	Spartakist Revolution crushed in Berlin
	March	Communist victory in Hungary (lasting only four months)
	27 March	Creation of the IIIrd International in Moscow
	28 June	Signing of the Treaty of Versailles
	19 November	The United States Senate refuses to ratify the Treaty
1920	7 September	Franco-Belgian Military Pact
	29 December	Creation of the French Communist Party
1921	April–May	London Conference on German war reparations. Ultimatum
1922	14 January	Poincaré's Ministry begins
	4 April	Stalin becomes Secretary General of the Russian Communist Party
	16 April	Germano-Russian Treaty of Rapallo
	29 October	Mussolini takes power in Italy
1923	11 January	Franco-Belgian troops enter the Ruhr. Passive German resistance
	12 August	Gustav Stresemann becomes Chancellor of Germany
	October	Separatist movement in the Rhineland
	December	Liquidation of the proletarian governments in Germany
1924	1 June	Poincaré replaced by Herriot after the electoral success of the 'Cartel of the Left'
	16 August	The Dawes Plan softens the reparations imposed upon Germany
	1 October	'Geneva Protocol' defines the mechanism of collective security as enshrined in the League of Nations
1925	March	'Geneva Protocol' rejected by the British Government
	17 April	Briand again becomes French Foreign Minister
	August	A plan for the evacuation of the Ruhr is formulated
	16 October	Locarno Treaty between Great Britain, France, Italy, Belgium and Germany
1926	10 September	Germany is admitted to the League of Nations
	17 September	Meeting between Briand and Stresemann at Thoiry
	December	Crushing of the 'Canton Commune' in China

1927	March	Chiang-Kai-shek liquidates the Communists in Shanghai
1928	27 August	Signature of the Briand–Kellog Pact renouncing war as means of international policy
1929	7 June	The Young Plan once again softens the reparations to be paid by Germany
	30 August	Decision to evacuate the Rhineland
	5 September	Briand proposes a European Union in a famous speech
	3 October	Death of Stresemann
	24 October	Wall Street Crash
1930	30 June	End of evacuation of the Rhineland by the troops of the Allies
1931	17 April	Proclamation of the Spanish Republic
	20 June	President Hoover proposes a moratorium of all inter-governmental debts
	9 July	Lausanne Conference. End of German reparations
	24 August	National Government is established in London under Mac-Donald
	17 September	Japan invades Manchuria. Great Britain abandons the Gold Standard
	11 December	The Statute of Westminster replaces the British Empire with a Commonwealth
1932	2 February	Opening of the World Disarmament Conference
	7 May	Death of Briand
	July–August	Ottawa Conference marks the end of British free exchange. Imperial preference
	24 August	Japan proclaims the new State of Manchoukouo
	7 November	Franklin Roosevelt is elected President of the United States
	20 November	Franco-Soviet Non-Aggression Pact
1933	30 January	Hitler becomes Chancellor of Germany
	24 February	Japanese aggression against China is the subject of inter-national moral condemnation
	27 March	Japan leaves the League of Nations
	June–July	International economic and monetary conference in London
	7 June	Signing of Quadripartite Pact (France, Great Britain, Italy and Germany)
	14 October	Germany quits the League of Nations and the World Dis-armament Conference
1934	6 February	Rioting in Paris
	17 April	France breaks with the World Disarmament Conference
	30 June	'Night of the Long Knives' in Germany
	25 July	Assassination of Dolfuss and the Nazi *'coup de force'* in Austria
	18 September	The Soviet Union admitted to the League of Nations
	16 October	Assassination in Marseilles of King Alexander of Yugos-lavia and M. Barthou
	1 December	Assassination of Kirov in Leningrad. The start of the Terror in the Soviet Union
1935	7 January	Laval and Mussolini's secret agreement in Rome
	27 January	The League of Nations decides to return the Saar to Ger-many
	16 March	Re-establishment of conscription in Germany
	27 March	Paul van Zeeland becomes Prime Minister of Belgium. Belgium leaves the Gold Standard

	11 April	Meeting at Stresa between France, Great Britain and Italy
	2 May	Franco-Soviet Mutual Assistance Pact
	7 June	Stanley Baldwin succeeds Ramsay MacDonald
	28 June	Results of the Peace Ballot announced
	3 October	Italy invades Ethiopia
	7 October	The Council of the League of Nations declares that Italy is in breach of the Pact by going to war.
	7 December	Laval-Hoare Plan
	28 December	Mussolini revokes the Rome and Stresa Agreements
1936	29 February	America passes neutrality laws
	6 March	Franco-Belgian exchange of letters about their military pact of 1920 in the light of the Locarno Treaty
	7 March	Re-occupation of the Rhineland and German revocation of the Locarno Treaty
	3 May	The *Front Populaire* in France. Leon Blum becomes President of the Council
	17 July	Start of the Spanish Civil War
	14 October	Speech by King Leopold III of Belgium declaring a policy of 'independence' (neutrality)
	25 November	Anti-Comintern Pact signed between Germany and Japan
1937	24 April	Belgium freed of her obligations under the Locarno Treaty by Britain and France
	18 May	Neville Chamberlain becomes Prime Minister of Great Britain
	16 June	Execution of Marshal Tukhachevsky in the Soviet Union. The 'purges' reach their zenith
	21 June	Fall of Leon Blum; replaced by Chautemps
	7 July	Incident on the Marco Polo Bridge. Start of the Sino-Japanese war
	13 October	Berlin declares its respect for Belgian neutrality
	5 November	Hitler announces secretly to his staff that he has decided to go to war
	6 November	Italy, adhering to the Anti-Comintern Pact, abandons Austria to her fate
	19 November	Meeting between Halifax and Hitler at Berchtesgaden
	3 December	Italy leaves the League of Nations
1938	12 February	Meeting between Schuschnigg and Hitler at Berchtesgaden
	27 February	Halifax succeeds Eden as Foreign Secretary. Chamberlain tells the House of Commons that the small countries can no longer count upon the League of Nations
	13 March	Germany occupies Austria
	18 March	The British Cabinet discusses the problem of Czechoslovakia and decides to leave it to negotiation
	8 April	Edouard Daladier becomes President of the Council with Georges Bounet as Foreign Minister
	24 April	The Czechoslovakian crisis is heightened by a speech at Karlsbad by Henlein, leader of the *Sudeten Deutsche Partei*
	28–29 April	Visit to London of Daladier and Bonnet
	21 May	High international tension. Mobilisation is ordered in Prague. London tells Paris that Great Britain will not be on the side of France if she intervenes
	12 September	Violent speech by Hitler at Nuremberg
	15 September	Chamberlain meets Hitler at Berchtesgaden and promises

		him the Sudeten lands. On the same day, Henlein pronounces their annexation by the Reich
	21 September	Franco-British ultimatum to Prague
	22 September	Chamberlain returns to Germany. Meeting with Hitler at Bad Godesberg
	29 September	Conference in Munich between Germany, Italy, France and Great Britain to discuss the dismemberment of Czechoslovakia without the Czechs being consulted. When faced with the ultimatum, they later capitulated
	30 September	Chamberlain signs an agreement of friendship and cooperation with Hitler
	9 November	*Krystalnacht*. Anti-semitic pogroms throughout Germany
	6 December	Ribbentrop goes to Paris to sign a treaty of friendship
1939	10 January	Chamberlain and Halifax in Rome
	15 March	German troops enter Prague and the Bohemian Protectorate is declared
	21 March	Ribbentrop demands the annexation of Dantzig
	23 March	Annexation of Memel by Germany
	28 March	End of the Spanish Civil War. Spain declares her adherence to the Anti-Comintern Pact
	31 March	London, quickly followed by Paris, guarantees the independence of Poland. Overtures made to the Soviet Union for negotiations
	7 April	Italy invades Albania
	28 April	Hitler renounces the German-Polish Treaty of 1934, claiming Dantzig and 'the Polish Corridor'
	3 May	Molotov succeeds Litvinov as Foreign Minister of the USSR
	12 May	Franco-Anglo-Soviet military negotiations
	23 August	Ribbentrop in Moscow. Signature of the Germano-Soviet Non-Aggression Pact and the secret protocol on the partitioning of Eastern Europe
	August	Final overtures to 'appease' Germany and to resolve the Polish crisis
	1 September	The Wehrmacht invades Poland
	3 September	Great Britain and France declare war on Germany

Neville Chamberlain with the 'No War' Pact at Heston Airport, 30 September 1938 (Associated Press).

PEACE
FOR OUR
TIME

Robert Rothschild

Translated from the French by
ANTHONY RHODES

BRASSEY'S DEFENCE PUBLISHERS
(A member of the Maxwell Pergamon Publishing Corporation plc)

LONDON ● OXFORD ● WASHINGTON ● NEW YORK ● BEIJING
FRANKFURT ● SÃO PAULO ● SYDNEY ● TOKYO ● TORONTO

U.K. (Editorial)	Brassey's Defence Publishers Ltd., 24 Gray's Inn Road, London WC1X 8HR
(Orders)	Brassey's Defence Publishers Ltd., Headington Hill Hall, Oxford, OX3 0BW, England
U.S.A. (Editorial)	Pergamon-Brassey's International Defense Publishers, Inc., 8000 Westpark Drive, Fourth Floor, McLean, Virginia 22102, U.S.A.
(Orders)	Pergamon Press, Inc., Maxwell House, Fairview Park, Elmsford, New York 10523, U.S.A.
PEOPLE'S REPUBLIC OF CHINA	Pergamon Press, Room 4037, Qianmen Hotel, Beijing, People's Republic of China
FEDERAL REPUBLIC OF GERMANY	Pergamon Press GmbH, Hammerweg 6, D-6242 Kronberg, Federal Republic of Germany
BRAZIL	Pergamon Editora Ltda, Rua Eça de Queiros, 346. CEP 04011, Paraiso, São Paulo, Brazil
AUSTRALIA	Pergamon-Brassey's Defence Publishers Pty Ltd., P.O. Box 544, Potts Point, N.S.W. 2011, Australia
JAPAN	Pergamon Press, 5th Floor, Matsuoka Central Building, 1-7-1 Nishishinjuku, Shinjuku-ku, Tokyo 160, Japan
CANADA	Pergamon Press Canada Ltd., Suite No. 271, 253 College Street, Toronto, Ontario, Canada M5T 1R5

First edition 1988

Library of Congress Cataloging in Publication Data
Rothschild, Robert.
Peace for our time/Robert Rothschild.
p. cm.
1. World politics—1919-1932. 2. World politics—1933-1945. 3. World War, 1914-1918 — Influence.
4. World War. 1939-1945—Causes. 5. Peace. I. Title.
D723.R67 1988. 909.82—dc19   88-14622

British Library Cataloguing in Publication Data
Rothschild, Robert
Peace for our time.
1. Europe. Political events, 1918-1938
I. Title
940.5'1

ISBN 0-08-036264-8

Printed in Great Britain by A. Wheaton & Co. Ltd., Exeter

I have set before thee this day
life and good and death and evil . . .
blessing and cursing; therefore chose
life that both thou and thy seed may
live

Deuteronomy Chapter 30: from
Verses 15 and 19

Contents

PREFACE ix

ACKNOWLEDGEMENTS xi

CHRONOLOGY xiii

1. The War in China and the Great Depression 1
2. Totalitarian Bewilderment 26
3. The Great Fear of the Decent People 46
4. Hitler's First Successes 58
5. Roosevelt and the New Deal 71
6. The Brief Halt at Stresa 83
7. The Ethiopian War 100
8. The Bankruptcy of the League of Nations 117
9. Berlin and Moscow 141
10. The Popular Fronts 154
11. Belgium Returns to Neutrality 170
12. The End of Austria 190
13. Two Hapless Men: Daladier and Chamberlain 217
14. Munich 235
15. Peace with Honour, Peace for Our Time 270
16. Mane, Thecel, Phares 287
17. The Jaws of Darkness 307

SOURCES 343

INDEX 361

Preface

'Peace for our time, peace with honour'—so ran the promise of the British Prime Minister, Neville Chamberlain, after the disastrous Munich Agreement in the autumn of 1938. Choosing between the humanist tradition, which appeared to have triumphed in 1919, and the martial ethics of the Machiavellis and Hegels—basis of the 'Nation State'—a number of European governments seem to have preferred the latter option. Others, alarmed by the changes in society brought about by the Great War, had lost the will to defend the best part of their civilization. For it is not true that it is through ignorance that the democracies had become entangled in Hitler's nets. They had known, but they had refused to believe. With the 'Unnecessary War', as Churchill put it, Europe ceased to be what she had been for four hundred years—the heir presumptive of Rome and the centre of the world. After 1945, a remarkable reversion gave her forty years of unprecedented peace, prosperity and liberty, and the prospect of renewed greatness. But today, she appears to be again losing her sense of unity and the confidence which goes with it.

Can the recollection of those sombre years protect us from the return of the evil geniuses of the past? It is in this hope that I have depicted inter-European relations at a time of excessive nationalism. Limiting myself to the watershed of events, I have not tried to rival the scholars who have explored the rich archives available to historians. Their patient efforts have uncovered the facts and changes of fortune which led to the Second World War. I doubt if it is possible to do better.

On the other hand, the whole truth is not confined to the archives. Some of them are deliberately misleading, sometimes with future historians in mind. Diplomatic notes, memoranda, reports of meetings seldom provide the explanation of enigmas bound up with the mixed thoughts and secret passions of statesmen, contradictory and sometimes unconscious; yet it is their personalities above all which, I believe, have determined events. It is equally difficult to find in the official documents the emotional climate of the time, so different from the one in which we live today that any narrative which does not take this into account would offer a false portrait of events.

Michelet saw in history—to quote his memorable expression—'A resurrection of life'. For Carlyle, history was 'the biography of great men'. I have attempted to follow these tenets without neglecting obvious connections between social conditions and diplomatic activities. I hope, too, to produce a 'European' image; for too many books have been inspired by the author's own country. I have frequently made use of personal memoirs, and those of many Frenchmen, Englishmen, Germans, Italians, Americans and Belgians, from all social strata, who have lived through these events, and with whom I have spent many hours recalling them. As far as possible, I have supported these recollections with written evidence. Sometimes I have added to facts as they were known at the time, information published later; but only in order to illustrate what was available to everyone, or at least to the newspaper reader. Even the Nazi dictatorship, for all its harshness and cruelty, was a more or less open society. Very little remained secret for long.

Robert Rothschild

London, 1988

Acknowledgements

My thanks are due first and foremost to all those, in several European countries, who so kindly agreed to spend many hours reminiscing about the Thirties. They are too numerous for me to list them all. I am also most grateful to those who read my manuscripts in draft and suggested numerous useful alterations or additions, particularly M. André de Staercke, formerly the Belgian Ambassador to NATO, Lieutenant General Sir Napier Crookenden, and Mrs Inga Haag of Germany.

I am specially indebted to Mr Anthony Rhodes for the English version of the original French text and to Brigadier Bryan Watkins who has devoted much care and time to editing and polishing it. Many thanks are also due to Mrs Monique Lang who worked with such infinite patience for several years upon an almost unreadable manuscript.

R.R.

CHAPTER 1

The War in China and the Great Depression

On 18 September 1931, at the close of a sunny autumn day, a Japanese General, the special envoy of the War Ministry, disembarked at Mukden. In Tokyo, the Government, composed of liberals and moderates, had wind of some unusual Japanese troop movements in Manchuria. The mission of the special envoy was to throw light on these, and to prevent any rash action on the part of the local commanders. On his arrival, he was invited by Colonel Seishiro Itagaki, Chief of the General Staff of the 'Army of Kwantung', to dine at the Kikubumi, the best Japanese inn in the town where, as was the custom, he would spend the evening with Geisha girls.

At 10 o'clock that evening, unknown to the envoy, a charge of dynamite exploded on the track of the South Manchurian Railway near the barracks of Peita Yin, occupied by the 7th Chinese Brigade. The incident was trifling; an express train soon arrived, undamaged at the station, having passed over the site of the explosion. Nevertheless, on the pretext of re-establishing order, Japanese forces surged out of their barracks to take possession of Mukden and, twelve hours later, of the principal strategic points in South Manchuria. Japan had dealt the first mortal blow to the great alliance for law and order founded at Versailles in 1919.

The fearful sufferings of the Great War had been undergone in the hope that 'the war to end all wars' would lead to the permanent disappearance of political oppression and international violence. In a world exhausted by the cruellest conflict of modern times, the Treaty of Versailles had been welcomed as the dawn of a new era. It is difficult nowadays to realize how much recourse to arms had been not only a legitimate choice, a natural attribute of sovereignty, but indeed one of the noblest qualities of the human race, until then, 'to die for one's country' sang school-children, 'is so wonderful that we all aspire to it'. From the epoch of Machiavelli, a powerful philosophical movement

1

had regarded war as a noble activity. Hegel saw the State as the representation of the 'Divine Idea on Earth', the battle field was the place of its accomplishment. Charles de Gaulle wrote in 1932, in *Fil de l'Epée*, 'Cradle of cities, sceptre of Empires, anathema of decadence, force gives the law to peoples and settles their destinies'.

By establishing the League of Nations, the peace treaties attempted to subject the cult of the State to the supremacy of humane values. For the first time in human history, a written rule abolished the ancient freedom to take up the sword, at the whim or ambition of some prince or nation. A system of 'Collective Security' was to impose peace on all bellicose States; the reign of law, as it existed in civilised society, was extended to international relations. A revolutionary notion it was, alas, not to be respected. Statesmen, powerless to free themselves from the habits of centuries, continued to prefer the anarchical jungle of conflicting national interests. The morrow of the Armistice was a tumultuous period, the reconciliation of ancient enmities slow and painful.

In 1923, the forced occupation of the Ruhr by Franco-Belgian troops had fanned the flames of hatred. In Paris, a Chamber of Deputies *bleu horizon* had furnished the most chauvinistic government the Third Republic had ever known.* It was presided over by Raymond Poincaré, the frock-coated and striped-trousered Cato of French nationalism, a frontiers-man steeped in detestation of Teutonism, whose crystal-clear logic concealed violent passions. On a futile pretext, his aim was to take over the industrial heart of Germany. To this Berlin replied with 'passive resistance'. Not so passive, in fact, because it led to violent incidents, with blood being spilled.

Soon, the occupation of the Ruhr was followed by attempts to cut off the Rhineland from the rest of Germany and to transform it into puppet states friendly to France and Belgium. The German Communist Party, broken up in 1919, had been allowed to raise its head. At Gelsenkirchen, in the occupied Ruhr, it had seized the municipality, shooting hostages in the presence of French troops, who were very slow to intervene. At Hamburg, Bremen, in Saxony and Thuringea, similar serious troubles occurred. At Munich, on November 9, 1923, Hitler attempted his first coup, the famous 'putsch of the *Bürgebraukeller*': 19 were killed. In the Rhineland itself, French and Belgians were encouraging autonomous movements, often competing

---

* This was the time at which Joan of Arc, canonised on 16 May 1920, officially became a national heroine and her feast-day a national holiday.

with each other. At Düsseldorf, 30,000 people demonstrated in the streets demanding an independent republic; there were casualties. In Aachen, Belgian troops fired at the police trying to expel rebels from government buildings: six policemen were killed. An ephemeral Rhinelandish state was proclaimed in Düren, Bonn, Trier, Wiesbaden, Krefeld. The crisis had overflowed from Germany, it had become European.

The German government had then given in. Gustav Stresemann had succeeded Chancellor Cuno in August 1923. Withstanding popular feelings, however, exhausted by the ordeal, the new Chancellor proclaimed an end to resistance and engaged in a policy of reconciliation with France. When, in the following year, Poincaré was replaced by Edouard Herriot, a compromise had been reached. Everything gradually returned to normal. The Ruhr was evacuated—not without leaving permanent scars. At the beginning of the crisis, Washington had recalled the 10,000 soldiers who still provided an American presence in Europe. They were not to return until 1944. In American and British eyes, France and Belgium were no longer victims of German imperialism. Their sympathies now went out to the Germans, as a nation unfairly penalised. The Foreign Office even went so far as to believe—according to the British Ambassador in Berlin—that the French Republic aspired to hegemony in Europe, on the Napoleonic lines after Tilsit.[1] However, from 1925 on, the bitter hatred generated by the Great War began to wane. When the famous exhibition of 'Arts Décoratifs' opened in Paris (where Germany was not yet invited), European diplomacy was conducted by outstanding men (Sir Austen Chamberlain, Gustav Stresemann and Aristide Briand) who preferred cooperation to 'insensate nationalism'.

The Frenchman in particular dominated the stage. For a time he was immensely popular. People would gather to look at his dishevelled mask of a benign lion, to listen to his speeches, clearly expressed and strongly emotional. 'The Apostle of Peace' was the idol of a young generation brought up to the horrors of war.[2] It was largely due to Briand that the ideals of 1919 began to take shape.* In October 1925, the principal Western European powers gathered in the small Swiss town of Locarno for a genuine reconciliation. They signed a number of agreements, of which the most important was a pact of mutual

---

* In October 1924, Briand had already been one of the moving spirits behind the 'Geneva Protocol' which sought to clarify and strengthen collective security. Approved unanimously by the 48 delegations present at Geneva, it would eventually be rejected by Great Britain.

assistance between France, Belgium and Germany upholding the frontiers enunciated at Versailles and the permanent demilitarisation of the Rhine's left bank. Great Britain and Italy added their bond.

France at last enjoyed guarantees of security which she had never known. Germany, no longer subject to a humiliating *Diktat*, made her entry into the League of Nations. At Geneva, in the Ariana park, looking out onto Lac Léman, arose the great palaces in which the senators of a new international republic were to gather.* During sessions of the League, the city, with its gaily beflagged streets, attracted hundreds of delegates, diplomats, journalists and tourists who came to listen to, and applaud, the political personalities.

On the morrow of the Locarno Agreements, the *New York Times* expressed the general enthusiasm with a huge headline, 'France and Germany have outlawed war!' This was to be confirmed three years later, at least on paper, by the Kellogg–Briand Pact signed by the principal powers. It was no more than a gesture, but a spectacular one, by nations who had, for a millenium, seen in the glory of arms the expression of the finest civic virtues. At the end of 1929 in Germany, a referendum was demanded by the nationalist parties to protest against Stresemann's policies. It resulted in a resounding defeat for hatred. Less than 6 per cent of the electors cast their vote for the enemies of reconciliation. In 1930, the last French troops left the Rhineland—four years before the date fixed at Versailles.

The ancient ideal of a united Europe, Roman, Christian or Humanist, had never been completely forgotten. Kept alive along the centuries, by the writings of legists and philosophers, it now acquired a powerful popular vogue in Germany as well as in France, Great Britain, Belgium and elsewhere. Associations were formed demanding the reconciliation of the enemies of the Great War, the enforcement of the rule of law, disarmament and a United States of Europe. Some included intellectuals, others were industrialists, Socialists, Conservatives and Christian Democrats.† Among the most influential was the Pan Europa Union, led by Count Coudenhove-Kalergi, a former Austrian diplomat, son of a Japanese lady and the descendant of an old aristocratic family of Flemish origin. Briand believed that the moment had come to learn 'to speak European'. Responding to the

---

* They would be completed in 1938—shortly before World War II.

† Among the industrialists, one should mention Emile Mayrisch, chairman of the important Luxemburg steel works ARBED, who tried to set up an international steel organisation from which was to come the idea of a coal and steel community.

interest aroused by his famous speech forecasting 'federal ties' between the peoples of Europe, he proposed a European Union with common institutions, a system of arbitration, security and guarantees, as well as the institution of a 'Common Market' (the term dates from then). But his project, alas, was premature, and soon buried in the dust of the Chancelleries. Only Yugoslavia and Bulgaria approved it without reservation.

Nevertheless, peace and prosperity seemed to have been consolidated. What Talleyrand had called 'the European Public Law' appeared to have been re-established on earth. But at this point, the Japanese colonels sounded their 'drums and fifes', and the disaster of the New York Stock Exchange announced the return of destitution.

★ ★ ★

For four centuries, within the walls of Whitehall and Westminster, the Speaker of the House of Commons, seated on his dais and wearing a white wig, directed the debates of the gentry and the merchants who had reigned over half a milliard human beings, scattered across the surface of the planet. An Empire on which the sun never set. The French Empire was almost as imposing. In 1931, the Colonial Exhibition in Vincennes, in all its magnificence, had triumphantly revealed its extent. In that year, England and France still reigned over the continents, and their navies policed the oceans. At Geneva they dominated the deliberations of the League of Nations. A year later, they revealed the vanity of great powers, built up over half a millenium, by renouncing global supremacy. The moment of decisive choice had slipped away; history had changed course.

The Manchurian Affair came as a sudden revelation. On the evening of the dinner at 'Kikubumi', an undeclared war had broken out for the possession of a territory as big as France and Germany combined. The Japanese conquered it. Soon they disembarked in the region of Shanghai, which was to become a zone of Japanese influence. In 1933, they took Jehol, and a little later other provinces. Finally, in 1937, they attacked China proper.

In this way, Tokyo violated the Charter of the League of Nations, violated the 1922 Nine Powers Treaty, and the Kellogg–Briand Pact, on which the ink was barely dry.* The cinema screens showed

---

* The Treaty of the Nine Powers (France, Japan, Great Britain, the United States, China, Italy, Holland, Portugal and Belgium), signed in Washington on 6 February 1922, guaranteed the sovereignty and territorial integrity of the Chinese Republic.

horrifyingly graphic scenes—of soldiers bayoneting people in the suburbs of Shanghai amid bursts of shrapnel, aeroplanes swooping from the skies in brutal bombing raids, straw huts going up in flames, columns of black smoke, mutilated bodies, children crying in the ruins. This was the first time that my contemporaries and I were faced by the reality of war, and we were completely overcome.

Article 16 of the League of Nations was the key to the system of collective security. Any member state having recourse to arms was considered *ipso facto* to have declared war on all the others, who were to ensure that the law was respected, using all means at their disposal, including economic and military sanctions. China having pleaded for help, the Council of the League (in which, for the first time, the United States was represented) demanded the withdrawal of the Japanese troops. Tokyo gave assurances that they would be evacuated and that there was no question of annexation or conquest. Fine promises! For the Samurai did not stop there. It was decided that a Commission of Enquiry under Lord Lytton should be sent to the Far East to find out what everyone knew. It took nine months to achieve its task.

In March 1932, Manchuria became Mandchukuo, a Japanese puppet state. The League of Nations refused to recognise it—an anodyne gesture, but one that was still sufficient to make Tokyo hesitate. It was not until September 1932 that the Japanese decided to go ahead and officially proclaim the existence of a new state. The following month, Lord Lytton submitted his report. An ambiguous document, which while confirming that Manchuria was Chinese, proposed to endow the region with an autonomous statute, with special rights for Japan. *Seventeen months after the Mukden incident*, the League Assembly unanimously adopted a resolution on these lines (with the exception of Siam). It was a useless gesture because no provision was made to help China or to re-establish the law. At no time was the application of Article 16 envisaged.

★   ★   ★

A dozen reasons have been adduced to justify the apathy of the European statesmen. In London, it was alleged that economic sanctions would not be effective—which was absurd, in view of the very limited industrial capacity of Japan (which had also been badly hit by the Depression) and her paucity of raw material, which obliged her to import all her petroleum products—as indeed is still the case today. Another reason was that sanctions would have led to an armed conflict. This seems unlikely because the Japanese leaders, deeply emmeshed in China, would hardly have been insane enough to throw down the gauntlet to the fifty Powers gathered in Geneva. Another reason given was that the British Fleet in the Far East, and the Singapore base, were not ready. Simply because war with Japan had been considered inconceivable for the next ten, fifteen or twenty years.

None of these explanations obscure the truth. The British politicians were not interested in what was happening beyond their own shores. In the House of Commons, the time reserved for foreign affairs or the problems of defence, was limited—two half-days in the Parliamentary session of 1931–32. Why bother? Harold Nicolson was a diplomat, Member of Parliament and journalist. In his celebrated diaries, there is not a word about the Manchurian war; he expressed the feelings of many when he noted at the end of 1931, 'What fun life is!'; and, at the end of 1932, 'I don't expect I shall ever enjoy a year as much as this one'.[3]

My wife, who is English, tells of the carefree days of her adolescence, of pretty debutantes and their *cavallieri serventi*, of their love affairs, and joyous marriages; the balls in the great houses, the fox-hunting in the green hills, evenings at the opera. A world of grace and civilisation, too contented to display anxiety. Energetic and outspoken political leaders could have shaken this complacency and made their countrymen understand the mortal dangers which threatened the elegant society in which they lived so unconcernedly. But such men were not in power. The 'National Government' of MacDonald and Baldwin had just obtained an electoral victory with more than 550 seats in the Commons. Its authority was exceptional, giving it almost unlimited liberty of action. However, its faculties of foresight and imagination *were* limited and it was more concerned with the problems engendered by the Depression, although, even not excessively witnessed. Tired of the complicated quarrels of continental Europe (which it could not completely ignore), it was now being asked to devote part of its attention and energy to the Far East.

While James Ramsay MacDonald was the first Labour Prime Minister to govern Great Britain, Stanley Baldwin, in fact, held the reins of power. He was the only son of an iron-master in Wilden, in the north of England, one of those ambitious and self-willed men who, from modest beginnings had made the industrial revolution—and their fortunes. Baldwin's father, a burly bearded prophet, lived with his family in a large Victorian house beside the factory. When the wind was in the east, a black and sticky dust permeated the house, an irritation which he accepted without demur because—so he would say—coal and coke were his family's bread and butter. Every day, throughout the year, at 7 o'clock in the morning he was to be seen at his desk. He became rich, and a Conservative member of the House of Commons.

After his father's death, Stanley had assumed his seat in Parliament and became head of the family business; for a long time without significant success. 'My place as leader fell to me after a succession of curious freaks of fortune, which I could not have foreseen, and never expected', he related. What were those freaks of fortune? 'He had neither ambition nor energy,' said one of his daughters. 'Without my mother, he would have been perfectly content in the country, going to the factory every morning and returning in the evening. He was terrified of big receptions and always tried to keep near the wall in case the floor gave way (he always feared the worst).'

Success was to give Baldwin the taste for high office, revealing an unexpected oratorical talent. But it never cured him of the morbid fears from which he suffered so severely.[4] In appearance, he was a tower of strength. Of medium height, thick set, clean shaven, his hair carefully brushed and parted in the middle, his neck encased in a starched, stick-up collar, a gold watch-chain across his stomach, a pipe in his mouth, he affected the bland style of a rural worthy. This gave him a reputation for silent strength, which he did not really deserve, and the air of the landed gentry to which he did not belong. He had high moral standards, which did not exclude a certain harshness, and a kind of integrity which did not exclude, on occasion, a little sharp preactice. 'We are a government of faithful husbands', he curiously flattered himself. Every morning, on awakening, he and his wife would kneel at the foot of the bed, and pray to God to allow them to do something beneficial in His service and in that of the Country.

Circumspect and unshakeable, 'a great mass of cotton-wool', Churchill called him ironically. When the Depression had struck his country, he accepted, without emotion, the unfortunate lot of the unemployed. His opportunism was based on a profound lack of imagination and a solid laziness. For he too preferred the futile discussions of electoral meetings, and lobby prattle, to the more arduous task of listening to experts and studying documents. Moreover, he distrusted the intellectuals, whose moral integrity he doubted. Anxious to please rather than dominate, Baldwin acquired great popularity by ignoring disagreeable realities, claiming, as did Dr Pangloss, that all was 'for the best in the best of all possible worlds'. One of his political friends said shortly after his arrival in Downing Street:

> Here is the man we have been waiting for, the typical Englishman. We've had
> enough of Welshmen and lawyers, of great brains and supermen. We want a
> statesman of the old school, honest, sensible and responsible, rather than a man
> whose intelligence pierces the future.[5]

Baldwin's personality, as much as that of MacDonald, explains why
they attempted to wash their hands of the need to find a solution to
the Manchurian Affair. Accommodation, of no matter what kind, was
preferable to defending the great principles of President Wilson, agreed
to so unenthusiastically in 1919. To Whitehall they appeared now no
more than the meanderings of a fuddled idealist. To hell with Geneva
and collective security, that 'fifth wheel of British foreign policy added
for ostentation,' wrote a distinguished English historian.[6] From then
on, the Chinese, who were weak, were regarded as importunate, while
the Japanese, who were strong, were to be cajoled. The Foreign Secretary, Sir John Simon, a Liberal, who had joined the National
Government, started by discrediting China—'A simple geographical
expression', was his description of that ancient empire. In the House
of Commons, he stated that the Japanese were undoubtedly in the
wrong to take the law into their own hands, but that they could be
forgiven for re-establishing order in Manchuria. A strange concept
from one of the most eminent lawyers in London.

The opposition was no more clear-headed. Attlee, the future Prime
Minister, a moderate, did not eschew demagogy, with 'No agreement
is possible in foreign policy between the Labour opposition and a
capitalist government.'[7] This was in fact untrue. The two Parties
were in complete agreement about not taking sides. When Labour
demanded an embargo on the sale of arms to the Far East—on all
arms, those to the victims as well as to the aggressors—the government
did not object. Just before the cease-fire, which temporarily stopped
the fighting in Shanghai, it forbade all shipments of war material *to
both belligerents*!

★　　★　　★

In Paris the same state of mind prevailed. Laval, a man of all
accommodations, headed the government in the early days of the
Manchurian crisis. His Minister of Foreign Affairs, Briand, aged 69,
old and sick, was reduced to impotence. Although he was President
of the Council of the League of Nations, he could only pronounce
fruitless calls to reason. In any case, he was to relinquish office in
January 1932, and to die two months later. Even more than the
London Press, the Paris newspapers sided with the aggressor. *Pertinax*,

the right-wing journalist with a great following, went as far as to say in the *Echo de Paris* that, 'If Japan has been forced to take extreme measures, it is the result of provocation by the League of Nations'.

When new elections brought the Left back to power, there was little change. Like Briand, Herriot had based his reputation on fidelity to international law. For ten years, he had made excellent speeches, condemning the recourse to arms and praising the sacred character of treaties. But he did nothing to put these fine principles into effect. 'Above all, don't annoy Japan', he telegraphed to the French Ambassador in Tokyo, recommending the greatest prudence.[8]

Because he promised a great deal and gave little, Edouard Herriot was one of the most disappointing figures of the Third Republic. Deprived in his childhood of the care of parents who led the wandering life of a military family, and brought up by an uncle who was a village priest, his first years passed in a devout atmosphere. This soon evaporated. 'Instead of doctrines which contradict one another', the future radical leader asked himself, 'would there not be a single human tradition based on the same ideas?' This convenient deism allowed him to side with the anticlerical factions of the Left; it would also facilitate his reconciliation with the Church just before he died. On the other hand, the reformist and internationalist programme of the Radical party owed a great deal to the teachings of the 'Ecole Normale Supérieure', of which young Herriot had been a pupil. He made himself a somewhat hypocritical champion of all this. He was a Tartuffe, never ceasing during his long life to sing the praise of the Republic, Liberty, Fraternity, etc. He was heard to attack the 'wall of silver' which was supposed to have blocked his administration, or to pretend to be deeply moved by the 'sick mother' whose sons 'should stop quarrelling at her bedside,' or to speak with tremors in his voice, of the humble clerics 'with their frayed cassocks'. An inimitable comedian, he even succeeded in fainting when he thought it useful, alarming only those who did not know his tricks.[9]

As head of Government in 1924 and 1932, he damaged his reputation by making futile attacks on the Church to prove his radicalism; and he substituted patriotic declarations for much needed reform. His connection with the party of progress did not prevent him from standing against them. In 1936, he opposed the Front Populaire. In 1940, when his beloved Republic was in mortal danger, he abstained from voting and appealed to his colleagues to rally to the authoritarian regimé of Marshal Pétain. The same ambiguities marked his foreign policy. Herriot claimed to be a champion of collective security; in fact, he regarded it only as a device for controlling Germany. Nothing good could come from the other side of the Rhine. The works of German philosophers were solemn stuff and nonsense. Listening to the 'barbaric themes' of Wagner, he discovered something irreconcilable between the French genius and 'that notion of becoming, which envelops the theories of Germany in its clouds'. Cranach 'confined in his methods, as in his thought, is a kind of peasant, heavy with crude but perfectly expressive outlines.'[10]

This aversion to Germany (which was to contribute to his objection to the European idea after the Second World War) brought him closer to the USSR, which was to exercise a strange fascination on this middle class conservative. Nevertheless, it also led him to establish friendly relations with London and Washington, to whom the Bloc National had shown no sympathy. He even went so far as to resign when the *Chambre des Députés* refused his request to honour the French war debt to America (his resignation was not without ulterior motives). In the favourable climate of Geneva, he contrived to camouflage his dubious policies with a fiery rhetoric which earned him the great ovations he desired, while presenting himself as a champion of peace and fraternity! It was certainly an improvement on the chauvinism of Poincaré and Tardieu. Unfortunately, it in no way corresponded with reality.

★   ★   ★

It was easy for London and Paris to justify their inaction during the Sino-Japanese war, by pointing to the example of Washington. But at this time, it was Great Britain and France who claimed the responsibility for maintaining world order. In any case, did the United States really display all the indifference with which it has been taxed? It is true that in 1919 it had refused to ratify the Covenant and had avoided any commitment in Europe. However, it had contributed to the Pact of Paris outlawing war. Moreover, it had signed the treaty of the Nine Powers, which guaranteed the integrity of China. Already, in 1899, it had announced the doctrine of 'The Open Door', which opposed all annexations by foreign powers in the Middle Kingdom. Admittedly the 'Open Door' favoured commercial interests there; but it was also inspired by the idealism which for a hundred years had caused thousands of young Americans, avid for sacrifice, and coming from all sects and Churches, to devote themselves to evangelisation of the Chinese and the improvement of their life. For the United States the Far East was a metaphysical colony, in the same way that, for the

Europeans, Africa and Asia were lands to exploit or populate. A powerful lobby in Congress defended the interests of the missions. The clause of Versailles handing over the German possessions in Shantung to Japan had caused an outcry in America (President Wilson had opposed the transfer). It is not impossible that, had this clause been omitted, the Senate might have ratified the Peace Treaty—including the Charter of the League of Nations.[11]

The attack in Manchuria had awoken latent emotions. Suddenly, tendencies hostile to traditional isolationism appeared. The White House felt itself authorised to take part in the conversations in Geneva—an unprecedented state of affairs. Here 'diplomatic pressure' and 'collective economic sanctions' were discussed; President Hoover, in favour of the first, would not support the second. Nevertheless, he authorised his Secretary of State to take soundings in London. Stimson had a somewhat confused telephone conversation with his British counterpart, Sir John Simon, which is to this day still a subject of controversy. Whatever was said, nothing came of it.

★   ★   ★

We were a generation haunted by the memory of the Great War, the sufferings of our fathers, the dead of the Yser, the Somme and Verdun, the cemeteries with the lines of wooden crosses stretching away into the far distance. Literary works, often of a high standard, fuelled our anger. Barbusse and Dorgeles were republished. New books, by Duhamel in France, Remarque in Germany, Aldington in Great Britain, Hemingway in the USA, sold in hundreds of thousands, in French, English and German, relating the fearful combat, the unspeakable horror, as well as the monotony, of trench warfare, the incompetence and the murderous frivolity of the Generals. The exaltation of martial glory, which was responsible for all this, was deeply repugnant to us. Although we seldom displayed our feelings violently, fundamentally, we were pacifists and anti-militarists. It was not necessarily a refusal to fight—but to do so only on behalf of a human ideal, for collective security, which seemed the only alternative to international brigandage.

The war in the Far East brought out these latent feelings and revealed ideological oppositions. Here and there, voices favourable to the aggressor were raised. Some expressed an innate respect for brute force. Others, such as Simon or Tardieu, believed that the Empire of the Rising Sun was the natural ally of the West against Bolshevism. Tokyo, well aware of this attitude, exploited it to the full—not without some success.* It represented the Kuomintang, Chiang Kai-shek's party, as an extreme left-wing movement—in spite of the latter's implacable suppression of Chinese communism. Washington's hesitation can be traced, in part, to the anti-USSR approach of London and Paris in their refusal to honour collective security.

From the beginning, Sir John Simon had told his colleagues that there was no question of applying Article 16. His permanent Under-Secretary, the future Lord Vansittart, did not blame him. We read in his memoirs, 'Simon—who has always looked as if he had just got out of a cold bath—showed no disposition to fight Japan for the benefit of Russia . . . no one thought seriously of fighting for yellow men'.[12] It was, in fact, in these terms that the question was asked, and the answer was a categorical 'No!' Neither Paris nor London were concerned about collective security, when it did not serve their immediate national interests. The long-term benefits, the stability which it would have brought to the world, including their own empires, completely escaped them.

For centuries, France and Great Britain had regarded themselves as heirs to the *Res Publica Romana*. Like ancient Rome, they had founded the legitimacy of their empire on a morality based, in spite of imperfections, on the defence of Law, material progress and respect for the human person—all of which Kipling called poetically 'The white man's burden'. It was this ideal which justified the participation of millions of white, yellow and black men, summoned from the distant bounds of their lands in the most murderous warfare known to history. It was in the name of that ideal that the supremacy of these two powers was generally accepted, after the Armistice, thanks to the human standards they promised. Countless men and women had given their confidence to them—and not only within their own frontiers. What credence could still be accorded to the fine sounding words of their statesmen?

★   ★   ★

The Manchurian Affair was not the only cause for concern. At Geneva on 2 February 1932, the few strollers chilled by the frozen fog rising from the lake, saw a strange procession wending its way through the narrow streets of the old town. Each member wore, on his arm, a

---

* When Chiang Kai-shek re-established diplomatic relations with Moscow in 1932 (after a break of four years), Tokyo claimed that this was a further proof of his collusion with the 'Reds'.

white ribbon bearing the letters PAX, and a green ribbon shoulder-strap carrying the name of their country. They carried large parcels containing petitions by millions of men and women demanding peace and disarmament.

The peace treaties had regarded the imposition of a strict limitation on the German armed forces, as the prelude to general disarmament. For seven years, technical committees had been working on lengthy preparatory plans. In spite of increasing scepticism, 2 February 1932 was a day of high expectancy. Afterwards, numerous solemn conferences followed one another, in Geneva, New York, Vienna and elsewhere, attempting to convert the old dream of disarmament into reality. None of them aroused such intense hope as that chaired by Arthur Henderson. But it proved a bitter deception! General Temperley, counsellor of the British delegation, wrote sadly afterwards, 'While we were taking our places, we seemed to hear the muffled explosions of the Japanese guns in Shanghai, and the crash of bombs on Chapeï, where millions of Chinese men, women and children were sent to their death—as a prelude to a new era of peace on earth'.[13]

On behalf of France, André Tardieu, Minister of War in a Laval cabinet, had at first proposed to replace all the existing armies by a great international army at the disposal of the League of Nations. 'So much journalism!' said Briand. The idea was not even studied. In the name of Germany, Brüning suggested reducing the armed forces of the principal powers to the level imposed on the *Reichswehr*. The British, who had virtually no army, acquired a certain notoriety by opposing any reduction in bomber planes, 'indispensable for policing operations in distant territories', meaning their colonies. The Japanese delegate had remarked that, as seen from Tokyo, Great Britain was a 'distant territory'. In the name of the Soviet Union, Litvinov demanded, in all seriousness, a general disarmament down to the last rifle.

After the great speeches aimed at impressing the public, the actors on the stage of history began complicated negotiations; from which Henderson and the representatives of the little nations—the only ones who really believed in disarmament—were carefully eliminated. Obliged to cool their heels in the Geneva hotel lounges and restaurants, they soon realised that the conference was confined to a confrontation between the Germans, demanding *equality of rights*, and the French demanding *security*, a confrontation which could only be resolved by the participation Great Britain on the continent—which she was not prepared to undertake.

★   ★   ★

When Brüning dejectedly left Switzerland immediately after the departure of the 'star' performers, Tardieu first, then Stimson and MacDonald, his days of government were numbered. The hardest blow he received, for all to see, was when, searching desperately for a diplomatic success, he tried rather foolishly to form a customs union between Germany and Austria. A much perturbed Paris saw in this a step towards the annexation of Austria—the *Anschluss*. Briand caused the two delinquents to appear before the Council of the League of Nations, where he gave them a good dressing-down.* The threatening shadow of Hitler undoubtedly justified prudence. But would it be possible to deny the Reich indefinitely the equality of rights which constituted the basis of the Geneva system? Was it conceivable that it could be kept disarmed for ever in a Europe armed to the teeth? Brüning inspired confidence. Even in Paris, he alone appeared capable of barring the way to Hitler. The inflexible rigidity shown to him, the absence even of the most elementary courtesy—were they not to lead to his downfall?

Perhaps, one day, unknown archives will reveal precisely what motivated Tardieu. What is clear is that his departure from Switzerland, followed by that of the other heads of government, sounded the death knell of disarmament. The Geneva conference went on amid growing public lack of interest. The Tardieu Plan, the Brüning Plan, the Hoover Plan, all abortive, were followed by the brusque recall of the German delegates by the new Chancellor Franz von Papen. When Herriot agreed to recognise for Germany 'equality of rights', on condition that the 'security' of France was guaranteed, this elegant formula settled the dialectical debate, but nothing else. Yet another German Chancellor, General von Schleicher, agreed to send his delegates back. The months passed by, Hitler took over. There was now a MacDonald Plan (elaborated by Eden), a Daladier Plan: 27 in all! To confuse matters further, a 'Four Power Pact' was signed (but not ratified) setting up a European Directorate consisting of France, Great Britain, Germany and Italy. This was an old idea based on the notion—which is still alive—that it would be easier for the major powers to settle their differences in the absence of the smaller ones. *Le club des charcutiers*, a French journalist called it. Substituting an illusory central authority to collective security would have sacrificed the many without assuring harmony among the great. In this way,

---

* Brought before the Court of International Justice at The Hague, the Austro-German treaty was declared illegal, and abandoned.

from 1932 to 1935, Geneva became the Tower of Babel, stigmatised as such by its critics.

★   ★   ★

1932. To a much greater degree than the war in the distant Far East, the miseries of the Great Depression plunged Europe into utter confusion. In Belgium, wild strikes occurred during the summer. Ignoring the appeal to order by their trade unions, the workers downed tools and took to the streets. In certain places, there were violent encounters with the police and a number of casualties. Such a thing had not been seen in Belgium for half a century.

I was 20 and doing my military service with the 2nd Lancers, as yet a mounted unit. During the summer manoeuvres, the regiment had been recalled to Brussels, and put on a war footing. One morning, in the great courtyard of the barracks, the quartermasters distributed iron rations and short range cartridges, for use in street fighting, to the squadrons. The cavalrymen, their rifles loaded, sabres flapping beside their saddles, patrolled the road approaches to Brussels, with orders to bar then to all unlawful assemblies. In the evening, in the guard-rooms set up in public buildings, the soldiers sat in small groups, their legs under blankets, and murmured among themselves. Officers and cadets, at first nonchalant, felt ill at ease. How would the conscripts respond, if the order was given to fire on the strikers? How would they respond themselves? Removed from the pleasure and ease of a privileged existence, their eyes were suddenly opened to the fearful realities of 'the Slump'.

In Great Britain it struck an economy that had already been for some time in decline. Suspended during the war, the convertibility of sterling into gold had been restored in 1925 at the (far too high) rate of the pre-1914 sterling-dollar value—for no better reason than prestige. Suffering from a deeply unbalanced domestic market (one percent of the population possessed two thirds of the national wealth), the old prosperity had depended largely on exports. With an over-priced currency, together with an out-of-date industrial structure, exports diminished. Even before the Wall Street Crash of 1929 and the Depression, production had stagnated and the number of unemployed exceeded a million. The Labour Party was in power. Ramsay Mac-Donald, knowing little of economics, had no longer the strength to study them, and allowed himself to be hemmed in by fashionable prejudices—convertibility of the currency into gold, budgetary equilibrium, deflation. Strangled by the increasing stagnation of business, fiscal receipts continued to diminish in spite of new taxes, while the pound sterling vacillated. 'The budget must be balanced, economies introduced', said the experts, convinced that the lowering of prices would automatically revitalise the market. In August 1931 the Prime Minister decided to reduce the pay of the civil servants, and the allocations for the unemployed. Ten of his leading ministers were opposed to these measures which would hit the least favoured members of the community, whom they represented in Parliament.

Things were now out of hand, and financial panic ensued. At the end of the month, the government disintegrated. MacDonald offered his resignation to the aged King George V, who asked him to form a crisis ministry, in which all parties would be represented. In this way, in spite of the opposition and reprobation of most of the Labour Party, the 'National Government' which, under MacDonald, Baldwin and Chamberlain, was to govern the country until 1940, was born.

A semi-official 'May Report' which inspired the budget of September 1931, in the words of J. M. Keynes, was 'compounded of prejudice, ignorance and panic . . . the most foolish document I ever had the misfortune to read'.[14] In spite of conforming with the requisite orthodoxy, the policy it induced failed to stop the financial haemorrhage. The stirrings of a mutiny among the sailors of the Home Fleet, whose pay was threatened, caused further terror. Holders of sterling again rushed to change it into gold. Was it not the only true currency? The reserves of the august Bank of England were almost exhausted and the government had to abandon convertibility. Surprisingly, the panic calmed down, and the pound sterling finished by stabilising at 70 per cent of its old value. But the financial crisis was only a symptom of the malady. Industry was suffering from a stagnation never known before. Exports had fallen by almost half. During the winter 1932–33 there were three million unemployed, 6–7 per cent of the population.

After nearly fifty years, unemployment has again become a nightmare. To master it, the authorities (and the Trade Unions) show little more courage or imagination than in the past. However, in spite of the pain it brings to those affected today, the sufferings of the Thirties were immensely greater. Allocations for the unemployed were minimal and mostly limited to 26 weeks, after which, the payment was more often than not reduced or cancelled. 'Hunger marches' and riots without any particular object, became everyday events—in Bristol, Manchester, Belfast, Liverpool and London. The clashes between demonstrators and the forces of law and order were often violent, with a number of dead. In his memoirs, Harold Macmillan, then a young Conservative Member of Parliament, wrote, 'The year 1932–33 was the worst that I can remember'.[15]

The problem remained acute until the improvement of the dole in 1936. Nevertheless, the clashes ceased. The British are one of the most patient peoples in the world.

In France, when the guns fell silent, the franc had lost half its value. After the Armistice, inflation increased. When a National Government concentrated on financial reorganisation in 1926, the dollar was worth ten times as much in francs as before the war and the cost of living was eight times higher than in 1914. Contrary to what had happened to the pound sterling, the government had the good sense to devalue the franc; an operation which dispossessed millions of small savers of four-fifths of their wealth, thereby creating a body of discontented people ready to listen to the demagogues of Left or Right, principally the Right. But, simultaneously it gave a powerful fillip to commerce and industry. By 1929 the index of industrial production—at 100 in 1913—had climbed to 139.[16] Floating capital flooded in. In 1930 the cash in hand in the Banque de France was 80 billion francs, an enormous sum, of which two thirds was in gold—a quarter of the world's gold. More than the United States, Britain or Germany, all devastated by the Great Depression, France then appeared to be the dominating Power of the world.

After 1932 France too was struck by the Great Depression. The devaluation of the dollar, sterling and other currencies, made the franc, in its turn, much too valuable. Exports diminished by 70 per cent; the number of registered unemployed reached 260,000 in 1932, 425,000 in 1935—that is, one to two per cent of the population, perhaps a little more. However, being less industrialised than her neighbours, the French Republic suffered less from the recession. It required the coming to power of Pierre Laval in July 1935, with his ferociously deflationary measures, and his relentless determination to defend 'a block of gold', to plunge the country into a stagnation from which the other countries were beginning to emerge.*

★　　　★　　　★

Germany was the country most hit by the Great Crisis. The young Weimar Republic, born of defeat, had hesitated to impose unpopular

---

* In July 1933, France, Belgium, Italy, the Netherlands, Poland and Switzerland had declared their common commitment to the gold standard.

measures for reducing the inflation caused by the cost of the war. When it decided to do so, the measures were inadequate. In February 1920 the dollar cost 100 marks, almost 25 times its price before the war; in November, 300 marks. In this dangerous situation, one of the greatest follies of the times was announced. Germany, judged responsible for the war, was condemned to pay reparations to the victors, over 66 years—three generations—a total of 132 billion gold marks (33 billion dollars), increased by 26 per cent of the value of its imports. A fantastic sum, it engendered in the vanquished nation a permanent rancour, which was to poison international relations for more than a decade. Anyway, as everyone knew, it would not cost Germany much because, in so far as she obeyed, she paid it with foreign loans (which she was never to repay). It might have perhaps been forgotten, if the question of credits granted to the Allies by the United States during the war had not added to the problem. Demanded vociferously by Washington, the repayment not only embittered transatlantic relations; it made Germany's European creditors more ruthless in their determination to 'make the Boche pay'.

The reparations, added to the expenses connected with the occupation of the Ruhr, had contributed considerably to German inflation. In 1923 the printing of banknotes was duly accelerated, soon digging a monetary abyss. The mark, at the rate of 18,000 for the dollar in January, fell to 100 million in September, to 840 billion on November 13, and 1260 billion on November 20.

Living conditions had become dreadful. Mountains of banknotes were coming out of the printing presses, to be sent all over Germany by rail, by road and sometimes by air. Everywhere people were waiting anxiously for their little pieces of paper to exchange them for basic goods—before galloping inflation deprived them of all value. The price of bread, vegetables, eggs and butter went up several times a day. When shopping, housewives needed baskets to carry their bundles of banknotes, as their value melted from hour to hour. Many shopkeepers soon refused to accept them. Barter became the rule. People had to give away jewellery, sometimes pieces of furniture, to acquire foodstuffs. Undernourishment was very near starvation level. Infant mortality reached dramatic proportions. 'Hyperinflation has made Germany a gigantic mad house', wrote a witness 'where the inmates are dancing a St Vitus dance of the billions'.[17]

When Stresemann had succeeded Chancellor Cuno, when he committed his government to reconciliation with France and Great Britain, when the currency was stabilised (and a little later the reparations made were more tractable), the new mark was exchanged at 1 billion old marks; a Caesarian operation resulting in the savage expropriation of the small and middle savers' cash. In 1914, more than 100 billion gold marks were invested in public loans, mortgage loans, life assurances, etc., the product of saving during a hundred years of unceasing labour and parsimonious living. It melted away like snow under the sun. Rentiers, widows, retired people as well as officers, civil servants, judges, professors and scientists, formed a class of worthy people who, once they had got over the shock of the fall of the monarchy, might well have formed the framework for a parliamentary republic. Inevitably, it was to its government that they attributed their ruin.

However, from 1925 to 1930 with the return of prosperity, the 'spirit of Locarno' gave German democracy a respite. Then the Great Depression had crashed as all over the world. In over-industrialised Germany, barely convalescent after hyper-inflation, several thousand business enterprises collapsed. During the winter of 1929, the number of unemployed increased to over three million. Chancellor Brüning's policies were marked by his strong convictions—unfortunately for the world. He was completely conversant with the technical aspects of government; but the frightening memory of hyper-inflation, together with his ascetic nature, led him into a policy of aggressive deflation. He reduced salaries, pay and pensions, causing great bitterness among workers, civil servants and pensioners. He also alienated the industrialists, the business community and the farmers by imposing price reductions. He introduced control of the banks, thus making resolute enemies of financial circles.

Brüning's two years at the Chancellery led Germany inexorably towards the abyss, marked at each step by the resounding collapse of the principal industrial and financial conglomerates. In June 1931 he visited London, in July Paris, then London again, in search of credit and an end to reparations. He met with diplomatic success in the English capital, where his courage and honesty were respected; but he obtained nothing concrete. In Paris, he made friendly contacts with Laval, the President of the Council, and with Briand, but not with Flandin, who remaind glacial, nor with Tardieu, who even refused to see him. Although the French ministers raised his hopes of a big loan, they demanded, in return, a solemn engagement by the Reich not to bring up the question of treaty revision for ten years—a proposal which Brüning was politically unable to accept. In the evening, when he was returning from Aix-la-Chapelle to Berlin in the darkened compartment of the *wagon-lit*, its curtains drawn, aware of the failure of his mission and fearful of hostile demonstrations, he had a moment of acute depression. 'So dejected was I,' he wrote later, 'that I dared not show my face at the window.'

This was understandable. Just before his visit to Paris, the giant *Darmstadter und National Bank* had, in its turn, closed its pay counters. A new tornado resulted in a desperate flow of capital out of Germany to Paris, Amsterdam and Brussels; 357 financial institutions, banks, savings banks and reserve funds suspended operations. The Chancellor was forced to decree the provisional closure of all banking establishments in the land. Economic life came to a standstill. An English journalist wrote:

> It is difficult to recapture or to describe the climate of despair which settled over Germany in the June days . . . I rode in the Tiergarten that Sunday morning and on my way to the Park I noted that larger congregations than usual seemed to be attending churches of all denominations. Their faces grey and drawn, men and women had reached the conclusion that prayer and divine intervention were their only source of salvation now.[18]

On the eve of the collapse of the world economy, President Hoover resigned himself, much too late, to recommending a moratorium of a year on all intergovernmental debts. It allowed Brüning to stifle the crisis with new and draconian deflationary measures (one of his favourite phrases). His strict orthodoxy had the merit of reassuring international capital. It also completed the economic collapse of the Weimar Republic. Incredibly, at the beginning of 1932, the State budget had been brought down from 12 to 7 billion marks. Indemnities for unemployment had been reduced or suppressed. Industrial production had fallen by more than a half, and salaries by a quarter. Of 60 million Germans, only two and a half million possessed the minimum taxable income. The totally unemployed numbered six million, 10 per cent of the population, to which were added countless partially unemployed.* The working class lived in fear of starvation, the middle class of proletarianisation.

The newspapers and foreign travellers were painting a grim picture of the German cities. In the suburbs, shanty-towns teemed with thousands of poverty-stricken human beings. Hosts of beggars stalked the streets, some reduced to singing on the squares and stations for a few coins. Others spent hours on end stretched out on benches in public

---

* For roughly the same population in 1982, the Federal Republic registered 2,250,000 totally unemployed.

gardens. At nightfall, the hungry were to be seen, resigned and silent, passing in front of the lighted restaurants, staring at those who were eating. The intellectuals were the hardest hit. 60,000 university graduates—some said more than 100,000—out of a total of 350–400,000 were out of work. Many others had to take on tasks unworthy of their qualifications. Publishing houses were on the brink of bankruptcy. The Universities and research institutes were obliged to dismiss all, or part of, their staffs. Many theatres had closed their doors, putting actors and musicians on the streets. Painters and sculptors found no clients. In Berlin, more than a hundred cinemas disappeared.[19]

The private militias, recruited from among the desperate and despairing, collided violently with one another, in particular the Communist 'Red Front' with Hitler's SA (*Sturmabteilung*). Nearly every weekend blood flowed. In July 1932, in the course of a particularly bad day at Altona, near Hamburg, the ambulances picked up 19 dead and 285 wounded. Brüning's decision to ban political militias aroused the hostility of the Right, and had to be postponed. The Brown Shirts numbered 400,000, of whom a proportion were armed by the *Reichswehr*. They ruled the streets, while awaiting the opportune moment to hoist their supreme leader on his shield. Parliament was paralysed, while Chancellor Brüning obstinately maintained his fatal policy. President Hindenburg had lapsed into the shades of senility.

When Brüning, the victim of palace intrigues and setbacks, was dismissed at the end of 1932 by the aged Hindenburg, whom he had just helped to re-election as President of the Reich, he was the most unpopular Chancellor that Germany had ever known.* In two years, effectively helped by Paris's pure blindness and London's indolence, he had succeeded, due to his determination and courage in bringing Germany to the brink of despair; which caused the Germans to repeat the words of a Major Schill who was executed in 1809 after an abortive revolt against Napoleon—'Better to have a horrible end than horror without end'. That horrible end—after the short and grotesque interludes of von Papen and Schleicher—was to be given then by Hitler.

Today, from one end of the earth to the other, in the capitals of the

★ ★ ★

* Threatened with internment by the National Socialist regime, Brüning went into hiding for several months, continually changing his refuge. Warned in June 1934 that an elaborate net was being cast to arrest him, he managed to escape to Holland, then to England and the United States. He was Professor at Harvard from 1939 to 1952, then at Cologne. He spent his retirement in New England, where he died in 1970.

industrialised nations, as in those of bamboo and puddled-clay in black Africa and Central Asia, the struggle against poverty, actively undertaken by the authorities, is based on the expansion of credit. Although the excesses of demagogy have often led this policy to doubtful ends, they have not deprived it of its fundamental virtue, when 70 per cent of the human race is still suffering from hunger. How shall we understand the leaders of the Thirties? The nineteenth century has created societies in the western world which, on the whole, appeared orderly, efficient and, from every aspect, admirable. They had led to a cultural explosion, vast empires, great material progress, and the emergence of new governing classes. For these, Science was preparing the millenium. The principle of *laissez-faire, laissez-passer* would lead to the greatest happiness of the greatest number. As for poverty among the less endowed, this was justified, as was the success of the élite, by the law of natural selection. John Stuart Mill had never doubted that the proletariat could better their condition by hard work and frugality, or 'by devoting their resources to the education of their children, instead of wasting them in excessive eating and drinking'. Fifty years later, Roger Martin du Gard's pére Thibault could still say:

> The proletariat revolts against the inequality of its condition, and gives the name of injustice to the admirable variety in life created by God. Is there not a tendency today to forget that a good man is always, or almost always, a man who possesses goods?[20]

The Great War had shattered, brutally, an order which had looked permanent. When the fighting stopped, the natural reflex of statesmen no longer young, brought up in triumphant societies, had been to efface the fearful 'interlude' or war, their hope a return to the lost paradise. Their watchword was 'Restoration'. Had not those former days constituted 'La Belle Epoque'? Prosperity and depression followed one another according to a natural cycle, they believed, just as the storm follows good weather. Such is destiny.

We should not forget that the study of economics was then in its infancy, and that the bankers—not always disinterested men—were about the only experts the politicians could consult. Admittedly, they lacked the statistical information indispensible for an appreciation of events. In Great Britain eleven different ministerial departments collected figures, all of them contradictory; it was not until 1939 that a Central Service of Economic Information was created. It was the same in France, where the first *Institut de la Conjoncture* was established in 1938, as in Belgium and elsewhere.

Ignorance had strengthened prejudice. For the Thibaults in France, the Forsytes of Galsworthy in Great Britain, or the Buddenbrooks in Thomas Mann's Germany, political economy was somehow a branch of bourgeois morality, rather than a more or less exact science. Did not M. Prudhomme or Mr Brown deserve reprobation when they ran into debt by living too luxuriously, or when their overdrafts resulted in their bankruptcy? Why should not this argument apply to the national economy? For Snowden* the Yorkshireman, and Brüning the German, one Protestant, the other Catholic, both deeply devout men, financial orthodoxy presented an almost metaphysical value. 'We both practice the same doctrine!' exclaimed Brüning joyfully after meeting Snowden. Lewis Douglas, Roosevelt's Budget Director, announced 'the end of Western civilisation' when the dollar went off the gold standard. He resigned when the social laws of the New Deal entailed large budget deficits.[21]†

In the most favoured strata of society it was sometimes suggested that unemployment was due to idleness on the part of the workers— a lack of compassion which is hardly surprising. The wealth of the upper class in France (but not Germany) had survived the ordeal. Their incomes had, it is true, been somewhat reduced, par- ticularly as a result of rising taxes, but this was compensated for by the lowering of the cost of living. Small notices in contemporary newspapers are indicative. One of them in the *Figaro* of 1933 ran: 'Require house-keeper, butler, cook for country house, region Nemours. Ten other domestic servants. Apply to . . .' This was relatively modest. Haddon Hall, the residence of the Duke of Rutland, employed 75 domestic servants, including gamekeepers.

> 'At Brissac,' its present owner relates, 'the menu normally included four meat dishes; dinner was accompanied by an orchestra playing on a specially erected dais. Among our forty gardeners and servants the sole task of two of them was to see to the oil lamps in the château, and of two others to carry up logs for the fires in the guest's bedrooms. There were twenty inmates in the house *when we were alone*. In the stables, horses were harnessed and waiting to be summoned by a footman on the terrace with a hunting horn'.[23]

In the most civilised countries of the world, living side by side with the rich, but as if on another planet, were 30 million workers, driven into inactivity and extreme poverty; with their families they numbered

---

* Philip Snowden, Chancellor of the Exchequer in the British Government.
† A report by the British Treasury in July 1930 stated that only loans invested in directly profitable enterprises were legitimate.[22]

more than 100 million abject human beings. Governments persisted in talking of overproduction when men and women were crying with hunger. Mesmerized by the magic of the past, they were content to await, as they had always done, the natural return of better days. Nevertheless, the confidence of many of them was secretly shaken; they were becoming aware that the old order was threatened. In fact, they exaggerated the dangers. But true enough, against their passivity could be heard, here and there, the rumblings of revolt. Seething discontent led to the search for new ideas or for men of destiny, 'no matter what kind of man, provided he can kick out the present regime!', cried one of the characters of Drieu La Rochelle, that fine but tragic writer who was himself a victim of the Fascist illusion.[24]

CHAPTER 2

Totalitarian Bewilderment

During Easter Week of 1933 (Hitler had been Chancellor for three months, and the Reichstag fire, most probably engineered by the Nazis, had taken place at the end of February) I made a motor trip in a second-hand car with two friends in the Rhineland. We were curious about what was happening in Germany. Descending the Rhine from Koblenz, we visited museums, churches and castles, the lovely and romantic Benedictine Abbey of Maria Laach and the Beethoven house.

In Bonn, before continuing to Cologne, we dined in a *Bier Halle* with some German students belonging, as we did, to a European action group. They appeared to have lost nothing of their ideals, but were all more or less in favour of Hitler. I shall never forget one of them, a naive and embittered youth, who wanted to destroy everything—and possess everything. He recited all the usual Nazi propaganda about the rottenness of the 'plutocracies' (one of his favourite words), and the need to destroy Bolshevism, not only Russia, but also France and Belgium (of which, in the latter, there was precious little trace.) Turning towards me, he spoke with rancour of the 'Judaeo-Marxist poison' which was corrupting the world and of Jewish conspiracies aimed at destroying Germany and of assuring through their gold the dominance of Zion.

The evening ended in disaster and we went back to the hotel deeply troubled. Apart from the anti-Semitism, which hurt me for obvious reasons, and offended my friends by its cruel and medieval simplicity, there were many points on which we could agree with our hosts. They were violently critical of the Versailles treaty. So were we, albeit less furiously; it was obvious that Germany had not been the sole country responsible for the Great War, and that many unjust clauses of the peace settlement had to be revised. They had put capitalism on trial. So did we ... daily, fully of revolt against a system which incinerated

wheat, destroyed cattle and poured milk in the rivers, while accepting
that a hundred million human beings should live on the fringes of
starvation. Like them we despised political regimes which did not seem
greatly concerned with preventing a new major war threatening the
world. We had no doubt that the famed 'moral order' of our fathers,
the pretence of virtue in a generation guilty of monstrous crimes, was
no more than contemptible hypocrisy. However, if in our hearts we
believed in the necessity of a mutation in society, our agreement
stopped there.

For our hosts, revolution was not a *means* to improve society, it
was an *end* in itself. They sought to plunge in its turmoil to avoid
having to think; and to achieve it, they had to reach a paroxysm of
wrath. Shortly after our return to Brussels, this was demonstrated for
the first time. On the night of 10 May 1933, some 20 to 25 thousand
books were burned on the famous opera square in Berlin, representing
'the non-German spirit'; similar demonstrations took place in Bonn,
Frankfurt, Göttingen, Hamburg, Cologne and Nuremberg. Although
it was raining in the capital, thousands assembled to celebrate 'the
historic greatness of the evening'. Amid the din of fanfares and orders
shouted from loud-speakers, students in the uniform of the SA put
torches to a pine-wood pyre doused in petrol; then, forming a human
chain, committed to the flames books brought to the pyre in truck-
loads—nearly all that was best in German thought. Illuminated by
the light of the pyre, the Propaganda Minister, Goebbels, promised
German youth that it would be 'educated and given the courage to
look life pitilessly in the eyes, and forget the fear of death'.

Freud, I think, foretold, 'Those who burn books will end by burning
men'. The *auto-da-fé* filled us with horror. In spite of relapses, the
passage of the centuries had been marked by *a slow improvement in
human behaviour*, a progressive triumph of the spirit over primitive
barbarism. Between this steady and rational advance, and the
impassioned virulence of a belligerent nationalism, between those who
would build a less harsh world and those who believe in ferocity, was
there not complete incompatibility? Had the booted militia in the
brown shirts any place in the great adventure which, since the dawn
of history, had progressively freed mankind from the law of the jungle?

Our mentors said 'No'. No religion or moral code, they taught us
has contributed so much to the automony of men, to their 'per-
sonalisation', as western civilisation. Not without being subjected to
a new servitude: the ceaseless questioning of things, the tiresome
obligation of having to choose between 'life and good, and death and

evil'. In this way, the pessimistic currents expressed in the totalitarian ideologies of the Thirties had become fashionable. They had been prepared by the Germans, Hegel, Schopenhauer, Nietzsche, the great names of a reaction, sometimes curiously marked by Asiatic thought, revolting against what they considered the ingenuous artlessness of the humanist philosophies. Also, although less eminent, were H.S. Chamberlain the Englishman, and Count de Gobineau, the Frenchman who invented 'scientific' racism.

George Sorel, the apostle of regeneration through violence also came from France. Then there was the most prominent, Charles Maurras, who died in prison in 1952 at the age of 80, serving a life sentence for collaboration with the enemy. What mysterious path had led the theoretician and inspirer of 'integral nationalism' to collaboration with the hereditary foe of his country?

A hypochondriac and infirm (Maurras assuaged his suffering with laudanum which was then considered harmless), his powerful intellect endowed this bard of the 'Goddess France', the exceptional strength which made him for forty years one of the leading figures of his country. The hideous chaos of a universe without God, the anarchy which he believed was growing around him, filled him with an obsession for order. There could be no beauty, no social life, without order; and no order without a hierarchy of values, no hierarchy without a strong authority to define and constitute its framework. It was, he believed, in ancient Greece that man had first found himself. After Athens and Rome, Paris became the home of the classical tradition, with its apogee in the seventeenth century, the *Grand Siècle*. French thought and language then ruled the civilised world. Everything foreign to that heritage was barbarous. It was therefore essential to abolish the democratic Republic and restore the ancien régime. This entailed the expulsion of everything defiling in thought or civic life; the purity of French classicism—such as the Romanticism of Germany and England, or the cosmopolitism of Kant, Tolstoi and Ibsen. Maurras referred to the 'four federated states', Freemasons, Protestants, Jews and Foreigners, an Anti-France Group which would defile the country's hierarchical, monarchist and Catholic essence. In short, he challenged modern life in all its aspects.[1] In the Europe of the Czars, the Kaisers and other moustachioed and plumed monarchs, the lay Republic was an anomaly. It was not surprising therefore to find posters of the *Action Française* on the walls of Paris in 1908 proclaiming that, 'the Republic is the government of Protestant pedagogues who have imported from Germany, England and Switzerland a system which brutalises and misleads the minds of French youth'. On the morrow of the Armistice, the exaltation of patriotic ardour made people forget what was anachronistic in Maurras's movement, and, for a brief moment it reached a zenith. Then, towards 1925, with the return of tranquility, it appeared to have retreated into the shades of the past.

Nevertheless, the 'Master' continued to be one of the principal personalities of the Parisian world of letters and salons. With the Fascist epidemic, he was to regain great notoriety. His newspaper, (*L'Action Française*) with a circulation in 1933 of 30,000 copies, had increased by 1936 to 70,000—as much as the venerable *Temps*. Some of his theories were similar to those of Hitler and Mussolini. Like them, he fuelled dissatisfaction, he execrated liberal society, idealised the past, and glorified the leaders. His faith in the superiority of the 'Goddess France' was expressed, as in Berlin and Rome, in extreme xenophobia—including hatred of the Jews. Nevertheless, the two approaches were very different. The Duce and the Führer attracted the lower middle classes but not the intelligensia—particularly not in Germany.[2] Maurras, on the other hand, had little appeal for the masses, whose suffrage he despised. But his brilliant reasoning, as much as his glorification of the elite, captivated the governing classes, who saw themselves as a 'plebeian aristocracy'. There were many whom he seduced in the literary world, the Church, the high civil service and the officer corps.

Whether through Maurras or some real Fascists in France, through Mussolini in Italy, Hitler in Germany, Pilsudski in Poland, Horthy in Hungary, Salazar in Portugal, Dolfuss and Schuschnigg in Austria, Mosley in Great Britain, France in Spain and Degrelle in Belgium— Europe displayed its bewilderment, its regret for lost security, its fear of the new or the unknown. Here and there, men clad in black shirts, brown shirts, blue shirts, green shirts, booted and belted, marched past, or goose stepped to the measured beat and sound of warrior songs. Here and there, they committed works of art and books to the flames which contradicted their incantations. When they had the chance, they imprisoned, tortured or assassinated anyone who persisted in believing in reason, or simply anyone they did not like. Nightmares of a frightful past, most of their names will be forgotten by history. But not those of Mussolini and Hitler.

A fortunate set of circumstances (and perhaps a spark of genius) had hoisted the Italian to the summit of power—until that morning in April 1945, when he met a sordid death with his young mistress in a sunken road on the slopes of Lake Como, shot down by tommy-guns. Their corpses were taken to Milan, where they were hung by the feet from the facade of a petrol station, exposed to the cruel derision of the passers-by.

Benito Amilcare Andrea Mussolini was born in Varano dei Costa, a malodorous little village on a hill near Predoppio in the Romagna on 29th July 1883, a Sunday. In his autobiography, written at the height of his success, he boasted, 'The sun had entered the constellation of the Lion eight days before'. His father, a part-time blacksmith, idle, partial to the rough wine of the region, addicted to facile amours (a quality which he bequeathed to his son) exercised by shouting, and sometimes by blows, a tyrannical rule over his family. Anarchist, socialist, no one quite knew which, he had done a spell in prison for subversive activities. The mother, a schoolteacher, provided the stable element in the household, and its subsistence almost single-handed. Father, mother and three children lived hugger-mugger in two dingy rooms in a former patrician house, half-ruined, known as the Palazzo Vorano, which also housed the village school. To the German writer Emil Ludwig, Mussolini said in 1932, not without a boastful touch, 'We very seldom ate meat. But hunger is a good teacher.'*

Angelica Balabanoff, a young revolutionary from Kiev, whom Mussolini had met in Switzerland, herself a bizarre personality, maintained close relations with the young rebel before collaborating with the socialist newspaper *Avanti*. To her we owe the portrait of a neurotic youth, extremely timid, at once ill at ease and yet vindictive, dirty and deliberately badly dressed, shaving only twice a week.

> 'In spite of his hatred of the privileged classes', she wrote, 'he did not regard himself as a proletarian but as an intellectual, a leader. The contrast between his high opinion of himself and his modest station in life filled him with self pity and an exaggerated sense of injustice. He was always complaining about his health, but at the same time was very proud of his virility.'[4]

She did not exaggerate. When still a schoolboy, he had been a regular client of the brothels in Forlimpopoli. He recounts himself how he:

> seduced Virginia, one of my first conquests. I followed her one day down the stairs, threw her on the ground behind the door and had her. She got up crying, and between the sobs shouted insults at me. She said I had violated her honour. Probably. But what sort of honour was it?

---

* After he came to power, Mussolini made much of his modest origins. Previously, he had prided himself on being descended from a family of the old nobility.[3]

He was to do the same with innumerable women, servants as well as princesses, wives of his collaborators or journalists, actresses or visiting foreign ladies, eager to prove to himself his contempt for the weaker sex. When still young, he contracted syphilis.[5] Before the discovery of antibiotics, it was almost incurable. To combat the agent of the infection, the 'pale treponeme', substances were injected—based on mercury arsenic, bismuth, in particular salvarsan—a treatment which lasted several years and was not without danger. Relapses were frequent; and each time the infection became more virulent. It finished by invading the brain and the marrow of the spine. The third phase of the infection seriously affects the personality of the victim, characterised by periods of great exaltation which cloud the judgement, followed by deep depression.

In 1904, after a long stay in Switzerland, the young Mussolini returned to Italy for his military service. He proved to be a docile and zealous soldier. After this, he resumed his career of itinerant teacher, always unstable, wandering from town to town, often drunk. As an extreme left-wing militant, he was kept under surveillance by the police. In 1911, at the time of the Libyan war, he appealed for an uprising and took part in a riot in the streets of Forli, for which he received a prison sentence. Released after five months, he published increasingly incendiary articles. He became known as a skilled polemist with a sharp pen, and an orator with a biting tongue. When the revolutionary leaders summoned him to Milan to edit *Avanti*, he launched into invectives against reforming socialism, as well as against the bourgeois state. When the first World War broke out, he condemned the 'imperialist' powers, and noisily demanded the 'absolute neutrality' of Italy.

Suddenly he turned his coat and advocated intervention. On 14 November 1914, a new paper, the *Popolo d'Italia*, appeared. In this, with his usual virulence, he preached Italy's entry into the war on the side of France and Great Britain. Ten days later, after a dramatic meeting, he was expelled from the Socialist Party. His motivations have never been thoroughly explained. Money certainly played a part. The *Popolo d'Italia* was originally financed by a group of industrialists, attracted by the prospect of military contracts; among them were the directors of Edison, Fiat and Ansaldo. Mussolini also received secret funds from abroad; from Paris through Marcel Cachin, the future French communist leader; from London, through Samuel Hoare, later the Conservative Foreign Secretary. It appears that he also asked for help from a Czarist secret agent; but the Russians did not trust him.[6]

In spite of this, the attraction of financial gain was not the whole explanation; he was never much interested in money. He told Emil Ludwig in 1932, 'The Trades Unions wanted war, because it would bring revolution, and I was with them.' For the first time, most of the nation adopted a position hostile to that of the Parliamentarians and political wheeler dealers.[7] In fact, powerful popular pressures led to intervention on the side of the Entente. They were strong enough to persuade Mussolini that his ambition could best be served by Italian patriotism—a yeast in the electoral dough as potent at that moment as socialism. His judgement proved correct and fortune smiled on him. The *Popolo d'Italia* was a great success. Reflecting most of popular opinion, edited by a journalist of exceptional talent, its influence contributed to Italy's entry into the war.

Called up in 1915, Mussolini was badly wounded after eighteen months by the explosion of a mortar bomb during an exercise behind the lines. Invalided out, he took to the pen again. After the Armistice, temporarily at a loss, he assumed the role of spokesman for the thousands of discontented ex-service men, embittered at not entering Paradise after escaping from Hell. With his usual ferocity, he attacked the peace treaties for not giving Italy her due. In March 1919, he founded the *Fasci Italiani di Combattimenti*. Because the workers remained faithful to their socialist leaders, the principal support and membership for the new Party came from the middle classes. With 17,000 members at the end of 1919, the Fascisti numbered 310,000 two years later. Benefiting from the feebleness and incoherence of the traditional Parties, they exploited to the full the unfortunate after-effects of the Great War. While their shock-troops donned black shirts (the old garb of the anarchists), and committed acts of violence, their leader proclaimed himself the champion of law and order.

The device worked. The movement grew astonishingly fast. In the 1921 election, Mussolini entered Parliament in the company of 35 colleagues from the *Partito Nazionale Fascista*. On 27 October 1922, on a cold and rainy morning, the Fascists marched on Rome—without their Duce. 26,000 Blackshirts (40,000 within the next few days) debouched on the streets, wet and famished, with little self-confidence, they could have been dispersed with ease. General Badoglio said later that a battalion would have done the job. But King Victor Emmanuel feared his Aosta cousin; who had joined the Fascists and aspired to the throne. He refused to declare martial law. Mussolini, in a state of anxiety bordering on hysteria, was in Milan awaiting the outcome of the venture. On receipt of a telegram, he rushed to the station and took the first train to Rome. After a night in the *wagon-lit*, he made his appearance before the King, wearing a black shirt, a hired frock-coat and white gaiters. The following day he obtained the King's approval to form a Ministry of National Union (in which, at the outset, there were only four Fascists). By a large majority, Parliament granted him full powers. Head of the government at the age of 39, Mussolini was to remain there until that day, twelve years later when the Fascist hierarchy and the King himself rid themselves of a director broken by illness and military disasters.

What was the secret of his extraordinary success? The political chaos at the time and the hand of the King undoubtedly played a role. As did his consuming passion for power—'this essence of joy', Nietzsche, for whom he had an unlimited admiration, had said. But also an almost inspired instinct which enabled him to base his dictatorship on a kind of national consensus. While fear of change weakened the moral strength of the democracies, Mussolini gave confidence by combining the promises of tradition and revolution. Fraudulent no doubt; but rather easy to do, by a regime which had silenced all opposition. Unlike Maurras, he extolled all social classes, promising every Italian a position of importance, and the wealth that went with it. It was the demagogy which the Communists had used so successfully with the proletariat, now applied to the whole nation.

In the very first manifesto of the Fascist Party, we find indeed the two principal themes of an extreme right-wing nationalism going hand in hand with the most radical socialism; on the one hand, territorial expansion in the direction of Austria and Dalmatia; on the other, the abolition of the monarchy, the Senate, titles of nobility, partial expropriation of wealth and distribution of land to the peasants. The rest? The setting of a comic opera—*A Noi! A Noi! Ulala!*, together with flags, uniforms, Roman salutes. It was not until 1926 that the Duce started talking about a 'Fascist regime', based on some of the ideas of Sorel, Maurras and Nietzsche—the divine nature of the nation, the mystical character of the leader, together with verbal hostility to capitalism. All this was expressed in those inept slogans repeated a thousand times, which Italians and foreign tourists could read on the venerable walls of Venice, Florence, Rome and Naples. 'An Italian peace in the shadow of Italian bayonets! Believe, Obey, Fight'; 'Mussolini is always right!', and much else. Towards the end of his reign, he made these slogans tally to a certain extent with the myths of National Socialism—the long-headed, blue-eyed blond heroes, brave warriors of the Aryan race!

In fact all these forthright exhortations concealed a very mediocre person. The giant who is 'always right', endowed with 'a logic of iron', 'a granite will' was in reality, the same tormented, indecisive creature whom Angelica Balabanoff had known, a 'pover huomo' his wife would write one day.

Mussolini found it very difficult to come to a decision, he was morbidly fearful of taking action. Superstitious manias reflected his sense of insecurity. He suffered severely from a stomach ulcer, which the strictest diet could not cure; it is well known that this is often caused by anxiety.[8] His amorous life, consisting of innumerable passing fancies, rarely moved him. After a six year liaison with one of his mistresses, Rachel, and the birth of a daughter, he married her. But she exercised little influence over him. He was without a real friend and confidant—with the exception, perhaps, of his brother Arnaldo, who died in 1931. 'I have no friends, I don't want any', he said in his informative conversations with Emil Ludwig. 'Of the many faces that pass before my eyes, not one has any effect on me inwardly. They move me no more than that table or this pile of paper.'[9]

This fathomless scorn for his fellow beings compensated his timidity. In his misanthropic loneliness he regarded them all as stupid or venal. That they might be moved by any idealism or altruistic motive, he would not concede. These convictions made him take risks which were alien to his nature. If he had not met Hitler, he would probably have remained what the Frenchman Paul-Boncour, with more wit than tact, called him, 'a carnival Caesar', a burlesque, if provoking figure, whom European cabinets would have to put up with. It was the meeting of the two Dictators which was to be the curse of Europe.

★　　　★　　　★

Hitler—what more is there to say about him? How to bring to life, for those who were neither the enthusiastic nor the horrified contemporary witnesses, the phenomenon of this inordinately evil career—of the man who deliberately, wilfully, brought about the Second World War? His career was meteoric and short; but when his calcined remains were buried in the concrete rubble of Berlin, he left behind more destruction than that caused by any other cataclysm natural or human. How shall we explain this character who was unique in the history of the West?

Hundreds of volumes have been written about him; but none has really explained this creature, unlike all other men. Have the historians been too recondite? Is not the mystery to be explained in the monstrous exaggeration of lineaments which many other maniacal demagogues have displayed—rather like an over-enlarged photograph? If we accept this notion, the enlarged print simplifies our understanding of his character. Psychiatric analysis, so presumptuous and dangerous in less defined cases, seems justified here; because the idiosyncrasies of the subject are easy to observe, it becomes possible, with less risk of error, to explain them.

It has always been stated that he was a paranoic. This, as is well known, is characterised by benign or serious disorders which psychologists attribute to a state of insecurity in early years, resulting from a derangement of emotional relations between father, mother and child. It is not very precise, and the term paranoia is often used loosely. However, Hitler's childhood was such that it could have caused the affliction—a tyrannical and brutal father, a mother who was a slave to the husband and inclined to an excessive love for her son, perhaps with incestuous undertones, subtle or more overt. In Hitler's behaviour we do indeed find most of the symptoms of the malady, in particular the sexual problems which are frequently an indication of it—linked perhaps obscurely with anxieties and morbid obsessions which stimulated the excessive hypertrophy of his personality.

Was Hitler maimed as a result of a war wound, did he suffer from illness of a syphilitic origin, or from impotence, or of anatomical malformation? It is known that he had only one testicle—a deformity without great physiological importance, but likely to have traumatic effects. Other more significant indications have led to diagnosing a sexuality brutally repressed over a long period, with the sadomasochist and homosexual tendencies, which are often the consequence.* We cannot be certain, but this hypothesis seems the best answer to all questions. Although much attracted by eroticism, the customs official's son displayed fear and repulsion when confronted with it. Like other paranoics who identify the flesh with evil, it weighed on his conscience, inducing an acute guilt complex. He had built up a pornographic library, and he liked looking at 'blue' films; he enjoyed questioning

---

* There is nothing to show that Hitler was ever an active homosexual. Nevertheless, the psychiatrists have discerned very clear tendencies in his behaviour. He was abnormally obsessed by it, and ferociously enforced the laws of the Reich repressing it. That he was, in other respects, the slave of repugnant sexual perversions is not in doubt. In 1941, they were revealed in a psychological study made by the American Secret Service, ancestor of the CIA. Other researches after the war have confirmed this.[10]

young women about their sexual life, and demanding detailed descriptions. At the same time, he displayed the most rigid puritanism.[11]

Shakespeare, that psychiatrist of genius, describes the torments of a Plantagenet, the future Richard III:

> Why, love forswore me in my mother's womb ...
> And am I then a man to be belov'd?
> O monstrous faulty, to harbour such a thought!
> Then, since this earth affords no joy to me
> But to command, to check, to o'ver bear such
> As are better person than myself
> I'll make my heaven to dream upon the crown ...
>
> Torment myself to catch the English crown
> And from that torment I will free myself
> Or hew my way out with a bloody axe.

His psychological problems were not eased by friendship, any more than by love. Something in his being encompassed him in solitude. Suddenly and brusquely, he had moved away from August Kubizek, who had shared his Bohemian life in Vienna. In his military career, he had always remained aloof from his fellows. He broke off all relations with his family—except with his half-sister Angela, a simple soul who acted as his house-keeper at Berchtesgarten. His relations with his closest collaborators, Göring, Goebbels, Himmler, Hess, and later with his generals, were frigid and distant. He only felt at ease in the presence of subalterns, secretaries, chauffeurs, aides-de-camp, with whom he would spend hours in monologue. Röhm, the chief of the SA was nearer to him than anyone, the only person who addressed him as 'Du'. Yet Röhm was to be liquidated in the first 'purge' of the regime. Hitler was never intimate with Göring, although he was to designate him as his successor.

Before the Great War, the solidly ordered structure of the old world could not have been shattered by the disordered paroxysms of a neurotic vagabond. Hitler had been seen wandering about the streets of Vienna, in and out of doss-houses and slums, filled with horror at living and fear of dying, haunted by extravagant dreams which compensated for the mediocrity of his life and the suffering of his flesh. Incapable of self-discipline or of mastering his ambitions, aspiring vaguely to be a great artist, one day a musician, the next a painter, then a architect, then a painter again, ranting at the depravity of society, true or imagined, expectorating to right and left the venom which filled his heart. A volunteer in the 1914 war, he proved a courageous soldier, being decorated several times. Four years of combat appear to have appeased his wrath. Then came 1919 and the collapse of the Central Empires. He was thirty, the age of Napoleon Bonaparte when he became First Consul. For lack of anything better, he stayed on as a corporal in the demobilised army, acting as an informer to the military police in Munich. He was instructed to infiltrate an obscure little Party of the extreme Right which was to become the NSDAP (*National-sozialistische Deutsche Arbeiterpartei*), the Nazis. One evening, when invited to address an audience of 2,000 in a beer-hall, the Hofbraühaus, he discovered his exceptional oratorical gifts. He has described the revelation which propelled him into his new vocation. In a disintegrating society, he had found a place for the expansion of his personality; then, taming the cosmic despair in his soul, he proceeded to the conquest of this paradise—that of Richard III, universal sovereignty.

In the middle of the Burning Bush of his frustration, God appeared to invest him with a divine mission. Comparing himself with Christ, Hitler insisted that he had been visited in 1919, when he was wounded and blinded in a military hospital, by a supernatural vision which ordered him to save Germany. He then was, he liked to relate, of the same age as Jesus at the beginning of his ministry.* *Der Führer*, the title he gave himself, was indefinable, unlike any other, possessed of a magical force. There is no doubt that he saw himself as the emissary of God, a Messiah destined to save his countrymen. His words in 1936 are well known, 'I follow the path traced for me by Providence with all the assurance of a sleep walker.'

Historians have attempted to discover the intellectual fountain at which the future master of Germany drank. A futile exercise. A temperamental and lazy adolescent, a mediocre student, he had shirked the *Abitur* (the German equivalent of the *baccalaureate*). Afterwards, he still avoided study, finding arduous tasks repugnant, even the simple examination of documents. He was unmethodical, undecided until he abruptly took a decision, moved by an often obscure impulse. Exalting in action, he had nothing but scorn for persons of reflective nature. In the hotch-potch of his writings and speeches are traces of Nietzsche, Hegel, Gobineau and other writers and pamphleteers of the same schools—even of Marx; but it is more than probable that he went no further than glancing superficially through them, gleaning here and there suitable arguments to justify his rages. On his own admission,

---

* Corporal Hitler, gassed in October 1918 on the Ypres front, was blinded, from which he recovered, only to lose his sight again on 9 November, at the time of the German capitulation. Were the origins of his malady hysterical?[12]

his mental attitude had crystalised when he was barely twenty years old. It is true that curiosity led him up a number of paths, from which he learned a good deal. But he lacked disciplined mental education, organised and systematised, which, departing from elementary data, leads to the highest levels, ending, as the Greeks contended, in the supreme talent of governance.

It was not therefore from a brilliant and intelligent mind that Hitler's strange charisma derived, a charisma which was to mesmerise millions of Germans and thousands of other Europeans; nor was it due to the magnetic flash of his blue eyes; nor the mysterious aura of which many of his flatterers have spoken. This comes with success, thanks to the natural emotions of simple souls in the presence of those who wield great power. In my youth in China, I saw European men and women (the women principally), sometimes racists, whose eyes dimmed when they touched the sleeve of that mediocre Asiatic potentate, Chiang Kai-shek. Among the many factors in the prodigious rise of Hitler was his promotion of the phenomenon of rejection which was characteristic of the 'totalitarian' ideology—The rejection of Christian moral forces, a liberation from 2,000 years of agonizing spiritual efforts to create a civilised world—what Oswald Spengler called a return to 'the primary psychic state'; the rejections of many new or foreign forms of thinking; also the rejection of intruding members of the community who demanded a more active participation in its working—among them women. The Great War had started the process of breaking the fetters which had always shackled them. National Socialism and Fascism proposed to send the weaker sex back to the 'kitchen, the nursery and the Church', in order to safeguard a masculine society inspired by virile virtues. Above all, was his success due to the mixture concocted more or less consciously by Mussolini—the only one of his peers for whom this monster of pride showed any respect all his life. More even than the Duce, the Führer was to render highly plausible the contradictory, even absurd, notion which constituted the originality of the two Dictators: that of the participation of everyone in the elite, *the promise to everyone, down to the humblest man in the street, that he could become a superman.* Probably one of the great ideas of the 'totalitarian' doctrines, it has made a contribution to contemporary politics, which have unfortunately not become completely free of it.

For the historical determinism of Karl Marx, Hitler substituted the determinism of natural force; for the class struggle, that of race.

> The 'brazen Law of Nature' requires a pitiless struggle of all against all, and the victory of the strong over the weak. Humanity can become great only through

mortal combat; this eliminates inferior races, to the advantage of nobler ones. From time immemorial, the Aryans have led the people towards what is most elevated politically, aesthetically and intellectually. Their empire is continually threatened by inferior races, in particular by the Jews. Mixing blood is the original sin. Since the Aryan renounced the purity of his blood, he has lost his place in the paradise that he had created for himself. People do not perish through losing wars, but by losing the strength which produces pure blood. Everything in this world which is not race is rottenness.[13]

Hitler spoke in glowing terms of a popular German community (*Volksgemeinschaft*), in which he described the finest of human societies. He had been invested by Providence with the sacred task of resurrecting it, returning it to its ancient greatness. War, total war, war of annihilation, was the natural condition for that resurrection. War was not, as the celebrated maxim claimed, politics carried out by other means, but an end in itself, an inevitable, metaphysical normality. 'All creatures drink the blood of other creatures, the death of one nourishes another . . . there is no reason to get excited by this.'[13] In his last radio speech, on 30 January 1945, when he was about to become silent for ever, he repeated that he had always known only one principle—strike, strike, and strike again!

The doctrinaire National Socialist did not hesitate to associate this eternal, unlimited struggle with the conquest of living space, *Lebensraum*—a contradiction which did not embarrass him. He had announced it in *Mein Kampf* in oft quoted words,

Only a sufficiently large space can assure liberty of existence for a nation. Germany does not possess it, she must acquire it . . . it can be gained only at the expense of Russia . . . Consequently, the new Reich must resume the road followed by the ancient Teutonic knights, to conquer with the German sword the soil owed to the German plough.

Was not this obsession with space—one of Hitler's fundamental ideas—closely linked with his pathological over-estimation of his ego, the irresistable need of aggrandisement? Or was it, according to the grosser explanation of the psychiatrists (who exaggerate perhaps—or do they?), due to a delirious desire to destroy everything around him.[14] What confirmed the hallucinatory nature of his ambitions was that they were devoid of any explicit content. Apart from the vague conception of the 'AA Line' (Archangel to Astrakhan), put forward at the time of the Russian campaign, in neither his speeches nor his writings do we find any more or less precise explanation of his long-term objectives. After having frequently promised to respect the western frontiers of 1919, he annexed Alsace-Lorraine, and intended to incorporate Belgium and Holland in the Reich. What would he have done with France and Great Britain? We do not know. All his life he talked about a great Empire in the east. Where would the limits of such an Empire have been? What would have become of Poland, Rumania, Yugoslavia and Greece? He never revealed this. He had made no study of the territories he intended to conquer, of their agricultural and mining resources, their strategic values, or of the statutes applicable to their population. Would they have all been liquidated? He had spoken gleefully of establishing German agricultural colonies in Russia, but had made no proper preparation for it. When Alfred Rosenberg became Minister of the East in 1941, no authority was conferred on him; to assure 'security', the all powerful police services confined themselves to massacring Slavs. Hitler showed the same imprecision about overseas colonies. Disdainfully rejected in *Mein Kampf*, they nevertheless occupied a high place in his ambitions, and he undoubtedly intended to try to conquer Egypt and the Middle East. Where would he be stopped?

Together with his need for space, the execration of the Jews was one of his principal obsessions, connected no doubt with his destructive mania. Anti-Semitism was an ancient and latent sentiment in Germany, as in many other countries. After the Great War, the trauma of an unexpected defeat, the humiliation of Versailles, the great immigration of Jews from the Polish ghettos, the destitution engendered by the Great Crisis, had concentrated resentments of all sorts upon the Jews. Unscrupulous politicians found it a paying proposition to denounce their imaginary depravity—as well as identifying them in all circumstances with the Bolsheviks, an allegation to which their relative importance in the communist parties of Eastern Europe seemed to give some ground. The visionary racist saw it differently.

> 'We are at the end of the century of reason', he told Rauschnigg.
> 'The sovereignty of the spirit is a pathological degradation of normal life'. This he applied to his hatred of the Jews, which was inveterate, frenzied and undying. 'Being "anti-humanity" (*Gegenrasse*) they cannot be regarded as human beings created in the image of an eternal God. They are the envoys of the Devil. In our defence against Jews, I am fighting for the works of the Lord.'

Sometimes he saw them gnawing at the social body, as tuberculosis gnaws at the human body. Convinced that, like Pasteur and Koch, he had discovered a new virus, he believed that it had opened the way to 'one of the greatest revolutions in world history'.[16] On one occasion, he surpassed himself. 'If the Jews, with the help of Marxism, succeed in conquering the nations of the world, their crown will be a mortuary wreath laid upon the tomb of humanity. As it was millions of years ago, the planet will gravitate into infinite space, drained of all human life.' This abonination of Judaism, in all its forms and aspects, was never to leave him. During the hours before his suicide, under the ruins of the Reich Chancellery, with the apocalyptical roar of the Russian guns outside, he dictated his will, which finished with the words: 'Above all, I recommend to the government of the nation strict observance of the racial laws, and pitiless opposition to the poisoner of all people—international Jewry.'[15]

These horrible maxims which were to send six million human beings to the gas chambers, could only emanate from a psychosis which will probably never be explained. It may also have been linked with Hitler's morbid sexuality. He cited: 'The young black-haired Jew, his face lit up with satanic joy, as for hours he lies in wait for the innocent young girl, whom he will soil by his contact, and abduct from the people to whom she belongs.' Or, 'These black parasites who methodically pollute our pure blonde young girls.' Or, 'The nightmare vision of hundreds of young girls seduced by repulsive bow-legged Jewish bastards.' This obsession is to be found again and again in his speeches and writings.[16]

We know that one of Hitler's grandfathers, whose identity is uncertain, may have been Jewish. Did Hitler, rightly or wrongly, perhaps believe this? The desire to conceal such an unspeakable blemish, an insane longing for redemption—did they constrain him to destroy all those whom he considered responsible for his misfortune? It is a psychologically valid hypothesis. Other men than Hitler have been driven to the most frenzied anti-Semitism by a secret repulsion for their Jewish origin. So it was, we are told, in the case of the cruellest of the Spanish Grand Inquisitors, Hernando of Talavera.

We may also ask whether the fact that Hitler succeeded, in exceptional circumstances, in becoming absolute master of one of the first civilised nations did not conceal the simple fact that he suffered from murder mania. All his ideology, with its mystical exaltation of war, his notion of limitless conquest, his sanguinary racism, tended to the 'annihilation'—a word often on his lips—not only of those who opposed his plans, but also of all those who offered the smallest possible pretext for being put to death. The Second World War gave him the opportunity to proceed—and not only on the battlefield—to slaughter on such a scale that it caused serious logistic difficulties for the conduct of operations themselves. For the Jews were not the only object of his ferocity—far from it. On 1 September 1939, the first day of the war, an order was issued for the liquidation of some 100,000 Germans, the sick and incurable, pensioners in hospitals and mental homes—so many redundant mouths to feed. In Poland, official statistics speak of six million dead. In Russia, the land of future colonisation, the slaughter of 'sub-men' Slavs as well as Jews, was even greater. Prisoners of war were also put to death or left to die in hundreds of thousands. In 1945 when there were no more Jews or Slavs to destroy, Hitler extended to 'Aryans' his murder mania. Confined ten metres underground in the Chancellery bunker, his body devastated by drugs, his hands trembling convulsively, his vision dimmed, his mind oscillating between moments of extravagant euphoria, and insane rages, his last orders were to slay prisoners, one of his former doctors, his brother-in-law, officers and soldiers who had retreated; finally he killed his mistress and himself.

Onto a rudimentary metaphysic he had grafted a doctrine of action, of which the National Socialist Party was to be the Church militant. It has been observed that its structure was inspired by Roman Catholic institutions. Hitler himself compared the role of the SS, his 'Black Order', with that of the Company of Jesus. Certainly, there were similarities—as also with the Communist Party of the USSR— but they were superficial. In 1934 the National Socialist Party had lost its old leaders, executed in the Night of the Long Knives; under the direction of Rudolph Hess, it continued to live on the fat of the land, but without any real authority.

As for the State, Hitler, with his fixation of race and nation, saw in it only a tool, soon to be blunted. Having concentrated most of the regional power in Berlin, he had taken under his exclusive domination the great public institutions, the Legislative, the Executive and the Judiciary. The Assemblies were abolished or converted into registry offices. The government was convened only at irregular intervals and, finally, not at all. The Ministry of Foreign Affairs had its double in the Ribbentrop Bureau, and the Ministry of Economy, a double in the Plan Commission. Only the General Staff (Ober/Kommando des Heeres—OKH) managed for a time to defend its identity; but it finally came under a Supreme Command (Ober/Kommando des Wehrmacht—OKW), directed by the Führer in person. No constitutional, legal or administrative rules now defined the rights of the citizens, or their relationships to one another. The solid pyramid of Bismarchian Germany, the powerful traditions of the old Prussian State, were destroyed. The Party institutions and those of the State were piled up in a chaotic mass of disparate bodies, on top of which, brooding and all-powerful, the little man in the mustard-coloured uniform sat alone. Such a state of affairs had never before been known in the West.

Hitler had not been interested in great economic questions. As with Maurras, to him they were entirely subordinate to 'politics'. 'On each occasion in Germany', he said, 'when political leadership has given a new injection of vigour, economic conditions have begun to improve.' After taking power, he launched out into vast rearmament and public works programmes, insisting that they would not lead to inflation. In a powerful monolithic dictatorship, after a long period of deflation, there could be temporarily some truth in this. Inspired unconsciously by the ideas of Keynes, he proceeded to 'reflate' on a grand scale. With the masterly technical assistance of Dr Schacht, this led to a revival of the economy and the reduction of unemployment—which contributed greatly to the popularity of the regime.*

Far more than industry, Hitler regarded agriculture as the real strength of Germany. For him, the peasants were 'the soul and blood of the people', the nation's stable element. By their labour, they enabled Germany to produce its own food without having recourse to the foreigner. They also made the best soldiers because they understood better than anyone else the need to defend the earth which they had watered with the sweat of their brows. The Third Reich showed great solicitude for them. It reformed the agrarian laws, instituted the *Erbhof*, an inalienable property of the family, and the support of a hereditary elite of pure-blooded peasant soldiers. *Blut und Boden* (Blood and Soil) proclaimed the Führer—empty meaningless words. That he should see the wealth of a nation in the soil, and not in the techniques invented by human intelligence; that he intended to ensure the prosperity of Germany by an agricultural colonisation which had been abandoned six hundred years before, this only emphasises the irrational nature of his thoughts.

Lebensraum and aggrandisement, war and extermination were, when all is said, the fundamental themes of *Mein Kampf*, the expression certainly of its author's subconscious. The book left no place for doubt. First, with Italy and Great Britain's help, the power of France would be crushed. The march towards the East would follow, with the annexation of countries inhabited by Germans (Austria, Czechoslovakia and Western Poland). Then the conquest of Russia could be

---

* In fact, the German economy had begun picking up six months before the Nazis came to power, thanks to the reflation brought about by Dr Schacht's 'bills of work'. Five million unemployed were put to work under the Third Reich; but most of their salaries remained lower than in 1929.

undertaken, to prepare the Great Empire of the Aryans of the Twentieth Century.[17]

★   ★   ★

Such were Hitler's ideas, proclaimed in two tomes of indigestible and muddled thinking, expressed in bad German, and presented after the manner of the Tables of the Law revealed to him by God the Almighty. All the same, they are well known, and events have given them a hideous validity. What seem astonishing today, and difficult to understand—even for those like myself who lived through the Hitlerian era—are the reasons for the scepticism and indifference, or complacency, with which European statesmen received the apocalyptical plans of the German Führer. And this, when the most inoffensive indications of ill-humour on the part of the Weimar Republic sufficed to make the French, Polish, Czech and Belgian leaders shiver in their shoes. Nothing much can remain secret. Informed by their Embassies and information services, they should have known that Hitler's statements, born of his hallucinations, nourished by his reading and conversations, had been perfected during years of struggle and discussion with his acolytes. No one could have failed to recognise the utter amorality of the man (nor his different set of morals), nor his extraordinary force of character nor his monstrous libido.

Nor were there grounds for supposing that the arrival in power of the Nietzschean hero would divert him from his plans, or moderate his rages. On its publication, *Mein Kampf* had only a limited success.* But during the twelve months after its author's entry into the Reichs Chancellery, a million copies were sold; and five more million between 1933 and 1940. Its sale was assured by the official services, and all Germans were encouraged, if not forced, to buy it—with the exception of young newly weds, to whom it was graciously presented by the registry official at their wedding. The French Ambassador in Berlin aksed Hitler personally on several occasions to modify with a footnote the violently anti-French passages; but he obtained no satisfaction.

Meanwhile all the acts of the Führer (with the exception of the occasional pacific or smoothing protestations)—the many confidential asides uttered by himself, or by his lieutenants, to many Germans and foreigners; together with the speeches and writings of Göring, Goebbels, Himmler, Streicher, and the media closely controlled by the

---

* Less than 10,000 copies of *Mein Kampf* were sold in 1925; 5,600 in 1927. During the Great Crisis the number rose to 54,000 in 1930, and 90,350 in 1932.

Reich Propaganda Ministry, which continued week after week, month after month, year after year—all these factors revealed the determined and inflexible will of the visionary to achieve his great ambition. 'I will do such things', said King Lear when near to madness, 'of which yet I know not—but they will be the terrors of the earth.'

CHAPTER 3

The Great Fear of the Decent People

'To give in to the temptations of the sirens is in the nature of man; but to be driven by despair to sleep with a crocodile is the privilege of our epoch'. With this graphic phrase Arthur Koestler referred to those who allowed themselves to be seduced—as he had been himself—by the fallacious promises of Communism. Today, we are surrounded by all sorts of crocodiles, which we often feed. We accept, without a murmur, disorder in its various forms. The word 'Revolution' itself has lost its horror, and may even imply something good. This state of mind in recent. All through the nineteenth and the first decades of the twentieth centuries, in spite of its past glories and apparent self-confidence, Europe never quite renounced the gnawing fear of the 'Great Revolution'.

After 1918, it had good reason for this. The victory of the Bolsheviks in Russia had unleashed a tidal-wave which threatened the Old Continent. In North Germany, Bavaria and Hungary, 'proletarian dictatorships' had taken over the public buildings. Poland was invaded by the Red Army. On the other side of the world, the flag of the Kuomintang (armed and dominated by Moscow, while directed by Chiang Kai-shek, then an honorary member of the Comintern), had been unfurled over the Old Celestial Empire.

In Italy, in 1920, extensive strikes had led to the occupation of hundreds of factories by 'Soviets', but the Communists and Socialists fell out, and the movement was short-lived. Nevertheless, the country remained apprehensive, under feeble and indecisive governments; domestic peace was beset with rival factions. France, too, during that year was restless, with more than 2,000 work stoppages, often accompanied by rebellious demonstrations. In Paris, in a single month, April 1920, 47 policemen and 19 police inspectors were killed during raids and riots. On 1 May, the capital was placed under a state of siege. Detachments of cavalry patrolled the popular quarters, barricades were erected at the Gare de l'Est, the *Mairie* of Saint-Denis was transformed into a 'Soviet'. The city was paralysed by an almost general strike. Soldiers responsible for maintaining order mutinied. In the Black Sea, the Bolshevik contagion led to a mutiny by the sailors of the French squadron. In camps and naval bases, orders were flouted. The courts martial pronounced heavy sentences. At the socialist Congress of Tours in 1920, most of the militants joined the Third International, Moscow's Comintern, and called for an armed uprising.

Great Britain did not escape the infection. A number of small groups unified, with the avowed intention of repeating Lenin's success and establishing a dictatorship of the proletariat. Their influence was felt inside the Labour Party which, while not collaborating directly with them, shared their views about class warfare and the approaching end of capitalism. There was much talk of a general strike. As in France, due to the political unrest and the appalling bungle made of demobilisation and the lack of employment, the troops could not be counted upon; units of the British Army in Russia revolted. On 22 January 1919, the Chief of the Imperial General Staff reported to the Cabinet that unpopular orders could no longer be given, and that discipline was a thing of the past.[1] These fears were enough to dissuade Lloyd George from going to the help of Poland, invaded by the Soviets.

For several months, Lenin, Trotsky and their friends believed that the Western world was about to rally to their side. Even peaceful Switzerland was afflicted by a general strike aiming at social revolution. Europe and the United States were on the verge of hysteria, fed by fearful accounts of atrocities committed by the Reds—mostly true, but some exaggerated. The most fantastic rumours were abroad; among them, that of the alleged 'nationalisation of women'.* All my contemporaries remember brochures on whose cover was depicted a bearded Bolshevik in a leather coat, the red star on his cap, a knife dripping with blood between his teeth. The myth circulated of a Europe on the point of being submerged by the 'Asiatic' barbarians—the end of civilisation!

The red tidal-wave ebbed very quickly. In Berlin, the Spartakist movement was crushed by a social democratic government, and its leaders, Rosa Luxemburg and Karl Liebknecht, were assassinated. Bavaria came under a reactionary regime. In Hungary, Bela Kun and his dictatorship foundered. In Poland, the Russian armies were thrown

---

* A rumour founded on a proclamation by short-lived Soviet anarchists in the city of Saratov, Central Russia.

back to the east. In Italy, Mussolini strangled the workers' movement. On the eve of the Depression, the Communists no longer presented a real threat. In the Reichstag, they had 45 seats out of 491; in the Palais Bourbon, 11 out of 612 and none, or insignificant numbers, in the British, Belgian and Scandinavian Parliaments. In China, the *volte-face* of Chiang Kai-shek before Shanghai in March 1927 had put an end to their venture. In Moscow, the struggle for power had ended with the victory of Stalin, a believer in 'Revolution in one country'. Trotsky, the advocate of 'Permanent Revolution' was exiled in Central Asia—finally to be assassinated in Mexico in 1940, with an ice-pick in his skull. For some time, the Kremlin muted its subversive activities, to concentrate on domestic problems.

Nevertheless, the trauma had been acute, the fear remained latent, nourished by the extreme brutality of the Soviet regime, the liquidation of the independent farmers (Kulaks), the obliteration of the national minorities, the anti-religious campaign; and after 1936, by the fearful purges perpetrated under Stalin's dictatorship.

★   ★   ★

Other deep causes added to the discomfiture of the West. Discoveries in physics threw doubt on rationalism, and on the generally accepted systems of thought. They seemed to confirm the pessimistic philosophies of Germany. Einstein had just shaken the notion of time and space. Heisenberg opposed the principles of indeterminism to the theories of determinism. Bergson, James and Unanumo stated that the human universe does not possess the scale of absolute values on which most western societies had hitherto been based. Many of the intellectuals were deeply perturbed.

Although the masses were not concerned with philosophy, they no longer subscribed blindly to regimes whose mentors were now so full of doubts. On one side of the barricade stood the great army of workers, many unemployed, the veritable 'damned ones of the earth', whose extremists, frustrated by poverty and full of fury, clamoured for a revolution—it didn't matter what revolution, provided it gave them back the bread they no longer had. On the other side, were those who still lived in the residue of the past, who anathematised the modern, more arduous times. The rich and powerful feared they would lose their wealth and authority. The less rich feared they would lose the privileges acquired at the time of the industrial revolution—and, of these, the prestige more than the income.

Above all, the white-collared *petit bourgeois* were terrified at the prospect of returning to the proletariat out of which they had climbed—they or their fathers—at such a cost. To those whose possessions had been affected by the consecutive devaluations following the Great War, bewildered by the disappearance of the old hierarchies, which had supported as much as oppressed them, appalled by the decline of the Churches which had consoled them since the death of Christ, unhinged in a rapidly changing society, the Nation State appeared to offer a new family, a new religion, a new reason for living. True enough, they were not the majority, but among them a number of young people and old soldiers allowed themselves to be carried away by the ardent mystique derived from the teaching of Hegel, Mazzini, Houston Chamberlain, Maurras, etc. They hovered between nostalgia for a former illusory perfection, and fear of a morrow draped in black. 'The future is the end,' wrote Drieu La Rochelle, 'because it prolongs nothing that we can call human'—La Rochelle, who committed suicide in order to 'drag himself from the atrocious wheel of modern life'. As for the survivors of the trenches, they were full of bitterness. Their unspeakable sufferings in the service of the Nation had made them the heroes of an epic universe; but now they found themselves back in an anonymous, indigent mob, their uniforms and decorations replaced by the banal and prosaic garb of the man in the street.

The *'Voyage au Bout de la Nuit'* a novel by F. Céline, published in Paris in 1932—significantly a huge success—expressed these emotions. For Bardamu, its nihilist hero, the world was ruled by evil human beings—odious puppets manipulated by an invisible and cruel hand. In Verdun, and at the Chemin des Dames, on the Somme, he had seen his friends sent by the hundreds of thousands to an obscene death, usually without any clear strategic purpose. Blood, lice and excrement had not only soiled their bodies, it had debased their minds. Love itself was but an hypocritical disguise for sex, a further pretext for men and women to set upon each other. As well as La Rochelle, he believed that 'Progress' was enslaving mankind rather than emancipating it.

To the Bardamus and their women, the elected representatives of the triumphant democrats had announced the long awaited hour—of great ideals, justice, peace, prosperity. A country fit for heroes to live in, Lloyd George had promised. But what had they been given? Cynicism, disorder and poverty; frequently without work, almost always without hope, many young people and veterans had come to scorn the betrayed promises; by the Conservatives and Liberals, whom they accused, not without reason, of the lunacy of uncontrolled capitalism; or by the Social Democrats, whom they reproached for their erratic incompetence. Consumed with fear and hatred, they were convinced of the need to overthrow their ancestral heritage. War itself, generally loathed, no longer horrified certain circles who saw it as an integral part, almost an essential part, of the cult of the Nation, a principal way of its self-assertion as preached by Hegel. Perhaps also a refuge from reality.

★　　★　　★

'Berlin or Moscow!' shrieked the miracle workers, 'You must choose!' Of the great European powers, only Great Britain and France repudiated this grotesque option, remaining faithful to the ethos which had created the grandeur of the West. They still seemed to dominate the world; but their authority was dwindling daily. The Manchurian Affair had revealed that the old gentlemen in their morning coats and stick-up collars no longer possessed the moral strength to oppose the despots in uniform. It was their lamentable failure which convinced Drieu La Rochelle that, 'Capitalism will not be reformed by its own means.'[2]

The two countries which had for so long, and so gloriously, upheld all the best in civilisation, could no longer escape the malady which was ravaging Europe. In Great Britain, the crisis was seen principally in the inertia of the old elite, and its retreat into the dream of a dying past. The intellectuals attempted to react, but by other means than those adopted by the democratic parties. The playwright Bernard Shaw (who was also something of a Fascist), John Strachey, the thinker and politician, the novelist George Orwell, Professor Harold Laski, the poets Auden and Spender, and others, having seen the light, had turned towards Moscow. Communism had little influence among the working class (only one or two Communists in the House of Commons); but it fascinated the youth of the Universities.

At Cambridge in 1933—I was told by an old member of the University—there were plenty of apolitical undergraduates who discoursed on poetry, a few Fascists too. But most of the support went to the extreme Left. A new journal, *Cambridge Left* had just appeared, full of red flags and marching proletarians. Some joined the Communist Party, an act which had an element of mysticism which inspired in some an awed respect. I was not surprised to learn at the beginning of the 50s that amongst them had been agents of the Soviet Secret Services. Apart from espionage, the situation was much the same in the other great educational institutions. At Oxford, the principal literary journal had disappeared, to be resurrected in a political form, the *New Oxford Outlook*, very much to the Left. Those who were then aged twenty will not forget the famous pacifist declaration of the students. That year, the Oxford Union, a venerable body and the forcing-house of imperial statesmen, solemnly expressed its refusal to fight for 'King and Country'. The reverberations were widespread.

At the other end of the political spectrum was the *British Union of Fascists*. This was founded in 1932 by Sir Oswald Mosley, descendent of an old and prosperous family, a hero of the Great War, an ex-Conservative Member of Parliament, then a Labour Member and finally Independent. He was exceptionally gifted and immensely ambitious. Forty years later I lunched with him in London. Although old and infirm, with a bloated face, he impressed me—in spite of my antipathy for all he stood for—by the fierce energy he still exuded. As a young Minister in MacDonald's homogeneous Labour cabinet, he had wanted to solve the economic crisis by bold measures, on the lines of the American New Deal. When his plan was rejected, he resigned from the Party in high dudgeon, and became converted to the 'National Revolution'. Soon the streets of London reverberated to the sound of his booted 'Blackshirts'. Nevertheless, the success of the British Union of Fascists (BUF) was limited. It appears never to have numbered more than 50,000 members, of whom 5,000 were active. Among them were very few intellectuals. Soon the parades of its militia in uniform and their violent demonstrations alienated even its sympathisers.

Other factions saw the light of day—inspired by the same admiration for Nazism or Fascism, and the same antipathy for everything Communist or Jewish (or French)—the *Imperial Fascist League*, the *National Workers' Party*, the *Nationalist Socialist League*, to name only some—small groups which seldom numbered more than a few hundred members. More influential were the *Anglo-German Fellowship* and the *Link*. The first, without being openly Nazi, undertook an active pro-German propaganda in leading London economic and political circles. The *Link*, headed by the ex-Admiral Sir Barry Domville (he made a number of visits to Hitlerian Germany, and was incarcerated during the war, had managed to establish several regional centres, recruiting 3–4,000 adherents—retired officers, old spinsters or landowners to 'assure peace through Anglo-German friendship'.[3]

Taken all in all, they were not of much importance. The extremist minorities, which revolted against the indolence of the traditional

Parties, failed to shake the latter's monopoly. Perhaps the monarchy, with its great prestige, and its ability to awaken emotions, restrained the general dissatisfaction with the old institutions. The festivities at the Jubilee of King George V in May 1935, celebrated with great fervour, revealed the loyalty of the people to the system.

★   ★   ★

There was no longer a glittering monarchy in France, where the polarization of extremist political feelings was gathering strength. The liberal humanism of the 'Republic of Professors', in which French thought had shone with unparalleled lustre, had to defend itself against furious onslaughts. As the Belgian novelist Charles Plisnier, an ex-Communist, wrote, 'On the Left, were those who had survived the slaughter-house who, convinced by the horror of what they had seen, cried out that a world which permitted such crimes must perish. Having read Marx, intoxicated because they saw clearly while others were fumbling in darkness, they gave themselves completely to him; they demanded a new, more mundane faith and trembled with excitement at the very mention of the words Moscow, Soviets, the International.' Among them were the leaders of the surrealist movement, Breton, Eluard, Aragon; and Malraux who, although not a Party member, had written in a Moscow newspaper, referring to a possible war, 'A rifle in my hand, I will defend the Soviet Union, the land of Liberty.' And Gide, who wrote in his journal that he 'longed with all his heart for the rout of capitalism, and of all those who cowered in its shade, its abuses, injustice, lies and monstrosities'.[4] Other circles, very similar in their criticism of capitalism and bourgeois culture were flourishing.

Opposing the predominant political scelerosis, a same desire for change could be discerned in certain right-wing groups. The democratic Republic had always had powerful enemies. Boulangism, the Dreyfus affair, the vitality of the *Action Française* movement, had revealed the strength of the old 'White Party'. Circumstances now endowed them with the means of making themselves heard as never before; *Ordre Nouveau, Esprit, Jeune Droite*, with others, united young intellectuals, mostly Catholic, who abhorred Marxism, but who displayed a sense of revolt no less profound and no less vehement. *Ordre Nouveau* wanted to abolish capitalism, interest loans, private property, the proletarian condition. The revue *Esprit* contended that 'the world was facing a total crisis of civilisation', and wished to regenerate it by a return to a Christian society purged of capitalism and Marxism. It was more or less the theme of the encyclical of 1931 *Quadragesimo Anno* in which Pius XI had opposed excessive state authority and free enterprise, for him the cause of class warfare.

Other coteries were more sinister, some of them clearly manipulated by the German and Italian Embassies—the *Comité France-Allemagne*, the *Cercle du Grand Pavois*, *L'Agence Inter-France*—they were not very different from those which had emerged in Great Britain, but they disposed of bigger funds and sharper pens. Robert Brasillach (who was to be shot in 1945 for treason) and Lucien Rebatet, were anti-Marxist, anti-bourgeois, anti-Republican, anti-Semite, and advocated violent action. Bernanos, Bainville, the Tharaud brothers, the young Thierry Maulinier, and some others, all imbued with an ill-defined rage against society, were roughly in the same category—their only precise aim being the destruction of the pacific, lustreless and ineffective liberal State. Quite recently one of their comrades wrote, 'It was a joyous time, when the pure and infrangible revolution seemed to knock at our doors.'[5]

'Leagues' proliferated, promising protection against Communism, the exaltation of national greatness, the restoration of order and prosperity—in short a remedy for all ills; the *Action Française* with its shock troops, the *Camelots du Roi*, the *Croix de Feu* of Colonel François de la Roque, and their *Voluntaires Nationaux*, *L'Association de Jeunes Patriotes*, whose members wore black berets and blue mackintoshes; *La Solidarité Française*, with blue shirts, boots and Sam Browne belts, and others. A part of the press was, overtly, as well as covertly, on their side; of which the principal weeklies, *Candide* and *Gringoire*, with a circulation of several hundreds of thousands, were the most influential, owing to the high standard of their articles.

As well as real Fascists, this New Right championed contradictory ideas—hatred and fraternity, anti-socialism and anti-capitalism, egalitarianism and elitism, a cornucopia in which everyone could find something to his liking. In particular, its attacks on 'plutocracy', of which it was sometimes (but not always, far from that) the secret expression, awoke echoes. It must be admitted that its success owed a great deal to the mediocrity of the traditional Parties. Their Ministries were formed and dissolved in a slough of intrigues, confrontations and wounded susceptibilities, which precluded any clear and coherent thinking. Between 1930 and 1940, there were twenty-four successive governments.

What brought the discredit of the regime to its climax were the frequent financial scandals, which besmirched the reputation of some of the highest dignitaries of the Republic. There was the Klotz affair, the Aéropostule affair, the Oustric affair, the Sacazan Affair. That of the *Mont de Piété* at Bayonne, had caused the greatest uproar. Stavisky was a crook and a jailbird whose name was linked with those of several Deputies and Ministers, among whom were the Chautemps brothers. He had succeeded in issuing 200 million francs in cash vouchers pledged on the *Crédit Municipal de Bayonne*, an official pawn shop which owned nothing more than some stolen or sham jewellery. Indictments poured in. The police announced that when they were about to arrest him, they found him dying, a bullet through the head. The reputation of the police was not good; scepticism increased, and the affair became a public scandal—but mainly in Paris.* Suddenly it revealed what lay beneath the surface, a deep unrest stimulated for months by a press hostile to the 'Republic of Comrades'. With the announcement of Stavinsky's death, public demonstrations degenerated into brawls with a number of injured. The government presided over by Camille Chautemps resigned.

Edouard Daladier, the new Premier, had the stature, it seemed, to deal with the situation. He was reputed to be incorruptible and unshakable, known as 'The Bull of Vaucluse'. Poor bull! Having long been accustomed to parliamentary *corridas*, he had learned to thread his way between the toreadors, rather than confront them. On 6 February, *L'Action Française* appeared with a huge headline, 'The robbers have barricaded themselves in their cave! Everyone this evening to the *Chambre des Députés*!' A number of newspapers, including *Le Temps* (Conservative) and *L'Humanité* (Communist), echoed this. The government replied by calling a state of emergency and putting the troops in the Paris region on alert.

In the afternoon, rioting broke out. In spite of the extreme cold, the weather was fine, and the crowds took to the streets. Several tens of thousands of demonstrators—among them the 'leaguers', but also, strangely enough, communist groups—assembled in the Place de La Concorde, determined to take the Chambre des Députés by storm. Blood flowed. Gradually, the forces of law and order had to give way, and fall back on the Pont de la Concorde. In the Palais Bourbon, the house was at fever-pitch, with Members yelling and shrieking, and,

---

* A little later, another 'suicide' was announced, that of Albert Prince, the magistrate dealing with the files on accomplices involved with Stavisky. His bound corpse was found on the railway-line, Paris–Dijon. In spite of their diligence, the police had great difficulty in explaining how the unfortunate man, after taking drugs, had managed to attach himself to the rails, and await the arrival of a train.

on several occasions, nearly coming to blows. Towards 22.30, Daladier obtained a vote of confidence with a large majority. On the streets, the police again opened fire. It was not until midnight that the demonstrators were dispersed. They left fifteen dead and several hundred injured.

The provinces had been less affected by the unrest. The 'leaguers', divided and disorganised, revealed that they were incapable of concerted action. The Duc de Guise pretender to the throne, an a pompous declaration, 'put himself at the disposition of the nation'; but he did nothing. Colonel de la Roque, at the head of the largest contingent, had proved that he was neither Julius Caesar nor General Monk. Maurras, who aspired to lead them all, had shown, at the height of the rioting, that if his pen was made of steel, his spirit was of a less well tempered metal. Taking cover in his office, the cantankerous little old man, isolated by his deafness, recommended to his excited henchmen who came for orders, 'I don't like people to lose their cool.'[6]

A few hours later, Daladier courageously announced that he was determined to defend the Republic. Then the Bull turned into a sheep. After interminable hesitations, capitulating to pressure by timid Ministers, he offered his resignation at the Elysée. For several days power was in default. At last, a government of national union, very much to the Right, was formed under the presidency of Gaston Doumergue, a smooth-tongued and colourless old man who was recalled from long retirement. In this government, Marshal Pétain (aged 78) made his debut in politics. On the 12 February, on the initiative of the Trades Unions and the Socialist Party, several hundreds of thousands of Parisians marched past in an orderly manner from Le Cours de Vincennes to the Place de la Nation; at the last moment, to everyone's surprise, they were joined by the Communists. A 24 hour general strike followed, to show the popular will to defend the Republic. In this, its supporters was the proof that, unlike Germany, it would not capitulate to its enemies—the latter admittedly being more inclined to bark than bite.

★   ★   ★

In Brussels, where particularly after 1914, France had always seemed to be the luminary of Western civilisation, the crisis shaking the Third Republic was observed with disquiet. An old Catholic land, Belgium was still much under the influence of the Church, and penetrated with the doctrines of *L'Action Française*. In his lifetime Cardinal Mercier, Primate of the Kingdom, a prime mover of neo-thomism,* did not conceal his admiration for Charles Maurras. The Jesuit colleges, the Catholic University of Louvain, the state University of Liege, were numbered among its strongholds. Young Catholics occupying key positions in Parliament, diplomacy, the administration, the press and high finance, were tainted with its dogmas—scorn for Parliamentary institutions, support for the authority of the executive, xenophobia. A dissident fraction of the Catholic Right soon offered a Belgian version of European Fascism. In the Flemish provinces, the awakening of a virulent regional nationalism was symptomatic of the uncertainty of the times. Several small extremist groups expressed it, sharing in common fervent Catholicism, opposition to Parliamentary regimes, and hatred of capitalism as much as of Communism.

In non-Catholic circles, the young intellectuals inclined frequently towards the Red, even the bright Red. A number of my contemporaries, imitating many of the French and English youth, became intoxicated to find in Marx—in the words of Charles Plisnier in one of his novels, 'a complete and coherent explanation of the terrestrial world, in its past, its present, and its future'. In contrast with the capitalist world, 'sweating blood and mud from all its pores', the Soviet Union radiated the mirage of justice, social progress and economic efficiency. It claimed to have vanquished the fatal laws of capitalism, that of 'supply and demand' and of the 'cyclical crises'. The Soviets also stated that they had put an end to family oppression and sexual taboos. They promised the emancipation of young women and men, love without constraint, easy divorce and legalisation of abortion. What seduced a youth obsessed by the Great War more than anything else was the promise of a fraternal universe freed from the nationalist passions which had stained the West with blood. Did not the Kremlin stigmatise the great hoax which, under the mask of patriotism, concealed the most sordid interests—in particular those of 'the gun merchants'—one of the myths of the time? Was not the Kremlin one of the most eloquent advocates at Geneva of collective security? Did it not support the campaign for disarmament and for the right of self-determination?

In reality, in spite of some intellectuals' naive infatuation, the Communists remained marginal parties in the countries faithful to democracy, without much influence on the masses. However, the governing circles continued to be haunted by a threat which, at that time, existed

---

* The modernised version of the philosophy of St Thomas Aquinas, fashionable at the time.

only in their imagination. Clinging desperately to the values of a past which was being destroyed by the irresistable pressure of modern times—and not by a Marxist conspiracy—they allowed themselves to be carried away on a wave of repulsion and fear, whilst concealing the real perils from themselves. In this prevalent feeling of alarm, lies probably the basic explanation of the democracy's refusal to face the risk of a confrontation with the Dictators.

CHAPTER 4

Hitler's First Successes

For a year, all was again clear and orderly in Germany; no more painful enquiries, harassing dissensions or uncontrolled disorders. The National Socialist 'Revolution' had given those who wanted it—and others—an answer to all questions. The federal and parliamentary Republic had been overthrown, fundamental liberties suspended, public meetings forbidden, postal censorship installed, the press forbidden or forcibly bought up, radio transmitters seized, the federated states subjected to the Central Power. The Reichstag fire, almost certainly instigated by Göring, had served as a pretext for arresting the Communist leaders. They were followed a little later by the Social Democrats and the leaders of the Trade Unions. What was left of the Parliament voted an enabling law authorising the Government, that is to say Adolf Hitler, to legislate by decree.

The SA, active for a time as auxiliary policemen, expelled the burgomeisters and civil servants of the old administration from the public buildings. On the streets or in their houses, all those whom the SA considered to be Communists, Socialists, Trade Unionists, Liberals, Jews, sometimes foreigners, often personal enemies, were attacked. Some 500–600 people died in street affrays, and more than 100,000 were arrested. At Dachau, near Munich, a charming little watering-place, whose castle had once been the summer residence of the Bavarian princes—and the Buchenwald—concentration camps engulfed their first victims. The political polic, the Gestapo, began to acquire its sinister reputation. *Gleichschaltung* (Nazification) was soon complete.

All open opposition was completely crushed, all power concentrated in the hands of 'the Führer-Chancellor'. In a few months, he had laid the foundations of the warrior autocracy of which he had dreamed for so many years, which would launch the German Aryans into the conquest of the 'Thousand Year Empire'.

Outside Germany, political circles attempted to minimise these events. The Communist parties, imbued with their slogans, supposed that Hitlerism was preparing the proletarian revolution. In Paris, Maurice Thorez, pleased rather than disquieted, spent his time reassuring the French, announcing the coming bankruptcy of Nazism. 'The abyss is opening beneath its feet', he claimed. On 7 March 1933 *Pravda* was still writing, 'Let the reactionaries tremble with rage! The internal and external contradictions of German capitalism are increasing.[1] The socialist Léon Blum proved no more perspicacious. Four weeks before Hitler came to power, he wrote in the *Populaire* that the candidate for the dictatorship had not only lost the hope of power, but even 'the shadow of the hope of power'. Blum continued to insist that the dictatorship was bound to collapse: 'I believe this, because I hope for this', he said—an attitude not without a certain elegance, but rather unwise in a statesman. It was also said that, conscious of his Jewish origin, he did not wish it to cloud his judgement. 'Hitler in power or Hitler in the wings, what does it matter?', asked a Radical Deputy.[2] Daladier, head of the government, also a Radical, had quickly entrusted an emissary, Ferdinand de Brinon, with the task of establishing secret contacts with the Führer. Some months later, to counter Georges Mandel, who described to the French the true nature of Nazism, he sent his protege on a second mission—which gave rise to a series of articles in *Le Matin*, praising the Third Reich.[3]

In London, the 'National Government' was presided over by MacDonald. Like Blum, he detested the Hitlerian tyranny with all his being but, unlike Blum, he discerned its dangers. This did not prevent him from inviting the Führer to Great Britain and promising him 'a warm welcome'.[4] The Labour Party was indulging in one of its periodical bouts of high-principled pacifism; it extolled unilateral disarmament and claimed that the world could be pacified by a good example. For many of its leaders, moreover the capitalist regime in all its forms, Democratic as well as Fascist, was the principal foe—the Beast. Because as Jaures had said, 'it exuded war as the storm clouds exuded rain', a choice was pointless. George Lansbury never tired of demanding total demobilisation of the Army, the Navy and the Air Force. Another, Clement Atlee the future Prime Minister, refused all 'national loyalty'.[5] Like Blum, he did not think the Hitler regime would last; like him, he continued to oppose all forms of rearmament. Bernard Shaw had set himself up as the spokesman of a dangerous demagogy, declaring that Great Britain must remain outside all 'imperialist quarrels'—a phrase which again comes into fashion here and there.

Although the politicians of the Left were not unduly concerned, those of the Right, haunted by the spectre of Marx—and not indifferent sometimes to the possibilities of the German market—were discreetly satisfied with the situation. In France, the hatred of Germanism was still alive; but it had now become curiously half-hearted. Barthou was one of the few politicians to deplore publicly that none of his colleagues had read *Mein Kampf* in its original form. A number of them liked to think that Hitler would help to make his country unpopular in Great Britain; and that he was not an enemy of France, only of the Jews—regrettable aberration, but of secondary importance—and of the Communists. A new war with the Reich would mean the appearance of the Bolsheviks on the banks of the Rhine.

The press had done nothing to destroy these illusions; the most chauvinistic were suddenly enthusiastic about moderation and peace. In *La Victoire*, Gustav Hervé, who had moved from the extreme Left to the extreme Right, predicted that 'Hitler will save Germany from the Red tide, in the way that Mussolini has saved Italy'. Gaxote in *Je suis Partout* wrote, 'No war of propaganda, no war of Democracies!' *Candide*, 'We have already had the war of Justice and Right. If this is war for spiritual liberty— thank you very much!' Even *L'Action Française*, long the inveterate enemy of Germany, expressed sympathy with the anti-Marxism of its new leaders.[6]

On the other side of the Channel, the Tories did not react much differently. They too wanted to remain apart from any form of 'ideological crusade'. Some of them brazenly announced that they preferred National Socialism to Bolshevism, which in their opinion was the only alternative. Stanley Baldwin, true to himself, refused to be ruffled. 'Worries', he said, 'are not good for the nervous system'. He was prejudiced against, and distrustful of, foreigners—all foreigners. Without any sympathy for the new German Chancellor, he was nevertheless pleased to see him as an effective enemy of Communism. He had lunch with Fibbentrop, and asked him to tea in Downing Street with MacDonald. The German, while insisting on the pacific intentions of his master, spoke in veiled terms of the return of the old colonies of the Reich, of its expansion to the East at the expense of the Soviet Union. The encounter lacked warmth, but it was not a total failure. MacDonald invited Hitler to Great Britain, and now Baldwin considered visiting Berlin, only abandoning the idea out of apathy, and so as not to annoy his Foreign Secretary.

As in Paris, the principal newspapers were busy reassuring their readers. The wide circulation papers of Lord Beaverbrook and Lord

Rothermere stated that there was no danger of war, that in any case Great Britain should remain apart from the affairs of the continent. *The Times*, stronghold of independent journalism, was openly in favour of National Socialist Germany until 1939. It censored any despatches which appeared to give an unfavourable image of Nazism, going so far as to dismiss one of its principal correspondents, Norman Ebbutt, because he told the truth. *The Observer* was opposed even more resolutely to promising the French anything which 'might lead Great Britain and Germany to destroy each other', and to 'establish Bolshevist supremacy in Europe and Asia'.[7]

★   ★   ★

Hitler was soon following the policy which he had announced so clearly in *Mein Kampf*. Immediately after his installation in the Chancellory, he dined with General von Hammerstein, C-in-C of the Reichswehr, and the principal military leaders. After the meal, he spoke for two hours about his plan (which he had repeated a hundred times in his speeches) to embark as soon as possible on the conquest of a new vital space in the East, where he would carry out 'a pitiless Germanisation'. He promised to re-establish compulsory military service as soon as circumstances allowed and, while awaiting the application of measures adopted in 1932, secretly to accelerate and triple the seven divisions of the Reichswehr.[8]

In public and with foreigners, the new master of Germany felt he must show moderation—but only briefly. Provisionally, he was powerless, without an ally. In spite of some clandestine infractions of the peace treaties, the Reichswehr had neither tanks, aeroplanes, heavy artillery nor trained reserves. It was said that Poland, through the medium of old Marshall Pilsudski, had discussed a preventive war with Daladier. Mussolini, in spite of some polite gestures, had remained circumspect about a disciple whose ambitions in Austria and the Balkans he feared. Hitler therefore lavished friendly gestures and amiable phrases upon Great Britain, France and Italy, even upon Poland, the Holy See and the USSR (which had, until now, been one of his principal *bêtes noires*). 'There was, without a doubt, no word' wrote Francois-Poncet, in the memoirs of his embassy in Berlin, 'that Hitler publicly pronounced more often at the beginning of his reign than that of "Peace"'.

Expressions of good will were soon contradicted by facts. On 11 May 1933 the Minister of Foreign Affairs, Baron von Neurath, declared unequivocally that Germany would acquire the armaments she considered necessary, whatever the outcome of the Disarmament Conference. The European governments became highly alarmed. Some days later, Hitler pronounced a speech full of soothing words ('War would be an unmitigated folly'). The European governments calmed down. In Geneva, the plenipotentiaries resumed work on Penelope's tapestry. Without avail. On 14 October, at the opening of the afternoon session, the President, Henderson, received a telegram from Berlin. In it the Führer announced that because the Disarmament Conference was unable to achieve its objective, owing to the ill will of the principal powers, he would take no further part in it. A little later, the harsh tones of his voice were heard over Berlin Radio. He was also quitting the League of Nations.

It was clear warning that the Reich would no longer submit to military restrictions; the end of all hope of limiting armaments. More than this, by quitting Geneva so ostentatiously, he defied all the rules of international behaviour. Indeed, Hitler boasted in a speech on 1 November, 'I have not become Chancellor of the Reich to act in any other manner than I have been proclaiming for fourteen years'. The first blow at Europe had been struck, and caused a tremendous uproar. On the shores of Lake Léman, the diplomats talked of war. Ina Germany, people were scared—very scared. They feared the sanctions laid down in the treaties, a re-occupation of the Rhineland, a Czech or Polish attack on their eastern frontier—operations which the Reichswehr would have been totally incapable of resisting.

The Führer alone remained imperturbable. Rauschning, then one of his close associates, found him in 'excellent humour, excellent form, the bit between his teeth'. 'War!' he had shouted with a scornful gesture, 'Nonsense! They wouldn't consider it seriously. These people assembled in Geneva are no better than a miserable flock of sheep.'[9] Adopting a method which was to become familiar, he made a few speeches full of soothing phrases, while submitting his decisions to a German plebiscite. Parades and martial ceremonies, a call to patriotism, were now to be seen or heard all over Germany. A huge success for the Führer, ninety per cent of the electors approved his insolent provocation of the Geneva powers. But the latter gave no sign of reacting. On the contrary, as with Japan the year before, they continued with polite negotiations, hoping for a magic formula which would transform the wolf into a respectable, law-abiding citizen. It was six months later that the Doumergue government declared solemnly that France refused to regard German rearmament as legal and that she had decided henceforth 'to ensure her security by her own means'. It was a bold gesture, even if ingenuous. But what did it amount to? Nothing—for this was the moment when the French government, a 'national' government, whose War Minister was the great Marshal Pétain, began to economise and reduce military expenditure.* The time was past when Paris could occupy the Ruhr in order to hasten the delivery of telegraph posts. As Wolfgang Stresemann, the son of the former Chancellor, said to a secretary at the French Embassy, 'In the time of my father, you protested when any rusty old cannon was discovered in Germany. Now France says nothing. She regards the treaties as a dead letter. She relies entirely on the eclipse of the Hitler regime sooner or later.'[10]

London remained even more phlegmatic than Paris. The leading circles—Left as well as Right—with the exception of some internationalist groups—continued to isolate themselves from a continent which was disturbing the peace. Refusing the requests of Paris, whom they accused of being one of the causes of the trouble, they were more sympathetic to Berlin. Anthony Eden, after his first meeting with Hitler in February 1934, found him 'almost shy, with a pleasant smile'.[11] He felt sure that the new Germany was better than the old. Lloyd George, who had been Prime Minister during the Great War, and who had talked of hanging the Kaiser, expressed the general opinion when he said, 'Germany has right on her side.' Agreed! General disarmament had proved to be a farce, and it was clearly impossible to keep Germany in a state of inferiority for ever. Nevertheless, was complete passivity the only alternative? The military heads of the three Services had not failed to give some warnings. A rule adopted after the Armistice, and subsequently prolonged, declared there was 'No possibility of war for ten years.' It had been abrogated in 1932; a petition of principle without practical consequences. The Royal Navy remained all-powerful, but its ships were rapidly becoming out of date. The Royal Air Force had some of the best aircraft in existence but they were far too few. The largest empire of all time did not feel threatened as the centre of its power; the bulk of its land forces was stationed in India and the Middle East and equipped accordingly. Only a token army, two or three ill-equipped divisions—less than in 1914— remained in the United Kingdom.

One fine day Baldwin stated, 'The greatest crime against our people

---

* Moreover, the military credits were not spent. In 1932 and 1934, when General Weygand was Chief of Staff, 59 and 33 per cent of the credits were not used; in 1935, on the authority of General Gamelin, 60 per cent; 5,000 officers were put on half-pay.

is to be afraid to tell them the truth . . . Our frontier is on the Rhine.'
Nevertheless, far from preparing defences, he kept repeating that there
was no danger. Deceiving Parliament, his followers and the country,
in 1934 he stated that the German Air Force was less than half the
size of that of Great Britain in Europe. Two years later, he had the
frankness to tell the House of Commons that he had deliberately
disguised the facts, so as not to have to rearm, adding, 'I cannot
imagine anything which would have made our loss of the Election
more certain.'[12]

On the continent, which was nearer to the danger, the drums beating
the alert were plainly heard. The friends of France moved further
away—at the very moment when unity become essential. In Brussels,
following the French example, the government had been very tough
with the Weimar Republic; but it now appeared most flexible. On 6
March 1934, the Comte de Broqueville, the Prime Minister, made
what he considered to be an important speech in which, defining
his policy towards Hitler's Germany, he simplified his dilemma to
absurdity. 'Either entente—or preventive war', he said; and the latter
was clearly 'unthinkable'. It was said that for this he had received the
approval of King Albert—given a few days before the fatal fall at the
foot of the rocks of Marche-les-Dames—and that of his successor,
King Leopold III. But not that of public opinion. Paul Hymans, the
Foreign Minister, noted in his memoirs, 'The following morning, the
press caught fire. There was a great outcry in Brussels, Paris and
Berlin'.[13] I was among those who wondered why M. de Broqueville
had not spoken like this at the time of Chancellor Brüning.

There was much talk of 'realism', a word now in fashion, but which
had not been used when Germany was weak and amenable. Those who
practised it most did not inspire unlimited confidence, in particular
Poland, which overdid it. After having discussed secretly, in Paris, a
preventive operation destined to destroy Nazism, without firing a shot,
Warsaw backtracked. On 20 January 1934 Pilsudski and Hitler, old,
implacable enemies, signed a ten-year pact of non-aggression. To the
uninitiated this new treaty appeared to align Poland with Germany.
This was an exaggeration. Nevertheless, without its being directed
against France it struck a blow at her system of alliances. The Warsaw
commentators left no doubt about the matter: their government had
adopted a position which was 'independent of idological bloks'. For
its part, the Soviet Union renewed the treaty of Rapallo with Hitler's
Reich, first signed with the Republic of Weimar. The Holy See consented to a Concordat with Germany. This was the time of the 'realists'.

On the 30 January 1934, the first anniversary of Hitler's accession to power, he spoke in the Kroll Opera House. Since the Reichstag fire, this was where the 'Parliament' was held, its members booted and in uniform. He was able to present an extraordinary balance sheet of his dictatorship. In eleven months, he had succeeded in consolidating such absolute power within his frontiers as had not been wielded by any Emperor in modern times. In foreign affairs, he had effectively shaken the diplomatic, legal and moral edifice which protected Europe. And this, by the strength of his character alone, without firing a shot.

★　　★　　★

It was not that the spilling of blood was repugnant to the Führer— of which he was soon to give atrocious proof. Having killed, imprisoned or exiled his opponents, he began to eliminate among his own followers those who had done most to bring him to power and who might therefore conceivably contest it. On Saturday morning, 30 June 1934, the crack of rifle fire and automatic pistols broke the sunny calm of a summer day. For forty-eight hours, Germany was delivered over to assassins. 'Humming-birds' was the poetic code-name given to this grisly operation, which had been decided upon at a secret meeting on the cruiser *Deutschland* between Hitler and his generals, all of them equally jealous of the political and military ambitions of the brown militia, the SA, under its redoubtable chief, Major Röhm.

The newspapers were full of the horror of the 'Night of the Long Knives', the last hours of SA authority. Apparently unsuspecting, Röhm and his principal officers had gathered at Bad Wiessee, a watering-place on one of the Bavarian lakes, to entertain and pay tribute to their Führer. The latter had flown to Munich that night in his private aeroplane. At dawn, having given his final orders and put his faithful SS on full alert he had taken the road to Bad Wiessee. A riding-whip in one hand, a revolver in the other, flanked by two bodyguards, he had burst into the bedroom of the lake-side hotel where his old friend was still asleep, with a cry, 'Röhm, you are arrested!' Only half awakened, Röhm stammered, 'Heil, Mein Führer!' 'You are arrested!', shrieked Hitler, a second time. The scene was repeated with the other SA chiefs. Only one of them Graf Spreti, put up any show of resistance. Hitler struck him to the ground with blows of his riding-whip. Heines, commander of the Silesian militia, was surprised naked, in bed, in the arms of his chauffeur; he was despatched with a revolver shot, as was his Ganymede. The others

were taken to the Stadelheim prison in a Munich suburb, where for
several hours, at irregular intervals, the firing of the execution squads
could be heard. The next day, Röhm, in his cell, was handed a revolver
with one round in it, and a copy of the *Völkischer Beobachter*,
announcing the failure of his alleged coup d'état. He refused to
commit suicide. Standing at attention in Cell 474, his shirt open on
his chest, he was shot down by two bullets fired through the door
grille.

In Berlin, a silent and frightened city, swarming with trucks full of
armed men, the carnage was presided over by Göring and Himmler.
The Ministries were guarded by soldiers in battle array, manning
batteries of machine-guns. At the headquarters of the Brownshirts,
the Minister of Air, in person, selected those to be liquidated. Others
were arrested in their homes and taken in vans to the cadet school at
Lichterfelde where, with blows from SS rifle butts, they were put up
against a wall, and immediately despatched. To facilitate the task of
the executioners, the shirts of the victims were opened, and their chests
marked with a black circle in the region of the heart. Shot down at
almost point-blank range, the bullets tore great holes in the bodies, so
that the wall behind was bespattered with pieces of bloody flesh. Karl
Ernst, chief of the Berlin SA division, had just been married (Göring
had been a witness at the wedding). He was arrested in his Mercedes
on the way to Bremen, where he was to embark with his young wife
for a honeymoon in the Canaries. Beaten black and blue, his face
swollen with pain, his arms crushed, he was taken back to Lichterfelde
and shot without any explanation.

The brown militia were not the only ones to be decimated. The
conservatives of the Right, who thought they had tamed the wild
beast, also payed dearly. The Vice-Chancellor, von Papen, only
escaped thanks to Göring, who intervened because of Papen's relationship with President Hindenburg. But his closest collaborators, Rose
and Jung, were executed, as was the President of the Catholic Action,
Erich Klausener. The ex-Chancellor von Schleicher was in his house
when it was invaded by ruffians in plain clothes, who shouted at him.
'Are you General von Schleicher'. His answer, 'Yes', was greeted with
a hail of bullets, which also shot down his wife who, hearing the noise,
had run into the room. Their blood-stained bodies were found by
their daughter, aged sixteen, on her return from school at lunch-time.
General von Bredow and the aged Gustav van Kahr, who had opposed
Hitler in Munich ten years before were also slaughtered, So, too, was
the Jesuit Father Stempfle, who had helped him edit *Mein Kampf*. The

inoffensive music critic, Willy Schmidt, was arrested and shot in error, being mistaken for his namesake, the SA divisional General Wilhelm Schmidt. And so it went on. The killings took place with as much nonchalance as brutality, in offices, apartment blocks, on the streets. Corpses were discovered weeks later in woods and streams. How many were killed? No one knows. Seventy-seven was the official figure. Several hundred certainly, perhaps a thousand.

On Sunday, having returned from Bavaria, Hitler gave a party in the sunlit garden of the Chancellory for the Party leaders and their families—while at Lichterfelde, a few kilometers away, the execution squad was still at work. The master of the Reich was apparently in the best of humours, walking about among his guests chatting, drinking tea and patting the heads of children. He had received a telegrame from the aged Hindenberg congratulating him on his courage. While General von Blomberg, Commander-in-Chief of the Reichswehr, had addressed an Order of the Day to the troops in his honour. To a civilised world this was unheard of; in the other capitals the politicians were embarrassed, preferring to look the other way—although they could not be entirely displeased at the elimination of the presumed radical element in National Socialism. Next day, the summer holidays began.

But the blood had not stopped flowing—nor would it cease flowing for the next ten years. Three weeks later, on 25 July 1934, in Vienna, the Chancellor Engelbert Dollfuss lay dying, his throat pierced by bullets, stretched out half conscious on a sofa in the salon of the residence on the Ballhausplatz from where Metternich had once governed the Austrian Empire. At about 12.45 pm the sentries in front of the palace gateway had seen a number of trucks arriving, full of men in the uniform of a Viennese regiment, the *Deutschmeister*. They were allowed to pass without verification. Once inside the courtyard, the imposters rushed into the buildings and arrested the occupants, including the Minister of the Interior. Dollfuss, who had received a vague warning of the impending coup d'état, was standing at the door, about to leave his office, when he was shot down by two revolver bullets.

Not far away, another group of insurgents had forced their way into the *Ravag*, the radio station. They killed one of the guards and forced the speaker, a revolver at his head, to announce the resignation of Dollfuss and his replacement by Dr Anton Rintelen, an Austrian Nazi. Hitler was attending a matinee of *Rheingold* at the Bayreuth Festival, where an ADC brought him the news from Vienna. Friedeling

Wagner, the grand-daughter of the composer, who was in a box near the Führer, told, after the war, of the wild exultation which took possession of him.[14]

It was to be of short duration. At the Ballhausplatz, Dollfuss, who had been refused both doctor and priest, died of a haemorrhage at 4 o'clock, having refused to the end to sign the letter of resignation which his tormentors attempted to elicit from him. The Vice-Chancellor, Starhemberg, was in Italy. However, Kurt von Schuschnigg, the Minister of Justice and Education, had evaded the conspirators. He made post-haste for the War Ministry, where he took control of the security forces. On his orders, the police launched an assault on the radio station. With grenades and machine pistols, they killed five of the Nazis, whereupon the rest surrendered. At the Chancellory which was now surrounded by the army, the insurgents, after lengthy negotiations, agreed to capitulate if their lives were spared—a promise quickly forgotten, when the body of the unfortunate Dollfuss was found, his throat torn by bullets, his face blue, a basin of blood beneath the bespattered sofa on which they had let him die.

Six weeks before this, the Duce had had a long conversation with Hitler, without witnesses or interpreters—first at Padua, then at the Venice Lido. Hitler did not speak a word of Italian. Mussolini spoke German, but less well than he liked people to suppose. He reported to his entourage that his disciple had talked at length in a sort of prophetic delirium, interspersed with tears; but that he had promised unequivocally that Austrian independance would be scrupulously respected. Did Mussolini hear what he wanted to hear?

Italy had joined the Great War to destroy the German empires, which for a thousand years had been threatening her; the Austrian Republic in the mountains of the north was a buffer state insuring against the reappearance of the threat. Informed of what had happened in Vienna, the Duce felt he had been cheated. In a telegram to Vice-Chancellor Starhemberg—given wide publicity in the press— he promised to come to the aid of Austria; at the same time he announced the concentration of several Italian divisions on the Brenner frontier. 'Mussolini was considering declaring war on Germany', related Sir Oswald Mosley, the head of the British Fascists. 'When I arrived in Rome, he was in such a rage that none of his colleagues dared speak about it to him.'[15]

Towards the end of the afternoon, the Italians appeared about to march. At Bayreuth, Hitler realised that the coup had failed. The Vice-Chancellor von Papen, summoned during the night to replace the disgraced German Minister in Vienna, found his master 'in a state of hysterical agitation'. 'A new Sarajevo!' he cried, terrified at the prospect of a war for which he was not yet prepared.[16] The Nazi Austrian Legion waiting in Bavaria was demobilised, the Vienna insurgents disavowed. Thirteen of them were condemned to death and hanged.

Dollfuss was not universally admired—far from it. His own hands were stained with blood spilled some months before the Putsch, when he had consolidated his dictatorship by shelling the Vienna working-class district, and by executing some of the heads of the Social Democrat opposition. But his courage in the face of death, and the barbaric savagery of the attempted Nazi coup, had awoken great sympathy for him. Nevertheless, the British and French ministers, who had become so excited two years earlier, when there had been the question of a customs union between Austria and Weimar Republic, remained placid spectators; even Barthou, who professed firmness, did nothing. Neither the crimes of Hitler in Germany, nor the criminal audacity of his attempted coup in Austria, nor his sudden retraction in the face of the Duce's threats, influenced their attitude. They confined themselves two months later, when all was over and Dollfuss forgotten, to a futile declaration recalling their attachment to Austrian independence.

★   ★   ★

This did not trouble the Führer. In June, he had got rid of those who aspired to be his equals. In July, he had suffered a temporary setback. But by August he had reached the summit. At dawn on the 2nd of that month, Marshal Paul Ludwig Hans Anton von Beneckendorff und Hindenburg, President of the Republic since 1925, died full of years and glory. At noon the same day, with that brilliant sense of timing, so different from the frequent wandering of his mind, Hitler caused a law to be promulgated, *dated from the day before*, combining in one person the roles of Chancellor and President. At the same time he spirited away the testament in which the illustrious deceased had recommended the installation of a constitutional monarchy. The former Corporal's new position gave him the supreme command of the armed forces. In all the barracks of the Reich, officers and men, lined up strictly at attention, two fingers of their right hand raised to the sky, took the solemn oath to Adolf Hitler which, since the beginning of modern times, the Prussian regiments had taken, swearing before God obedience and loyalty to the Hohenzollerns.

In an atmosphere of mystical exaltation, inspired by the ancient Germanic legends, during a nocturnal ceremony illuminated by a

CHAPTER 5

Roosevelt and the New Deal

At Latitude 40.33 North and Longitude 55.55 West, the little steamer ploughed through the heavy swell of the Atlantic. New York was not far away. Since our departure from Antwerp nine days before, at the beginning of September 1934, the weather, with the exception of a spectacular thunderstorm, had been superb. In brilliant sunshine and with the sea clement, the crossing on the 'Pennland' was most agreeable. I had looked forward to this voyage which was then much less common than it is today. Why did I want to go to America? Certainly, in part due to a curiosity to visit the four quarters of the globe, which has inspired me all my life; but also, because of an intense political interest. Convinced of the decadence of the capitalist system, even momentarily attracted by the Russian revolution, I had quickly overcome these seductions. Had not Roosevelt and the New Deal opened up a third way, between the extreme Right and the extreme Left?

The remarkable economic expansion of the United States had contributed to its prestige. The First World War had transformed it into the greatest industrial and financial power in the world. On the eve of the Depression it was producing more than two-fifths of the world's manufactured goods.* In new industrial sectors, such as the manufacture of automobiles, four-fifths of world production issued from its factories.[1] This success had not been achieved without problems. During the Great War, the level of production in Europe had fallen, while the demand had increased. The farmers of the New World had got into serious debt, in order to purchase new lands and machines, tractors and harvesters, to replace horse traction. At the end of the Twenties, the production of cereals in the United States and Canada was one-third higher than before the war and exports had doubled. The demand had then diminished, partly because people ate less bread

---

* The gross value of manufactures produced per head of population in the United States was nearly twice as high as in Great Britain or Germany and more than ten times as high as in the USSR or Italy.

than before, partly because European production had returned to its old level. It was the same for most other agricultural products; and 30 per cent of the population lived by agriculture. In industry, the techniques of mass production had increased the hourly output of the workers by 40 per cent; but the remuneration of the consumers, peasants, workmen and employees had not progressed in proportion; 5 per cent of the most prosperous citizens disposed of 30 per cent of the personal incomes. Unequally divided, these were not put to sufficient use. The enormous increase in production had surpassed the purchasing power of the consumers. A recession was inevitable; at the beginning of 1929, certain indicators told that it was not far away.

On 24th October, the notorious Black Thursday, the crisis was initiated by the collapse of the New York Stock Exchange due to immense inflation of credits and unbridled speculation. The story of the fearful panic which seized Wall Street has often been related, of the rush to rid themselves, at all costs, of the pieces of paper, which often represented the owner's entire fortune, and which were losing value every minute. Nothing could arrest the collapse of the market, which had soon fallen by a half. Bankruptcies increased, the consumer market was further cut down. Orders to industry were drastically curtailed, putting millions of men out of work. Herbert Hoover, a Republican, was in the White House. He was not a bad man, but massive, ponderous and narrow-minded. From modest beginnings, he had become a civil engineer, and then went abroad, where he had amassed a vast fortune. Returning to the United States, he had been Secretary of Commerce before becoming President. Confident in his personal success, he sincerely desired that all Americans should become rich, convinced that nothing could prevent it if they displayed the same assiduity and frugality as he had. He worked eighteen hours a day and, to set an example, had his own salary reduced. Hard on himself, he saw no reason why he should not be hard on his compatriots. Of strict and formal manners, he was said, even when alone with his wife, to dine ceremoniously, clad in a dinner jacket, a boiled shirt and stiff collar, surrounded by rigid and silent footmen.[2]

As with Brüning, MacDonald and Laval, Hoover's outdated ideas were based on the traditional conception of natural economic cycles; public intervention could not affect them. If business declined, people must wait for the returning upsurge, which could only be helped by the State reducing its expenditure and keeping the currency stable. For more than three years the President allowed these precepts with moralizing obstinacy—'a conventional wisdom', commented the economist Galbraith 'destined to aggravate the situation'. And so it did. United States Steel, the basis of heavy industry, was working at 20 per cent of its capacity. The American Locomotive Company, which, in prosperous times, had sold six hundred locomotives a year, sold only one in 1933. A large number of famous automobile firms closed— Stutz, Auburn, Pierce-Arrow, Cord and Locomobile, for example. In the spring of 1930, Ford cut its working week from six days to five; and to three days in August of the same year. General Motors, which in 1929 had produced five and a half million vehicles, produced only two million in 1931. At the beginning of 1933 there were, officially, thirteen million totally unemployed—as in Germany, these represented 10 per cent of the whole population, or 25 per cent of the active sector. *Production had declined by half, the national income by two-thirds.* Prices had fallen to the level of 1668, the epoch of Louis XIV or Charles II.*

Between one and two million vagabonds roamed the streets all over the country—the so-called 'hobos' or 'bums'. The railway police ceased locking the doors of freight trains to enable them to travel without paying. In the countryside, the ruined farmers could no longer feed their cattle; the cows stopped yielding milk. Unsold pigs were incinerated and transformed into fertiliser for lack of purchasers, vegetables and fruit rotted on the ground and trees. Worst of all, several years of exceptional drought had transformed large areas of the West into 'dust-bowls'. In Kentucky and Virginia, regions which had always been under-developed, dire famine killed off hundreds, principally children and old people. With benighted selfishness, financial establishments and mortgage holders forced innumerable businesses to be sold at auctions as their proprietors, deeply in debt, could no longer face their obligations. John Steinbeck in *Grapes of Wrath* has described the fearful condition of families who had been expelled from their homes, and were on the road in thousands, in dilapidated vans, piled with their bags, mattresses and a few bits of furniture salved from the ruin, wandering aimlessly across the vast continent.

In New York, an urban microcosm, hordes of men and women converging from every part of the continent added to the local unemployed. Without shelter or resources, they took over the abandoned warehouses, or the lawns of public parks. Riverside Drive, near Columbia University, and central Park, became shanty-towns, or 'Hoovervilles' as the New Yorkers called them. Seven thousand 'shoe-

* The London *Economist*, in a study on 18th June 1978.[3]

shine boys' wandered about the streets, boxes of brushes on their shoulders, hoping to pick up a few cents. Swarms of unemployed descended on the public soup-kitchens, organised by charitable organisations or the municipality—an unimaginable humiliation for a society based on success, for which poverty was a shameful stigma.

Year after year, the crisis deepened. With inflexible determination, President Hoover opposed all intervention by the central power on behalf of the unemployed, convinced that dole subsidies would encourage idleness, and undermine the American 'rugged individualism'. With millions and millions of unemployed, 'rugged individualism' had led to the collapse of salaries, often by a half, and to the disintegration of the Trades Unions, rendering a strike action impossible.[4] More than a quarter of the population possessed only a nominal purchasing power, another quarter a much reduced income. Consumption continued to diminish, the Depression to worsen.* The very web and woof of society was becoming frayed. The revenue from taxes declined, because between 20 and 30 per cent of the tax-paying public was insolvent. Deprived of an important part of their resources, crushed by the cost of social assistance, the municipalities were no longer able to fulfil their normal role. Roads were not kept up; the police force had to be reduced, and schoolteachers dismissed in large numbers. In 1932, more than 300,000 children were without schooling, owing to lack of funds. A woeful song, 'Halleluia I'm a bum!' symbolised the destitution of the period.

By the end of that year, disorder had become general throughout the Union. As in Great Britain and Germany, the patience of the hungry was exhausted and they took to the streets. In industrial centres, they clashed with the police; many fell to the ground, never to rise again. In the countryside of the Middle West, serious disturbances took place when farmers blocked the roads, attempting to cut off food supplies to the towns.

Just before Franklin Roosevelt took his Presidential oath, a new tornado of exceptional violence descended on the American economy. The country was virtually without a government, and the new President refused to cooperate with his predecessor who treated him with contempt. Panic took hold because many of the banks, lacking liquidity, were unable to satisfy massive withdrawals. In February, the

---

* Exact statistics are lacking. The review *Fortune* (September 1934) estimated that out of a population of 122 million, 34 million men, women and children had no salary. These figures do not include 11 million rural families.

authorities in Michigan and Maryland were obliged to decree the temporary closure of all financial establishments. While the Reichstag was burning in Berlin, and the Japanese were bombing Shanghai, the banks in seventeen States of the Union had ceased all transactions; elsewhere, they were forced to limit withdrawals to five per cent. Ten thousand closed their doors, of which half were to disappear completely. The richest and most stable nation in the world had appeared about to sink into ruin, despair, and perhaps, revolution.

★   ★   ★

My last evening on the 'Pennland' had come. Before returning to my tiny cabin, I took a last stroll on deck in the company of an American girl I had befriended during the crossing. She was an ardent supporter of the New Deal, imbued with a patriotric faith in the future of her country. 'Yes,' she said,

> the United States has gone through a dreadful crisis, which has shaken it from top to bottom—a crisis no less serious than the Civil War. But we have emerged from it stronger than ever. From the first days of his accession, President Roosevelt gave us the confidence and dignity we had lost and now his first concern is to restore prosperity by imposing structural reforms, to efface the blemishes of uncontrolled capitalism. Tomorrow, the United States will again be for all the oppressed peoples of the world the haven it has been for more than a hundred years.

I needed only a few days to discover that her optimism was not unfounded. The country had certainly surmounted the crisis, economic, political and moral. It was now climbing the steep and difficult slope to prosperity again, but gradually and not painlessly. This had obviously been due to Roosevelt—from the moment of his inauguration speech—the magnificent speech of 4 March 1933 in which he launched his famous challenge to adversity: 'the only thing we have to fear is fear itself, nameless, unreasoning, unjustified terror . . .' A clarion call! The new President had at once thrown himself into the struggle. In his first 'Hundred Days', his dynamic action galvanised the nation. Assuming a much increased presidential authority, which no one in those circumstances would have dreamed of questioning, his aim was to raise prices and revitalise purchasing power—thereby scorning the sacred dogmas of the time. He injected large sums into the economy by launching a huge public works programme. He introduced a control of the banks, he increased aid to threatened enterprises, he encouraged the negotiation of collective agreements and the Trades Union movement. He imposed a minimum legal salary, limiting the weekly working hours, and forbidding the employment of children. A federal law for social security formed the basis of a pension scheme for the unemployed, the aged and invalids. Farmers benefited from low-level interest loans, while being subjected to a severe production discipline. The gold standard, the sacred cow of liberal orthodoxy, was abandoned. The complete antithesis of everything which the Hoovers, MacDonalds and Lavals had stood for.

A whirlwind—with rules, decrees and laws pouring out of Washington like water from a spring. Some proved ineffective, some inopportune, even harmful. But by the time I arrived in America, more than four million unemployed had found work; purchasing power had increased by 15 per cent and most enterprises were again showing profits. Industrial production, which had fallen by a half, had risen to 80 per cent of its old level. Agricultural prices were picking up, and exports increasing. All signs of poverty were not yet effaced, far from it. In New York, three hundred yards from the smart Fifth Avenue, one would come upon extreme poverty in the Bowery, with its tramps and drunkards stretched out day and night on the pavements. But if abundance had not fully returned, the movement of decline had been reversed; the future could be regarded with optimism. 'Happy days are here again!', sang the Roosevelt enthusiasts during his electoral campaign; and the nation took up the refrain.

★   ★   ★

One evening I made the acquaintance of Erik Lundberg, a Swedish student. For $200 we bought a two-year-old Ford Cabriolet (new, it would have cost double); and at the beginning of October, we set off on the conquest of the continent. As well as being an agreeable holiday, the trip proved an enriching experience. Erik asked innumerable questions about the resources of the places we passed through, how the locals voted, their professional activities and political views. Most of them replied frankly, simply, confidently, sometimes a trifle boorishly. They were modest as well as self-satisfied, generally interested in politics, being strongly in favour of, or strongly opposed to, the New Deal.

From these conversations, it was clear that the Democratic Party had cut the ground from under the feet of the Left-wing extremists. Compared with Roosevelt's 23 million votes, the Socialist Party, under its leader Norman Thomas, a moderate idealist, had obtained only a million; the Communist Party barely a hundred thousand. The influence of certain 'Leftists' in Minnesota or Wisconsin was limited to the popularity of their local leaders. For the extreme Right, it was somewhat different. In the south, Senator Huey P. Long, 'the mad dog of Louisiana', dominated the scene. At the age of thirty-five he had succeeded in getting himself elected Governor of his native state. Utterly unscrupulous, he managed to control the National Guard and the police force. The tommy-guns of his bodyguard ensured the fidelity of his electors, and the discipline of the journalists. 'The Constitution—I *am* the Constitution' he would brag. As Hitler and Mussolini, he spent money like water on hospitals, schools and highways (of which incidentally the State was much in need), not without enriching his supporters.

The demagogue announced a redistribution of wealth, so as to give evey family a capital sum of $5,000, and an income of $2,000, as well as guaranteed salaries, reduction of working hours and pensions for the aged. Games and books were distributed for recreation; agricultural land was transformed into golf-courses. 'Every man a King!' Aided by the great crisis, these grotesque promises conferred on Huey Long a popularity which went far beyond the bounds of Louisiana; nor did he conceal his White House ambitions. But he was to die in 1935, murdered in mysterious circumstances.

At the other end of the country, at Royal Oak in Michigan, another man of the same ilk flaunted himself, Father Charles Coughlin. Born forty-three years before in Canada, he was of Irish origin, and had been ordained in 1916. The Archbishop of Detroit had given him the modest parish of Saint Teresa of the Little Flower. Endowed with natural eloquence and a radiophonic voice, he contrived to have his sermons broadcast through a small local transmitter. He did not confine himself to edifying homilies, but preached against 'the pagan God of Gold', against the tycoons of Wall Street 'who starve the people', against the intellectuals of the Eastern establishment. Money flowed in, from voluntary contributions, and by the sale of crucifixes which, he claimed, had 'been in contact with a piece of the True Cross'. He built himself an enormous church (illuminated at night by thousands of electric light bulbs), in which his secretariat, numbering several hundred, worked. On the wavelengths of dozens of commercial radio stations—listened to, he boasted, by 40 million listeners—he denounced the world conspiracy of the bankers, the Communists and the Jews. The movement he founded, the *National Union for Social Justice*, had six million adherents in 1934, to whom he offered the same cocktail of tradition and revolution which had intoxicated the Germans and Italians. But when he openly announced his support for

Fascism and Nazism, his popularity began to wane. During the war, he indulged in vehement isolationist propaganda, which did not cease even after Pearl Harbor, and he lost most of his influence.

But at the time of my stay in America, the resistance of the Right to the New Deal was very strong. Big business circles, reassured that the revolutionary danger was now past, reacted against the controls of the free hand they had enjoyed. For them, Roosevelt became the incarnation of evil, Satan in person. 'My Wall Street colleagues', recounted Averill Harriman (himself a rich banker, but a generous spirit) who had rallied to the New Deal, 'would cross the street to avoid having to shake hands with me.'[5] Some friends of my father, with whom I occasionally spent the weekends, had a charming house with a Georgian portico outside Philadelphia, at the end of a street called 'Roosevelt Lane'. They moved house to remove themselves from the abhorrent name, in this case funnily enough, the name of the former Republican President.

★   ★   ★

Like Hitler, *only with a much larger electoral majority*, Roosevelt had come to power on a wave of hope, carrying a people at bay. Also like Hitler, he benefited in the first months of his Presidency from unlimited authority. No power then existed which could have prevented him from assuming dictatorship. But during his twelve years in the White House—including four years of war—he never restricted the freedom of radio or press, although, until Pearl Harbor, they had nearly all been hostile to him. Nor did he ever attempt to strangle the opposition, to silence public meetings, nor to attack the Constitution.

His nature displayed a fortunate combination of faults and virtues, of shameless opportunism and breadth of vision, which made him one of the most complex, as well as one of the most remarkable, figures of the century. 'A born arbitrator of vices and virtues', wrote a Roman contemporary of the great Emperor Hadrian. Roosevelt's shortcomings if not his vices, were far from insignificant—among them an unscrupulous tactical sharp practice, and an often frightening casualness in defining his objectives. In the management of men, he displayed an almost cynical skill, being careful to entrust identical tasks to different members of his cabinet, so as to put one against the other, and so oblige them to appeal constantly to him for arbitration. He was a ready liar, confiding to Orson Welles good-humouredly, 'You and I are the two best actors in America.' There are plenty of anecdotes about his insouciance. When in 1933 he realised that the price of gold must be manipulated, he would fix it every morning at breakfast in bed, in the company of two of his collaborators; one morning, while eating his boiled egg, he decided on a rise of 21 cents, 'because three times seven is a lucky number'. Another time, on a cruise in the tropics, he became enthusiastic about bamboo, and planned to use it for making armoured cars.[6] Of the geography of Europe, he had but the slightest notion. This did not stop him during the war from suggesting the oddest ideas for her future, including the farcical project to replace Belgium by a 'great Wallonia', which would include a part of northern France and stretch to the Swiss border.[7] He worked in an atmosphere of total disorder, his desk littered with files which he hardly ever read, interrupting his audiences with frivolous monologues, always ready to answer the telephone, spending much of his time listening to the chatter of importunate visitors to whom he happened to have taken a liking.

The story of his life, the moral and intellectual quality of his entourage, his achievements during the long years at the White House, reveals a thread of steel running through the tissue of his somewhat flexible character—in spite of the cruel illness which had reduced him when still young to being a permanent invalid. General ideas and abstractions bored him. Relatively uncultivated, his reading was confined manily to adventure stories; but his ever alert imagination, marked by an insatiable curiosity and notable taste for novelty, was set alight when faced by concrete, human facts. Most of his reforms were dictated, not by his principles, which were vague, but by his emotions, which were strong. The poverty of the aged farmers in the neighbourhood of Hyde Park, his country property, was responsible for his old-age insurance measures. The high cost of electricity at War Springs, where he took the cure, was in part responsible for his programme of the electrification of the countryside. His travels in the West, which had been devastated by the agricultural crisis, revealed to him the need for large scale rural irrigation and rehabilitation.

Some bold minds—in particular the Englishman, John Maynard Keynes—condemned the traditional economic doctrines, all of which tended to regard the wealth of nations as a cake to divide between the citizens—an antique notion which still continues, consciously, or unconsciously to exercise an influence, particularly on Socialist thinking. Keynes saw it on the contrary, as a dynamic mass, enlarged by the work and intelligence of man, and nourishing itself on its own developments. However, it was not until 1936 that Keynes published his principal work (without incidentally attracting the attention of the leading politicians). To President Roosevelt, the economic sciences were of no more interest than geography or history. His only interview with the English economist in May 1934 was not a success. 'I thought he was better informed', remarked the professor politely at the end of the conversation. The pragmatist had complained of having been baffled by the mass of figures thrown at him.

'I am a Christian and a Democrat', Roosevelt described himself to a journalist. 'His faith was a simple one', confirmed one of his ministers and a close friend, Mrs Perkins. 'As far as I could see, it knew no doubt.' It lacked any metaphysical inspiration, but was a solid basis for his political beliefs. Talking to Maxim Litvinov, the People's Commissar for Foreign Affairs of the USSR, he would sermonise him. 'Max, you must tell Stalin he is wrong to follow an anti-religious policy. God will punish him, if he goes on persecuting the Churches.'[8]

He defined the place he occupied on the political chess-board as 'a little left of centre', a sentimental remark which describes his personality better than the most learned analyses. His greatness derived in fact from an almost sensual perception, preceding reasoned understanding; it told him (and he was the first of the heads of government to be aware of this), that social justice is a practical necessity, born of the technological revolution, as much as a moral imperative. Together with his love of humanity, and a natural liveliness from which his energy sprang, he possessed those gifts of intuition which make him, I think, among statesmen, the greatest creative genius of the century.

Thomas Jefferson, one of the principal authors of the American Declaration of Independence, and who was the United States envoy in Paris from 1785, helped Lafayette to draft the *Déclaration Universelle des Droits de l'Homme* which has become the charter of political liberty in Europe. Franklin Roosevelt gave the world a pragmatic social justice which had been largely absent in the liberal societies of his time, and which had deprived democracy of a large part of its substance. The New Deal saved free enterprise, submitting it to new laws, and curbing its excesses and follies. By denying the Marxist pretention to be the sole repository of scientific truth, by renewing the morality, as well as the efficacy, of free societies, Roosevelt gave the prodigious impetus which has made our epoch, in spite of its many imperfections, one of the happiest in the history of the West.

★   ★   ★

In May 1935, no longer having any reason for prolonging my stay in America, I again embarked on the 'Pennland'. On this occasion there were few other passengers, and the sea was stormy. In the warm smoking-room, listening to the creaking of the ship's bulkheads, I endeavoured to put my notes in order, and drew up a balance sheet of my time in the United States. One of the factors which had most impressed me was the idealism in American public life. Many Europeans are inclined to see in this no more than a hypocritical disguise. For them, a nation is not only an expression of the general will, but an almost metaphysical entity, transcending the citizen. They remain faithful to the old concept of the Fatherland, attachment to the soil, devotion to a Prince, an instinct from a distant past which, in spite of the advance of humanism, they cannot completely overcome. Consequently, they resign themselves without much difficulty to seeing in politics, as did Machiavelli and Hegel, only a question of power, more or less foreign to morality. 'Right or wrong, my country!'

In quite a different way, the American nation was born of an ecumenical message. No Capet, Tudor or Hohenzollern has shaped it from within a '*pré carré*' (a fief) or the shores of an island's seas. What brought the colonists together and unified them, was a human ideal deriving from the Old Testament, stamped with the wisdom of Rome, the traditions of England, and nourished by the Encyclopaedists. The 'Covenant' drawn up in Philadelphia by the Founding Fathers of the Republic had its source in the Ark of Alliance, the mysterious monument erected by Moses, at once the throne of Jehova and the receptacle of the Tables of the Law; it embodied the links between the Creator and His people, as well at the rules enabling men to live in an organised society. That the United States is a nation is due to this credo which its citizens, in spite of their different origins, continue to revere. Without it, the Union would lose its cohesion and vitality, in the same way that France would cease to be herself without the Hexagon, or Great Britain without its monarchy.[9] Undoubtedly, like all human enterprises, it has its defects. In its recent history there have been—and there will be again—the Longs, the Coughlins, the Macarthys and other smaller sharks who have used the national ideal for personal advantage. There have been grotesques. There have also been sections of public opinion which have doubted the value of the ideal, or who have bitterly attacked it. This is the consequence and the price of liberty. But on the whole, its ideal has been, and will remain, the solid cement, the raison d'être of the American Republic.

It is here too, from all evidence, that resides the principal reason for the division of the two great families of the West. Although they may exaggerate it, the Americans often see the world of their ancestors as

CHAPTER 6

The Brief Halt at Stresa

In the first days of May 1935, the 'Pennland' sailed up the muddy waters of the Scheldt towards Antwerp. With more emotion than I had envisaged, I returned to the polders of Flanders, the flat land with its lush meadows and placid cows, beneath a lowering sky and steady rain, the poplars bending to the eternal winds of the North Sea. Returning from an America with its clear-cut outlines, I became aware of the European disarray. Germany and Italy had, I gathered, increased their prestige, while France and Great Britain uncertain of themselves and fettered by contradictions, appeared to be drifting.

For their part, the Belgians were beguiled by 'Rexism', their own brand of Fascism. Its leader, Léon Degrelle, had suddenly acquired a dubious notoriety. Active for a number of years, the chief of 'Rex' had long been regarded as a busybody of little importance. At the Catholic University of Louvain, where he had begun his legal studies (without completing them), he had read the works of Charles Maurras, the pamphlets of Léon Daudet, and the diatribes of the *Action Française*, which were widely circulated in the Catholic schools. Following their example, he attacked those whom he described as 'rotters' or 'banksters', namely the leaders of the political and business world in general. The demogogue announced, 'We desire everything, we shall take everything, the press, the radio, the cinema, the government.'*

---

* Degrelle was arrested in 1940 by the Belgian authorities. Liberated during the German occupation, he joined the Walloon Legion, became a Colonel in the SS, and fought with the German Army in the east. After the Allied victory, he managed to take refuge in Spain, where he is living today. He was condemned to death *in absentia* by the Belgian courts.

Curiosity prompted me to go and listen to him. On the podium of the huge Palais des Sports in Brussels, lit by floodlighting, surrounded by bodyguards armed with symbolic brooms, he enacted his noisy turn before a credulous mob. In vulgar, colourful phrases, he expatiated on 'the future of our children', and the 'white hair of my poor mother'. Although he did not impress me, it was clear that he combined a natural eloquence with an exceptional gift of invective, to the extent that one ignored the emptiness of his thought. He naturally sympathised with Berlin and Rome, from where he obtained important subsidies.[1] Although he kept secret his encounters with the Dictators, he did not conceal his sympathy for them. He was, of course, against Democracy; against the League of Nations, against Freemasonry (the habitual scapegoat of extreme right-wing movements), against the 'Reds'—Social democrats as well as Communists, against the French Republic (from which his family originally came). His real *bête noire* was Great Britain which, for the extremists of all shades, symbolised 'Imperialism'—much as the USA symbolises it today.

Far more than Degrelle or his few rivals in the Flemish provinces, it was the dissensions and vacillations of the great Democracies which caused them to lose their credibility. Where was Paris going? What did London want? The French Minister of Foreign Affairs was the aged Barthou, who had the reputation of a *bon viveur* with a taste for pretty women; also of being intelligent, courageous and energetic. But his attempts at an Eastern pact inspired by Locarno were only half-convincing; and his inactivity when the Nazis had attempted to lay hands on Austria was inexplicable. Anxious to revive France's Eastern alliances, Barthou had invited King Alexander of Yugoslavia to make a State visit. On 9 October 1934 he was at Marseilles, to welcome the sovereign. While the cortège was proceeding up the Canebière, a Croatian terrorist managed to empty his automatic pistol into them both, putting an end to the lives of these resolute enemies of the Third Reich.

Although a tragic episode, the Marseilles assassinations were quickly forgotten; but French prestige suffered. Soon the affair of the Saar occupied the centre of the European stage. For centuries, the French and Germans had disputed the ownership of the valley of the Saar, a rich coal and metallurgical basin of great strategical importance. By the peace treaties, it had been provisionally administered by a League of Nations commission, while associated economically with France. A plebiscite was to decide its permanent future. In January 1935 the moment for this arrived. An international corps, composed of British,

Italian, Dutch and Swedish troops, was despatched to the Saar by the League of Nations to supervise the suffrage—the first time in history. Of more than 500,000 voters, less than 3,000 favoured France. On 1 March, the SA and SS made their clamorous entry into Saarbrücken, accompanied by the Nazi bosses, Hitler at the head. The church bells rang, swasticas hung from all the buildings. It was a facile and spectacular success for Nazi Germany—another humiliation for French prestige.

★   ★   ★

With the Saar affair settled to his satisfaction, the Führer took a further step, a decisive one, on the road which he had always planned. Two days after his triumph, he announced the formation of the *Luftwaffe*. A week later, in the absence of any reaction from London and Paris, he decreed compulsory military service. It meant the reconstruction of the armed forces of Germany, forbidden by the Versailles treaty. A military parade that evening Unter den Linden gave Berliners the opportunity to manifest their enthusiasm.

The seven divisions allowed by the treaty were increased to thirty-six, a peace-time army of 550,000 men. The reasons given by Hitler to justify his decision were: the failure of the disarmament conference, the rearmament by the other powers, the need for protection against the Soviet Union; all pretexts to calm the simple minds, but in reality devoid of any real foundation. It was true that, in London, a 'White Paper' had recommended an increase in defence expenditure at the beginning of March: but little had been done about it. In the United Kingdom, with the exception of two or three poorly equipped divisions, there were no land forces. In Paris, Parliament had passed a law prolonging military service to two years; its object was not to increase the numbers called up, but to maintain them at their old level, which had beem affected by the lower birth-rate during the war years. Far from increasing her military strength, France was concerned with reducing it. As for the so-called Russian danger, it was at this time non-existent.

While making Europe ring with martial sounds, the Führer not only announced the reconstitution of a powerful army (which European public opinion, sympathetic to Germany's right to equality, would have accepted in time); he raucously announced that his army would be larger and more powerful than any other. To this end, he devoted enormous sums of money, almost half the 1935 national budget infinitely more than France and Great Britain.* These figures were not unknown in the West; indeed they were discussed in the Parliaments, and often exaggerated.

The great fanfare with which the rearmament of the Reich was accompanied caused a considerable stir in the West. It would seem that the time had come for the pacific countries to undertake an examination in depth of the military situation—preferably together. Nothing. In France, the Ministers gnashed their teeth; in Britain, they chose to ignore the facts; in Belgium, total silence. Of consultation between former allies, there was no question.

Paris, which had refused the 200,000 men demanded by Brüning, now accepted the 500,000 men Hitler so crudely arrogated to himself. Flandin confined himself to fiery speeches in the Senate and—a futile initiative—to send the case to the League of Nations, in one of those typical protests couched in energetic terms, the classic document 'for the record'. Even more futile, he simultaneously sent a note to Berlin stating that he was prepared for conciliation and all efforts to 'dissipate the misunderstanding'.[3]

An even feebler protest came from London. Sir John Simon and Anthony Eden insisted on going to Berlin to discuss the situation. The visit had been envisaged previously, but Hitler had deferred it, rather flippantly, under the pretext of a 'sore throat' at the time of the British White Paper on rearmament. When it took place, it was a strange encounter, the first at such high level since Disraeli had met Bismarck in 1874. The newspapers quickly announced that the meeting, far from being stormy as simple souls might expect, had been marked, in the words of the official communiqué, by 'frankness and friendliness'.

Hitler, calm and self-confident, presented himself as a man of peace. He was accused of violating the Treaty of Versailles? How could he have done so, as he had not signed it? He had no territorial ambitions; he asked for nothing more than equality of rights, and the means of assuring the defence of the Reich against 'the Bolsheviks'. The ex-

---

* In 1926–27, British defence spending was £116 million. By 1932–33, it had fallen to £103 million—the lowest figure between the two wars. In 1933–34, in an almost derisory gesture, the allocation for the Royal Navy was increased by £8 million and that for the Royal Air Force by £10 million. As a proportion of the national budget, the figures for defence in 1934–35 represented 15.5 per cent, rising 17.7 per cent in the following year. In France, defence spending during the period 1921–36 varied between 25.6 and 27.3 per cent of the whole. In sharp contrast, the German defence budget rose from 23 per cent in 1933 to 49 per cent in 1934 and no less than 74 per cent in 1938.[2]

change of views also touched on an Eastern pact, the return of the Reich to the League of Nations; Austria, on which Hitler made clear his designs; on the restitution of the old colonies; and the 'vital space' which Germany required to live. There was also talk of lasting political cooperation, which meant an alliance between the two countries. All these topics were totally unconnected with the treaty violations, which the British ministers confined themselves to mentioning 'in a very friendly and pleasant manner', in the words to the German interpreter.[4]

The conversation lasted seven hours, followed by a State dinner at the Presidential Palace. In the great rococo drawing-rooms with their decorated ceilings and damasc-covered walls, the Führer, in the guise of a man of the world, clad in evening dress with a white tie, circulated among the guests surrounded by footmen in livery and powdered wigs. Chatting with Eden, the two men discovered that they had been opposite one another in the trenches on the Oise in 1918. When the French Ambassador, François-Poncet, learned of this curiour occurrence, he remarked to Eden, 'How could you have missed him?'[5]

The second day was devoted to the military situation. Hitler stated unequivocally the he would not retract his determination to equip Germany with an army of 36 divisions; that question was not negotiable. As for the air force, he wanted parity with France, then the principal European air power. In passing, he indicated that the Luftwaffe (whose creation had been announced only a few days before) had already attained the same level as the British Royal Air Force—causing a moment of startled silence among the guests, according to reports. As for the navy, Germany would be satisfied with a tonnage representing 35 per cent of the British fleet.*

That evening, at a smaller dinner in the salon of the old Chancellory built in the time of Bismarck, Eden found himself sitting next to the King of Italy's daughter, Princess Mafalda of Hesse (who was, one day, to find herself in the Buchenwald concentration camp, where she died). Hitler was a charming host. Why not? He had every reason to believe he had initiated an understanding with the British, one of the principal aims of his grand strategy. In spite of his impudence, perhaps

---

* Military circles in London adapted themselves without difficulty to the idea of a German army of 36 divisions, which they apparently believed would not endanger the balance of power. They were much impressed by the announcement (a false announcement), of the size of the Luftwaffe. As for the Admiralty, it was satisfied with a *Kriegsmarine* limited to counter the Soviet fleet in the Baltic.[6]

because of it, Simon and Eden seemed affable and understanding, prepared, apparently, to transfer their old relationship with Paris to Berlin.* The despatches of the German Ambassador to the Court of St James relating the sympathy felt in London for the third Reich encouraged Hitler's optimism. In particular, the Prince of Wales was extremely well disposed. In April, he confided to von Hoesch his disapproval of the 'prejudices' of the Foreign Office, and he assured the German Ambassador of his complete understanding of the position and aspirations of Germany.[7]

★   ★   ★

If the words of the Prince of Wales reflected the views of certain pro-Nazi circles, the attitude of the British politicians was more influenced by an age-old repugnance for the affairs of the continent. 'Wake me up when the next item on the agenda comes up', said Baldwin, closing his eyes when such matters were considered in the Cabinet. Eden believed there was nothing to fear from Hitler, while Sir John Simon saw him as a timid and reserved man, an 'Austrian Joan of Arc with a moustache'.[8] Most extraordinary views! The Nazi regime had never attempted to conceal its objectives; from the very outset, it had, indeed, boasted about them.

Wing-Commander Winterbotham, the ex-chief of the Air Section of the SIS (Secret Intelligence Service) is responsible for a curious piece of information. Thanks to Alfred Rosenberg, with whom he maintained continuous contact, he had a long interview with the Führer in February 1934.† After recalling 'the great days of the war', the ex-corporal suggested a partition of the world among the three principal powers, the United States, the British Empire, and the Reich, the latter to dominate Europe. 'All we ask', he said, 'is that Britain should be content to look after her Empire and not interfere with Germany's plans of expansion.' Later, invited to lunch at Hörchers (the Berlin Maxim's), Winterbotham heard General von Reichenau, one of the officers closest to the Führer, explaining his plans and giving a number of details about German rearmament. According to the

---

* After leaving Berlin, Eden prolonged his trip in Eastern Europe (without Simon). He was warmly received in Moscow by Stalin. It was the first visit of a British Minister to Russia since the time of the Czars.

† Alfred Rosenberg, the Nazi regime's theoretician, and author of *The Myth of the Twentieth Century*. During the war he was High Commissioner for the Eastern Territories. After being tried at Nuremberg, he finished up on the gallows.

Wing-Commander, all this was communicated to the French intelligence services through Colonel (later General) Georges Ronin.[9]

It was not the first time—far from it—that Hitler, or those close to him, had spoken of giving free play to Great Britain in exchange for recognition of the Reich's predominance on the continent. Ribbentrop had referred to it when he had tea with Baldwin in 1933. The Führer spoke of it in barely veiled terms when he met Sir John Simon and Anthony Eden; it was the same in conversations he held with many other personalities, such as the ex-Prime Minister Lloyd George, the historian Arnold Toynbee, Lord Londonderry and Lady Vansittart. This did not trouble Whitehall. Baldwin echoed a widespread opnion when he confided to a group of Conservative MPs in 1936 that his 'heart would not be broken if Hitler marched east'.[10]

Some politicians endowed with more vision (among them Churchill) and many diplomats perceived the danger, demanding a more vigorous policy and an army capable of supporting it. They were not listened to. Many others, and the military establishment in particular, full of horror at the carnage of the Great War, decided that it would not be repeated. They suggested a maritime strategy, 'in accordance with British traditions', which would render large land forces unnecessary. Their views were expressed in a number of writings, sometimes brilliant, which were widely supported. With their help, the responsible ministers managed to silence the bothersome internationalist groups, using methods which were not always overscrupulous. Under the influence of the Conservative party, which at each of its congresses voted resolutions in favour of rearmament, they agreed, with ill grace, to improve the defence of the British Isles by a small increase in the Royal Air Force; but they would not agree to the formation of a land force, which alone could have been seen by the Third Reich as an unbreakable deterrent.

★　★　★

In 1935, Pierre Laval occupied the centre of the political stage in Paris. Ten years later, in the courtyard of Fresnes prison, he was to end his career before a firing squad. In the early hours of 15 October 1945, lawyers and magistrates found him in his cell, with glazed eyes and mouth contorted, a phial of cyanide in his left hand. There is a rule that sick men cannot be executed. He was accordingly taken to the prison infirmary, where a doctor attended to him. Towards 11 o'clock, after seventeen stomach pumpings, the condemned man regained consciousness. A macabre communiqué announced, 'Laval is no longer in danger!'

The funeral rites prescribed by tradition could now be followed. The ex-Premier confessed, and the prison chaplain gave him absolution. He was dressed. His body shuddering with spasms, he had the courage to ask for a comb and a mirror to put his hair in order. Leaning on his lawyers (his right leg, half paralysed by the poison, no longer supported him) . . . he left his cell for the place of execution. On seven occasions, the lawyers related later, the procession had to stop to allow the condemned man, bent double and tossing his head from side to side, to vomit and swallow a glass of water.[11] In the courtyard, the execution squad stood waiting for him; beside them, an open coffin. A chair was brought forward, but he refused it. He requested the presence of the judges who, appalled by the hideous spectacle, had taken cover behind a van. He also asked to be allowed to give the order to fire; this was refused. Riddled with bullets he fell. A sergeant gave him the finishing bullet in the head and his remains were quickly placed in the coffin.

It was death which, in spite of its indignity, revealed a strength of character unsuspected in his life-time. Born at Chateldon, a small country town in the Basse Auvergne, the son of a common innkeeper, Pierre Laval was put to work as soon as he left his primary school at the age of eleven. After lengthy family wrangling, he was allowed to go to Paris. Having obtained the *baccalauréat*, he became an assistant teacher in a Lyons *lycée*, where he joined the extreme Left wing of the Socialist Party. After completing his military service, he studied natural science and then law. Called to the bar in 1909, a candidate for Parliament but unsuccessful at a by-election in 1910, we find him four years later, at the age of thirty-one, Deputy for Aubervilliers. He now acquired a rather dubious reputation. Invalided from the Army, he escaped the horrors of the trenches. In Parliament, he inveighed loudly against militarism, with revolutionary speeches. But, at the same time, he was beginning to move to the Right, rapidly mounting the rungs of the ladder to power, while amassing a considerable fortune on the way. In 1931, he was at the head of a Right–Centre government, including Flandin, Maginot, Briand and Tardieu.

What was Pierre Laval really like? Small, thick-set, with a lustreless brown complexion, blubber-lipped, with protruding ears and heavy-lidded eyes, his physical appearance was repulsive, accentuated by the eternal damp cigarette-end hanging from his lips. His career had been remarkable. From 1925 to 1936, and again during the Vichy regime, he was always in the forefront of the political stage, a member (or the Premier) of nearly all the governments. In the saraband of the Third Republic Ministers, something must have distinguished him from the others—a hidden strength which was difficult to identify, perhaps a more desperate eagerness to climb than that of the others; it also explains his vast fortune. The latter caused some raising of eyebrows; but it was by no means rare to find the bank account of a business lawyer much inflated due to the holding of a public office. Admittedly, not very pretty, it was not illegal. Did he sell himself to Mussolini at the time of the Ethiopean war, as the Secret Service and the British Government contended? It is not improbable, but unproven.

'He had been treated with great contempt, so that he was full of it', Chateaubriand remarked of Talleyrand. In Laval, contempt was mixed with a secret anxiety, a dangerous mixture that stimulates ambition in many men. Contempt which had grown with success. 'I know people, I am the cleverest, Hitler is a child . . .' Anxiety, reflected by his hesitant nature, his cupidity, his duodenal ulcers, his strange superstitions.* Devoted to his wife if not always faithful, a loving father, he had no real friends, and remained secretative and suspicious, a loner in spite of his pretence of bonhomie. 'The upper classes have always thought of me as a monster, an odd defector of anarchy', he complained. 'They have never accepted me. Only among the peasants of the Auvergne, or the steel workers of Aubervilliers, do I feel comfortable.'[12] As a matter of fact, as a minister in 1930 in a conservative government, he was to introduce, for the first time, a law on social security intended to transform the condition of the proletariat. At the same time, deeply impressed by the hereditary aristocracy, he prevailed upon the Pope to give him the title of Count.

Albert Thibaudet, I think, the Geneva professor and author of *Republique des Professeurs*, said of Laval, 'He automatically left to the other party the benefit of the spiritual element, the category of the ideal.' His amorality sprang from a sort of innocence nourished by ignorance. He hated files, 'so much waste paper', he called them, and he flattered himself that he never read the reports of his colleagues, or of his ambassadors. 'He spent most of his time in conversation', recounted Léon Noel who worked closely with him. 'So that his principal secretary had to imitate his signature, with his approval, in

---

* Among his superstitions, a terror of the figure 13 or of a broken mirror, his addiction to a white tie, to the colour blue or to an old coin from which he was expecting a particular protection. He was constantly consulting fortune tellers, seers, astrologers.

order to ensure the smooth working of his office.' Lacking any real culture, he would say 'a cowherd with common sense knows more than my officials'.

One of Laval's ambitions was to follow in the steps of Briand and acquire the same popularity as the 'Apostle of Peace'. In the last years of his life, he showed a sort of deep despair, which cannot but inspire compassion. He was probably inspired by a real and sincere horror of war. During the conflict of 1914–18, he had been one of the rare Zimmerwald pilgrims, that curious encounter in neutral Switzerland where the pacifists of Europe challenged—in vain—the governments bent upon pursuing the carnage. Pity for the underprivileged might also have given him a taste for the cocktail of socialism and nationalism that went to the head of so many of his contemporaries. But more than anything else, what brought him under Hitler's spell, and eventually to face a firing squad, was a frenzied hatred of the British Empire—together with his hunger for power and his thirst for revenge.

Prime Minister of Vichy, he could give free vent to this, and he did so ferociously. He had always detested '*La perfide Albion*', perhaps since the days when he was a militant of the extreme Left, and regarded Britain as the principal 'Imperialist power', the evil genius of Marxist mythology. He assumed that Britain was in decline, an irreversible process. At the same time, in contradiction as it were, he accused her of isolating France, and forcing her into a state of inferiority. The incompatibility between Laval and his Whitehall counterparts was complete. The patricians of London were offended by his manner and methods; they distrusted him and made no effort to conceal it. Stanley Baldwin, by no means a dandy, compared Laval with the peasants he met while walking in the Alps near Aix-les-Bains. Chamberlain considered him the most dishonest politician in France. 'Laval, who appeared at ease with everyone in all situations revealed himself to be extremely uncomfortable and embarrassed on these occasions', wrote Léon Noel, after a visit by his Minister to London. 'He had an instinctive horror of the country of the Lords, of worldly manners, of gentlemen and the monarchy.' Well before 1939, he had become convinced that he was the victim of an international conspiracy organised by the British Intelligence Service.[13]

★   ★   ★

With Mussolini, the situation was reversed. With him, Laval forgot his complexes. Everything which separated him from the British brought him closer to the Duce—their deprived childhoods, their revolutionary past, their *volte-face* from Left to Right, their nimble Latin minds, the same vulgarity which made then guffaw at the filthiest jokes.

In January 1935, shortly after the Saar plebiscite, the two cronies met in Rome. Laval had not yet become a partisan of Hitler's. The immediate successor of the unfortunate Barthou, he was following his halting policy of erecting a coalition against Germany. As for Mussolini planning to conquer Ethiopia, he distrusted the aims of the Reich with regard to Austria—a buffer state protecting Italy's northern frontier. The differences between Rome and Paris were therefore resolved without difficulty. The bargain struck, secret military protocols transformed it into a real alliance—to which London was not privy.

Twenty-five years later, when holding a diplomatic post in Yugoslavia, I had the good fortune to meet one of the former officials of the Fascist regime, Flavio Suvich, at the house of some friends in Trieste. Born in the city and having retired there, Suvich had been Under Secretary of State for Foreign Affairs in Rome at the time of the African expedition and spoke readily of the past.

'In 1935', he said, 'the Duce had become bored. He was no longer interested in power as such, he wanted to taste fresh excitements. Moreover, being relatively uncultivated, history was a kind of cartoon to him, a series of brilliant images. Among these was the Roman Empire—the most colourful one and one to revive. He therefore *had* to have Africa, beginning with Ethiopia. At the time he was prepared to pay anything to obtain it—and this demanded the connivance of France.' I asked Suvich the obvious question, 'Could the cooperation have remained permanent?' He shrugged his shoulders. 'For Mussolini nothing was ever permanent. *Ma chi lo sa?*'

An idea of the British but prepared by the meeting in Rome, the conference of Stresa in the Italian Alps, took place on 11 April 1935. The Duce, piloting his hydroplane, descended from the skies to welcome his French and British colleagues in the scented gardens and noble palaces of the Borromean Isles. In spite of the long and incoherent speeches of MacDonald, whose mental condition was deteriorating, the three governments appeared united. Stigmatising the violation of treaties, emphasising their fidelity to the Locarno pact, they reaffirmed their concern about the integrity of Austria. A few days later—proof of the immense authority they still wielded—they obtained from the League of Nations an almost unanimous declaration condemning German rearmament in the severest terms, and stating that all acts likely to threaten the peace of Europe would be met with appropriate counter-measures. Only Denmark abstained. This was not all. Soon the Soviet Union, which had just joined the League, signed treaties of mutual assistance with France and Czechoslovakia. Soon after, Laval was warmly received in Moscow by Stalin.*

In this way, the Stresa Front was formed, a brief but unique and impressive coalition to make collective security a reality. It was inconceivable that the Führer would risk a confrontation with it. It might even prepare the way for his downfall. Obliged to obey the law like anyone else, he would indeed lose his *raison d'etre*. Would not the German people soon become tired of an impotent tyranny? A simple and convincing piece of reasoning, it created many illusions. The information coming from Germany seemed to support them. It was reported that consternation had replaced arrogance. Never since the start of the Hitler regime had its Ministers and dignitaries, or the German journalists, appeared so distressed and discouraged.[14]

The spectre of war appeared to be receding. A month after Stresa, Hitler made a speech very different in tone from his usual diatribes. Alsace-Lorraine, he said, was French; he did not intend to annexe Austria; he was in favour of a general limitation of armaments. He reaffirmed that the treaty of Locarno, including the demilitarisation of the Rhineland, remained the corner-stone of European peace. In June, Baldwin succeeded MacDonald as head of the British Government. Sir John Simon became Home Secretary, replaced at the Foreign Office by Sir Samuel Hoare and Anthony Eden (then Minister without Portfolio) who had the reputation of being a firm upholder of Geneva and the League of Nations.

The general situation had improved. The economic crisis had eased, the wheels of industry were turning again, workers and intellectuals were finding employment (except in France where stagnation had worsened owing to new deflationary measures). In the United States, Roosevelt and the New Deal were proving that it was possible to revive a depressed economy without recourse to dictatorship. Great Britain confirmed this by overcoming its deflationary policies; the number of its unemployed fell by nearly a million. Germany, too, had emerged from the slump, thanks to the skill of Schacht, the Minister of Economy; and also, a sad paradox, due to the ferocious deflationary

---

* Returning from Moscow, Laval stopped in Warsaw for the funeral of Marshal Pilsudski. Here, he had a cordial conversation with Göring. During this, he thought it clever to denigrate Stalin, and to minimise the pact he had just signed with him. The German diplomats were quick to repeat this to Moscow.

measures imposed by Brüning which permitted enormous new expenditure without excessive damage.

Simultaneously, an extraordinary event took place in the United Kingdom—'The Peace Ballot'. For several months, a private organisation under the auspices of *the League of Nations Union* and inspired by Lord Cecil, had undertaken a popular consultation on the subject of collective security. On June 27 1935, the results were published in an atmosphere of great enthusiasm at a monster meeting in the Albert Hall. More than 11 million Britons, about half the electoral body, had replied spontaneously to five questions. More than 11 million declared in favour of reduction of armaments through international agreement. More than 10 million said 'Yes' to collective security, including the application of economic sanctions against any aggressor state. To the last question about the eventual application of *military sanctions*, the answer was less clear. Nevertheless, 6,750,000 Britons approved of them. Only 2 million, less than 20 per cent were against.

A manifestation of the popular conscience unimaginable today, it appeared to prove that the true realists were not the cynics ready to surrender at the first crisis. The true realists were those who put their faith in an international order presided over by the power of France and Britain.

★　　★　　★

Not so. Soon, the Nazis were back with all their old arrogance. Great Britain had signed a pact with the Reich, and the Stresa front foundered. On 18th June (the anniversary of Waterloo, it was pointed out bitterly in Paris), Ribbentrop arrived in London as a special envoy of the Führer. In a matter of hours, almost without bargaining, he obtained what he had brazenly demanded originally: the agreement of His Majesty's Admiralty to the construction of a German navy 35 per cent the size of the Royal Navy, and an almost unlimited German submarine fleet. In return, Ribbentrop gave a solemn promise that the submarines would never attack merchant shipping.

This time it was not Hitler who tore up the *Diktat* of Versailles. It was France and Italy's old ally who, in total disregard of the renewed agreement two months before at Stresa and without even consulting Paris or Rome, conceded to the Dictator the right to rearm on the seas, as he had arrogated to himself that right on land and in the air. On his return to Berlin, Ribbentrop was feted like a new Bismarck. Had he not succeeded in breaking the ties which since 1914 had linked France and Great Britain? Had he not laid the basis for a permanent cooperation between London and Berlin? Never before had any Chancellor of the Kaiser obtained such a triumph.*

The Germans in their delight, and the French in their fury, exaggerated the political importance of the naval agreement. But the British had given them every reason for so doing. In March, after their Ministers' meeting with Hitler, they had spoken of 'candour and friendship'. In April at Stresa, they had joined a coalition against him; now, in June, they had made another *volte-face*. What made them do this? Still, today, after so many years, and with access to most of the contemporary archives, it is not easy to give the question a clear answer.

★   ★   ★

The peoples of Europe were shaken by these political events. But, as is natural, it was the work and joys of daily life which, more than anything else, occupied their minds. The Brussels World Fair in the summer of 1935 was one of those great international to-dos which delighted all worthy souls. It was opened by the young King Leopold III—slim, good-looking, romantic, who had just succeeded his father Albert, the sovereign so revered for his conduct during the great War, who had been killed in a climbing accident. In his open carriage, escorted by a squadron of Guides, the King was accompanied by his beautiful wife Astrid (she too destined to die in an accident a few months later). It was the last time, I think, that he appeared at such a ceremony of ancient pageantry.

Everywhere were signs of an astonishing change in society, the first indications of a new, more popular culture. Imperceptibly, the masses were walking towards a more pleasant life—when they had a job. The movies particularly attracted them. In Great Britain alone between 1932 and 1937, 890 new cinemas opened, bringing the grand total to 5,000. Many of them were enormous, sumptuous, built, in the words of the time, 'in a Babylonian-Spanish-Cubist style, enlivened with chromium and bakelite'. From negro America came jazz, exuberant, melancholic, enriching the musical world with its 'ragtime', 'blues' and 'spirituals'. Opening their doors to an expanding clientele were the dance-halls. In 'Dance Marathons', couples rivalled one another in endurance, to gain notoriety and prizes. They danced ten, twenty,

---

* Germany made purely formal concessions. The tonnage to which she agreed to limit her pretensions was beyond her construction capacity. By the outbreak of the Second World War, it had not attained even a half of the authorised tonnage.

thirty hours on end until, worn-out, famished, haggard, they could do no more, sometimes collapsing on the floor.

Holidays abroad, still more or less the preserve of the privileged classes (but not for long) were greatly extended. The young roamed the countryside on foot or bicycle, sleeping under canvas, or in the youth hostels which sprang up on all sides. A novel by Dekobra, *The Madonna of the Sleeping-Cars*, another by Agatha Christie, *Murder on the Orient Express*, selling in hundreds of thousands of copies, romanticised continental railway travel. Honegger's railway symphony *Pacific 237* was a great success. A taste for escapism was taking hold of social classes hitherto confined within strict limits.

In spite of the Great Depression and the political confusion, it was an epoch of great intellectual ferment. Literature, painting, the theatre, music, all thrived and scintillated as seldom before—more in the United States, France and Great Britain than in other countries, certainly more than in the totalitarian regimes. The sciences, particularly the applied, made enormous progress. Synthetic substances were invented—artificial rubber, fibrocement, plastics, ersatz petrol. Nylon contributed ladies' stockings as fine as silk, and much less expensive. Medicine benefited from new drugs, curing, in a matter of days, illnesses which had before been fatal: insulin, vitamins, sulphonamide. Diesel locomotives began to replace steam engines, in rivalry with electric traction. In America, Schick invented the electric razor. Other gadgets (the world was new) came into general use: electric blankets, ball-point pens, photo-electric cells, neon lighting. The radio became part of home life, and politicians found it a powerful instrument of propaganda. In Great Britain in 1936, the BBC transmitted the first regular television programme, addressed to 2,000 receiving sets.

The 'conquest of the air' impassioned the masses, much as space flights do today, Lindbergh's great exploit in 1927, connecting New York to Paris, had started its extraordinary upsurge. Amy Johnson, the daughter of a Hull fishmonger, flew solo in twenty days from London to Australia, in her second-hand *Gypsy Moth*. In 1933 Wiley Post, an American, went round the world in seven days, eighteen hours and forty-nine minutes. An Englishman, Lieutenant Boothman, won the Schneider trophy, attaining the extraordinary speed of 340 miles per hour.* The French, Germans and Italians emulated him. Networks

---

* His Supermarine plane was to serve as a model for the Spitfire, which played so great a part in the winning of the Battle of Britain in 1940.

of regular airlines began to cover the globe. On one of the busiest, between Paris and London, Air France served a hot meal at lunchtime. On the New York–Los Angeles flight, with Dakota bimotors, couchettes could be hired. Spacious long distance aircraft took to the skies. The flying-boats of Imperial Airways carried 24 passengers to Asia and Africa: to Karachi in 1929, the Cape in 1932, Singapore in 1933, Australia in 1935. With luxurious couchettes, smoking compartments, lounges and tiled lavatories, they were slow and irregular (seven days from London to Karachi, or from Cairo to the Cape). The Pan American 'Clippers' began a service in 1936, but they did not cross the Atlantic until just before the Second World War.

The lighter-than-air dirigibles had not yet been abandoned. The German 'Zeppelin', experimented with apparent success in the Great War, now had imitators. The British took six years to construct a enormous airship, the prototype of a future fleet. Propelled by diesel engines (something new) provided with all technical innovations, the R.101 could transport a hundred passengers in comfortable cabins at a speed of more than 70 miles an hour. Its luxurious salon was decorated like the Ritz hotel, with gilded columns and potted palm trees. Inaugurated with a great fanfare on 4 October 1930, it crashed on its maiden flight after a few hours, near Beauvais. In America, the Macon and the Akron were to share the same fate in 1935. Only the Hindenburg of Dr Eckener continued to ensure a transatlantic service until it, too, caught fire when landing at New York in 1937.

There was much talk about new methods of warfare. According to the newspapers, the Russians were experimenting with parachute drops *en masse*. General Douhet, an Italian airman, published a book in 1931 foretelling the massive deployment of aerial squadrons which could destroy entire cities. Lindbergh, the 'Lone Eagle', misanthropic as a result of the murder of his small son, foretold great disasters ahead, contributing to the general popular apprehension. The frightening myth, 'The bomber will always get through', was accepted even by politicians. The bomber seemed an absolute weapon, against which there was no defence save massive retaliatory measures of the same kind.

In the German Army, perfected radio techniques, kept strictly secret, were transforming communications on the battlefield. Colonel Guderian endeavoured without much success to persuade his superiors of the need for large formations of armoured vehicles. The work of scientists among whom were the Joliot-Curies, the James Chadwicks, the Rutherfords etc, had led in 1932 to the identification of the neutron and the positron. Even in less informed circles, there was talk of splitting the atom, and a future in which apocalyptical appliances could be put to use.

Apart from the Reich, most countries remained faithful to more conventional methods of warfare. Imaginative military minds in Great Britain and France advocating the 'fighting engines', General Fuller, Captain Liddell Hart, General Estienne or Colonel de Gaulle were not listened to. During the summer of 1935, I was recalled to the colours. The cavalry corps having been motorised, its reserve échelons were seconded to other units. Transferred to a light infantry regiment, I spent four weeks in a camp at Beverloo on the Dutch frontier. Our men helmeted, entrenching tools at the side, gasmasks slung on the back, rifles over the shoulders (the whole weighing more than 70 pounds) and clad in uncomfortable great-coats, were being trained for the wars of Napoleon—but without their offensive spirit. In their marches and counter-marches, they covered 4 kilometres in 50 minutes, with a 10 minute halt once an hour. The normal march was 30 kilometres; forced marches once or twice a week, over 40 kilometres. The regiment went laboriously along the main roads, or on the sandy tracks of the camp area, each battalion preceded by its commander on a horse, followed by the machine-gun waggon and field kitchens, abandoning the footsore by the dozens beside the road, sitting in the ditches. There was of course, no question of motorised transport, less still of tanks and aeroplanes. On one solitary occasion, field artillery batteries appeared for the grand manoeuvres, that apotheosis of our recall period, galloping across the moors like the gunners of the *Grande Armée*.

CHAPTER 7

The Ethiopian War

'War elevates human energy to its highest degree', proclaimed the Duce. 'It imprints the seal of nobility on all peoples who have the courage to engage in it.' To live dangerously was the Nietzchean precept in which Mussolini saw the guiding light of his existence. At the beginning of 1935, not long after his meeting with Laval, perhaps even before it, he had decided to launch the great adventure.

Ethiopia (or Abyssinia, from the name of its principal region) was to mark the first stage in Mussolini's imperial ambitions. Italy, already installed in Eritrea, had long fixed its gaze on Ethiopia where, in 1896, it had suffered a crushing defeat. A predominently Christian land (Coptic), the mythical kingdom of Prester John was governed by feudal princes, the 'Ras', under the suzerainty of the Negus Neguesti, the King of Kings, Haile Selassie I, Power of the Trinity, Conquering Lion of Judea, who claimed descent from King Solomon and the Queen of Sheba. The oldest and last of the independent African nations, barely emerging from the Middle Ages, it had been admitted to the League of Nations in 1923, on the proposal of France and Italy. Among the strong feelings of sympathy it stimulated, the colonial question played no part. The British Empire, the colonies of France and Portugal, the Dutch East Indies, the Belgian Congo, appeared in 1936 as entities destined to last forever. Few people doubted their legitimacy. 'In the Empire', said Lord Curzon, Viceroy of India, 'we have found not merely the key to glory and wealth but the call to duty, and the means of service to mankind'.[1] At the French *Ligue des Droits de l'Homme*, an influential organisation far from being dominated by the Right—a motion in favour of 'civilising colonisation' had been approved by 70 per cent of its members. In spite of certain abuses, no-one doubted that Europe had brought to backward peoples the benefits of a better civilisation—as Rome had in classical times to Europe. Only the Communist parties disagreed, except in the USSR itself.

On the contrary, what was to call down universal condemnation—Ethiopia or no Ethiopia—was once again the shameful violation of international law. The League of Nations consisted principally of Europe, our Europe, whose domination extended over three-quarters of the globe. The United States had excluded itself; the USSR and the Latin American states played only a secondary role in it. Through Briand, Cecil, Stressemann, Hymans (the Belgian) etc., the League imposed on nations a code of law and correct behaviour, similar to the one governing the life of citizens in a democratic state. Many saw in it the advent of a new Golden Age, the resurrection, in the words of Pliny the Elder, of the 'immense majesty of the Roman peace'. It was a matter of faith. Although there were obviously certain blemishes in the League, and there were those who doubted its efficacy, to a great many people, as much on the Continent as in Great Britain, Geneva was a holy city. Between collective security and the return of carnage—of which youth would be the first victim—there was no third way. The invasion of Ethiopia did not inspire an anti-colonial or anti-Fascist operation; it inspired a crusade for peace.

The Duce was most unpopular in liberal and social-democratic circles. However, if he forbade any display of political opposition, he stopped short the absolute totalitarianism current in Germany. Waste, muddle, and corruption, with a good dose of anarchy, tempered his dictatorship, and the mass of the Italian people were left in peace.* He seemed a less disagreeable character than the Führer. The Foreign Office was inclined to see in him an element of stability, in a country apparently not yet fit for Parliamentary democracy and Italy was not listed among the potential enemies of Great Britain. The Quai d'Orsay, not without reason, distrusted her ambitions in North Africa, where they conflicted with French interests; but at the same time, France was anxious to keep her in the camp of her old allies. Certain right-wing circles regarded Mussolini as 'a Hercules engaged in a struggle with the Reds'. To the man in the street, more aware of reality, the Duce appeared a somewhat comic figure. Diminutive in stature, pot-bellied, affecting flashy uniforms, his skull shaved to hide his baldness, rolling his eyes dramatically, he loved to stand arms akimbo haranguing 'Oceanic Crowds'; or perched on an enormous horse, to review the Black Shirts or the Bersaglieri. His evocation of the Roman Empire,

---

*Political oppression lacked in Italy the general and cruel nature it held in Germany. From 1926 to 1932, the tribunals for the Defence of the State pronounced 7 death sentences and 1,617 prison sentences, plus many more of exile; 12,000 accused persons, recognised as innocent, were set free.[2]

his grandiloquent rhetoric, his tendency to exhibitionism could not fail to make people smile; he was to be seen on the cinema screens running on foot at the head of a squad of his perspiring Ministers or, his torso naked, threshing corn in a farmyard. Abroad, people laughed good-naturedly at the unfortunate she-wolf exposed in a cage on the Capitol, to recall the glories of an ancient past.

After 1935, with the decay of international order, and Mussolini's obsession with appearing as formidable as his German counterpart, perhaps also as a result of the advance of his neurosyphilis, he gave free play to all his extravagances. Seldom seen in society, without a friend or confidant, remote from his wife and children, believing increasingly that he had been invested with a supernatural mission, he would take no advice. He promoted the growing cult of his own personality, encouraging the newspapers to print in capital letters his self-styled title DUCE. At the Villa Torlonia, a banal building isolated in a small park, tastelessly furnished, he led a simple and lonely life, even preferring to have his meals by himself. But at the Palazzo Venezia, his official residence, he insisted that his colleagues should march smartly up to his desk across the twenty metres of the immense Mappamondo Hall, then stand to attention, click their heels and give the Roman salute. His speeches became more and more extravagant. 'War is for the man what maternity is for the woman', he stated. 'Man is the dunk-heap of history!', he exclaimed on another occasion to the acclamations of his listeners. His entourage went further, protesting against the British presence in the Mediterranean, beginning to lay claim to French North Africa, Corsica, Savoy, Nice and Malta.

★　　★　　★

In December 1934, an incident at the oasis of Ual-Ual, on the frontier of Italian Eritrea and Ethiopia had caused the death of some thirty askaris, native soldiers of the Italian Army. Further incidents followed. The Fascist government no longer concealed the fact that it was preparing for war, using all means of propaganda at its disposal— public speeches, the press, radio, the cinema. A law introduced compulsory military service *from the age of eight*. General De Bono was nominated C-in-C in Eastern Africa, and reservists were recalled to the colours. Troops and war material in large quantities were dispatched to Eritrea and Somalia, to 'protect them against Ethiopian aggression'. They passed through the Suez Canal, where French and British personnel were in a position to check them, taking along 59 tons of toxic gas. There could be no doubt of the Duce's intentions.

The European governments had none. During his visit to Rome in 1935 (a few weeks after the Ual-Ual incident) Laval had had a *tête-a-tête* with Mussolini at a dinner in the French Embassy. Although what precisely passed between them is unknown, it appears certain that the Frenchman, when informed of Mussolini's intentions, assured him of his approval—tacitly or explicitly. That the British Ministers, for their part, were aware of the Duce's plans is not denied either. At the beginning of the year, a committee of experts had been set up in London, under the chairmanship of Sir John Maffey, to study the implications of an Italian seizure of Ethiopia. It concluded that it would not seriously endanger British interests.[3]

On the eve of Stresa, the British had considered bringing the matter up with the Duce. But the difficult decision had been postponed in the hope of a more favourable turn of events and Sir John Simon had limited himself to delegate one of his assistants to discuss the matter with his italian counterpart—the usual 'document for the record'. It is also noteworthy that the final communiqué of the Stresa Conference referred to the maintenance of peace 'in Europe'. In view of the care which these documents are drawn up, it appeared that peace 'in Africa' was not under consideration. Mussolini has assessed it that way. At the railway station, where he bade farewell to his guests, after the train had left, he turned irritably to Grandi, his ambassador in London. 'You told me the English would reply "Yes" to Austria, and "No" to Africa. Well, what has happened is that their answer for Austria is "No", and for Africà "Yes".'[4]

The Italian secret service had confirmed it. One of its agents, a butler in the British embassy in Rome, had managed to cut away the back of the Ambassador's safe and to replace it by a moveable panel.* Among the papers he obtained was a full copy of the Maffey Report, of which the Duce was able to take full cognisance. He had no faith in the power of ideas, and nothing but scorn for everything represented by the League of Nations; he had founded a newspaper, *Anti-Europe* to mock the high ideals of Briand. If even the British considered their interests were not threatened, why should they worry about Ethiopia— any more than they had about Manchuria? Dino Grandi, a party man rather than a diplomat, frequented circles in London which were almost all sympathetic towards Fascism. Grandi coveted a title of

---

* It was some months before the Ambassador discovered that his safe had been plundered—and then only as a result of the theft of the diamond tiara which his wife had been wearing on the evening of their daughter's wedding.[5]

nobility (he was to obtain it in 1937), and he was anxious to please. In spite of several warnings by the Foreign Office, he preferred not to alarm his master.

The months passed, and Italy openly continued the mobilisation of nearly a million men. Visiting London, Edda Ciano, Mussolini's elegant daughter, made no attempt, at numerous dinner parties, to conceal her father's designs.[6] This did not prevent Sir Samuel Hoare from taking the initiative of sending a friendly letter to the Duce. Added to which, Eden was sent off to Rome to offer him—without consulting Paris, let alone Addis Ababa—an entire province of Ethiopia, the latter receiving in return an access to the sea. Mussolini rejected the gift disdainfully; he was not interested, he said, in 'a few acres of desert and a dozen palm-trees'. What is more, this son of the Predappio blacksmith, took pleasure in snubbing the young English aristocrat who had not been deferential enough. When invited to a lunch given by the Cianos on the seafront at Ostia, the great man declined the invitation to appear later during the meal, standing up mockingly in a motor-boat a few metres from the restaurant terrace. 'I thought he was going to dive in to join us', wrote Eden. Not amused, he prolonged the lunch deliberately, so as to arrive late at the *rendezvous* arranged with Mussolini in the afternoon. Here, the Duce had made it clear that he wanted the whole of Ethiopia, whether by a protectorate, a mandate or otherwise—a cold shower, an Italian witness would report.[7] Eden would always deny it but it may be assumed that he never forgot the snub.

What reason had the Duce to worry? He had been assured by Laval of the complicity of France. The advances of Hoare and Eden made him believe that he had nothing to fear from Great Britain either. In August, Paris and London confirmed it by offering him Ethiopia under the guise of a protectorate. Now extremely self-confident, Mussolini affected indignation, referring to a 'humiliation of the worst kind'. From Baron Aloisi, his *chef de cabinet*, he no longer concealed that, with France and Britain neutral, he aspired to the glory of a victorious war, 'even if they give me everything'.[8]

In London, the Peace Ballot had revealed the strong popular concern for collective security. The government could not altogether ignore it. On the other hand, it did not want a conflict with the Duce, whose Mediterranean fleet could threaten Britain's communications with the Indian Empire. While deploring Mussolini's intemperate outbursts, it was equally afraid of undermining his authority, to the advantage, perhaps, of the Communists. These were contradictions which Baldwin could resolve only by ignoring them. 'The Prime Minister', wrote Hoare in his memoirs, 'thought of nothing but his holidays, and of keeping out of the affair at any cost.' Giving the impression of being older than his 68 years, Baldwin was slightly deaf. Suffering from high blood pressure, he often complained of insomnia and rheumatism. He was also inclined to nervous depressions, which he treated by stuffing himself with medicines and which occasionally hampered his mental faculties for weeks.[9]

In London, it was to the Foreign Secretary, in a capital deserted by most of the Ministers, who had gone off on their holidays, that the task of unravelling the Ethiopian imbroglio fell—a task too heavy for his frail shoulders. The eldest son of a rich banker, intended by his father for a great career, Samuel Hoare had, after a spell in municipal politics, been elected Conservative MP for Chelsea, at the age of thirty. An advantageous marriage contributed to his success. Having broken with a young provincial beauty, he had married Lady Maud Lygon, the youngest daughter of Lord Beauchamp, descendent of an old and powerful family. The young couple, propelled by a voracious appetite for success—Lady Maud was as ambitious as her husband—had launched on the ascent of the long and slippery slope leading to 10 Downing Street. It had been brutally interrupted by 'the guns of August' in 1914. Hoare joined up but was soon graded as unfit for active service on grounds of ill health. Appointed an intelligence officer, first in Petrograd and later in Rome, he had been the horrified witness of the collapse of the old regime in Russia and of the birth of Bolshevism. In Italy, the rioting and turmoil which marked the end of the war made him fear a repetition of events in Russia.* He was deeply affected by this. In 1919, he wrote to Churchill (not yet a detested rival), 'The entire future of Europe, indeed of the world, depends upon settling the Russian affair and the destruction of Bolshevism.'

Hypochondriac, crippled by psychosomatic pains, arthritis, nervous depression and apparently causeless fainting fits (which did not prevent him from reaching the age of eighty), he had little defence when faced with trials and tribulations. Until now, he had been able to circumvent unpleasantness by the methods of a wily Parliamentarian, namely to avoid all confrontation, to talk, to please and to wait. But this no

---

*Among the personalities subsidised during the 1914 War by the British Secret Service in Italy was the young Mussolini. In 1925 when Hoare was Secretary of State for Air, he passed through Rome and was received by the Duce who treated him as an 'old friend' and recalled their relationship. In 1935, Hoare hoped this would help him settle the Abyssinian Affair.

longer sufficed. Abandoned by the head of the government (Baldwin
had left for Savoy after having seen him fleetingly on 6 August, but
without leaving him precise instructions), the poor man fell ill and took
to his bed. Mussolini did not appear to be retreating; the Assembly of
the League of Nations was about to go into session, delay was impossible. Gathering up his courage, Hoare decided to respond to the
pressures of expectant public opinion, which clamoured for the application of the Charter, while at the same time being careful not to offend
the Italians, and to do nothing without the complete collaboration of
the French—so he wrote to his friend Chamberlain 'a limitation which
made his valour safe', noted Vansittart.[10] The Foreign Office had
prepared him a speech. Baldwin, taking his walks in Aix-les-Bains felt
he must return for a day in England to consult with his Foreign
Secretary. Hoare relates the conversation he had had with Baldwin at
Chequers, perhaps exaggerating a little. 'When I arrived we chatted
for a while, comparing the delights of Aix with those of the English
countryside. We walked in the garden and had tea. Then Baldwin, as
if thinking of Geneva, said, "You have a speech to make there? . . .
Let me have a look at it." When I gave it to him, he gave it a quick
glance and said, on handing it back to me: "That is alright. It must
have taken you a long time to make it up", and that was all.'[11] On 22
August, a restricted council of the Cabinet approved the speech and
intentions of the Foreign Secretary.

In Geneva, on 11 September, completely unaware of the contradictory and ulterior motives of the British Ministers, the delegates
listened to Sir Samuel Hoare's speech in which he expressed his country's determination to respect 'in its entirety' the Charter and the
obligations enshrined in it. It was the first time since 1919 that His
Majesty's Government had shown itself clearly and resolutely decided
to uphold collective security. In the Assembly Hall, sustained applause
broke out (surprising the orator, unaccustomed to such success). The
enthusiasm of the delegates revealed that they were not simply being
polite, this time they were deeply moved in their approval. The small
powers, in particular, had always seen, in the machinery of Geneva,
the surest guarantee that they would not one day become the Ethiopia
of one of their big neighbours; with the countries of the Commonwealth, with Scandinavia, Holland, Spain and the Little Entente they
loudly endorsed the British. The Prime Minister of Belgium, Paul van
Zeeland, made a courageous speech (he was not to pronounce another)
confirming that Belgium would go 'to the very end' to fulfil her
obligations.

The idea that the Duce would now persist in his plans seemed absurd. Morally the issue was clear, clearer than it had been over Manchuria, certainly clearer than over the reintroduction of conscription in Germany. Materially, the circumstances were also favourable. Italy, in spite of its bombast, was a spectacularly weak country, its standard of life equivalent to that of Northern Europe at the beginning of the nineteenth century. Its agriculture was still absorbing 50 per cent of its work force, an underdeveloped industry produced only 2.8 per cent of the manufactured goods of the world. She had to buy abroad nearly all her minerals, coal and oil, even a large part of her food; 70 per cent of her exports went to member states of the League of Nations. Might was on the side of Right. The Royal Navy, the redoubtable fleet which had for centuries policed the oceans, could drown Mussolini in his 'Roman lake'.* A glance at the map reveals the extreme vulnerability of the Italian armies, operating thousands of miles from their bases. Nothing would have been easier than to cut their lines of communication by closing the Suez Canal, the narrow throat through which they breathed. The canal was administered by an international company dominated by Franco-British interests; British soldiers camped on its banks. In the west, the Straits of Gibraltar formed another bolt capable of locking Italy in to face starvation; 80 per cent of her supplies passed through it. Great Britain could, on her own, have forced the aggressor to capitulate. Never had the League of Nations been in such a strong situation.

But no, the Duce did not withdraw; he *knew* that the risk was slight. He was in almost constant contact by telephone with Laval. For his part, Hoare had informed him at the end of September that the closing of the Suez Canal and military sanctions were not envisaged, adding that he did not wish to humiliate him or diminish his prestige.[12] On 2 October 1935, the church bells rang throughout Italy, the drums beat, the sirens screamed. The Duce had proclaimed *l'Adonata*, general mobilisation of the population. The next day at dawn, three Italian army corps invaded Ethiopia, without any declaration of war.

This time the British lion appeared tired of having his tail twisted. At Geneva, Britain showed proof of the immense authority she still possessed when she chose to use it. On 7 October, on the proposition of Anthony Eden, the Council of the League of Nations unanimously (less the voice of the aggressor)—followed by the assembly with an

---

*The British, who had mobilised a fleet of 800,000 tons in the Mediterranean, found that they were short of ammunition. On the other hand, the Italians, with 500,000 tons had no armour piercing shell. They had no aircraft carriers; their submarines were obsolete, slow to dive and lacking modern instruments.

immense majority—recognised that Italy, having had recourse to war in violation of the Charter, came under the interdiction of article XVI. Laval, captive of a Parliamentary coalition supporting collective security, and flanked by Paul-Boncour and Herriot, could not oppose it. The mechanism of sanctions was put in motion. Since the Manchurian affair, the Secretary General of the League had carefully prepared its technical application. The ponderous machine rolled slowly forward.

★   ★   ★

World reaction was overwhelming. In several capitals, as in Brussels, street demonstrations protested against the Fascist aggression. In Marseilles, San Diego, the Cape and Alexandria, the stevedores refused to load ships abound for Italy. Even in distant and reticent Sweden, voices were raised, among them that of the Primate of the Lutheran Church.

In France, the extreme Right led a violent campaign against the League of Nations and Great Britain. *L'Action Française* threatened death to Deputies who voted for sanctions and recommended its readers to assassinate them, in default of a guillotine. Other papers denounced the war party forming in Great Britain, composed of the Left, the Trades Unions, the Freemasons, the militant Jews, the Liberals of the Lloyd George persuasion and the Conservatives of Eden. However, in Parliament, the parties insisting on the application of sanctions had a clear majority. They had qualified representatives in the cabinet; the Trades Unions and many newspapers not devoted to the Fascist cause supported them. Numerous groupings of different tendencies demanded that an end should be made of Fascist aggression.

In the United States, which had withdrawn into isolation since the Manchurian fiasco, public opinion was nevertheless favourable to Ethiopia. If sanctions had been firmly applied, the Neutrality Act of 1935, in spite of its object, would automatically have had consequences much more damaging to Italy than to her victim. The USSR, through Litvinov, took its stand unhesitatingly among the countries demanding the application of the Pact. Germany, although no longer a member of the League, was prudent. 'I really don't know what to do', said Hitler to one of his henchmen, while pacing up and down in his Berchtesgaden chalet. 'It's too difficult a decision to take. I would prefer to ally myself with the English. But history shows that they are unreliable allies. If I go with them, all will be finished between Italy and us. Then the English would drop me, and we shall fall between two stools.' He therefore sold arms to the Negus and coal to Italy.[13]

In Great Britain, the results of the Peace Ballot were confirmed by hundreds of letters to MPs demanding the enforcement of the Covenant. The press, the political associations, the confederation of Trades Unions and the Churches, were unanimously in favour of sanctions. Overnight, the apparent firmness of the Foreign Secretary and the Prime Minister had endowed them with a popularity they had never known before—an opportunity seized by Baldwin to announce new elections, based on the theme of collective security. 'No government had ever been in such a strong moral and political position', Harold Macmillan was to write. 'The Prime Minister's prestige was higher than it had ever been . . . He stood on a pinnacle.'[14]

On the Continent, pro-Fascist newspapers wrote of 'Hypocrisy, selfishness, imperial interests, concern about the route to India, the sources of the Nile', and so on. But those who knew the British well felt that there was much more to it than that. In any case, how important was it? They had made themselves the defenders of order and justice, as enshrined in the ideals of Geneva, the guardians of the honour of the world.

The military situation in Ethiopia encouraged a firm line by the League. After an initial success, the Fascist troops had run into unexpected resistance, and they were marking time. Mussolini had always distrusted the army and his generals, coveting for himself the glory to be gained on the battlefield. He had therefore entrusted the campaign not to his general staff but to a committee set up in the Ministry of Colonies. Confusion was exacerbated by the Duce himself who, convinced of his strategic genius, bombarded the Commander-in-Chief day and night with telegrams. The latter, General De Bono, an old man of 69, one of the *quadrumviri* of the March on Rome, owed the command to his age, and to never attempting to eclipse his master. He had asked for three divisions; he was given ten and, by the end of the campaign, twenty-five. Between five and six hundred thousand men, and two million tons of material were sent to Africa.

It constituted a gigantic effort for Italy, resulting expenses which largely outstripped her limited resources. Her economic situation was deteriorating. The falling Lira had to be devalued by a quarter, a serious blow to the prestige of the Duce, who had repeated a hundred times that his currency was as sound as gold. By the end of autumn, news from Africa, in spite of the strictest censorship, confirmed the scale of the enormous difficulties being encountered. Old De Bono was replaced by General Badoglio, a professional soldier; but he too marked time, and there were rumours that he intended to withdraw to the old frontiers.* In Italy itself, disillusion replaced the enthusiasm stimulated by the early victories. Journalists and travellers returning from Italy reported discontent, and told of catcalls in the darkened cinemas when the face of Mussolini appeared on the screen. In fact, he was losing his nerve. Pointing his finger at his temple, he spoke to the French Ambassador of shooting himself rather than capitulate.[15]

To those who did not read the diplomatic despatches, the situation had never before appeared more propitious to the maintenance of international law. Nevertheless, once again it was to be flouted. The planned sanctions became a mockery. In theory, they should have halted all commerce between member states of the League and Italy by cutting credit and forbidding access to the principal raw materials. But Laval, a master of legal niceties, put forward a hundred good reasons for postponing, week by week, the measures which would have quickly checked the aggressor—an embargo on iron, steel, copper, lead, zinc, cotton, wood and oil—all indispensable for the war industry, and resources which Italy lacked. 'I'll give a kick to that shanty-town called Geneva', quipped Laval to a Spanish delegate, Salvador de Madariaga (who was not slow to repeat his words).[16] It was really a kick under the table, to avoid provoking his colleague Herriot, who was making splendid speeches on the sanctity of treaties, and whose support was essential for the survival of the Cabinet. But all Herriot did was mildly to blame Laval: 'I was astonished and piqued to find Laval so scornful of Great Britain', he said, coming out of a meeting of the Council of ministers at the end of October. Not a word for the victim of aggression, Abyssinia! From all this we may well say, 'Undoubtedly, the weak are always in the wrong.'[17] In fact, all through the crisis, Laval would make the British feel that they could not rely on France in case of an armed conflict with Italy.

In contrast, Baldwin, Hoare and Eden started by looking like towers of strength. (Were not the British elections approaching?) To the electors, Eden said: 'The League alone can create a new order, which will prevent any nation from ever resorting to war as a political instrument, while Baldwin promised 'Collective security and moderate rearmament'. Pressing for sanctions, to satisfy the good people, the Ministers were careful not to propose measures which might be

---

* In retirement General De Bono was made a Field Marshal. During the last session of the Fascist Grand Council on 24 July 1943, he voted for the replacement of the Duce. Later he fell into Mussolini's hands, and was condemned to death, together with Ciano and three other members of the Fascist hierarchy. Bound astride chairs, the five men were shot in the back.

unacceptable to Laval or to Mussolini—that is to say, only futile and ineffectual measures. 'Aimed at depriving Italy only of what she does not need', in the mocking words of Lloyd George, who admitted that he had for a short while been hoodwinked by them. Cargoes destined for Italian ports continued to pass without interference in front of the guns of Gibraltar. Between Port Said, Ismailia and Suez, from the decks of the transports sailing under the green, red and white flag towards Africa, the Fascist militia men derided the British sentries on the canal by urinating into it.

In Geneva, as at the time of the Disarmament Conference, the Great Powers were engaged in secret negotiations, from which the other states were excluded. Two facts were patent: First, the decisive sanctions which the League had voted were being continually postponed. Second, France and Britain were responsible for the postponement. Laval refused to apply sanctions in the absence of a British guarantee against any German attack on France, which Baldwin and Eden would not give.[18] There was suspicion too that Paris and London were still trying to side-step their differences by abandoning Ethiopia, or a great part of it, to the aggressor.

Nevertheless, the Geneva machine could not be entirely swayed by them. At the beginning of November, its competent commissions recommended an embargo on coal, iron and steel, with oil products to follow. For the first time Rome seemed apprehensive, 'An embargo on oil is war!' thundered the Duce. He even spoke of bombing the Riviera. The clamour was loud. In view of his economic and strategic problems, this sounded ridiculous, impressing only those who did not want to hinder him.* Laval and Hoare now seemed resigned to the enforcement of the League. Seemed—for were they really? Why not, they suggested, postpone the application of the decisive sanction for a few more days, until the 18th November (the British General Election was to be on the 14th), and take advantage of the delay to explore, for the last time, a possible area of agreement between the Duce and the Negus? To everyone's surprise the Belgian Premier, Paul van Zeeland, had jumped to his feet and proposed that Paris and London should undertake a last mission of conciliation. Although vexed, the other delegates could not refuse. Once again, and not for the last time, the principal sanctions were shelved.

★   ★   ★

* Mussolini was fully aware of the enormity of his gamble. At the Munich Conference in 1938, he admitted to Hitler that an embargo on oil would have had a disastrous effect, and forced him to capitulate within a week.

The little Italian King, Victor-Emmanuel III, had longed to become Emperor of Abyssinia, and he did all he could to support his 'President' (as he called Mussolini). Letters passed between the courts of Europe. In Brussels, King Leopold III, brother-in-law to the Crown Prince of Italy, felt it his duty to intervene. Already, on 19 October, his Prime Minister, van Zeeland, had lunched in Paris with Laval and submitted to him his 'suggestions for putting an end to the conflict'. These had been 'well received'—which indicates their trend. On 2 December 1935 King Leopold, after a rough Channel crossing, was entertained as a private guest at Buckingham Palace. In spite of their family links, relations between the two royal houses lacked warmth. King George V had not forgotten that his father, on a journey in Belgium thirty years before, had nearly fallen victim to the bullets of an assassin— who was then judged very leniently in the Belgian courts. Nevertheless, he listened sympathetically to his royal colleague, and did not discourage him. The next morning, before returning to Brussels, the King of the Belgians had a long interview with Sir Samuel Hoare, who assured him that he too wanted to help Mussolini extricate himself from his present unfortunate predicament.[19] Hoare was as good as his word. With the General Election won and behind him,* he made even greater efforts to avoid confrontation with the Duce. We know now, through the archives, that the prospect—improbable as it was—of a war with Italy and without the backing of France terrified the ministers.

On the eve of Hoare's conversation with King Leopold, the British Cabinet, after a confused session, authorised him to meet Laval and discuss new attempts at conciliation, as proposed by van Zeeland. The Ministers (including Eden) had again talked of re-establishing peace in Africa in line with the League of Nations.[20] Short of immolating Ethiopia, it was tantamount to squaring the circle. Hoare again fell ill. On Saturday 7 December 1935, on the way to convalescence and rest in Switzerland, he stopped off in Paris; he was accompanied by Sir Robert Vansittart. In the French capital he met several of his experts who had been exploring with the French diplomats, a way to placate Rome. Eden was not there—a stroke of luck for the young Minister's reputation for everything points out that he was, like his

---

* Baldwin won 432 seats in the Commons, a majority of 247, confirming the state of mind of the electorate. Labour regained some hundred seats lost in the 1931 Election. But it too had campaigned for collective security, although not for rearmament.

colleagues in the cabinet, ready to abandon the Negus. Actually, the Foreign Office (and Laval) had kept the Duce fully informed of their intentions which had seemed to satisfy him. On Sunday, a short comunique announced that the French and the British had agreed on a 'formula' for settling the Italy–Ethiopia conflict. On Monday the Paris newspapers leaked its principal items. Italy was to be given nearly two-thirds of Ethiopia (much more than the territory conquered by her troops); in exchange, the Negus would receive a small opening to the sea, the famous 'camel corridor', in the mocking phrase of *The Times*.* That Monday morning, at the breakfast table, one of the experts who had returned to London showed Eden the text of the Hoare–Laval plan (in French). If he was appalled—as he later claimed—he nevertheless accepted responsibility for it along with his Cabinet colleagues when they were summoned that evening. He confirmed himself to requesting that the plan should be shown simultaneously to both the Negus and the Duce—something which had not been intended. It was said—but it was not true—that the British Ministers had not bothered to verify the extent of the concessions made to Italy on the map.

After his stop in Paris, Hoare boarded the midnight train for the Engadine and the sun of the Swiss mountains. Stretched out in a compartment of the sleeping car, lulled by the whirring of the wheels, he pondered over his great triumph. Had he not found the way to stop the war in Ethiopia? When he arrived at his destination, he immediately made for the skating rink. A little later, weaving pretty arabesques on the ice, he had a fall. Irony of ironies—he broke his nose! While the unfortunate man lay once more in bed, ministering to his nasal appendix, his magic formula unleashed stupor and revolt— the former in the Chancelleries, the latter in public opinion. Only three days earlier, the Italian Air Force had bombed the Ethiopian lines and destroyed an American hospital run by the Red Cross. An immediate application of the embargo on oil was expected in order to make the overstretched aggressor surrender unconditionally—instead, it was upon his victims that the blow of the law had fallen. In France, despite approving cries from that section of the press which was subsidised by the Italian Embassy, there was a general storm of indignation. In Parliament, Georges Mandel and Paul Reynaud, both Conservatives, Yvon Delbos, a Radical, and Leon Blum, a Socialist, attacked the

---

* To avoid all competition with the Addis Ababa–Djibouti line, run by a French company, it was stipulated that Ethiopia could not construct a railway in the corridor.

'suburban Louis XI' for having betrayed the policy of France, at the very moment when Great Britain appeared to be rallying to it. Paul Reynaud made a prophetic pronouncement. After enumerating the falacious pretexts that Hitler would proffer to justify aggression against Austria, Czechoslovakia, Poland, Yugoslavia and Rumania, he cried: 'What we need is a formula that cannot be debated, which will put a full stop to the aggressor, whoever he may be, whatever the violence.' One of his colleagues wrote, 'I see Reynaud gesturing with his outstretched hand, an unusual gesture for him. His normally nasal voice has changed. . . . And I see that ground-swell of surging Assembly opinion confronted by the true issue. All his adversaries were applauding him, with his friends hesitant, apprehensive, in conflict with their consciences.'[21]

But it was in Great Britain that the uproar was loudest. Stanley Baldwin had just been elected on a programme based principally on collective security. Then, three weeks later he had trampled underfoot the very principles which had led to his electoral victory. The influential 'Union for the League of Nations', the Archbishops, the press including *The Times*, a large number of Conservative MPs, among them the young Harold Macmillan and the aged Austen Chamberlain, the Trades Unions and most of the Labour MPs, protested vigorously against 'the propositions of peace' elaborated by Messrs Hoare and Laval. The Cabinet came close to resignation.

A large element of the public anger was directly against France, who had sabotaged the Covenant and where much of the press kept attacking Great Britain in the vilest terms. In a letter to Herriot, a French professor at London University summed up the situation. 'By defaulting and obtaining the signature of Sir Samuel Hoare, France has lost the support of the English people, both those in favour of the League and those who are not. Our public cannot know Great Britain if it thinks that their leaders could support us at a decisive hour, if it would not be in the defence of an ideal.'[22] For generations, reported the London correspondents (even of *Le Temps*), no question of foreign policy had caused such confusion.

The Hoare–Laval plan (rejected incidentally by the Duce, as well as by the Negus) was buried in Geneva. To salvage the British Government, Sir Samuel Hoare, despairing and in tears, was inelegantly sacrificed by his colleagues. Shortly after, Laval was forced to resign. 'Vomited by the Chamber', were his own furious words. Anthony Eden and Pierre-Etienne Flandin succeeded them at the Foreign Office and the Quai d'Orsay. Meanwhile, talk of an embargo on oil went on.

A report by the experts in Geneva on 12 February stated that if the United States agreed to limit its deliveries to the level of the preceding years, Italy would quickly be reduced to unconditional surrender. The American law of neutrality did not forbid this, and President Roosevelt had let it be known that he would cooperate.* But, with the exception of Eden, the Ministers, including van Zeeland, were making friendly, if discreet, signs towards Italy. On one occasion Flandin, appeared ready to agree to the embargo on the condition of unreserved support by Britain in the event of a German reoccupation of the Rhineland. This time, it was Eden who refused—on 5 March, two days before the *Wehrmacht* crossed the Rhine.[23]

Italy continued to obtain the indispensable fuel, and General Badoglio was able to mount a new offensive. The only Ethiopian military force organised on western lines was the Imperial Guard, six battalions trained by Belgian instructors (paid by the Negus), whom van Zeeland had courageously recalled when Italy attacked. Most of the troops 'belonged' to the great feudal lords who obeyed the orders of the Emperor only when it suited them. The Emperor's son-in-law, the Ras Gugra, had gone over to the Italians; the aged Ras Mulugueta, the Minister of War, the aged Ras Kassa, the C-in-C, and the young Ras Desta had been over confident. In rash and disorderly offensives, they launched their warriors against automatic weapons, quick-firing cannon and armoured vehicles. The Italians dropped mustard gas in large quantities from the air, which burned the naked feet, bodies and eyes of the Abyssinians. Their armies, in spite of displaying the greatest courage, finally disintegrated. On the afternoon of 5 March, Marshal Badoglio at the head of a mechanized column marched triumphantly in the burning capital. Reporting the event, the Belgian Minister in Addis Ababa asked Brussels by telegram, 'Should I pay him a formal visit, or should I leave my card?'

Four days later in Rome, towards 10.30 in the evening, a deep growl went up from the 'Oceanic' crowd of four hundred thousand assembled in front of the Palazzo Venezia. Mussolini appeared on the balcony. After announcing the victory of Fascism over the 52 nations coalition of the League, he proclaimed Emperor the tiny Victor Emmanuel. He remained for some time on the balcony, on the warm spring night, motionless, triumphant beneath the flood-lights, while from the crowd arose the savage cry 'Duce! Duce! Duce!' In illuminated Rome, only

---

*In the absence of international cooperation, the USA actually increased their sales of petroleum products to Italy.

the Vatican remained in darkness; Pius XI would not take part in the barbaric celebration.

In June, the unfortunate Negus pleaded the lost cause of his country at the rostrum of the League of Nations. Small of stature but full of dignity, his shoulders covered with a large black cape, his exotic bearded face impassive, the vanquished Emperor pronounced, in a recently inaugurated new palace, a moving but ineffective speech, interrupted by catcalls of 'Long live the Duce!', and by the shrill noise of whistles which Italian diplomats had distributed to a dozen Fascist journalists infiltrated into the assembly hall. 'I was seated beside him', wrote a Belgian diplomat. 'The League of Nations had recognised his defeat. I could only share the silent embarrassment of my colleagues.'[24] Shortly after, at the Cornavin Station, a few delegates and journalists came to salute for the last time the unfortunate monarch who, expelled from his own country, was now expelled from Switzerland. The Helvetian government, no less realistic than the others, had given him four hours to leave the country. He took refuge first in Great Britain, where King Edward VIII refused to see him.

The disaster was complete and irreparable, the collapse of collective security a hundred times graver than in the Manchurian Affair. Voting *nolens volens* sanctions, in a dramatic crescendo of tension, the statesmen had given new vigour to the old European idealism and had brought back to the Charter of Geneva a confidence that it had not known for years. But in making the law inoffensive, in transforming it into a hypocritical semblance of itself, they had ruined its credibility.

It was from that moment on that Adolf Hitler felt himself freed from any rules. Never again would the faith be reborn which had inspired the West with the promise of a true world order.

CHAPTER 8

The Bankruptcy of the League of Nations

A few weeks before the fall of Addis Ababa, on Friday 6 March 1936, a grey, cold day which barely gave a hint of spring, I left Brussels by car with friends to spend the weekend in the forest of the Ardennes. On Saturday at midday, wearied by the continuous bad weather, we took refuge for lunch in a restaurant in the little town of Bastogne. There was great excitement. Since dawn, German troops had been crossing the Rhine bridges and occupying the left bank, which had been demilitarised in perpetuity by treaty. The restaurant reverberated with noisy conversation, inspired by fear and indignation. 'Are we going to let the Boche get away with it yet again?', exclaimed one of our neighbours.

Much perturbed and with mixed feelings, we hurried back to Brussels, where we found our anxious families in front of the radio or feverishly reading the papers. On Sunday evening we heard the French Premier announce gravely in a strongly worded speech: 'We shall not allow Strasbourg to come under the German guns again.' On Monday morning, the Press reported the movements of French troops. The Maginot Line was put on a war footing. Returning hurriedly from Paris friends reported that Sarraut's speech had been well received, and that the French population, although deeply apprehensive, was prepared for any eventuality.

This was also true of the Belgians. Some, ignoring the faults of their own government, blamed Paris for the revival of German nationalism. Others, previously most hostile ot the Weimar Republic, suddenly discovered that the claims of the Third Reich were not all unjustified. They smiled at an article in the *Canard Enchaîné* entitled 'German troops invade Germany'. They agreed with Lloyd George who, I gathered, had approved of the German reoccupation of their 'back-yard'. But, in general, healthier and more instinctive reflexes prevailed. The Japanese and Italian aggressions had transformed the emotive horrors

117

of war into concrete, palpable reality—that scourge, that malediction which the Nazis never ceased to glorify daily in all their demonstrations. An enormous force, sinister and perverse, could be seen increasing on the other bank of the Rhine. What was particularly ominous was not so much the presence of German soldiers in the Rhineland (they had been infiltrating it for some time, and it would have been doubtless impossible to exclude them for ever), but the Führer's new and impudent challenge to the established rules, when he could have obtained what he wanted without too much trouble by patience and negotiation. People were undecided but also exasperated, ready to respond to the call of their leaders.

★   ★   ★

That call did not come. As is known, the demilitarisation of the left bank of the Rhine and of a 50 kilometre strip of territory on the right bank, had been imposed on Germany by the Treaty of Versailles. She had accepted this of her own free will, by the signature of the Locarno agreements. Hitler himself has solemnly and publicly recognised these obligations, confirming them on a number of occasions. In terms of the treaty, their violation constituted an act of unprovoked aggression comparable to an invasion. France and Belgium were authorised to take all appropriate actions; Great Britain and Italy were committed to implement their guarantee and to co-operate in the mutual assistance provided by the League of Nations.

Although Berlin had not spoken of a revision of the treaty, it was clear at the beginning of 1936 that an attempt against the demilitarised zone was contemplated. The warnings were becoming more frequent. The Belgian Consul-General in the Rhineland had reported disquieting signs for months, as had his French colleagues in Cologne and Düsseldorf. In Paris, the military intelligence had informed the Quai d'Orsay that, 'the repudiation of the Rhineland statute must be expected in the autumn of 1936 at the latest'. In Berlin this was reported, albeit with the reservations of a cautious diplomat, by André François-Poncet.

In Brussels the government had been alerted by its Chargé D'affaires in Berlin, and its Ambassador in Paris, Count de Kerchove de Denterghem. The latter had already reported, on 30 January, that the question of the reoccupation of the Rhineland zone was 'entering a critical phase'. A few days later after an interview with the French Foreign Minister, he renewed his warning adding that, without the support of Great Britain, France would probably act prudently. On

27 February, Count de Kerchove reported a further conversation with the Minister. A number of indications, including rumours from Rome and Moscow, suggested that Germany intended shortly to enter the demilitarised zone with 'a grand fanfare'. Flandin, however, had not given him the impression that he was prepared to take positive action.[1] On the other hand, the British Foreign Office told Belgian diplomats that, in its opinion, Germany would not confront Europe with a *fait accompli*; the risks were too great. In addition, Germany would not want to create a disturbance in Europe on the eve of the Berlin Olympic Games, planned for the summer. The question would be treated 'entirely in the diplomatic field'.[2] Meanwhile, in Ethiopia, General Badoglio was launching the attack which was to take him to Addis Ababa. Flandin and Eden continued to argue over sanctions against Italy, and Brussels, Paris and London waited to see what Hitler would do. But no preparations were made.

The waiting time was short. Early on the morning of 7 March 1936, detachments of the Wehrmacht had marched through the principal Rhineland towns. According to the Belgian Consul General in Cologne, they received a cold welcome from an anxious rather than a joyful population.[3] At 10 o'clock that morning, the diplomatic representatives of France, Great Britain, Italy and Belgium were summoned to the Wilhelmstrasse. The Minister of Foreign Affairs told them that the signature of the Franco-Soviet act of mutual assistance constituted a violation of the Locarno agreement; consequently, Germany was reoccupying the Rhineland with 'a symbolic force'.* The same day Hitler summoned the Reichstag at the Kroll Opera House for one of those sittings, at once frightening and ridiculous, with which he celebrated his triumphs. In the semi-circular hall, surrounded by gold-plated eagles and gigantic swastika flags, the 'Members of Parliament', booted and in brown uniform, greeted him with outstretched arms and repeated cries of, 'Heil Hitler, heil, heil Sieg heil!' In the presence of imperturbable Ambassadors, he delivered an hour and a half speech, frequently interrupted by the vociferous audience leaping repeatedly to their feet with outstretched arms. When he announced, 'The Treaty of Locarno no longer exists', the enthusiasm gave way to the stamping of feet, loud shouts and a wild demonstration of approval. But the military hierarchy behaved differently. The cor-

---

* The treaty of Franco-Soviet mutual assistance, proposed by Barthou, signed by Laval, had been approved in the Chamber of Deputies by a large majority on 27 February 1936—333 votes against 164, with no abstentions.

respondent of the *Daily Telegraph* reported that the Commander-in-Chief, Werner von Fritsch, was in a state of agitation, perspiring and nervously polishing his monocle. His American colleague William Shirer wrote, 'On the way out, I ran into General von Blomberg. His face was livid, convulsed by nervous tics.' When night fell, a great torchlight tattoo lit up the darkened avenues of the capital.

In Paris, early that morning the Premier had summoned his senior Ministers to consult with General Gamelin, the highest military authority in the land. In the afternoon, a smaller meeting took place in Flandin's room at the Quai d'Orsay, and the following morning, a Council of Ministers was held at the Elysée under the presidency of Albert Lebrum. 'At lamentable disarray', Flandin was later to comment, exaggerating perhaps in order to justify his own pusillanimity.[4] We know that no counter-measures were envisaged.

The attitude of the military leaders was the main cause of the paralysis. General Maurin, the Minister for War, and General Gamelin, the Chief of Staff, amazed and dismayed the Ministers by stating that no military action could be undertaken without full mobilisation and the collaboration of Great Britain, Belgium and Italy (most of the latter's army was in Africa). The Chief of Staff drew a depressing picture of the situation. The German forces in the Rhineland, he said, numbered 295,000 men, the equivalent of 21 to 22 divisions. General Gamelin admitted later that he had made it a personal rule always to present what he called *bulletins de couverture* to the ministers, reports designed to protect himself against all possible blame, in which he unduly exaggerated the difficulties ahead, 'in case things went wrong'.[5] On this occasion, he disguised the truth by including in his calculations certain formations, such as the SA and the SS, which had no proper military training (apart from goose-stepping), no cadres, no arms, and which would require many months before they were ready for combat. Indeed, the regular army itself was little better prepared, being in the process of complete reorganisation.

Sarraut wanted a police action to expel the 30,000-man German force which had entered the Rhineland. Gamelin wanted to put more than a million men in the field, together the entire Air Force and Navy, to fight a war against Germany of which the probability existed only in his imagination. It was a decisive moment, the hour of truth for a policy pursued since 1919. General Gamelin, the man responsible for the defence of France, could not have been unaware of this; for months he had taken part in staff discussions envisaging such a situation.

Gamelin will not be forgotten in history because, more than any other soldier or politician, he had presided over the French grand strategy during the crucial years; also because in 1940, at the head of the armies, he suffered a defeat of the dimensions of Waterloo. For those who knew him, as much as for historians, his was a difficult character to fathom. 'A nobody', said George Monnet, a member of the Government in 1939. 'A pot-bellied little grocer', said the British Air Marshall Barratt. 'A noodle', was the opinion of a French staff officer.[6]

In 1906, on the recommendation of his father, Gamelin had become ADC to General Joffre, then in command of an infantry division. It was his chance of a lifetime, but also the main cause of the 1940 defeat. A close relationship developed between the young Captain and the future Marshal, who saw 'an outstanding officer ... to be promoted as rapidly as possible' in his ADC. In the gravest, but also most glorious hours of 1914, Major Gamelin was Joffre's close collaborator and confidant. With his own hand, he had written the orders which led to the victory of the Marne; rightly or wrongly, he was also credited with helping to formulate them. At the time of the Armistice he was a General in command of a division. From then on, he was destined to rise to the summit. In 1930, the Premier, André Tardieu, required a successor to Marshal Pétain, who was approaching the age of seventy-five. General Weygand was appointed Chief of Staff, a natural promotion for the right-hand man of Marshal Foch, the victor of the Great War. Tardieu did not like him, finding him too impulsive, so he placed at his side General Gamelin, Joffre's man. It was a subtle move, satisfying both the political parties and the factions within the Army. The following year, Pétain retired and Weygand took his place, yielding his own to Gamelin.

Weygand belonged to a proud and haughty military caste whose relations with the Republic had always been uneasy.* Clemenceau said of him: 'He is somebody. An ugly, ungainly, outlandish and tortured character, he must have often been beaten as a child. But he is intelligent, there is something in him, a smouldering fire ... profound and sensitive.'[7] One day, to emphasise his point in a conversation with politicians, his face red with anger, he took a dagger inscribed with a swastika out of his pocket and planted it on the table. He was reputed to favour a return of the monarchy. To be sure, he did not hide his

---

* Maxime Weygand was born in Brussels in 1867, entered in the birth register 'of unknown father and mother'. Brought up in France, a foreign cadet at St Cyr, he did not take French citizenship until he became a regular officer. He was said to be an illegitimate descendant of the Belgian royal family, but this appears unlikely.

hostility towards the Ministers of the Republic; he irritated them and made them feel uncomfortable.[8] Maurice Gamelin, on the other hand, was charming, affable and flexible. In contrast to his chief, from whom he discreetly kept his distance, he never said 'No'. Serious, reserved and modest, he gave the impression of having a philosophical mind—a true Republican General. Reynaud, who saw through him, said, 'A Bishop rather than a soldier'. But when Weygand retired from active service in 1935, Gamelin, aged sixty-three, was his unquestioned successor.

The laws of the Republic enact the incontestable supremacy of the civil power; its Ministers have the last word in all major strategic decisions. The young Colonel de Gaulle reminded Leon Blum of this at their only meeting in 1936. 'National Defence', he said, 'is the responsibility of the government.' Nevertheless, Ministers did not presume to participate in the esoteric cult and rites of that church which was the French Army. The institutions where they met the Generals, the Permanent Committee for National Defence, and the Supreme War Council, were feeble and not very strongly stuctured.*

The first of these bodies assembled around the Premier and consisted of the Ministers of Foreign Affairs and of the three services and the principal military chiefs, but it was a purely consultative affair and rarely met. The second, under the chairmanship of the Minister of Defence comprised the titular holders of the high commands. It was assisted by a secretariat in charge of strategic studies in the widest context. However, this body would lose much of its purpose in 1936 when it was integrated with the General Staff. Daladier left it to be run by the inevitable Gamelin. He chaired it but once between 1935 and 1939. Mindful of the sensitivity of the designated C-in-C, he did not even convene it at the time of the invasion of Poland.[9] Nor did he venture to consult the Members of the Council individually, with the exception of two generals who were attached to ministerial private offices.†

In Paris during the Thirties, the fate of the French Army, of France and of Europe, depended on one man: General Gamelin. Over him, stood a Minister concerned only with obtaining vast credits from a docile Parliament, but unconcerned with the use to which they were

---

* In Great Britain, the Chiefs of Staff (sea, ground and air) were under a ministerial committee (the Committee of Imperial Defence) presided over by the Prime Minister and assisted by a secretariat.

† When Daladier under the Vichy régime, was hauled before the High Court at Riom, he pleaded the non-responsibility of the government in strategic matters.

put. Gamelin had no one at his side, apart from ADCs. Under him were submissive subordinates, an obedient hierarchy which crushed any dissent. 'Encased in an intellectual iron collar', said General Beaufre, 'the Army had not studied the general problem of war, even less of strategy.' To the questions which Beaufre had asked in 1935, when as a young captain, he had been posted to the General Staff, his colonel replied, 'My poor friend, you are clearly new here. Get it into your head that there is no programme, nor will there ever be a programme. All we can do is our best according to the circumstances.' General Weygand says the same in his diary at the beginning of 1940.[10]

'I am a strategist', General Gamelin used to say haughtily; but the skills he claimed to possess demanded arduous preparatory work, precise analytical effort and an imaginative synthesis. No trace of these is to be found in the archives. Neither is there any systematic study fathoming the main aims of the enemy, no dissertation on the psychology of dictators, and above all no plans of counter-measures. The overruling general idea was for static defence, while waiting for Germany to exhaust herself. In May 1940, General Gamelin forgot this, and threw his best troops into Belgium and the Netherlands in a rash manoeuvre, based on a Plan D, hastily approved by the Supreme Council in November 1939, sketchily prepared and ignoring the most elementary precautions of military art.[11] At this supreme moment, he shut himself up in the Château of Vincennes on the outskirts of Paris, complacent and detached, *without radio communication*, assisted only by a handful of liaison officers, far from the General Headquarters, even further from the battlefield. It was here, while his armies disintegrated, that he pronounced on 19 May, the celebrated directive, ' . . . not wishing to interfere in the conduct of the battle now under way.' Colonel de Villelume, his liaison officer to the Quai d'Orsay, said the C-in-C was 'the authentic heir of the Platonic theory that movement is only an inferior alternative to immobility, just as the act of being is an inferior alternative to nothingness'.[12] A Swiss doctor, Dr Pierre Rentchnick, wrote in a book that Maurice Gamelin, having contracted syphilis, had been treated in the neuro-psychiatric department of the military hospital in the Val de Grâce. Although not having the complete medical file, he claimed he could diagnose the preliminary symptoms of 'general paralysis' which the disease causes, basing his opinion on the treatment Gamelin received, and also on his lethargy, lapses of memory, lack of synthesis and precision in his statements.[13] If true, the disease may explain the more surprising aspects of his behaviour.

★   ★   ★

In the crucial hours of the weekend of 7 March 1936, the British Ministers left the capital as usual for their country homes without bothering to meet. Only Anthony Eden remained at his post. To the surprise—of the public at least—this fervent advocate of collective security, who had striven for months to impose international justice on Italy, was now making frantic efforts to prevent its imposition on Germany, indeed, for weeks, he had been whispering to the Germans that he might agree to remilitarisation of the Rhineland in exchange for an air pact.* The French Ambassador was summoned to the Foreign Office to be lectured. The British Ambassador in Paris was told to warn the Quai d'Orsay immediately against any hasty action. The Belgian Prime Minister, Paul van Zeeland, was requested by telephone to support these exhortations—which he did.

Sunday 8 March. While German troops were completing the occupation of the demilitarised zone unimpeded, the hours were passing in indecision in Paris. The Secretary General of the Quai d'Orsay, Alexis Leger, who had taken part in the formulation and negotiation of the Locarno Treaties with Briand, insisted that, in accordance with the terms of those agreements, France must take immediate action, if necessary on her own and before any recourse to the League of Nations. He threatened to resign and, with a vigour bordering on desperation, insisted that acceptance of the *fait accompli* would give Germany domination over Europe.[15] No one denied this. However, the French did nothing apart from lodging (with Belgium) a complaint to the League of Nations.†

The newspapers were not good. They condemned the *coup de force*, but did not encourage resistance to it. Maurras wrote in *L'Action Française*, 'We must not march with the Soviets against Hitler.' The *Populaire*, organ of the Socialist party, and *L'Humanité*, the Communist paper, declared against any counter-measures. On the other hand, the populace prepared calmly and resignedly for the grave events which Sarraut's speech had foretold.

---

* Recalled only four days later, the British Cabinet heard Eden recommend half-heartedly and unsuccessfully, the application of the Charter. Baldwin complained that France had been 'most unfriendly' in placing Great Britain in an embarrassing situation.[14]

† Eden contended that Great Britain, in her capacity as a guaranteeing power, could not associate herself with the Franco-Belgian protest. In fact, Whitehall had abandoned its responsibilities as a guarantor in order to play a mediating role between Paris and Berlin, an attitude which was maintained until 1939.

Monday 9 March. Eden, hoping to defuse the crisis, was trying to procrastinate; under some pretext, he declined to attend a meeting of the Locarno powers due to be held in Paris. On that day, Sarraut summoned his closest Ministers and the Chiefs of Staff to his house once again. Again, the soldiers claimed that they could do nothing without general mobilisation; but the Ministers feared that this would antagonise the public just before the elections to be held at the end of April. General Pujo, head of the Air Force, alarmed everybody by painting a fearful picture of the aerial bombardments which would threaten French towns. Nevertheless, the Minister of War was instructed to study the possibility of an operation to seize Sarrebruck or Kehl as 'a security'.

Tuesday 10 March. A meeting of the Locarno signatory powers was held at the Quai d'Orsay. While the Ministers (except, of course, the Germans) were conferring, General Gamelin was giving a luncheon for the military attachés accredited to Paris in the fashionable restaurant 'Drouant'. The Wehrmacht was represented by Colonel Kuhlental, a courteous officer who was proud to recall the French origins of his family. Over brandy and cigars, Gamelin spoke affably about the reoccupation of the Rhineland. He referred to 'military camaraderie'. 'I disapprove of your brusque methods', he told the German officer, 'but I fully understand that the honour of the Wehrmacht would be deeply offended if it was obliged to go back across the Rhine.'[15]

In the salons of the Quai d'Orsay, Flandin, less mindful of German susceptibilities, invoked the treaties to demand economic and military sanctions against Germany (the sanctions which he had rendered ineffective against Italy when he replaced Laval). However, he did not press for an immediate decision, which, in any case, Eden was determined not to take. Von Zeeland, representing Belgium, predicted that war was inevitable if the German troops were not evicted from the Rhineland. He sided with Flandin—but not for long. Faced with the dilemma of having to choose between France and Great Britain, with gymnastic agility he managed, in his own words, to 'squeeze between the two so as to bring their points of view closer together.'[17] As these points of view were diametrically opposed, the result was stalemate and an implicit acceptance of the *fait accompli*. Italy, although already condemned as an aggressor, was invited to the meeting as a guaranteeing power. Her representative did not open his mouth. The meeting was adjourned, the only decision taken being that they would meet again. It was all over. The decisive moment had passed. Hitler had won.

In a statement to the House of Commons the evening before, after a routine allusion to the sanctity of treaties, Eden had already stated that the reoccupation of the Rhineland 'brought with it no threat of hostilities' and suggested that it might even offer an opportunity for reaching a settlement. He had been secretly in contact with Hitler, asking him to withdraw his troops in return for the promise of a new statute for the Rhineland.[18] A clumsy gesture, it was quickly leaked to the Press by the calculated indiscretions of the Wilhelmstrasse. It angered the French and confirmed the German view that London would remain neutral. In the end, as is well known, nothing was attempted except for futile conversations, which went on for weeks, and brief staff talks between Britain, France and Belgium—not to be repeated until 1939—and even then without the latter.

★   ★   ★

The Führer was greatly relieved. Once again, ignoring all adverse advice, he had gambled and won. Visiting the 'liberated' Rhineland to the sound of pealing bells, he celebrated his triumph. In Cologne, the crowds gathered in front of the cathedral were dazed by his hoarse cries broadcast from the loudspeakers; now that the danger was over, they applauded wildly. Hitler in his special train exulted; 'My God, how pleased I am that it all went off so well! The world belongs only to those who dare.—God supports them!' To soothe his ruffled nerves, he then listened to a recording of Parsifal. Later in a speech he was to admit to his anxiety during the early hours of the operation—'the toughest hours of my life.' To Mussolini he confided, 'If the French had shown sign of action, I would have had to retire, my tail between my legs.'[19]

It was understandable. The French Army in metropolitan France numbered 360,000 men; which could in theory be increased in a week by the mobilisation of troops known as 'covering forces'; and on general mobilisation by several millions.* The Army was composed of some 30 regular divisions, seven of which were motorised, and one light armoured division (a second was to come into service the following month). After witnessing their manoeuvres in Champagne, Colonel van Overstraeten, the military adviser to the King of the Belgians, spoke highly of their readiness.[21]

* General Beaufre states in his memoirs that a partial mobilisation was however impossible, because the recall forms for individuals had been catalogued in terms of military units. Consequently, the recall of one or two classes would have involved a gigantic classification operation.[20] But could it have been done by radio?

Almost certainly, the Belgian Army, comprising 14 divisions, 8 of which were regular, could be counted upon, as could be the British naval and air forces. Churchill considered it would be inconceivable that Great Britain (or Belgium) would no nothing if the situation deteriorated. Alexis Leger, the Secretary General at the Quai d'Orsay, took the same view; and Fernand van Langenhove, his Belgian colleague, thought that he was 'probably right'.[22] Other allied countries had shown willingness to intervene. Czechoslovakia, one of the first military powers in Central Europe, and Yugoslavia had immediately promised their whole-hearted support, More equivocally, Poland through its Chief of Staff and its Minister for Foreign Affairs, had pledged 'to mobilise to fight'. They did not retract until they realised that Paris would do nothing. The USSR aligned itself beside France, with which it had just signed a treaty of mutual assistance. Pope Pius XI himself, who had previously protested at the Franco-Belgian occupation of the Ruhr, told the French Ambassador on 16 March, 'If you had sent 200,000 troops into the zone reoccupied by Germany immediately, you would have done a great service to everyone.[23] In short—200 allied divisions (not counting the Soviets) would have faced a handful of ill-prepared German units.

The German High Command was well aware of this. They considered that the risks the Führer was taking were unjustified and they made desparate but vain efforts to dissuade him. Although devoted to his master, General von Blomberg, the Minister for War, resigned himself to the venture on the express condition that if the French moved, he could withdraw his troops immediately. When, on the Sunday evening, the Maginot Line was put in a state of alert, he panicked and rushed to the Führer, insisting that all resistance was impossible. He returned a second time, on 14 March, when the League of Nations made a (purely verbal) condemnation of Germany. The Nazi dictator, now convinced that he had won the day, told him brutally that the conduct of political affairs was the sole responsibility of the Chancellor.

The cabinets and the general staff of the western powers were well aware of the differences between the Führer and his generals, and the fears of the latter. Sir Eric Phipps, the British Ambassador in Berlin, knew of them—'with all details' he confided to his Belgian colleague, who had also been informed by his own military attaché. The Polish Ambassador was aware of them. Even the French knew! But nothing, neither the German Army's lack of preparation, nor the overwhelming superiority of the forces of the French and their allies, could persuade

Sarraut, Flandin and Gamelin to confront Adolf Hitler. It was the day of the realists.[24] The greatest military power in the world was reduced to impotence by a few poorly armed battalions.

★   ★   ★

Belgium was in the grip of a fever—the Fascist fever. In the 1936 elections, held a few weeks after the Rhineland coup, the partisans of Degrelle, after a Nazi-style campaign, gained 21 out of the 202 seats in the House of Representatives at a stroke—almost as many as the old Liberal Party. 16 seats were won by the Flemish nationalists. It was an unprecedented situation and the emulators of Rome and Berlin clamoured more loudly than ever for the severance of all foreign ties and the withdrawal from the League of Nations. At the same time, the Government was undertaking a detailed reassessment of Belgium's foreign policy. The notion of neutrality was in the air. It had deep roots. Imposed by the great Powers in 1839, the statute of guaranteed neutrality had brought Belgium nearly a century of peace and tranquility. With the passage of time, it had become engrained in the minds of the people, not only as a fundamental law, but as a kind of national expression. Although they had been trampled underfoot by the Germans in 1914, it still had its supporters. During the Great War, King Albert had been careful not to identify Belgium's cause with that of the principal powers. 'Belgium', he noted on 10 November 1914, while the battle was raging, 'must not give its allegiance to any power, neither to Great Britain nor to France. We were neutral before the war, and the mass of the population want no links with any of their neighbours.'[25]

At the time of the Armistice, it was true no more. The Government, Parliament and the public no longer wanted a neutrality whose frailty had been laid bare by the German invasion. In addition, neutrality would have been incompatible with the nation's obligations to the League of Nations, to which both the Flemings and the Walloons had rallied enthusiastically. From then on, the main concern of Belgium diplomacy had been to obtain from London and Paris a promise confirming the enforcement of collective security. Great Britain agreed to guarantee Belgium, but only on condition that she returned to her pre-war neutrality—a condition unacceptable to Brussels. The Belgians resigned themselves to reliance upon France alone. After difficult negotiations, the two governments, through an exchange of letters in 1920, pledged themselves to come to one another's assistance, 'in the event of an unprovoked German aggression'. The exchange of letters was made public, but complemented by secret agreements between the two general staffs.

From the moment of signature, this agreement attracted criticism. The Socialist Party, and Flemish circles in particular, feared that the Army and the diplomacy of the small kingdom would come under the undue influence of France. Then, in 1925, the Treaty of Locarno brought Great Britain back onto the Continent and Belgium's foreign relations seemed better balanced again. Anxieties were calmed; in March 1931 Paul Hymans, the Minister of Foreign Affairs, obtained the approval of Parliament without difficulty, when he defined the obligations of his country as enshrined in Geneva, Locarno and the Franco-Belgian military convention. He stated that the latter (previously agreed to in Paris), was not an alliance, but a form of technical co-operation, as envisaged by Locarno and the Geneva Pact. He ended it by stating, 'Belgium will only take up arms to safeguard its territory and independence, and *to fulfill the duties dictated by its statute.*'* In December 1933, he repeated to the Commission of Foreign Affairs in Parliament that, 'the Locarno agreements, and the Franco-Belgian military agreements, remained the basis of the country's foreign policy'. The Comte de Broqueville, Head of the Government, also confirmed (before changing his mind) that 'the entente with the French Republic remains the corner-stone of our policy'.[26]

With the renaissance of German might, and the renewed dangers that accompanied it, what had seemed clear—though never completely—was now enveloped in a cloud. King Albert had never given up his predilection for neutrality. Patiently he had redoubled his efforts to rally his leading Ministers to his point of view. After his father's death in 1934, King Leopold continued this policy. 'My father deplored Belgium taking part in the discussions between the Great Powers', he stated to his secretary. 'Our geographic position alone has enabled us to avoid domination by a neighbour ... This trump card is more important than any treaty of guarantee or defensive alliance.'[27]

Political circles took some time to be convinced. Two years had gone by. With Hitler becoming increasingly threatening, the strengthening of the Army became essential. Both the Socialists and the Flemings were reticent, on account of their misgivings over the secret agreements of 1920, as well as their deep-rooted pacifism. Paul van

---

* The defenders of 'political independence' were later to invoke the first part of this phrase without insisting on the second (author's italics) to emphasise that Belgium's foreign policy has never varied—which was indefensible.

Zeeland intended to reassure them. On the eve of the reoccupation of the Rhineland, after many weeks of discussion, he had initialled a new exchange of letters between Paris and Brussels, annulling those of 1920. It was in no way a rupture, but a simple readjustment dictated by the changing situation. The close relations between the two general staffs were to continue in the framework of the Locarno agreements. However, the next day the Reich repudiated these, and German troops appeared on the Belgian frontier.

The demilitarisation of the Rhineland, together with the Franco-Belgian entente, had until now made the French Army the police force of the continent. Stretched out between Bâsle and Montmédy on the impregnable Maginot Line, they had had the means, in the event of war, to strike with impunity deep into the heart of Germany and to seize the Ruhr, the mining and industrial centre essential to Germany's war economy. Now, with the Rhineland again militarised, and the Maginot Line faced by a 'Siegfried Line' under construction, the balance of power had been transformed. But Belgium, if not the exiguous Helvetian plain, always remained the natural battlefield of Europe. 'The pit of the stomach of Europe', Clausewitz called it; or as the diplomats said, 'The line of the Paris–Berlin express'. Geography had thus conferred on Belgium a role in history, out of all proportion to her actual power.

Noblesse oblige. The repudiation of the statute of Europe and the reoccupation of the Rhineland in defiance of all the treaties, should have given Paul van Zeeland an exceptional opportunity to justify the role which his predecessors had played in less stormy times. If he had had the courage to raise the voice of righteousness—as I believe it was his pressing duty to do—he might well have been able to persuade the hesitant French Ministers to adopt a firmer line; it certainly was the opinion of several responsible Belgian diplomats, among them Count Geoffroy d'Aspremont-Lynden, his diplomatic adviser at the time.[28]

In any case, the Belgian Government would have been assured for a long time to come of an estimable reputation. Instead, he chose to use its influence in favour of doing nothing.

From March 1935 onwards, Paul van Zeeland was King Leopold III's Prime Minister and Foreign Minister. The monarch has been judged, severely and sometimes unjustly; we need not do so again. His concern for the nation was beyond doubt. His great mistake was not to shake off the dust of the past, to allow himself to be influenced too much by the teaching of King Albert, whom he revered. From him he had learnt that in the nineteenth century Belgium had had to be equally suspicious of Paris and Berlin. 'Belgium is a ripe pear which will fall into our mouths', said Napoleon III, and he had bargained with Bismarck for its possession.* Leopold was well aware that Belgium had been saved by her neutrality during the Franco-Prussian war of 1870. It had also helped her to acquire a vast colonial empire in Africa. Its violation in 1914 had bestowed on her, during her ordeal, a privileged place among the nations.

King Leopold, thirty-seven years of age, was inexperienced, too good-looking and over-confident int he almost divine right of his crown—the source of a mystical reverence which the constitutional texts had not erased. He believed that he had to remain faithful to a system which had served the country and his ancestors so well. Curiously, this young man identified himself with his elders in their nostalgia for the past; but was this not the tendency of the time? Like so many statesmen, he was unaware of the revolutionary violence pent up in the myth of National Socialism. He believed that the situation could be handled by the old, calculating, astute diplomacy. This concept no longer applied to the times; but weak Ministers did not press him to abandon it. The greater the danger, the surer he felt that it was the only hope of salvation.

The day after the *coup de force* in the Rhineland, the King was heard to say rejoicingly, 'This will be an exceptional opportunity for Belgium to regain her international statute.'[29] At the time of the defeat in 1940, inspired more than ever by the certainty that he was right, and pursuing his illusions to their logical conclusion, he broke with his unanimous Ministers, thereby laying himself open to the severest criticism. But until then, in Belgium, as in other constitutional monarchies, the old adage remained: 'The King can do no wrong'—the Ministers alone were responsible.

In 1936, van Zeeland's intellect and experience of public affairs placed him high above many of his peers. Economist, university professor and banker, chosen by the King, he had reached the summit at the age of forty-two. As Prime Minister, he appeared for a short time to have been sent by Providence, the only politician perhaps in Belgium's history to have achieved much prominence.

But his fame was short-lived; he died in 1973, and few people now remember him. He craved too much for power, as well as for wealth

---

*Belgian schoolchildren learnt that Count Benedetti, Napoleon III's Ambassador in Berlin had received from Bismarck a vague promise to give Belgium and Luxembourg to France in return for French neutrality during the Austro-Prussian war.

and honours. European democracies do not approve of such intemperance. By failing to opt for one of the three alone, he neither achieved real power, nor made a great fortune, and was awarded only ordinary honours. He was exceptionally gifted, and should have played a distinguished role in Europe; but his talents were impaired by an obsession to identify himself with a hereditary aristocracy to which he did not belong. This would have been unimportant, had it not had a profound influence on his politics. It was in these faults, rather than in a lack of lucidity, that the explanation of his diplomatic mistakes is to be found. When Ethiopia was attacked he started, as we have seen, by strongly supporting collective security; but he almost immediately regretted this and capitulated without a struggle before the attacks of Mussolini's sympathisers. Influenced by his birth, he was not prepared to antagonise the *Quartier Leopold*—the Belgian establishment— which tended to be indulgent to Italian fascism, a view he was too intelligent to share. Nor did he wish to displease King Leopold, brother-in-law to the Crown Prince of Italy, by recommending a course of action which his monarch was not prepared to like.

By the time of the reoccupation of the Rhineland, van Zeeland's energies had ebbed. To choose between Paris and London was certainly painful, but by no means impossible. Loath to raise his voice outside the narrow confines of his country, Paul van Zeeland failed in the European role to which Belgian Ministers had aspired since Versailles and Locarno. He also lost the opportunity to gain the great acclaim which his rare talents deserved.

★ ★ ★

'The statesman can only listen to the footsteps of the Lord down the road of universal history, grasp the hem of his cloak, and hold onto it a little way along that road' wrote Bismarck. A striking formula which integrating the fatality of history and the role of human effort, sums up my experience of events. During the 1930s, European statesmen proved singularly inept at grasping the hem of the Lord's garment. They had certainly had the opportunity; first at Manchuria, then again under the most favourable circumstances in the Ethiopian war; a third time, during the re-occupation of the Rhineland, and perhaps yet again during the Czech crisis.

Why were the seats of power occupied for seven consecutive years by men whose influence was generally so baneful? Why on one side were the evil geniuses, mentally diseased and full of fury, and on the other, puny men paralysed by an equally morbid fear to act? Many historians quoting the adage 'People get the government they deserve', contend that the masses in the democracies were responsible for the faults committed by their leaders. This is too facile and over-simplified, too general and too pre-emptory. Nor is it based on convincing or precise analysis. It is notable that none of the great international crises was marked by any public demonstration of defeatism. It was not the voter who between 1925 and 1932 made disarmament unworkable; it was not the electorate who subverted collective security by opposing sanctions against Japan and Italy. Nor was it the electorate who opposed action when the bridges of the Rhine were being crossed by a few Wehrmacht battalions. On the contrary, there is much evidence that had the British, the French and the Belgians been fully informed, they would have, dolefully but resignedly, followed resolute leaders. Churchill and other writers have confirmed this for Great Britain. Why not believe them? Barely four months had elapsed since Baldwin's government had won a resounding electorial victory with the motto 'Collective Security'—a victory which had ratified the Peace Ballot of the preceding year. The first soundings of public opinion, made by Gallup in 1937, revealed the the lucidity of the British people: 83 per cent were convinced that their country would eventually be involved in war; 74 per cent considered that the government should remain faithful to the League of Nations.*

Were the French less determined? Much has been made of the protestations in the newspapers, 'unanimous in their desire for peace'. *L'Action Française* had headlines such as 'Out with Sarraut and Flandin!'; 'Clear off, you gang of cuckolds!'; 'We don't want war!'; and so on. *Le Populaire*, of Léon Blum, the Communist *L'Humanieté*, and others declared less violently but with equally strong feeling that they were 'on the side of peace'. Experienced diplomats are well aware that the Press does not always reflect public opinion. It was, of course, true that the French, the British, the Belgians (and probably a majority of the Germans) felt a deep repulsion at the mere thought of a repetition of the carnage of 1914–18. Nevertheless, to regard a police operation in 1936 in this light was an error or a deliberate falsehood—as much as pretending that the arrest of an assassin would lead to more murders. To have pushed the Germans back across the Rhine would not have been a declaration of war. On the contrary, it would have eliminated the probability of war with very little risk; but a risk, which petrified timid governments.

* Asked also to which country they had most sympathy, only 15 per cent of the British said Germany.[30]

It is easy for those who have wielded power to justify their mistakes by blaming public opinion. But on this occasion who would have dared to do so? Not Blum, who confessed later to feeling 'a kind of remorse'. Not Sarraut, nor Flandin who attributed their passivity to the defeatism of the generals and the absence of British co-operation. Nor Eden, who had been such an ardent supporter of non-intervention, and who later regretted the pressure he had brought on the French Government to break his will.[31] Indeed, six weeks later, the *Front Populaire* won the elections with the promise of the consolidation of collective security. Certainly there were other factors which favoured the parties championing the old French Republican idealism; but the commitment to a more definite and coherent foreign policy undeniably played a significant role.

★   ★   ★

Statesmen who appear coldly calculating are often moved by erratic instincts of anxiety deep in their very natures. The obstinacy and dynamism which separates them from the horde of vulgar self-seekers is rarely accompanied by the gift of sagacious speculation. Indifferent and barely aware of what Malraux called, 'the exquisite music of existence', in the excitement of power they seek an elixir which will anaesthetise the torments plaguing their nerves and sometimes their bodies.

Were Herriot, Laval, MacDonald, Baldwin, Hoare, Eden, van Zeeland, and later Chamberlain and Daladier, all of the same ilk? Inexorably from year to year, their errors of judgement accumulated to the point of astounding those who today try to analyse them, in spite of all the rational explanations which have been given. Their apologists claim that they were always concerned with the public well being. No doubt—but any such motive was confused with the neurotic promotion of their own personalities. They were obsessed by the electorate, of which they had little understanding, despising it while, at the same time, courting it. They had eyes only for their immediate concerns, the coterie with which they identified themselves, the political party which sustained their career, and finally the country where they were born. Their main concern was the tactics of the day, to the exclusion of long-term objectives or collective European interests in particular, the fear of change made them tremble. In the words of Diderot, they were, 'narrow-minded, lost souls, indifferent to the fate of the human species and so concentrated in their small society, which is their nation, that they see no further than its immediate interests.

They think we should regard them as good citizens. This I will concede, if they will allow me to call them evil men.'[32]

Ignoti nulla cupido. We do not like what we do not know. Our 'evil men' were imbued with the most curious prejudices. Poincaré showed deep vexation when Briand played golf—a foreign sport—with Lloyd George at one of their meetings in Cannes. Laval was surprised when, on an official visit to Berlin, he was served sauerkraut; he believed it was the daily dish of every German. He hated the British, whom he considered were the real enemies of France. Daladier, a firm supporter of the *Etente Cordiale*, disliked them almost as much—'Tigers' he called them. Mussolini also had detested them ever since the day he thought he had been snubbed during a visit to London in 1922. 'London is a nightmare', he said, and hoped he would never have to set foot there again. He never did. He had rendered himself ridiculous by quarrelling with some journalists and making a scene at Claridge's because he did not consider his suite corresponded to his rank. Like Laval, he believed that the British had lost all combative spirit. Did they not drink tea every day, dressed in dinner jackets—a sure proof of their decline? Chamberlain believed that the Americans were so 'rotted' that he was indifferent as to whom should be Ambassador in Washington. Simon wondered what sort of language 'Belgian' was. Baldwin had such a horror of foreigners that he always tried not to sit next to them at meals. When he retired from politics, he rejoiced that he would never have to meet any French statesman again.[33]

These anecdotes might be amusing, did they not reveal a national egocentrism bordering on xenophobia. Most puzzling and most serious was the irrational incomprehension which divided the French and British Governments at a time when so many common interests should have united them. In Paris, a number of politicians saw in collective security only a pretext for a coalition against Germany; they bitterly reproached the British for not joining them in it. A school of dissidents (a minority) believed that the British Empire was the greatest of all threats to France. At the time of the Ethiopian crisis, these fears crystallised to the extent that the possibility of a war between the two coutries was envisaged. General Beaufre reported that the French General Staff was instructed to study the eventual consequences for French overseas territories which might arise from it—disastrous. The extreme Right, anti-Protestant and anti-Parliamentarian, indulged in an orgy of invective. *Gringoire* snarled, 'I hate England by instinct and tradition. I state, and I repeat, that England must be reduced to slavery.' The *Je suis partout* stated, 'The Bellicose Judaic masons are propelling France towards war, at the orders of British colonialism and Russian Bolshevism, and in the interests of Ethiopian negro cannibals.' *L'Action Française*, in an article addressed to the Catholic élite, was indignant about the 'disastrous alliance of England with all the revolutionary forces which aim to spread disorder in Europe'.[34] Paradoxically, in Marxist demonology *Perfide Albion* was the imperial and reactionary power *par excellence*, the root of all evil.

In Great Britain many people felt that Germany had been too harshly treated, for which they readily blamed Paris. Haunted by the spectre of French hegemony in Europe, they wished to preserve 'the balance of power'. While afraid, with some reason, of another confrontation between the two great continental powers, they feared equally that Germany and France might get on too well. To an American diplomat, MacDonald said, 'We don't want them to make war on one another, but we also don't want them to be friends.' The British General Staff, like the one in Paris, had drawn up plans for a possible Franco-British war. British bombers had not the range of action for striking at Germany, because they had been designed for use against France.[35] It was not until 1933 that British diplomatic and military circles realised that Germany and Japan, not France, were their potential enemies. But the politicians were slow to come round to this view, or to establish better relations with the French. The future Lord Hankey, Secretary to the Cabinet and an influential *eminence grise*, voiced a widely held opinion when he stated that he preferred simple patriotism and autonomous defence to great principles. He was opposed to all that Geneva stood for, in particular to the use France wished to make of it. The Labour Party, as much, if not more, than the Tories, accused Paris of ambitions which were responsible for the European tension. They had not forgotten the occupation of the Ruhr. Laval's underhand intrigues during the Ethiopian crisis and his refusal to support London and collective security, had greatly contributed to the supine acceptance of the *coup de force* in the Rhineland.

This was the opinion of most of the Ministers. It was also to be found in a number of newspapers. *The Times* and *Observer* stated that Great Britain and Germany were natural allies, and had been so through many generations. The big circulation newspapers owned by Lords Beaverbrook and Rothermere, which flooded London with acres of newsprint every day proved just as nationalistic as those of Paris. In scarcely less violent terms, they recommended withdrawal from the continent and they attacked the League of Nations as 'a moribund institution, an instrument of powerful and unscrupulous ambitions'—this being a reference to France. The advent of the *Front Populaire* led to hysteria. I have before me a copy of the *Sunday Despatch* dated 21 June 1936 which—it seems incredible—reported over five columns, 'Imminent end of France and Belgium'. It described the alleged excesses of the strikers, the riots and bloodshed, the scenes of horror, and the tourists fearing for their lives.

Daladier and Chamberlain were masters of their foreign policy at this time more than at any other moment. They exercised a strong influence on the Press, and their diplomats were most anxious to collaborate. Dislike perhaps, but no hatred, separated the two people; nor was there any real clashes of interest—only a strange psychological incompatibility rooted in the rivalries of an ancient past. Without apparent logic, while the 'Great Fear' led certain Parisian circles to oppose the British, the same deep-rooted prejudices led to feelings of aversion for the French in London.

★ ★ ★

Among the selfish, capricious and unstable men who occupied the heights of politics only one, the young and handsome Anthony Eden, stood out as different. His aristocratic origin, his gallantry in the trenches of the Great War, his polished manners, his youthful political success, all these transformed him into a romantic figure. Imbued with the finest traditional values, he also appeared most resolute in promoting the ideal of common good which his elders promised without believing in it.[36] In a little book, full of sensitivity and very moving, Eden has described his childhood—so rich in material goods and so poor in tenderness. After an unhappy spell at Eton, shortened by the great storm of 1914, he enlisted in an infantry battalion when barely seventeen. Then followed the years of indescribable misery in the trenches of Flanders and on the Somme, the premature death of his father, the loss of two brothers killed in action—the eldest in a cavalry regiment in 1914, the younger a midshipman on board HMS *Indefatigable*, sunk at Jutland. A Captain at the end of the Great War, Eden left the Army after some hesitation and went to Oxford to read for a degree in Oriental languages, with the intention of becoming a diplomat. However, in 1923 he entered the House of Commons—on the extreme Right of the Conservative Party, possibly a posthumous challenge to his father, who had displayed radical tendencies.

Almost the whole of Anthony Eden's career was to be with the Foreign Office, which he joined in 1926 as Parliamentary Private Secretary to Sir Austen Chamberlain. Under Secretary of State in 1931,

Lord Privy Seal, Cabinet Minister for League of Nations Affairs, he had soon answered the call of Geneva and moved gradually to the centre of his party to become a dedicated champion of collective security. It was that reputation which led Baldwin to appoint him Secretary of State for Foreign Affairs after the enforced resignation of Sir Samuel Hoare. Erudite, poly-glot, interested in art, particularly modern painting, his inclination for a humanist European civilisation made him seem born for it.

The public admired his slim, elegant figure, and listened attentively to his moderate and sober, if not particularly original, rhetoric. What a contrast with the vulgar duplicity of Laval, the confused verbosity of MacDonald, the histrionic over-statements of Mussolini, the hysteria of Hitler! His popularity at home and on the Continent was immense. However, his undeniable talents hardly concealed the flaws in his personality. Psychiatrists (who should be listened to, although their perspicacity should not be exaggerated) might be inclined to assign his neurotic disposition to an early youth deprived of tenderness. One so often finds him pathetically and painfully seeking an approbation to sooth his anxieties. Poor Eden—so incapable of giving what he as a child had not receive, so anxious to please the Right, the Left, the Centre, and therefore so indecisive. Throughout his life he remained secretive and impenetrable. Adverse to solitude, he surrounded himself with companions; but he had very few real friends, holding at arm's length those who tried to approach closer.

Hypersensitive, when facing great difficulties, he fortified himself with stimulants. Apart from his political activities (and modern paintings) few subjects interested or amused him. He did not care much for holidays. Even when ill and confined to bed—which happened frequently—he was never without his documents, and he summoned his collaborators to his bedside. Although he enjoyed fame and admiration over a long period, he was not always liked by the diplomats who served him, some of whom criticised his versatility, his lack of human warmth, his violent and unjustified fits of temper. Apart from a serious operation in 1953, which left deep and permanent after effects, some of the maladies from which he suffered in the difficult moments of his life are attributed to nervous instability, more especially his stomach ulcers.[37]

His desire to please, his agile and supple intelligence, made him an oustanding diplomat. But he tended to concentrate on detail, showing little interest in the long-term aspects of a problem. The British Empire remained the centre of the world; he would never have any feeling for a European commonwealth. Adrift in the immediate upheaval of the day, obsessed by his own image, Anthony Eden lacked the vision and force of character of an architect of the future. For most of the time, he showed himself aware of the unique importance of collective security; but only when he felt it served short-term British interests. 'The Covenant, the whole Covenant, and nothing but the Covenant!', he proclaimed. Yes, against Mussolini, whom he hated ('the anti-Christ', he told his secretary), but not against Hitler, whom he did not hate.* In the case of Italy, whose armed forces were far from insignificant, he accepted the risk of a conflict. In the case of Germany, at that time militarily impotent, he resolutely opposed honouring the engagements contracted at Locarno (even before consulting the Prime Minister or his colleagues). A little later, however, he was to declare in the House of Commons, 'I do not intend to be the first British Foreign Secretary to repudiate our signature'. How can we understand him?

The regrets Eden expressed after the war, the publication of his memoirs and the official documents—these should provide us with an explanation of his German policy. But it still remains a mystery. The analysis on which he based his actions were often perspicacious, but when the time came to apply them, they were forgotten. In a document of 1936 addressed to the Cabinet and entitled, 'The German Danger', he wrote: 'Hitler's aims are the destruction of the peace settlement and the re-establishment of Germany as the dominant Power in Europe.' At the same time, he stated that the Führer was too occupied with domestic problems to contemplate war. In Baldwin's time, he was one of the principal advocates of 'appeasement' (a term he invented). With Chamberlain, he conceived a 'general settlement' to resuscitate the normal times of the Weimar Republic—and which would assure a Conservative victory in the elections planned for 1940.[39]

What a melancholic destiny, so many rich expectations, so long awaited, only to be pulverised in the crash of Suez and then to be followed by nearly twenty years of lonely and bitter retirement. 'We travesty our impotence and weakness into calculation and systems', wrote Benjamin Constant—words which so aptly described the British

---

* Something in Eden's personality led him to accept the rise of Hitler, and later that of Stalin. In his memoirs he wrote, 'I knew that Stalin was merciless, but I respected his intelligence, and even felt a certain sympathy for him, *which I have never been completely able to analyse* (author's italics). It has been suggested that the Red Czar exercised over him the psychiatric fascination of a paternal image.[38]

CHAPTER 9

Berlin and Moscow

In 1936 Mussolini, victorious in Africa, revived the abominable glories of war, in Bernanos' fearful words, 'By having a few niggers boiled'. Hitler celebrated his first successes at the Olympic Games, contemplating his great conquests, forging the Rome–Berlin Axis, and fraternising with Japan. Beyond the Pyrenees, Franco's star was rising on battlefields littered with corpses. In the same year, Edward VIII renounced the royal and imperial throne for the love of Wallis Simpson, a twice divorced American lady, no longer in her first youth, possessed of a grating voice. Stalin increased his execrable massacres by executing the old Bolsheviks, accused of counter-revolutionary plotting. Léon Blum inaugurated the tumultuous era of the *Front Populaire*.

On looking back over the Thirties, we find all the elements of a classical tragedy: the initial errors, the tyrannical forces and ever mounting passions which relentlessly propel mortals to absurdity and crime, leading finally to disaster and death. All this was prepared in the fatal months of 1936. It is, however, only after the tragedy, when order has been destroyed and the 'Kings' have departed, that the moment chosen by fate is revealed. For those of us who lived through these events, 1936 was only another year of crisis and anxiety. An obscure force and an instinct for self-preservation still inspired hope. Yet the more perspicacious were well aware of the forces of destruction gathering, of war approaching—a war to destroy civilisation.

★　　★　　★

On the morrow of the reoccupation of the Rhineland, amid the clamour of mammoth demonstrations, a new plebiscite was held in Germany, so that the people might renew their confidence in the swastika; 99 per cent of the electorate did so. And why not? Thanks to Hitler's unlimited impudence, his new relationship with Italy, a burgeoning German economy and, above all, thanks to the complacency of his adversaries, the Führer now dominated the European stage. That summer reverberated with his glory and renown. On 1 August 1936, with the coup of the Rhineland forgotten, people flocked to Berlin to witness the Führer presiding over the opening of the Olympic Games. A huge and magnificent stadium had been constructed at Wannsee, on the threshold of the capital, in the midst of lakes and forests (not far, either, from the Oranienburg concentration camp). The President of the International Olympic Committee was a Belgian who had had no intention, whatever the circumstances, of renouncing his role. After some hesitation, the official representatives of Paris and Brussels, who had been openly affronted in March, joined the 100,000 visitors converging from all quarters of the globe. Determined on this occasion to appear respectable, Hitler had given orders to the Nazis to be courteous to foreigners. In the trains, trams and buses, men were to give up their seats to women, 'even if they appeared Jewish'.[1] The new potentates, Göring, Goebbels, Hess and Ribbentrop, entertained the world's grandees lavishly with champagne and caviar. King Boris of Bulgaria, the Crown Prince of Sweden and other Scandinavian princes, Prince Paul of Greece and, in particular, the Prince of Piedmont and Mussolini's sons, ambassadors and ministers, the old wartime leader Lloyd George, the historian Arnold Toynbee, Charles Lindbergh, the conqueror of the Atlantic, and other less illustrious names made the pilgrimage to honour the ex-Viennese tatterdemalion, the man of the 'Night of the Long Knives', the assassin of Dollfuss, the subverter of the European statutes. Fascinated and dazzled, the credulous visitors sang the praises of the new Reich, celebrating its radiant blond youth, its orderliness, the munifence of its leaders. The beautiful Leni Riefenstahl, an actress and cinema scriptwriter, mistakenly thought to be Hitler's mistress enacted a dazzling film, *The Gods of the Stadium*, which was shown all over Europe, contributing further to Hitler's fame.

★　　★　　★

These Grecian games were to be, as enacted in their charter, 'a festival of peace', a short interval in the history of the Thousand Year Reich. For the latter very quickly reverted to its martial predilections. At the beginning of September, the most extravagant display of the cult of National Socialism unfolded in Nuremberg amid the annual rites of the Party Congress. One of the main towns of the Holy Roman

Empire, the old city awoke a romantic chord in the heart of every German. Every year now, hundreds of thousands of men and women came, in hundreds of special trains, from the four quarters of Germany, to blazon forth in blind collective hysteria. Another of Leni Riefenstahl's films, *The Triumph of Will*, still exists, enabling us to recapture the atmosphere, both ordered and frenzied, whilst not devoid of a certain savage beauty, of a liturgy answering to the oldest instincts of the human soul.

Homage to the dead constituted one of the dramatic moments of the solemn ceremony. Hitler's attraction to funerals was well known; they obviously appealed to his morbid apocalyptical '*angst*'. On these occasions, he wore the Party uniform, brown shirt and jacket with the swastika arm-band, sloppy boots, bare-headed or with a peaked cap, which was too high and pulled down to the ears. To the strains of *Deutschland über alles* and the *Horst Wessel Lied*, attended by two ADCs, he would inspect the lines of the SS and SA drawn up in battalions as far as the eye could see. On the granite rostrum, he would then hear the call of the heroes who had died for the Nazi movement. Before the 'blood-stained flag'—relic of the victims of the 1923 *Putsch*—he would stand, a solitary, hierarchical figure, deep in meditation, in the presence of the tense and silent cohorts.

For the man with the Charlie Chaplin moustache, the Party Day provided the occasion for an orgy of eloquence. His harangues, which were veritable oratorical trances, have been described. Frequently delivered at night-fall, generally later than the appointed hour, they thereby increasing the suspense and tension in his audience. After listening to his spate of disjointed but frenzied utterances, the human sea surging at his feet would respond with the ineluctable Nazi litany— 'We salute our Führer. We love our Führer. We belong to our Führer! One people, one nation, one Führer!'

His speeches always followed the same pattern, an introduction with a long recital of the injustices and mortal dangers to which the German people had been subjected, followed by a call for unity and fraternal communion, inspired and directed by 'The Elected One'. The peroration repeated his cast-iron determination to lead the people to the promised land. These philippics often lasted two hours or more— with a remarkable range of tone, from a low, almost wheedling murmur to a stentorian outburst of corncake-like shrieks and cries, accompanied by violent gesticulations which left him foaming at the mouth, in a bath of sweat, breathless and exhausted. All this produced a state of ecstasy, drowning any demands on reason; in the words of the French Ambassador, 'almost convulsionary', a delirium in which hundreds of thousands of voices were raised to the skies in minute-long shrieks of communion with the celebrant, '*Heil, Heil, Heil! Sieg Heil! Sieg Heil!*'

During 1936 something akin to panic seems to have taken possession of the man. He had always been a hypochondriac, but now his fear of illness became acute. A few months before, at the age of 46, when he imagined he had cancer of the throat (one of his permanent obsessions), he drew up his first will and testament. He complained of insomnia, cardiac disorders, eczema and stomach pains. He often interrupted an interview for half an hour or more in order to lie down. His collaborators had the greatest difficulty in obtaining access to him. The most senior of these, and those with urgent problems, often had to wait two or three hours in the ante-chamber, while their master dozed on a sofa, or paced up and down in his study. They found him in a sombre mood, cantankerous, irritated by the slightest contradiction, relying increasingly on astrological or providential guidance.

The doctors who treated his minor nervous complaints were replaced by Dr Morell, a retired venereal disease specialist with a dubious reputation. Adipose and scruffy, he claimed to be the authentic inventor of penicillin which, he contended, the British Secret Service had stolen from him. Hitler, impressed by the mystico-scientific prattle of this charlatan, took him as one of his closest companions. Monell treated him with all manner of drugs and injections, often dangerous ones, some morphine-based and some narcotic. Since the suicide of Geli Raubel, Hitler followed a strictly vegetarian diet, which was supposed to prolong his life. Haunted by the thought of death, which he believed imminent, he feared assassination as much as illness. He was tormented by the rapid passage of the days and wore no wrist-watch; he rarely wound up the old chronometer in his waistcoat pocket.[2]

He felt that time was against him, and he had to act urgently. On 24 August 1936, in spite of the reservations of the General Staff, he increased military service to two years, upgrading the already ambitious plans drawn up during the previous year. His new programme envisaged the mobilisation of 102 divisions by 1940—3,612,000 men, a much larger army than the Kaiser's 2,142,000. Some days later, at the Nuremberg Congress, in a particularly violent diatribe against the Soviets and the Jews, the master of Germany announced a four year economic plan. In an explanatory memorandum, for the benefit of his Ministers, which he had dictated himself (a rare occurrence) he concluded, 'First, the Army must be operational in four years. Second, the German economy must be prepared for war in four years.'

The memorandum remained secret, but Western governments had full knowledge of the plan and its objectives. The Nazi Press gave it wide publicity, with much technical detail. In a speech which made a great stir, Göring proclaimed, 'Some people in the international field are hard of hearing. They will listen only when they hear the guns. We shall have guns. We have no butter, comrades. But I ask you—do you want guns or butter?'

In this way, with complete candour, the Nazi dictator informed the world. This was the man whose 'supreme quality' Lloyd George admired, postulating a man of the same calibre to lead Great Britain; this was the man who had not displeased Eden, whom Laval thought he could bamboozle, whom Halifax and Chamberlain thought they could cajole, whom the 'realists' everywhere imagined they could seduce by affability and patience.

★　　★　　★

The vulgar ostentation of Nazi Germany contrasted with the mystery of the Soviet Union. Nevertheless, a skilfully orchestrated propaganda and a few illustrious visitors, who had been lavishly entertained (among them Bernard Shaw and André Gide), praised the Five Year Plans which, by exposing the aberrations of the famous 'natural laws', enabled the economy to be run for the first time by rational guidance. These intellectual idealists, praising the immense effort which was transforming mediaeval Russia, let themselves be hoodwinked. The liberal German journalist, Emil Ludwig said that he could readily confide the education of his children to Stalin. The English Socialist writer, H. G. Wells, contended that, 'No one is afraid of him and everyone trusts him.'[3] But for the elderly gentlemen who ran the world, Moscow was still the capital of a nether world. Baldwin, Chamberlain, Poincaré, Petain and others, like them, were nineteenth century men. They had grown up during the reign of Queen Victoria and the Czars and were attached by their surroundings and upbringing to the Christian moral code of their youth. Such men could not allow Bolshevism to overthrow all that was for them most sacred—God, Country, Family and Fortune.

Certainly, the enormity of Stalin's crimes (and those of Hitler, particularly after 1940) made these years one of the most hideous periods in a world history that has never been short of atrocities. In Russia, the brutal collectivisation of land between 1928 and 1932 had cost the lives of five million peasants. On 1 December 1934, another thunderbolt struck the Russian people. Serge Kirov, one of the regime's leading personalities, a brilliant orator, a member of the Politburo and the Leningrad Party Secretary, was found lying in a corridor opposite his office in the Smolny Palace, drenched in his own blood, with a bullet in the neck. At his side lay a young Communist named Nikolaev in a faint, a revolver beside him.

How had Nikolaev managed to pass through the closely guarded doors to reach his victim unimpeded? Ever since the elimination of Trotsky, Kirov had been Stalin's only real rival. Had Nikolaev been acting out the orders of the NKVD? Or had he killed Kirov because, as was rumoured, the man was the lover of his wife? The Soviet Press spoke of a 'White Guard plot instigated by a foreign consulate'. The public soon learned that the assassin, with his accomplices, had been tried and executed. Under what conditions, and with which accomplices, we do not know.

The body of Kirov was brought to Moscow and interred with due solemnity. Stalin let it be known that the murder would be avenged. At the same time, the political friends of the murdered man, together with a number of persons who had been in gaol well before his death, were summarily executed. A strange way to avenge! Then in January 1935, Zinoviev and Kamenev, two of the closest companions of Lenin, were condemned with seventeen other Old Bolsheviks (Oppositionists) to terms of from five to twelve years' imprisonment for moral responsibility in the so-called Nikolaev plot. Zinoviev 'confessed' his crime, Kamenev did not. Judged again after a short interval, they were sentenced to a further five years' imprisonment. In August 1936, the Military Tribunal of the Supreme Court of the USSR judged them once again, hauling them out of their gaols, this time in the company of fourteen party dignitaries and a few unknown men accused of being Trotskyist terrorists. After five days of public debate, they were condemned to death and immediately executed. Six months later, a second trial (23–30 January 1937), and again fifteen months later, a third trial (2–13 March 1938) arraigned dozens of the régime's dignitaries. Some were as important as Bukharin, favourite of Lenin; some of them belonged to Stalin's immediate entourage. They were accused of the most extraordinary and heinous crimes. Among these were complicity in the murder of Kirov and other personalities such as Gorki (he had died in 1933, probably poisoned on Stalin's orders);

association with the 'Judas' Trotsky; conspiracy with Hitler and the Emperor of Japan, with a view to re-establishing the capitalist régime. Most of them were condemned to death and executed. Some escaped with long prison sentences; but of these nearly all finished their lives in prison, assassinated like Radek (well known in diplomatic circles), who was found with his skull stove in by a fellow prisoner. The confessions and evidence of the accused, often incoherent and manifestly false, were the only basis for the indictments.

The military men were soon to follow the politicians. On 11 June 1937, the Soviet radio announced that Marshal Tukhachevskii, Vice-Commissar of the People for Defence, Commander-in Chief of the Soviet armies, hero of the civil war, had been arrested with seven other high-ranking officers, and was to appear before a court martial held in camera. Accused of having plotted the disruption of the Red Army, they confessed and were shot. In the following months, thousands of officers of all ranks were executed or sent to concentration camps— some 30–35,000 it was estimated, or one-third of the officers corps, five out of seven Field-Marshals, 90 per cent of the Generals (including most of those who had taken part in the court-martial responsible for the execution of Tukhachevskii), 80 per cent of the colonels, nearly all of them veterans of the civil war. It was a fearful slaughter, more lethal for the officers corps than the Second World War was to be.[4] It caused great consternation in the western capitals, not only because it revived all the horrors inspired by Bolshevism, but also because it posed a most serious question: 'Can the Soviet Union still be a great military power?'

The accusations which led to the execution of Tukhachevskii and thousands of officers (posthumously rehabilitated in the Kruschev era) are still shrouded in mystery. It would appear that Benes, the President of Czechoslovakia, handed over to Stalin a document with information about the Russian military chiefs. What was the source of this 'document'? Did it emanate from the Gestapo, aimed at weakening the Soviet army, as Kruschev was later to allege? Or from the NKVD, which had it 'planted' by a White Russian General, N. V. Skobline, a secret double-agent in the service of the Soviets, while being simultaneously a leading member of the Paris association of Czarist officers, the ROUS? We do not know.*

---

* The President of the ROUS, General Miller, was kidnapped in Paris in September 1937, lured into a trap by Skobline, who was his adjutant. He disappeared, as had his predecessor, General Kuticpof. In 1930, Skobline, who was under suspicion, took flight and was never seen again. His wife, arrested by the French police for complicity, was convicted of espionage for the Soviets and sentenced to twenty years in prison.

When the third trial opened there was great surprise over the finding of Jenrihk Yagoda, the People's Interior Commissar and head of the NKVD, the man who had prepared the condemnation of Zinoviev and Kamanev, amongst the accused. He was detested by the Party leaders, and had no authority save what his master conferred on him. He too ended up before the firing squad.

After Yagoda had been 'purged'—and with him his principal adjutants and hundreds of NKVD agents—he was replaced by Nikolai Yeshov, a deformed dwarf with a reputation for sadism and sexual perversion—another of Stalin's cronies. His nomination in September 1937 was to coincide with what the Russian people call Yeshovchina, the era of the Great Purge. The Soviet Communist Party was ravaged, its 2,900,000 membership in 1935 had fallen to 1,500,000 by 1939. The Politburo, its supreme organ, lost almost all its members. Nearly two-thirds of the Central Committee were liquidated.[5] Yeshov also struck at circles which were completely apolitical—the Universities, artists and writers; ethnic minorities of every race, religion and colour suffered especially—victims of a Russian nationalism which confuted the Soviet claim to universal fraternity. The Ukranians survived, Khruschev stated later, only because there were too many to kill. He should have known; he had been in charge of the Great Purge in his own province. Yeshov himself was to finish punished for punishing others; in his turn, he became an enemy of the People, was arrested and hanged or, it was suggested, struck down in a criminal lunatic asylum.

Those nearest to the Red Czar found no protection from his murderous caprices. Together with two other eminent doctors, he put to death Dr Levin, head of the Kremlin medical services, who had occasionally treated him and his daughter Svetlana. As his personal valet, Stalin employed a certain Pauker, a former Hungarian barber who had become a secret police agent. He alone was allowed to shave the Dictator and cut his hair, amusing Stalin with his clowning and obscene stories. Promoted Head of the Bodyguard and NKVD General, he managed to make himself indispensable. Always at the side of his master, he saw to his well-being, his food and drink—the latter in considerable quantities. He flattered Stalin's vanity by supplying him with padded shoulders in his jackets and boots with high heels, which made Stalin appear more imposing than his small stature warranted. He also procured erotic photographs and drawings, to which the former seminarist was partial.[6] But all these services did not protect him from being accused of spying for Germany and being shot. Many others were struck down, including Alexis Kepler, the first first love of Stalin's daughter, a Jewish cinema scriptwriter who was deported to Siberia because the Marxist dictator disliked the Jews. Stalin's brothers-in-law, Svènidze and Redens, high dignitaries of the régime, were also liquidated, as too, possibly, was his second wife, Nadya Alliluyeva, who was discovered one morning, after a night of drunkenness and violent conjugal altercation, with a bullet in her head.[7]

Amongst the particularly nauseating circumstances surrounding the GreatPurge—without mentioning the tortures to which prisoners were subjected—was a decree extending the death penalty to children from the age of twelve upward. Another decree (which was unpublished) enacted the collective responsibility of the family for every individual accused of treason; this led innumerable innocent people to the gallows or the concentration camp. When Field Marshall Tukhachevskii died before the firing squad, his wife and brother were also put to death, while his mother, his daughter, a divorced wife and three sisters were incarcerated. When General Jakir, Commander of the Ukrainian Military District, was executed, his wife, brother, brother-in-law, nephew and other relations suffered the same fate. Only his son, aged fourteen, survived; but only to spend long years in prison and the Arctic camps. There were thousands of others.

The prisons were overcrowded, the concentration camps (called 'labour camps' as in Germany) proliferated, from the outskirts of Moscow to the far reaches of Siberia. The internees were crammed together in appalling unhygienic conditions, under-nourished, inadequately clad, forced to the hardest labour in temperatures often below $-25°C$ or above $35°C$, under the supervision of common criminals and brutal, sadistic gaolers. At the same time, millions of anonymous persons, as well as those well known abroad, members of the Politburo and the Central Committee, People's Commissars, ambassadors, generals, scientists, doctors, writers and Commintern agents, disappeared—in the words of Solzhenitsyn 'buried naked in a common ditch, without a coffin, only a ticket attached to one of their toes'.

The world had to wait until the death of Stalin to hear Khruschev's famous speech at the 20th Communist Party Congress, an official voice which described the fantastic peripeties of the sanguinary madman, 'The Greatest of the Greats'. In all, four to five hundred thousand people shot; at least five million swallowed up in the 'Gulags', perhaps ten to twelve million, of whom, according to serious historians, two-thirds perished.* 'One death is a tragedy,' said Stalin, 'A million deaths is a statistic.'

★   ★   ★

While this savage terror ravaged the Soviet people, Moscow made great efforts to extricate itself from its diplomatic isolation. Sergei Kirov had led an oppostition alarmed by the rebirth of Japanese and German imperialism. He had been killed, almost certainly at the behest of Stalin; but the Dictator could not entirely ignore the process set in motion. In 1934, the Soviet Union had joined the League of Nations. Pacts of mutual assistance with France and Czechoslovakia dated from 1935. In that year, while the purges were raging, the USSR gave itself a constitution guaranteeing public liberties, 'the most democratic constitution in the world'. In the same year, the 7th Congress of the Comintern overturned the resolution of 1928, which had confirmed the old anathema against Social Democracy.† It decided unanimously (as always) to adopt a new strategy, that of the *Front Commun* or *Front Populaire*. Instead of vituperating *en masse* against the 'Imperialist instigators of war', the agents of the Communist International limited themselves to denouncing the 'Fascist aggressors'. In Asia, as in Europe, they concentrated on regrouping the Left—all the Lefts.

In France from 1920, Leon Blum's party had been the principal target for their attacks. 'The most faithful supporters of the bourgeoisie', almented Thorez in 1928 (after the 7th Congress of the Comintern). 'It supports by every possible means the ideological and material preparation of an imperialist war . . . it takes up a position on the side of the owners against the claims of the workers.'[8] In 1928, the Social Democrats were the enemy to strike down. In 1935, the same Thorez suddenly became the fervent champion of the unity of all democratic forces.

Who was this 'Son of the People', the title of an autobiography published at the pinnacle of his career? Born at the turn of the century, the natural son of the daughter of a miner and fostered by another miner, his first years in the mining villages of *le Nord*, in a united family, were poor but not wretched. Quite young, Thorez inclined

---

* In the nineteenth century, the odious Czsarist secret police executed some dozens of political prisoners; some hundreds, or at the worst thousands, died in prison or exile.

† In Germany, in particular, the refusal of the Communists to vote in the Reichstag with the Social Democrats allowed Hitler to obtain the Parliamentary majority without which he would probably not have acceded to power.

towards revolutionary action, first as a Trotskyist, before marrying the niece of a leading Communist and submitting to the official line of the Party (which he was to follow throughout his life, in all its sinuosities). At the age of twenty-eight, his zeal was to be rewarded by nomination to the Executive Committee of the Comintern, before which he displayed the most abject docility and which, in return, elevated him to the highest posts. Meanwhile Moscow had imposed on him a guardian angel, the mysterious 'Comrade Clement', a Czech whose real name was Eugen (or Desider) Fried.*

A strange tandem! The tall, slim Czech with the saturnine expression, was an ex-chemist who had become a permanent agent of the Comintern, which he had served on various secret missions, in Czechoslovakia (where he had done a spell in prison), in Belgium and Germany. He had the reputation of being a lover of fine books and antiques; he was always elegantly dressed, affecting a grey felt hat and a long dark cloak, carrying an ivory-headed knobstick—an idealist and enthusiastic intellectual. The Frenchman, on the other hand, was restless, cunning, calculating and not without vanity, but despite an awkward, stolid appearance, also over-sensitive; on one occasion, when reprimanded by the Soviet Secretary of the Comintern, in full session, he broke down in sobs.

It was in the backwash of the Stavinsky Affair that the new policy of the Comintern had made itself felt in France. On 6 February 1934, on the morning of the riot, *L'Humanité*, still faithful to the old 'line', called on its militants to demonstrate alongside the League 'against the Fascist bands, against the government . . . against Social Democracy, which enfeebles the working-class by dividing it . . .' On 7 and 8 February, the newspaper of the French Communist Party continued on these terms; Thorez still rebuffed the advances of Blum. But by 9 February, all had changed. Suddenly, the Party Bureau demanded fraternal friendship with the old Socialist enemies. On the 12 February, the boulevards witnessed an explosion of popular rejoicing at the amalgamation of the forces of the Left.

This sudden *volte-face* has never been properly explained. Thorez was not present at the decisive meeting of the Party Bureau on 9 February. He had disappeared the evening before without informing anyone— not even his mistress, who had been waiting for him in vain at their *rendezvous*, a Métro station. He was away for a month. When

---

*Fried was assassinated almost under the eyes of Madame Thorez in Brussels in 1943—officially a victim of the Gestapo, more probably of the Soviet Secret Service.

he resurfaced, he had been converted. The conversion seemed a bit slow—too slow for the Comintern, which chided him, demanding from him, 'unity of action at all costs'.[9] On 27 July, the two workers' parties signed a pact of collaboration. With the first hurdle cleared, the 'United Front' offered participation to the 'Radicals', the bourgeois Reform Party. The Communists had no difficulty in transforming themselves into defenders of the middle classes, their only enemies now being the 'oligarchies', the 'two hundred families'.*

They even abandoned their traditional anti-militarism when Laval, by signing a Franco-Soviet pact, obtained Stalin's agreement to the French defence policy. If Thorez and his friends did not yet speak of 'Eurocommunism', they were the first to enunciate its principles. 'The destiny of France,' he stated, 'will not be determined in any foreign capital, not even in Moscow'. He went further, holding out a hand to the Catholics praising the 'progressive role' they had played in the Middle Ages!

On 14 July 1935, the *Assises de la Paix et de la Liberté* were celebrated in Paris. After a mammoth parade at the Bastille, Daladier Blum and Thorez, in the presence of hundreds of thousands of Parisians, took the oath, 'to defend this day which recalls the first victory of the Republic, and the democratic liberties won by the people of France—to give bread to the workers, work to the young, and to the world the great peace of humanity'. This was followed by the elaboration of a common programme. It contained nothing revolutionary: the defence of Republican institutions, a plan for grandiose public works, the stabilisation of agricultural prices and reform of the Banque de France to withdraw it from the control of the financial oligarchy (the two hundred families) who had run it since its creation. No nationalisation measures were included—with the sole exception of the armaments industry. In foreign policy, they advocated the consolidation of collective security, the imposition of sanctions on aggressor states and confirmation of the Defence pacts. Curiously, the common programme did not envisage paid holidays, nor the 40-hour week, which were to be its principal achievements. On the first Sunday

---

* The evolution of the Chinese Communist Party on the other side of the globe had been identical. In July/August 1935 Mao Tse-tung changed position, calling for the union of all democratic forces. 'Our struggle is against imperialism and feudalism, not against capitalism,' he said. 'The Socialist revolution—that is a task for the future'. In December 1936 Chiang Kai-shek, who had been taken prisoner at Sian, and threatened with death by a rebel general, was saved by Chou-En-lai. The incident gave birth to the 'Anti-Japanese National Front'.[10]

of May, the *Front Populaire* won the election, with a swing in its favour of 5 per cent of the votes, following the usual alternation of parties in a Parliamentary regime (in England, 'The Law of Buggins's Turn'). The real victors were the Socialists and Communists. With 146 seats, the former became the principal party in France, the latter doubled its voices, going from 30 seats to 72. For the firts time, universal suffrage designated, in an unexpected manner, the leader of the Socialist party as President of the Council. For the first time Leon Blum, aged sixty-four, came to power.

CHAPTER 10

The Popular Fronts

Ramsay MacDonald, Franklin Roosevelt and Leon Blum were the principal figures who represented the Ciceronian ideal of 'the tenderness which binds the human race' between the two World Wars. In 1936, MacDonald, who had come round rather early to conformism, had sunk into senility. Roosevelt had immured himself in America. While Hitler and Mussolini were blustering, Blum alone held in his frail hands the promise of a less violent world.[1]

He was born on 9 April 1872 in the rue Saint-Denis, Paris, in a modest apartment above the family shop; it was almost in the shadow of the church of Saint-Eustache where, during the Revolution, the famous Cult of Reason had been celebrated—and not far from the synagogue, where the Blum family performed the religious duties of their faith. His father, Abraham Blum, a native of Alsace, had come to Paris in 1845 at the end of Louis Philippe's reign. He married Marie Picart, whose mother kept a small bookshop patronised by lawyers and students. Abraham (who was to call himself Auguste) was now able to take over the small shop, 'Silks and Velvets', in which, for fifteen years, he had worked as an employee. His business prospered, assuring a comfortable existence for the household and his five sons. Auguste was a good-natured man, a lover of flowers and music; he is reported to have invented the opera hat. Marie was more cultivated and original, with a passion for justice, 'meticulous about it', recounted Leon Blum, who was very close to her.

After benefiting from the best educational system in the world, Leon Blum, *licencié en droit*, came second in 1895 in the examination for the Conseil d'État, one of the most prestigious bodies in the Republic. He remained there for twenty-four years, gaining the reputation of a wise and upright jurist. The Law was one of his vocations. The other, for him the more important, was literature. Essayist and journalist, he became one of the prominent figures in the world of letters. His principal works are *Du Marriage* (1907), and *Stendhal et le Beylisme* (1914). The first is an indictment of the stifling and oppressive manners of the contemporary bourgeois society. *Stendhal* is an auto-biographical essay on the happiness a man can find in the pursuit of an ideal, although well aware that it is unattainable. Married, the father of a contented family, Blum was not without his problems. Although he had abandoned the faith of his fathers, he remained very conscious of his Jewish origin. At the same time, he wanted to be as completely French as those around him. This required constant adjustment, which was not always easy.

Among his close friends was Lucien Herr, the Marxist librarian of the Ecole Normale. Leon Blum was drawn to Socialism when he became aware of human suffering at the age of fourteen. 'It was Herr', he wrote, 'who crystalised all the different tendencies in me. It is to him that I owe a profound reorientation of my individual and anarchical conception of Socialism.' However, more than a doctrine, this was to remain a generous disposition in him. 'He is a Socialist', wrote the writer Martin du Gard (who was not one), 'because he hates war, oppression by the powerful, deceit—in a word, violence.'[2]

It was also Lucien Herr who, in 1896, introduced Blum to Jean Jaures, Professor of Philosophy at Toulouse and a member of the *Chambre des Députés*, then well on his way to becoming one of the leading figures of the European workers' movement. It was a decisive encounter. For eighteen years, until the day upon which Jaures fell beneath the bullets of a madman, he and Blum were inseparable. The trio made Blum's apartment, where he lunched several times a week, 'his restaurant, his library, his laundry and his bath house'. In the young man he found a pupil and a friend whose sharp intelligence was a fount of knowledge. For his part, the young man found in the older the elementary powerful inspiration necessary for his 'delicate sensibility'. In 1906, they founded *L'Humanité*, which became one of the principal journals of European Socialism, until the Communists managed to take it over.

Jaures was assassinated on 31 July 1914. Some days later, when the first battlefields were covered with the dead and dying, Blum, the pacifist preacher, came down from his ivory tower, and issued a call to arms. As in Germany, Great Britain and Belgium, a deep-rooted instinct swept aside all the ideologies; the rally to *La Patrie* was instantaneous. When the aged Jules Guesde, a veteran of the Commune and a former anarchist, became the principal figure of the

Socialist Party, Leon Blum appeared to be the spiritual heir of Jaures. With the return of peace, the way ahead for him was clear. He left the *Conseil d'État* for the Paris bar, and entered Parliament. At the famous Tours Congress in the following year, impelled by some interior force, he felt incapable of following the old party leaders who had rallied to the Third International of Moscow. This was the great schism, a disaster, it seemed, for the moderates. The militants joined the new Communist Party *en masse*, bringing with them their subscriptions, their newspaper and their organisation. Nevertheless, in the 1924 elections they obtained only 10 seats in the *Chambre*, while the Socialists had 105, two more than in 1914. When Jules Guesde died in 1922, Leon Blum became the natural leader of one of France's principal parties.

His success was in part due to the 'Cartel of the Left', the electoral alliance he had made with the Radicals. Logically, the victors, following the lead of the voters, should have together formed the government. Many Socialists favoured this. But not Blum; he was already in the blind alley where he would later be trapped—faced with the impossible choice between dictatorship of the proletariat and classical capitalism. By temperament a reformer, he persevered in his revolutionary rhetoric; by refusing on the grounds of his ideology, 'his sacred treasure', to govern with the Radical party, he forced the latter to look to the Right. It is true that, in the 1932 elections, 130 Socialists entered the *Chambre*, but nearly a third of them rose against the 'orthodox verbalism' of their leader, and his systematic refusal to join a government. They soon broke away and founded the *Parti Socialiste Français*. But Leon Blum still pursued his course.

'Leon Blum does not know, he is always searching, groping, he has too much intelligence and too little personality', wrote André Gide, one of his close friends.[3] Nearing the top, he continued to 'search and grope', divided between his religion of humanity, and the thought system by which he wished to rationalise it. In 1936 he was at the head of the government, a figure of outstanding distinction, not concerned with 'a radiant crown', but a Stoic impregnated with classical wisdom, a good, peaceable man, loving his family, his country and the human race. But was he also endowed with inspired intuition, that divine spark, that peerless quality of the great leaders of men?

★   ★   ★

Shortly after the electoral victory of the *Front Populaire*, and well before the formation of his ministry, the 'sit-in strikes' began, characterised by the permanent occupation of the factories. On 1 June, there were more than a million strikers, a high figure but, in terms of the six or seven million industrial workers, a minority. Most witnesses confirm this: a sudden outburst after several unhappy years, there was nothing revolutionary about it. In any case, the workers were not politically motivated; only 200,000 had joined the Communists, who, under the orders of the Comintern, accepted as much as anyone else at this time the laws of democracy. On the other hand, Blum and Thorez were the disciples of neither Lenin nor Trotsky.[4]

Scrupulously following the rules of the Constitution, Leon Blum did not form his government until 4 June, and then without the Communists who, while promising their support, refused to participate in it. The strikers, in spite of their peaceful mood, exercised an irresistible pressure. On 7 June, a Sunday, the delegates of the owners and of the Trade Unions met at the Hotel Matignon in the presence of the head of the government, the first meeting of its kind in the history of France. On the same day, towards midnight, in an atmosphere of mutual understanding, agreements were signed granting salary increases of from 7 to 15 per cent, extending Trades Union liberties and recognising collective work contracts. In the following weeks, Blum obtained from Parliament the principal articles of his programme, to which he had appended paid holidays (15 days), and a 40 hour week. The workers gradually began to evacuate the factories and to return to work. By the end of June, the situation had almost returned to normal.

With the same energy, the government undertook the modernisation of the armed forces, which had been seriously affected by the economies of the previous years. In September, following the German decision to increase military service to two years, the government obtained a vote in the *Chambre* for doubling the strength of the armed forces, between 1936 and 1940. This would absorb almost one-third of the Budget, an effort, in view of the financial difficulties, not far short of heroic.* The three departments, War, Air and Marine, were regrouped in a Ministry of National Defence under the authority of Daladier. Unfortunately, the structural reforms stopped here. Although the disaster of the Rhineland had indicated the overwhelming need for a re-examination in depth of defence problems, the President of the Council, lacking courage or vision, did not heed it.

---

* The military expenditure represents 16.1 per cent of the French budget in 1987.

He received Colonel de Gaulle, whose writings were beginning to be read, and listened to him attentively. Nothing came of it, and the benumbed General Gamelin—'the old woman', his officers called him—was not disturbed.

How to explain the failure of the 'Blum experience'? His government had inherited a disastrous situation, comparable with that which Roosevelt had found three years earlier when he entered the White House. Laval, by his fidelity to the gold standard, and his policy of savage deflation, had led the economy to the brink of disaster: falling production, excessive imports, disequilibrium of the balance of payments and a serious budgetary deficit; the flight of capital had begun. The gold reserves of 80 milliards of francs had fallen to less than 60 milliards in September 1936. Like Roosevelt, Blum perceived the principal cause of the stagnation, announcing that the authority of the State, 'must operate not to reduce production, but to support consumption'. He put all his hopes in a revival obtained, as in America, by an increase in purchasing power. The revival failed because Blum's 'monetary patriotism' retarded the indispensable devaluation for months. The economist Sauvy stated that 'The fundamental obstacle to economic recovery was that French prices were higher than foreign ones. It is useless to increase demand if this involves more imports.'[5] At the end of summer, that summer so full of hope, exports were falling again, production was contracting and higher prices had eroded the increase of salaries. The crisis had followed the classical evolution, to end what was then its natural paroxysm: the flight of capital.

In September Blum had resigned himself to devaluation—too late and too little—in a framework of financial agreements with London and Washington, the first agreement of its kind. Almost immediately, industrial production was stimulated (10 per cent in two months), exports increased, unemployment declined and gold and capital began to surge back.* It was a brief respite because it was thwarted by an accumulation of economic and monetary mistakes due as much to incompetence as to ideology. They were responsible for severe inflation (28 per cent between September and January), a diminution of purchasing power and a new wave of strikes. Production slowed down and the number of unemployed increased again. The haemorrhage of capital returned, more acute than before, aggravated by the dis-

---

*The economic revival in the autumn of 1936 invalidates the facile and often advanced theory of the 'capitalist plot' against the *Front Populaire*.

heartening fiasco of the 'Universal Exhibition'.* By the spring of 1937, the crisis had returned in all its severity. Leon Blum, the captive of his dilemma, revolution or orthodoxy, refusing the first was obliged to return to the second. He announced 'The Pause', in other words classical deflation, which had failed everywhere else, and which was to fail again in France.

Not without contradicting himself, Blum had been greatly attracted by the New Deal. 'By watching Roosevelt in action', he said, 'France has an example to follow. We should do so, adapting it to the conditions and resources of our country.' Although the leader of the *Front Populaire* lacked the genius of his American model, the disarray caused by his setback must not make us forget the progress he had made when he took office. The *Chambre* adopted, with a majority much larger than those of the governmental parties, social improvements whose humane nature appealed to most thinking men and women. The law for paid holidays was passed unanimously. The Cardinals and Bishops—not exactly men of the Left at that time—issued a Pastoral Letter in October calling for Christian fraternity, charity and reason. This amounted to approval of the *Front Populaire* reforms.

They were not the only ones who approved. Besides Bertrand de Jouvenel, who had come over from Radicalism, there were genuine Socialists like Brossolette, progressive Catholics like Mounier, and even Fascists like Drieu La Rochelle. 'Everybody wanted the same thing', wrote Claude Roy, then a member of the extreme Left, 'a Socialism which is not like the Soviet brand, a national Socialism which will confront National Socialism, a Communism which is strong but not dictatorial.' Maurice Duverger, then on the extreme Right, stated, 'In the twilight of a world . . . this light occasionally causes the demon of the evening to be bright.' In his unforgettable style, General de Gaulle summed up the situation, 'In the troubled times through which the nation was passing, and which politics framed in an electoral and parliamentary combination entitled *Front Populaire*, there was, so it seemed to me, a psychological element which could enable it to overcome passivity.'[6]

Among the great achievements of the *Front Populaire* were the paid holidays. Unknown before to the French workers, they had existed for some time in the totalitarian states. Today, we no longer think

---

* Announced with a great fanfare and inaugurated ceremonially, when it was still only a muddy building site, it seemed to confirm the incompetence of the government, and rebounded to its discredit.

about them, they have become a part of ordinary life; but they are a fundamental liberty, the right to be one's own master for several weeks, a great boon for millions of men and women. Among innumerable expressions of joy and gratitude, Leon Blum published a letter from an old unnamed worker, which said, 'Thank you! Owing to you, I have been able to see the sea before I die.'

★   ★   ★

Compared with the rest of Europe, Spain had been a backward country for centuries. The big landlords, the Army and the Church benefited from privileges comparable to those which they had enjoyed in France before 1789. Spain was 72 per cent agricultural, of which more than half the land belonged to the privileged 1 per cent. The domains of the Duke of Alba were almost as extensive as the area of Belgium; 40 million peasants did not possess an acre. The rural economy was very primitive. It was without machinery, lacked irrigation and, preferring pasture to cultivation, produced only one harvest a year. The industrial proletariat was no better off. The number of illiterates was 45 per cent, the highest in Europe (Portugal excepted). In Madrid alone, 45,000 children were without schooling. The world economic crisis had reduced three-quarters of the Spanish population to indescribable poverty.

Abuses abounded. The Army, with 219 Generals and 14,000 officers (more than three times the numbers in the German Army at the time of Versailles), absorbed a quarter of the national budget. The Catholic Church, with more than 100,000 monks and nuns, most of them salaried by the State, possessed vast territories and considerable interests in banking and industry. It exercised an almost complete monopoly of education and, of course, of religion. The Holy Inquisition was not abolished until the collapse of the monarchy in 1931.

The young liberal Republic had been confronted with enormous problems: a failed military *coup d'état* in Madrid and Seville in 1932; a rebellion in Catalonia; a miners' uprising in the Asturias in 1934. A climate of perpetual anarchy prevailed. In the 1936 elections, the combined parties of the Left in the *Fronte Popular* had a majority in the *Cortes*. It was not a revolutionary coalition—formed of only 14 Communists, 85 Socialists and 157 moderate Republicans of various shades. Facing them were 140 Deputies of the Right and Centre. Unrest continued. The Falangists on the extreme Right, and the anarchists on the extreme Left, committed a series of abhorrent excesses. It was said that more than 100 churches were destroyed or pillaged. There were multiple political murders, priests assassinated, nuns raped and repeated strikes. At the doors of the *Cortes*, ushers frisked Deputies to ensure that they were not carrying arms. The time was ripe for a *coup d'état*. The Generals were preparing it.

On Saturday 18 July 1936, the evening papers announced a *pronunciamento*. After this the storm broke, degenerating into civil war. In Madrid, the leader of the rebellion, General Fanjol, committed the fatal error of shutting himself up in the Montana barracks. Besieged by the Left militia, subjected to fire for five hours from two pieces of artillery drawn by a beer wagon, he had to capitulate. Many officers were massacred on the spot, others were thrown out of upstairs windows to be despatched on the street. There was a horrifying spectacle in the armoury, a dozen officers spread-eagled on the ground, bullet wounds in their heads, revolvers in their hands; they had committed suicide to avoid surrender. The capital had remained in the hands of a ministry of the Left Centre, presided over by Jose Ginal, a moderate Republican and a chemist by profession. Nevertheless, the militias already dominated the streets. Immense portraits of Lenin were hoisted on the façades in public places. Fifty churches were set on fire.

It appeared that the military coup had failed. But not for long. In Seville, General Queipo de Llano, assisted only by an ADC, managed to rouse the garrison and take possession of the town. The same happened in Cadiz and Algeciras. From Saragossa, Pampéluna, Burgos and Valladolid, which had fallen to the rebels, columns of soldiers and 'Falangists' in blue shirts moved off in the direction of Madrid.

The deciding factor was the entry of the Spanish zone of Morocco on their side. General Franco, in exile in Teneriffe, escaped in a private aeroplane, a Dragon Rapide, hired from an English firm. Having to stop over at Agadir and Casablanca, towns under the French Protectorate, he wore civilian clothes and carried a forged diplomatic passport. Two young English beauties completed the *mise-en-scène*. After passing the night quietly in Casablanca, he went on to Tetuan where the insurgents welcomed him exultantly. There he found 30,000 mercenaries, those of the *Tercia*, the Spanish Foreign Legion and the *Regulares*, the Moors of the native regiments commanded by a hardened old warrior, General Astray, well known for his absurd war-cry, *Viva el Muerte*! (Long Live Death!)

For several days Franco had to mark time. The sailors of the Fleet, having shot their officers, or thrown them into the sea, were in control of most of the warships and blocked the sea routes. On 30 July 1936, a few antiquated Breguets bombed the Republican vessels anchored in the port of Malaga. The demoralised crews, without officers, refused to go to sea. By air or boat, the Moroccan regiments crossed the straits. On 6 August, the future Caudillo installed his headquarters in Seville. With his African mercenaries, he was soon the uncontested leader of the insurrection. As we now know, he led it to its conclusion with pitiless resolution. Starting in the first weeks of the rebellion, 40,000 Republicans in all, including six generals, were executed. On the other side 75,000 rebels—or putative rebels—were killed by partisans of the government.[7] For three years, the Spaniards fought one another with unparalleled ferocity. Certainly, the poor and the rich; but also the regionalists and the centralists, the Trades Unions and the military, the free-thinkers and the Catholics. When the guns finally fell silent, nearly a million dead had been interred, 'in the great cemeteries beneath the moon'.

★   ★   ★

When the first fighting broke out on 20 July 1936, an uncoded telegram had arrived at the Presidency of the Council in Paris, 'Surprised by dangerous military coup. Ask to consult with a view immediate furnishing arms and ammunition. Fraternally Giral'. The request was in no way irregular, Franco-Spanish agreements signed by Laval in 1935 envisaged the provision of war material to the Iberian Republic. After consulting Daladier and Delbos, the Ministers concerned, Blum promised 20 aeroplanes, 8 75 mm field guns, 50 machine-guns, 1,000 rifles and the ammunition demanded. Shortly after this, political circles were plunged into a state of frenzied excitement. On 23 July *L'Echo de Paris*, having been informed by the Spanish Military Attaché, reported the promises made to Madrid. In *L'Action Française* Maurras, with his customary vehemence, wrote an article entitled, 'Blum is leading us to war'. For once in full agreement with him, all the Right, a large section of the Radicals, and even several Socialist Ministers, showed hostility to engaging the country in a cause which, in the early days, seemed a dead-end.

It is said that Leon Blum was so discouraged that he wanted to resign and that only the urgent requests of the Spanish Republican leaders dissuaded him. It might have been so, but only briefly. Already, by 25 July 1936, at a Council of Ministers convened in urgency, far from recommending help to Madrid, he regarded himself as a referee. The Government decided not to involve the State—while allowing the private sector the freedom to sell arms to Spain. On 1 August a second meeting took place, for new factors had emerged. Three big Savoia-

Marchetti hydroplanes, painted white with no national markings, had made forced landings in French territory on the African coast. When the survivors, Italian military and civil personnel, were arrested for breaking the rules of aerial navigation, they admitted being part of a squadron sent by Rome to help the rebels.* Another important factor was that Baldwin's government being firmly neutral, had unequivocally indicated its desire to be followed by Paris. Drawn up by the Quai d'Orsay, a European pact for controlled 'non-intervention' appeared to Blum the only way of reconciling the various moral and political exigencies of the situation. A majority of the Ministers, including several Socialists, agreed. While waiting for it to come into effect, Paris delivered important quantities of war material to Republican Spain. A week later, in response to urgent demands from London, a decree forbade this.

One by one, the powers subscribed to non-intervention. An international commission, based in London, was to organise its mechanism, define the frontier controls, supervise the arms embargo and prevent the recruitment of foreign volunteers. Very soon, like the Conference of Disarmament and the sanctions against Italy, non-intervention was transformed into a disgraceful sham. The Germans, Italians and Portuguese on one side and the Soviets on the other, sent massive aid—the French slightly less.

The Duce was the more cynical. Without any precise object, but hungry for easy glory, he came down completely on the side of General Franco. The Ethiopian war had given him exquisite agony, the inexpressible delights of those who gamble for high stakes. Why should he give them up? In December a first detachment of Black Shirts, 3,000 men, disembarked at Cadiz at the same moment that Mussolini—God knows why, perhaps due to a deep-rooted reflex of wisdom—signed a gentlemen's agreement with Great Britain, confirming the *status quo* in the Mediterranean. 'Mussolini is always right!' announced the walls of the Italian cities—and he had persuaded himself that this was true. 'Don't contradict me!', he reprimanded one of his Ministers. 'You disconcert me. I know that my animal instinct is never wrong.'[8] An inveterate gambler, incapable of limiting his losses, he continually increased the stakes. By June 1937, he had put 50,000 men, 250,000 rifles, 2000 guns, 750 aeroplanes and several thousand machine-guns, in all about a third of the resources of the Italian Army, at the disposal

---

* The survivors were condemned, in spite of the protests of Rome, to a month in prison, and a conditional fine of 200 francs.

of Franco, who had not asked for so much. In the aftermath of the Ethiopian campaign—where, moreover, the fighting was not yet completely over—it was a gesture out of all proportion to his means and one which the Spanish were never to repay.*

Simultaneously with the adventures on the battlefield, Mars was sacrificing to Venus. The new Caesar had fallen desperately in love, perhaps for the first time in his life, with the voluptuous Clara Petacci, thirty years his junior. In the midst of all the European crises, it was a silly infatuation between the chest-thumping Dictator, violent and jealous, but secretly ill (his stomach ulcer was extremely painful), and the simple little woman with the cropped black hair, the grey-green eyes and the generous bosom. Like a love-sick schoolboy, he telephoned her at all hours. He wanted daily contact on her constant presence in the audience at the opera or at official ceremonies, in order to receive her admiring glances. Soon he had her installed in the Palazzo Venezia in an apartment, a short distance from the Mappemondo Room, where he paid her homage in the intervals of giving audiences to Ministers and Ambassadors.[10]

Hitler, who was not in love, was more discreet.† Displaying once again his tactical ability, which contrasted so strangely with the deliriums of his long-term objectives, he had calculated his part in the Spanish intervention most carefully. Operation *Magic Fire* involved the despatch to Spain of the Condor legion, a group of bomber planes, fighters, a reconnaissance squadron and anti-aircraft units, supported by an army unit and a battalion of armoured vehicles, about 10,000 men—'tourists', as they were blandly described by the German diplomats. While helping Franco these 'tourists' gave the Wehrmacht battle-experience and prepared the ground for an economic agreement by which the Reich could obtain minerals, the copper, iron and tungsten which its war industry desperately lacked.

Above all, it was the destablisation of Europe, and the consolidation of his ties with Mussolini which the Führer had in view at this time. In fact, the Duce, who had been horrified by Hitler in Venice in 1934, and who had sided with his adversaries at Stresa in 1935, began to yield to his entreaties in 1936. Was not the German the only one

---

* Some of this material was later sold secretly to the Yugoslav government by Franco.[9]

† Nevertheless, it is a curious fact that, in that same summer of 1936, Hitler installed the young Eva Braun (with whom he had been having a clandestine liaison), permanently in his chalet at Berchtesgaden.

among his peers to encourage his fanciful plans? Count de Kerchove, the Belgian Ambassador in France (and later in Italy) reported with clairvoyance, 'The situation of Mussolini with regard to Hitler has something truly tragic about it because by instinct, by nature and by temperament he is irresistably and inevitably drawn to the German, almost all of whose views he shares. In spite of himself, he is condemned to love and hate his emulator and disciple simultaneously.'[11] It was to fall to Ciano, Mussolini's son-in-law and Minister of Foreign Affairs, to prepare the union of the two regimes.

Ciano was a commonplace character. A good family man, generous towards his friends, he was not really evil. Cultivated, clever, capable of charming and not without intelligence but of inordinate vanity, he was a sensualist, avid for personal advancement and without principles. He became a Fascist because he was born in Italy; in Germany he would have become a Nazi; in the Soviet Union, a Communist. Completely amoral, he liked amusing his friends by describing how, as an airman in Ethiopia with his squadron, the *Disperata*, he winkled out enemy soldiers concealed in the high bush of the savana. 'A first burst of machine-gun fire, and they think they have been seen. They rush out of their hiding places and run in all directions. Then you can spot them easily and make short work of them.' Was this extreme frivolity? Ambassador Guariglia, when he was appointed as Italian Ambassador to France, ironically relates the story of an interview he had with Ciano on the eve of his departure in 1938:

Me: What am I to do in Paris?

Ciano: Nothing.

Me: That will be difficult, but I will do my best.

Ciano was a typical product of his time—an adept at Machiavellism for whom politics was simply pillage. He considered the disappearance of Austria to be 'disagreeable but inevitable'—the demise of Czechoslavakia, Switzerland and Belgium would follow.[12]

Personal success was the beacon of Ciano's existence. As the guardian of that beacon was the Duce, he attached himself to the Dictator's fortunes—not without conspiring to take his place. His valuable secret diaries, published after the war, are effusively flattering to the Duce (to whom he doubtless showed them). However, as the Second World War was approaching, he was far-sighted enough to point out the dangers as well as the advantages of neutrality. That lucidity did not prevent him from following his father-in-law on his insane course—until the day on which he finally revolted and was shot, on

the Duce's orders, one glacial morning in November 1944, in a moat
in Verona.

In October, 1936, Galeazzo Ciano, in the full flush of his success,
returned the visits of German ministers to Rome in Berlin and Berchtesgaden. At the Berghof, inspired perhaps by the magnificent scenery
of the Bavarian Alps, the Führer let himself go for several hours in
one of those vaticinatory harangues so dear to him. He expatiated on
sharing out the planet between Rome and Berlin, and on his plans for
eastern conquest, promising Mussolini ('the greatest man in the
world') the Mediterranean and Africa. Intoxicated by his rhetoric, the
young Ciano signed a secret agreement with him. It was, in fact,
extremely vague. Nevertheless, several days later, in an emotional
speech in Milan, the Duce alluded to a Rome–Berlin axis around
which the world would rotate. Although people were not fully aware
of it, the destiny of Europe was sealed.

★   ★   ★

About to fall in September, Madrid continued miraculously to hold
out. While the rebel regime in Burgos, under the presidency of General
Franco, benefited from the massive aid bestowed in Berlin, Rome
and Lisbon (Salazar put 20,000 men at his disposal), the Spanish
Republic received the more modest support from France and the
USSR. Before the non-intervention pact came into force, some 50
French fighter planes had crossed the Pyrenees; there were to be
200 in all. They were followed by artillery, machine-guns, rifles and
ammunition. The French authorities also facilitated the transit of large
quantities of Soviet material, when the Spanish ports were blocked.
Unloaded at Dunkirk, Boulogne or elsewhere, they were transported
in sealed convoys, escorted by specially selected customs officials,
to the Pyrenean frontier posts.

After a hesitant start, the intervention of the USSR had increased.
Bombers and fighter planes, some 300 it was thought; armoured
vehicles, technicians and airmen, about 2,000, made their appearance
on the battlefield. But these figures did not reflect accurately the
true scale of the Soviet involvement. From August on, an enormous
Russian Embassy, headed by Marcel Rosenberg and General Berzin,
was installed in Madrid. The former had been Ambassador in London,
an experienced diplomat, but without any real authority. Ian Antonovich Berzin was a more outstanding personality. A Latvian, the leader
of a band of partisans at the age of 16 during the 1905 uprising, he
had been wounded and taken prisoner; condemned to death, he had

been spared on account of his youth. Deported to Siberia, he escaped and lived in hiding. In 1917, he had joined the Red Army and advanced his career rapidly as the aide of the future Marshal Voroshilov. Head of counter-espionage on the General Staff, he had been chosen by Stalin himself to organise and direct the armed forces of the Spanish Republic. One day, not far distant, his mission accomplished, he was to be recalled to disappear, like Rosenberg and so many others, probably before a firing squad.

His task had been immense. Two-thirds of the Spanish Army, its 14,000 officers (all but 200), and two-thirds of the *Guardia Civile* had defected to the rebels. Berzin had to place the celebrated 'International Brigade' on a war footing. It was an autonomous force which had recruited some 40,000 men, of whom the majority were Communists of various nationalities—10,000 French, 3,000 Belgians, as many Americans, 2,000 English, Yugoslavs, Scandinavians, Italians and German refugees—but no Russians. Recruited by Comintern agents (among them Tito, in Paris, then called Josip Broz), subjected to an iron discipline, the men of the Brigade, the bravest of the Republican soldiers, were also—willingly or under pressure—the Praetorian Guard of the Communist Party. 10,000 of them were never to return (among them a friend of mine, Brachet, a young Social-Democrat lawyer, who had joined up to defend Liberty—and only Liberty!).

Another entirely Communist corps was the 'Fifth Regiment', 8–10,000 men, nearly all Spanish. It was commanded by Enrique Lister and Juan Modesto (old revolutionary workers who had undergone military training in the USSR), and El Campesino (The Peasant), a bearded giant, who had achieved fame at the age of sixteen for killing four gendarmes with his own hands. His real name was Valentin Gonzales. He would take refuge in Russia after the collapse of the Republic. Promptly sent to a concentration camp, he was to escape during the war to Persia, where the British arrested him and handed him over to the Russians. After a series of picaresque adventures, he got away a second time.

In the great confusion of the Civil War, the strength and cohesion of the Fifth Brigade and the International Brigade enabled the Soviets to impose their own hierarchy, above that of the legal authority. When, in September, the Centre–Left Ministry of Jose Giral was replaced by the Socialo-Communist coalition of Largo Caballero, the *Frente Popular* became identified with a Bolshevist regime. In Madrid, abandoned by the 'Government of Victory' and the political parties (with the exception of the Communists) a Republican regular officer, General Miaja, found himself subordinate to an imposing Russian team in which, besides Berzin, figured a mysterious 'Miguel Martinez', probably the future Marshal Rokossovski. Another group ruled in Barcelona under Vladimir Antonov-Ovseenko, notorious for having commanded the Red Guards in 1917 when they sacked the Winter Palace in Patrograd. (He too was to disappear after his return to the USSR.) The Soviets were more or less in control.

★   ★   ★

More than the Ethiopian conflict, more than any event since the Armistice, the Spanish Civil War aroused the deepest emotions. Europe looked on, torn by sympathies for the Right or the Left, fascinated, ready in the first months to take sides. In the tragedy, Europeans discerned, in a dim way, the paroxysm of a crisis which rocked the entire continent, scarcely less severely than Spain itself. In general, public opinion sided with the Republic—as indicated by the high figure of the foreign volunteers in its ranks, and the correspondingly low figure for those with Burgos. This was also revealed by an opinion poll in Great Britain, which revealed 86 per cent opposed to official recognition of the Franco regime, and only 14 per cent were in its favour.[13] However, the savage religious persecution, tolerated if not encouraged by Madrid and Barcelona, aroused indignation in many people who had no sympathy with Fascism.

Faced with the various shades of opinion, ill-defined and often contradictory, Western governments were powerless to adopt a definite line or, more precisely, adhere to it. In London, responsible circles with the exception of Eden, felt nothing but antipathy for the Loyalists, and little sympathy for disagreeable realities. In Paris, the *Front Populaire* was shattered by being unable to intervene on the side of its Spanish brothers. Its leaders saw clearly that it would have been madness to risk an ideological war, in which the Soviet Union would be France's only ally. It would have been repugnant to almost everyone, even to those hoping for a Republican victory.

'Leon Blum did not accept non-intervention as an obligation imposed on him, but because he was in favour of it personally', said Jean Zay, one of the Ministers most vigorously opposed to non-intervention. This was confirmed by the English Labour Member of Parliament, Hugh Dalton, whom Blum took into his confidence.[14] Because non-intervention was, in fact, the only common ground for the various tendencies dividing Europe. Blum's fault, and Baldwin's, was not that they supported it—no other course was possible—their unpardonable sin was to fail to oblige Rome and Berlin to respect it. There is no doubt that the governments in Paris and London would have been supported by public opinion. This was made very clear when, in the summer of 1937, after the Nyon conference, the two democracies acted energetically (the only occasion) against 'unknown' submarines which were torpedoing merchant vessels outside Spanish ports. Fifty French and British destroyers swept the seas and quickly put an end to this piracy—to the general satisfaction of all.

As for the ill-applied non-intervention, the public was well aware of what it was—a hypocritical expedient, a shameful strategy invented by politicians to camouflage their pusillanimity. It increased discontent—while reinforcing in Hitler and Mussolini, and soon in Stalin, the conviction that the Western powers no longer counted. 'France is old and sick,' said Mussolini to one of Hitler's emissaries. 'A country where *la cuisine* has become one of the national arts.' He saw England in much the same way (the culinary art excepted). 'As degenerate as France, ruined by alcoholism and sexual perversion. With 11 million citizens over 50, and 2 million spinsters, it's finished!'[15]

Impossible to explain or define to the public, on account of its ambiguity and secretiveness, Leon Blum's Spanish policy, quite as much as his economic incompetence made him increasingly unpopular. On the Left, his tactics had been shamelessly exploited by the Communist Party. On the Right and Centre, he lost the credibility which his rectitude and integrity had conferred on him. To his irreconcilable enemies, he was no more than a dangerous demagogue, confirming what they had seen in Herriott—the incapacity of the Left to manage the national economy.

CHAPTER 11

Belgium Returns to Neutrality

Near the Parliament in Brussels and opposite the Parc Royal, the Foreign Ministry at 8 rue de la Loi dated, as did the entire district, from the reign of the Empress Maria-Theresa. Whilst not devoid of distinction and elegance, it operated in a ceremonious and antiquated fashion in keeping with the architectural style. Hierarchical, secretive, courteously disdainful, the 'Department' was isolated from the vulgar noises of the forum—and from the realities of life. Without a research section, its main decisions on foreign policy were taken in a more or less intuitive way by three highly placed officials under the authority of Paul Henri Spaak. They were known respectively as 'The Booted Cat', 'Teddy' and 'The Black Man', nicknames for Fernand Van Lengenhove the Secretary General, Edouard Le Ghait, the 'Chef de Cabinet', and Baron van Zuylen the Political Director. The last named was the most influential. His sobriquet was apt. Always sombrely clad, with a swarthy complexion, black hair, a lugubrious expression on his face, he affected the preoccupied air of a man on whose shoulders rested the destiny of the world. He had a 'realist' conception of international relations drawn from Maurras, seeing it as a jungle in which only the fiercest and most cunning survive. This led him to a presumptuous chauvinism which concealed from him how weak Belgium really was. An ultra-conservative Catholic, haunted by the spectre of Bolshevism, he detested republican France and, to a lesser degree, Protestant England. During the 'phoney war' his wife, who shared his views, expressed them indiscreetly one evening at the dinner table. 'Just think of it! To have to fight on the same side as such people!' One of her sons heard her objurgations, and later joined the Waffen SS to slay the Soviet dragon. He lost his life in the attempt.

Tradition conferred upon the King of the Belgians a privileged authority over diplomacy and the Army which was rarely questioned. His entourage—Baron Capelle, his secretary, Colonel (later General) van Overstraeten, his military adviser and a few others constituted, with Baron van Zuylen, a camarilla which in a semi-clandestine manner, handled the foreign policy of the country—not without occasionally exceeding the directives of the sovereign. Most of the Black Man's influence could be traced to his personal relations with the head of the principal Belgian diplomatic missions abroad: they feared him and generally recognised his ascendancy.

Paul Henri Spaak, himself respected van Zuylen's presumed knowledge of the arcane mysteries of diplomacy. This was understandable. He was aged 38 and, although born into a family of lawyers, politicians and artists, he had no preparation for foreign affairs—probably one of the reasons why van Zeeland chose him. Apart from France, from which he had derived many of his ideas, and which he often visited, he was not well informed about foreign countries. Even the United States meant little to him. I was astonished when, as a silent witness at confabulations between the minister and his senior officials, I realised how little regard they had for that immense country. An unfortunate chance had contributed to this. The careers of Pierre van Zuylen and Fernand Van Langenhove, which had been passed almost entirely in the central administration, had not prepared them to temper the provincialism of their master.

It was during the Second World War, when Spaak was in exile in London, that he discovered the great world around him. From Churchill, who took a liking to him, he learned that without lyricism and without courage no one can be a real statesman. When he visited the USA for the first time, he became aware of the vitality and optimism of a youthful people, and the extent of its formidable power. Curiously his only meeting with Roosevelt—whom he resembled in many respects—was not a success. 'Hard and hasty', he said of Roosevelt in private. However, the New Deal was a discovery which was to have a marked influence on his political thinking. In it he saw a form of Socialism which suited him, a Socialism which was heart-felt rather than a doctrine, which placed its confidence in the individual rather than in the State, which encouraged an economic expansion permitting prosperity for all, instead of imposing egalitarian austerity.

In the clash of battle, the nation states realised that they had reached the ultimate point of their predicate—reciprocal annihilation. In 1941, Spaak put forward in a letter to an English Member of Parliament the notion of a European union under the aegis of a victorious Great Britain. Two years later, in the venerable setting of Oxford University where Thomas More, Erasmus and others had expounded Western humanism, he made a speech calling on the peoples of western Europe to federate. In December 1944 he summed this up in an important diplomatic note. The Communities which saw the light when peace returned constitute the great achievement of his life. Others also contributed extensively to them, Monnet, Schuman, Adenauer, de Gasperi, Beyen and also Truman. But without Spaak, their ideas and efforts would have ended only in unfulfilled hopes. Fragile as it still is, the economic community, the 'Common Market', is the basis of European cooperation. Without Spaak, it would not have been born.

In June 1972, he was my guest in Paris. He had a bad cold and I found him greatly aged, but with his vitality and abilities intact. At a European meeting, he made an impromptu speech for thirty minutes. With relentless logic and exquisite courtesy, he demolished the classic themes of nationalism. Two weeks later when holidaying in the Azores, he was struck down by a heart attack. Conveyed dying, in an American hospital aircraft, he expired in the arms of his wife, his mind lucid to the end, sadly aware of losing a life he so loved. In accordance with his wish, he was buried in the communal grave of a cemetery in a Brussels suburb.

★   ★   ★

I began my career in 1937, in the most sombre political climate. The previous year had seen the unpublished reoccupation of the Rhineland and the bankruptcy of the League of Nations. 'Fear,' said Sir Samuel Hoare somewhat ponderously, 'made the alarm call of the trumpets resound in our ears'. Franco's legionaries and Moors were within 30 km of Madrid. In a blacked-out Paris on the evening of 16 October, a large-scale exercise simulated an aerial bombardment. In Brussels, the coterie around the King was surreptitiously encouraging a return to neutrality.

The head of the government, Paul van Zeeland, was not among those who believed that the shortest way between two points is a straight line. In 1935 (before the reoccupation of the Rhineland), he had received Ribbentrop secretly at his private house, where, seemingly, he raised the German's hopes that Belgian policy would henceforth be less inclined to Geneva, Paris and London.[1] In June 1936, presenting to Parliament his second Ministry, he boldly announced a policy of Belgium's total independence, while at the same time respecting the obligations of international cooperation, namely collective security and the Treaty of Locarno. Simultaneously he authorised fresh discussion between the Belgian and French general staffs. These were completed at the beginning of July with a plan for common defence—a very concrete plan, which in both Paris and Brussels was regarded as the consolidation of the Franco-Belgian military cooperation.

Some days later, on 20 July, Paul Henri Spaak, who had just become Foreign Minister, addressed the public. He still had only a hazy knowledge of foreign affairs (a shortcoming shared, incidentally, with most of his compatriots), consisting of a profound repugnance for Hitlerian Germany, a great sympathy for France and England, and above all a detestation of war. It was a sentiment rather than a policy. Aware of his lack of experience, and contrary to his habits, he read a text prepared with the help of his collaborators, and checked by Paul van Zeeland. He said a great deal about the horrors of war, about realism and unity, beginning, 'I want only one thing, a policy which is exclusively and wholly Belgian'. These were the only words which hit home. In pronouncing them—it must be admitted injudiciously—this Socialist Deputy, yesterday a member of the extreme Left, today a member of a government of national union, had no other intention that to reassure the Catholic Right by promising a policy which, in his own words, 'will not be that of the Second International'. Spaak confirmed this before the competent commission in Parliament. He was certainly not thinking of *neutrality*, an idea which was at that time completely alien to him.[2] But he had no objection to a *policy of independence*, an increasingly ambiguous conception which his entourage recommended to him, while assuring him that he was not doing anything new, nor was he contravening the military cooperation with France which had just been confirmed.

There is no doubt that Spaak was manoeuvred by his crafty Prime Minister. Close examination of his 20 July speech, reveals several key phrases taken word for word from a letter addressed a week before by the King to van Zeeland. Spaak was not aware of it, but it confirms beyond all doubt that it recommended a return to the true neutrality which the dynasty had always favoured. That the head of the government preferred at this stage to let Spaak show the ways is confirmed by the misleading words which he whispered in confidence in the ears of foreign diplomats. To the French Ambassador van Zeeland stated that Belgium would remain loyal to collective security, and that 'the backwash caused by the Foreign Minister's speech was a storm in a tea-cup'. He even told Blum that the declarations by his young colleague had 'surprised and irritated' him.[3]

Step by step, the Prime Minister followed his tortuous path. On 9 September he addressed the country in a radio speech. Skilfully repeating Spaak's words, he gave them this time their full meaning—the royal meaning. On 14 October, the King himself presided over a council of Ministers, to whom he read a memorandum which he had drawn up by Colonel Van Overstraeten and approved by Paul van Zeeland. Its principal purpose was to recommend the strengthening of the Belgian armed forces, made necessary by German rearmament. To convince and reassure the Socialist and Flemish Ministers—traditionally the most opposed to military expenditure—but not, one presumes, without ulterior motives, he stressed the independence of Belgian foreign policy, 'on the lines of the proud and determined examples of Holland and Switzerland'. The aged Socialist leader Vandervelde suggested that the Head of State's speech should be made public. With the exception of van Zeeland, the Ministers had not *read* it; they had only *heard* it, without being fully aware of its significance. The government now decided, without informing friendly capitals, to allow the journalists who thronged the anti-chamber of the Royal Palace to see the text.

King Leopold's unexpected declaration caused a sensation. Well received in Belgium (which showed how quickly public opinion had veered) it reinforced and confirmed latent attitudes which were still not well defined. In Berlin, the Nazi newspapers were jubilant. The *Deutsche Allgemeine Zeitung* wrote, 'Twenty years of French Security collapses. King Leopold proclaims Belgian neutrality. End of the policy of alliances'. The Italian Press also rejoiced that, 'Belgium overturns the myth of collective security'. In London there was some concern. Although van Zeeland had sent Eden a personal letter of embarrassed explication, the Foreign Office recommended him on several occasions to handle France carefully. Indeed, in Paris there was consternation and anger. Hitherto, Belgium had always appeared a steadfast ally—even more, a sister state, with the same language, the same ideas and culture.* In the late King Albert, *Le roi chevalier*, the French, encouraged by war propaganda, had seen a symbol of Right and Justice (of which they sincerely believed themselves to be the defenders). And now, at a crucial moment, his son, without a word of warning, had terminated a unique relationship. The Belgian Ambassador in Paris, reported sadly, 'Belgians in this country have now become no more than likeable foreigners, from being the close brothers in arms they had been since the first Prussian Uhlans entered

---

* Feelings which, in reality, were not shared by a significant part of the Flemish population.

Belgium on 4 August 1914.' In a somewhat cavalier manner, the French had regarded the close ties with the little kingdom as those of a dutiful satellite. They were therefore all the more startled when Belgium abruptly broke those ties. Even in Moscow, it was seen as 'a distinctive shock' to collective security.[4]

From the publication of King Leopold's speech, in London as well as in Paris, suspicion and irritation arose, explaining in part, the unjustified accusations of treason made at Belgium after the disasters of 1940. Not that Brussels diplomacy had made exorbitant demands; they were consistent, I believe, with the chauvinistic egotism prevailing, at the time. But by frequently contradicting itself, and taking pleasure in mystery and secrecy Belgium gave the impression of duplicity. Blum who was never to pardon the monarch (no more than would Churchill) permitted the newspapers to refer to him in the harshest terms. Brussels, taken by surprise, assumed an air of wounded dignity. Spaak had not foreseen anything like this, and he was forced to tone down the more exaggerated interpretations of his policy. To Baron de Cartier de Marchiennes, the Belgian Ambassador in London, he wrote, 'I think it would be useful to emphasise that there has never been any question of our country—nor will there ever be— withdrawing from the international engagements we have contracted and which link us.' Other Belgian diplomatic missions received similar assurances, with instructions to make them known. In the Chamber of Representatives the Minister confirmed publicly, 'Belgium's earlier commitments are still extant ... conversations between the French and Belgian General Staff go on.'[5]

Perhaps. However, the staff agreements had become accessories to the Locarno Treaty of 1925. A pact of *mutual assistance*, it had been hastily reconfirmed by France, Great Britain and Belgium when Germany had denounced it, thus becoming, in fact, a defensive alliance against the Reich. As incompatible with neutrality, the Rue de la Loi aimed at disengaging itself from it—but without losing the guarantees that went with it. In other words, Brussels wished to obtain a promise of *assistance without reciprocity*.

Difficult negotiations were undertaken in the winter of 1936, presided over by Paul van Zeeland in person. Impelled forward by some, restrained by others, not sure of the support of a far from unanimous Parliament, the Belgian Prime Minister manoeuvred behind a thick smoke-screen. After telephoning Paris, he visited the city secretly (why secretly?) to confer with Blum and his Foreign Minister. What did he say to them? If we are to believe the report of the honest Delbos to the competent commission of the *Chambre des Deputés*, he assured them that King Leopold's words were no more than a gesture, and the Franco-Belgian Alliance was still in force. Of course, there had never been a real 'alliance' between the two countries. But with that restriction, it was more or less what Spaak (who did not doubt the good faith of the Prime Minister) was also telling the French Ambassador: nothing had changed fundamentally, it had been necessary to calm Flemish opinion. Belgium would respect her engagements.[6] In December Blum and Delbos had a final conversation at van Zeeland's house—again in secret and again abortive.*

In London, things were easier. The Foreign Office, annoyed by the simultaneously vague and peremptory methods of the Belgian Government, feared at first that Belgium might slide into the German sphere of influence. Reassured on this point after a private visit to Britain of King Leopold, the Foreign Office became resigned to Belgium's return to a situation akin to its traditional neutrality, very close also to England's own policy.[8] In short, France and Britain yielded. In a joint note of 24 April 1937, they freed Belgium from the obligations she had assumed at Locarno, while confirming those of Paris and London. In October, the Germans stated in a unilateral declaration that, 'the inviolability and integrity of Belgium are of common interest for the western powers'. The only counterpart demanded from the Belgians was an engagement to defend themselves against any foreign invasion. This went without saying—but it also implied that friends and foes, the law abiding and the aggressive sides, were regarded by Belgium in the same light.

During these months, the discussions in Brussels with the French military had continued. After stating that these in no way contradicted the new status of the country, the trustees of governmental wisdom discovered that the staff agreements had to be repudiated. The senior officials at the Foreign Ministry, the highest military authorities, the royal coterie, the Prime Minister, the Sovereign himself, all assailed Spaak. King Leopold gave him a dressing down. 'The General Staff agreements', he wrote his Minister, 'can only compromise our policy while contributing nothing to our military situation.'[9] Gradually, under the joint pressure of the Head of State and the Head

---

* Returning to Paris, the vehicle of Blum and Delbos skidded on the icy road near Compiègnes, and turned over in a ditch. They were lucky to emerge alive. I can find no reference to this meeting in the Belgian archives. Mentioned in Leon Blum's memoirs, it was confirmed to me by Spaak many years later, with a dejection made more acute by his high regard for Blum and Delbos.[7]

of Government, who exercised a powerful influence over him, Spaak's hesitations were dispelled. On 29 April 1937, three days after Eden's visit to Brussels, he declared, 'The era of General Staff agreement is over.'

Belgium's place on the European chessboard has radically changed. At Versailles, the neutrality of 1839 had been replaced by the solidarity defined in the texts of Geneva and Locarno, and rendered enforceable by the Franco-Belgian military agreements. Now, the Rue de la Loi recognised no other agreements than those of the Charter of the League of Nations (with the exception of Articles XVI and collective security, which were interpreted in the most restricted manner). 'Our hands are free', Baron van Zuylen flattered himself—What he had said, of course, implied the rejection of the rules governing a genuine world order.[10] Free hands? It was not even true. In terms of her neighbours, Belgium now found herself in an almost contractual situation, which was distinguished from the status of 1839 only by minute legal points. Her frontiers closed to those who would not keep their word, she would have only a weak militia to ward off those who ridiculed such integrity. Germany's raucous approval of the new Belgian policy was significant. It was so indiscreet that Brussels had to ask for it to be toned down.[11]

History will rightly summon before its tribunal the leading Belgian figures as well as those of France and England, and accuse them all of criminal negligence. As far as the principle of 'an independent policy' is concerned—if not in the way of conducting it— Belgium may well, I think, plead attenuating circumstances. Together with the continued irresolution of London and Paris, an argument which influenced her more than any other, and which for reasons I do not understand has not been underlined, was Brussel's conviction that its neutrality would have no ill effects on the strategic situation of the French and British; rather the opposite. In spite of this growing disenchantment, the Belgian Government had no doubt about the military superiority of its old allies. A sentimental attitude no doubt, but it was confirmed by the assessment of its generals. In a small country with no martial aims, the Army is not the chosen place for original thinkers; there were few of these in the Belgian General Staff. As in Paris, a defensive strategy was an unquestioned dogma, the result of the influence of French military thinking, as much of the lessons of the First World War. Also the logic of neutrality. The only serious debate within military circles concerned where the principal defence line should be positioned: on the frontier, on the Albert Canal, on the Antwerp–Namur line, etc? Each had its advocates. The matter was never settled, so that when the German attack came, the defence system was spread piecemeal. Nowhere in Belgium would there be a solid fortified line.

The government was not directly concerned with the strategic options. The doctrine and conduct of military operations lay within the competence of the King who was Commander-in-Chief; he guarded his prerogatives carefully. Between him, the civil power and the General Staff lurked Colonel Raoul van Overstraeten, Leopold's military adviser. A secretive and presumptuous man, greedy for authority, he saw himself as the Jomini or Clausewitz of the Brussels Court. Although exercising no command, he was assured by the prestige of the Crown of a preponderant influence in military circles. An owl rather than an eagle, he had a piercing vision, but did not see very far. Not opaque to new ideas, which he taught competently at the École de Guerre, he appeared unaware how inconsistent they were with the defensive strategy which was a part of neutrality; perhaps he did not dare to point it out to the King or the General Staff. For the latter the only conceivable form of warfare was what they had learned on the battlefield: 'Dig in and wait!', or 'Fire power has precedence over movement'—the two intangible dogmas of trench warfare.

For this purpose, the High Command prepared to mobilise 22 divisions (an enormous effort: in 1940, the British had only 10). They were supposed to deter any aggressors; but without armour and with very few aircraft (offensive arms, and therefore useless), they were hardly in a position to do so. Nevertheless, in the context of the times, a neutral and resolute Belgium, according to its soldiers or the diplomats, would present an insuperable barrier, an unbreakable lock. If the Reich respected Belgian neutrality, the frontier to be defended by the French armies would be halved; if it violated it it would constitute a strong glacis upon which the aggressors would have been mauled. This reasoning was generally accepted even in Paris and London. The extremely prudent General Gamelin resigned himself to it without too much protest. As for the British General Staff (with some reservations among the airmen) it considered that a neutral and armed Belgium would be an important strategic trump. Would it not be a return to the good old days before 1914? Until the first months of 1939, London did not discourage this Belgian version of appeasement. Was it an insane judgement? Of the German general who breached the French front at Sedan in 1940, the well-known English historian, Liddell Hart, wrote, 'Guderian had a tremendous impact on the course of events of our time. Without him, it is possible that Hitler would have met early frustrations in his offensive efforts when he embarked on war.'[12]

Many historians now agree with this view and regard the attack on Sedan as a gigantic gamble. But have not most of the great battles of history been won or lost on such terms?

★   ★   ★

Contrary to what has often been said, it was the secret action of the 'camarilla', much more than popular pressure which initiated Belgium's return to neutrality. Public opinion was undecided—which explains the serpent-like prudence with which the Prime Minister had to thread his way.[13] Even the Fascist outburst, which had appeared to encourage it, quickly died down. In 1937, Leon Degrelle, who had hoped to triumph in a by-election, was beaten decisively by van Zeeland, the only candidate from the traditional parties—for once united.

The famous *Zeitgeist*, the spirit of the times, the new breath which Nazi propaganda exalted, was no more than a glacial wind from the Dark Ages. The sunlit visions of the Olympic Games were substituted in the popular imagination by those of the terrifying mass demonstrations at Nuremberg, the blond athletes replaced by *Landsknechts*, encased in leather and iron, stamping the ground to the rhythm of their great drums. In particular, the intellectuals were shocked at the inauguration, with great pomp of a House of German Art in Munich that year. The newspapers described sarcastically the monumental halls in which hung the canvases of Matisse, Cézanne, Nolde and Munch, torn from their frames and hung askew or upside down, scattered among works by unknown eccentrics, and described as 'Jewish art'. Works of German art were hung in adjoining halls, the apotheosis of the neo-realism beloved by Hitler, flat oil paintings in strident colours, gigantic statues of conventional nudes, sexless women with perfect breasts, men with enormous pectoral muscles and minute penises. Curiously, this was precisely the pretentious, banal style favoured by the Russian Soviets.

Once neutrality was adopted, the inconsistencies of the great democracies, as much as fear of Hitlerism, dissuaded the Belgians from questioning it. Apart from rare exceptions, this was the attitude of the Foreign Ministry.* The Belgians were extremely Anglophile, even

---

* No important personality of the great traditional parties, with the sole exception of Henri de Man, was to 'collaborate' with the occupation authorities.

Anglomaniacs. Everything that came from the other side of the channel was perfect: the black Homburg hats from Lock (soon known as 'Anthony Eden' hats), umbrellas from Briggs, suits from Savile Row. Pax Britannica was the heir to Pax Romana. The most conservative found in England the beauty of romantic tradition; the more liberal revered the moderate institutions inspired by the sterling English respect for the human person. The diplomats, too greatly influenced by historic memories (a frequent failing in diplomats), tended to see in England the supreme rampart of Belgian sovereignty. Had it not been so in the time of the Valois, Louis XIV, of Napoleon?

Contrasted with the apparent lackadaisical attitude adopted by France, and the German frenzy, the majesty of the British Empire seemed highly impressive. In the spring Spaak, returning from the coronation of George VI, recounted admiringly (unusual for this sceptic) the religious splendour of the ceremony beneath the immense Gothic vault of Westminster; the presentation to the dazzling congregation, of the immobile monarch at the foot of the throne of Edward the Confessor, symbolically naked before being recognised by his subjects, then donning the golden cloak, and taking his place on the throne. And then the antique ritual which, from the hands of the Archbishop of Canterbury, conferred on him the holy oil and the attributes of sovereignty, the sword, the sceptre, the globe and the crown, to make him the Lord's Annointed, Defender of the Faith, King-Emperor.

As it was, in the years after the First World War, Belgium could hardly congratulate herself on her relations with her powerful and haughty neighbour. Distrustful of ties too close for their liking between Brussels and Paris, the British had refused relations of a similar nature which Belgian diplomacy had hoped for. In May 1934 Paul Hymans, in the British capital to obtain guarantees against Hitlerian aggression, had been advised by Sir John Simon to conclude a non-aggression pact with the Reich! Several subsequent propositions for conversations between the two staffs of the two armies were rejected by London— as Eden wrote in an *aide-memoire*, so as not to give the Germans a pretext for reoccupying the Rhineland. The propositions were rejected again in the summer of 1936.[14]

The only agreement reached between London and Brussels was: to do nothing. Ambassador Bullit confirmed in a letter to President Roosevelt, 'Belgium, at the present time, is the little brother of England. Van Zeeland is, to all interests and purposes, a representative of the British Government.'[15] Bullit exaggerated, but certainly the example of Great Britain influenced Belgian diplomacy. Ribbentrop, who represented the Third Reich at the court of his Britannic Majesty had received 'a very warm welcome' in August 1936. So wrote the Belgian Ambassador, adding that the Führer's favourite had rented the house of Neville Chamberlain in Eaton Square while waiting to occupy his official residence. After a visit to England by Colonel Beck, the Germanophile Polish Foreign Minister, the communiqué announced, 'No formation of opposing blocks, no rigid alliances, no engagements beyond the effective power of the signatories.' There is little doubt that a different attitude by Great Britain would have made Belgium hesitate in the months before she took her decision on neutrality and might, perhaps, have prevented her return to isolation.[16]

Towards France, the feelings of my colleagues were more complex. We were nearly all Francophone, penetrated with French culture and often proud of it, conscious also of an ancient fraternity in arms. But at the same time we suffered from the inferiority complex of provincial cousins. We were conscious, too conscious, of the designs on our little kingdom expressed now and then in Paris, quite irresponsibly, by more or less important persons—feelings which were emphasised by the absence of true political cooperation between our two countries.

In 1937, Brussels had certain grievances against Paris. The first was due to Marshal Pétain who, on a number of occasions, had thought it appropriate to tell the Belgian Ambassador that the French Army would not hesitate to enter Belgium if need be, *with or without Belgian permission*. It was an uncalled-for threat, and it caused quite a flutter. In the political class, it was the recent Franco-Soviet treaty of mutual assistance which caused the divide. To Catholics—the great majority of the population—the USSR was still the Empire of the Devil. Brussels was one of the last capitals to establish diplomatic relations with Moscow, in 1935. The notion was widespread that Belgium could be dragged by Paris onto the side of the Soviets, a notion which became a nightmare when the *Front Populaire* came to power.

Other suspicions of a quite different order arose from secret relations between Paris and Berlin. The Rue de la Loi had learned through the usual indiscretions (diplomats are among the most garrulous people in the world) that Dr Schacht, the German Minister of Economy and one of the principal personalities in the Third Reich, had been received in the greatest secrecy in April 1936 by Leon Blum. The two men had apparently discussed a general European settlement, to be accompanied by a redistribution of colonies in Africa. Would this include the Belgian Congo or Ruanda-Urundi (the latter a former

German colony administered by Belgium on behalf of the League of Nations)? All that the Quai d'Orsay had to tell us was that, 'the question was progressing well', which was hardly reassuring.* The colonial question, as confirmed by reading the Belgian diplomatic correspondence in which it was discussed almost daily, was to remain one of Brussels' major preoccupations until the outbreak of war. That Laval had deliberately sacrificed Ethiopia to the greed of Mussolini did not dissipate our distrust.

In the summer of 1937, it was the unexpected presence in Paris of General Beck, chief of the Wehrmacht General Staff, which caused surprise; as much as did the courtesy shown to General Kuhlenthal, the Reich's military attaché in France, who spoke freely of 'unexpressed collaboration' between the two armies. So too did a visit by General Milch, second in command of the Luftwaffe, who was received at Le Bourget with a guard of honour to the strains of *Deutschland über alles*.[17] (the first German to be so honoured since 1870). There was also the coming and going of suspect emissaries whose doings were hidden from us. The possibility of a Franco-German rapprochement—or on the other hand of an Anglo-German rapprochement—at the expense of Belgium or her colonies, could never have been far from the minds of men as suspicious as Baron van Zuylen and his friends.

★   ★   ★

A junior private secretary, as I then was, dealt with all manner of subjects, without ever going into any of them in depth. Nevertheless, one specific task occupied a great deal of my time, the secretariat of an enquiry entrusted to Paul van Zeeland by London and Paris into the possibility of 'a general reduction of obstacles to international trade'. The First World War had forced the governments to intervene vigorously in the interplay of economic forces. After the Armistice, prompted by a nostalgia for the past, they had returned, more or less, to economic liberalism. But the Great Depression had sounded the knell of *laisser-faire, laisser-aller*, it was the cause of too much

---

* H. Schacht and A. Francois-Poncet both mentioned this episode in their memoirs. In agreement with Hitler—who is said to have predicted to Schacht that the initiative was bound to fail—Schacht had asked the French Ambassador in Berlin to arrange the interview with Blum. The prospect of expansion overseas, he said, might have turned Hitler away from his design on Czechoslovakia, whose conquest haunted him. Blum did not reject Schacht's proposition immediately. In London, where any redistribution of colonies was categorically denied, the matter was taken much more seriously than in Paris.[17]

suffering. A new conscience was developing, hastened by the Socialist, and even the Fascist, parties. It demanded that 'something should be done'. But what?

Buffeted by pressures from the employers as well as from the Workers' Movements and anxious not to shake the ancient structure, the governments had taken the easy path, of protectionism—that is, increase exports and reduce imports. The most militant enunciated an economic doctrine which they called *autarchy*, a new word whose learned sonority camouflaged its rudimentary xenophobic egoism. The United States had set a bad example in 1922 when they introduced a high customs tariff, which they increased again in 1930. Great Britain, for long the paragon of *laisser-faire*, took the same course; in 1931 and 1932 it abandoned Free Trade, which had enriched it for a hundred years, in favour of an illusory imperial *autarchy*. Opposed to the stabilisation of currencies, it caused the pound sterling to 'float', thereby artificially favouring exports. Germany submitted all her exterior exchanges to the authority of the State. France protected herself with a formidable apparatus of customs duties, compensatory surcharges on exchanges, anti-dumping measures and quantitative restrictions of all kinds. Dozens of other countries, in particular the successor states of the eastern empires, German, Austro-Hungarian and Russian, overlaid Europe with exchange rules and customs barriers. 'Buy Belgian!', 'Buy French!', 'Buy British!', chanted the authorities. Between 1929 and 1932, world commerce declined by a quarter.

Some attempts were made to remedy the situation. In June 1933, the King of England solemnly opened a world economic congress (to be joined, most unexpectedly by the United States) in the Natural History Museum in London. After long preparations, presided over by Ramsay MacDonald, it aimed at resolving the principal economic problems, customs barriers, raw material prices, war debts, convertibility of the currencies and the like. For several weeks, the great men launched into platitudes denouncing the evils of protectionism. However, hopes of a vast economic agreement quickly evaporated. On 3 July, in a curt message, Roosevelt virtually put an end to the London conference. On the same day Belgium, France, Italy, Holland, Poland and Switzerland immured themselves in the ruinous 'Gold Block', turning their backs on the Keynesian theories which were to be applied successfully in the United States. The Natural History Museum could now place Free Trade beside the skeletons of the dinosaurs and iguanodons.

Four years later, after the violent political backwash of 1936, a sort of calm descended on Europe. The Depression was receding, the Great Powers were attempting to appease Hitler. Paul van Zeeland had succeeded on a small scale in the reforming experiment which the *Front Populaire* had not been able to accomplish; at the pinnacle of his career, London and Paris agreed to entrust him with an economic investigation whose unavoided aim was the reintegration of Germany into Europe. He began his task by instructing Maurice Frère, a well known Belgian expert, to sound out the capitals. On several occasions I had to carry his bags, passing long hours in *wagons-lits* and *wagon-restaurants*, studying arid files, drafting memoranda and discovering cities that I did not know.

Beginning in Paris, we were received from 19–23 April 1937 by Vincent Auriol the Finance Minister, Georges Monnet the Minister for Agriculture, Spinasse the Minister of National Economy, and by senior officials, among them Leger, Couve de Murville and Alphand. All were in favour of a European agreement, although they entertained few illusions about it. Vincent Auriol defined the fundamental problem. 'Germany', he said, 'cannot modify its policy of *autarchy* unless it proceeds to large scale devaluation and a new stabilisation of its currency. For that it must receive credits. These cannot be granted until Germany is prepared to offer political guarantees. It is inconceivable that we should help Germany economically so that she can build up her armaments. The economic problem is dominated entirely by the political one.'[18]

From Paris, Maurice Frère proceeded to Berlin, without me—it was considered inappropriate to exhibit me in the capital of anti-Semitism. He left Brussels with a heavy heart. That morning the newspapers had reported the annihilation by the Luftwaffe of Guernica, the holy city of the Basque Catholics, with many civilian casualties. An experience in new methods of terrorist bombing, 'carpet bombing', it created a wave of deep resentment.

'With Schacht,' related van Zeeland's emissary, 'the first conversation was in the form of a monologue; it could be summed up as a polite refusal of international collaboration as long as Germany did not receive satisfaction over her colonial claims.' Other German demands followed, including the revision of the frontiers; with Belgium in the region of Eupen and Malmédy (two cantons ceded by Germany at Versailles); with Denmark in Schleswig. Danzig must go back to the Reich, which would in return formerly, recognise the 'Polish Corridor'. 'Raising his voice', Dr Schacht told me solemnly, 'What I am saying now is not my personal opinion, but the Führer's, when I saw him three days ago. He adopted this position at the last Party congress. If the German colonial claims are not met, your mission will be fruitless. The concession of a colonial domain to Germany is, in any case, the only possible way of resolving present difficulties, without upsetting the political equilibrium.'[19]

When Maurice Frère was received the next day by Göring, he was appalled at the German's ignorance of affairs. Göring had in his hand a report of the conversation with Schacht the day before, but he appeared ill-informed on the reasons for the van Zeeland mission. Frère found him 'jovial, smiling, relaxed'. 'They say abroad', stated Göring, 'that I dream of making war. That is untrue. I will make war if I am forced to, but my greatest wish is to confine my warrior activities to hunting and artistic matters.' He categorically contradicted Schacht, of whom he spoke with scorn. The colonial question, he said, was irrelevant.* The status of Eupen and Malmédy was already definitively settled. 'We are very pleased with the Belgian attitude,' he said. 'She has shown that she really wants to be completely independent ... we will see how she organises her defences, and if they are directed against all frontiers, not only ours'. Just as Vincent Auriol had done, the Führer's Dauphin emphasised the political problems, on which the economic ones depended; they could not be envisaged separately, as van Zeeland seemed to suggest. Göring then made a curious demand— for a pact making it unlawful to seize private property, even in an enemy country, even in time of war. In view of his later acquisitiveness, this question is not without a certain piquancy. To sum up, the Berlin visit brought no new elements, emphasising only that the political claims of the Reich rendered economic problems insoluble.[21]

Italy being not yet converted to racism, I was able to accompany Frère to Rome, being very curious to see the Fascist regime from close to. Its prestige was not at its zenith. Mussolini had just made a theatrical visit to his Libyan colony, where he had himself photographed on a horse, brandishing the Sword of Islam, surrounded by Moorish guards carrying Roman emblems.† A chance incident added

---

* However in October 1936 Göring had himself claimed publicly the restoration of the colonial territory 'stolen' from Germany. He also emphasised to the Belgian Ambassador a speech by Hitler in January 1937 officially making the claim. Ribbentrop, for his part, speaking in Leipzig, did not hesitate to announce that the German people would 'have recourse to force', if its claims were not satisfied.[20]

† The Duce had also an equestrian statue erected in the principal square of Tripoli of himself adopting the martial attitude of Colleoni. Today it has been replaced by a statue of Colonel Gaddafi.

to the ridicule. One of his many mistresses, a French journalist, something of a spy and somewhat hysterical, Magda Fontanges (her real name was Magda Coraboeuf), had pretended to poison herself after he had rejected her unceremoniously. She was soon well. She then seized the occasion of visit to Paris of the Comte de Chambrun, France's very solemn Ambassador to Italy, who she thought was responsible for her misfortune, to fire a shot at him; she only grazed his nose. Given a light sentence, she pursued her vengeance by publishing, to the delight of all Europe, articles full of spicy details, true or false, about the private life of her illustrious lover.

On the evening of 13 May, the Rome Express deposited us at the new Central Station, one of the regime's legitimate sources of pride. The Eternal City glittered in all its beauty, the streets animated and noisy, the café terraces crowded. After a night at the Excelsior hotel, we began, on a sunlit morning, with a visit to the Governor of the Bank of Italy, Signor Azzolini, to several senior officials and to the Finance Minister, Count Thaon de Revel. All, with remarkable candour, gave us most detailed and technical reports, revealing a disastrous financial and economic situation. The currency reserves, 12 billion Lira in 1928 had fallen to 4 billion, in spite of the most rigorous control. In addition, poor harvests resulting in large purchases of cereals abroad, forecast a new deficit in the commercial balance of more than 3 billion for the current year. 'In all branches of industry,' ran the report drawn up on the instruction of my chief, 'the reserves of raw materials are much reduced, often insufficient to guarantee regular activity.'

Where was Italy going? Engaged up to the hilt in the Ethiopian adventure, plunged in economic and financial stagnation, how could she bear the further burden of participation of the Spanish Civil War? But if the economic experts showed great anxiety, the politicians seemed almost care-free. In the venerable Palazzo Chigi, seat of the Ministry of Foreign Affairs, the coming and going of the bureaucrats, clad in bedizened military uniforms, some booted and spurred like cavalry officers, seemed part of the décor of some operetta. Count Ciano in a dark uniform, with gilded insignia, accompanied by his secretary in a pale green get-up and a black shirt, gave us a short audience. Courteous, smiling, with an offhand, airy manner, Mussolini's son-in-law revealed nothing of his character defects—with the exception of a certain frivolity. From this interview which was limited to a few generalities, nothing of importance emerged.[22]

The end of May saw us in London, Warsaw and Prague. In the British capital (where Baldwin had been replaced by Neville Chamberlain) we passed four hours in the company of a team of senior officials presided over by Sir Frederick Leith-Ross, the principal economic adviser to the government. Our conversation was serious and technical. Leith-Ross confided to Frère that he thought the moment had come to attempt a general stabilisation of the currencies; he hoped he could convince his Ministers, including the inevitable Sir John Simon, the Chancellor of the Exchequer. Sir Otto Niemeyer, one of the heads of the Bank of England repeated his proposal, which was not new, that a common monetary fund should be created.*

We arrived in Warsaw after a seemingly endless journey through forests and over steppes. Here and there along the railway line, we saw dusty earthen tracks, *isbas* with thatched roofs. At the station halts were bearded peasants in smocks, their women's heads covered with shawls and the inevitable gendarme with a sabre at his side. The Polish capital, in spite of the French elegance of some of its avenues and the Hanseatic charm of *Stary Rynelk*, the old market, struck me with the curious atmosphere of 'old Russia'. In the streets there were few motor-cars but innumerable carriages drawn by famished horses, hand-carts and a mass of hirsute beggars. The conversations which Frère had with a number of Ministers, including the stiff and starchy Colonel Beck, yielded little. Our short stay left the impression of a very poor country which, without huge foreign investments, could not for a long time be integrated in the European circuit.

Prague, nestling in its bowl of hills on the banks of the Voltava, made a very different impression—with its city hall and Gothic cathedrals, ancient churches and synagogues, sumptuous buildings of the old nobility, dominated by the Hradcin, the palace of the Kings of Bohemia. The well-kept streets were alive with motor traffic, and along the pavements walked well-dressed men and elegant women. In the evening, the brasseries were crowded, resounding with conversation and the music of orchestras. M. Hodza, the President of the Council, a Slovak, bald, wearing pince-nez, looking like a professor, explained in perfect French, a plan for a Danubian economic agreement and cooperation, to which he hoped to give his name. The President of the Republic E. Beneš received us in the Hradcin in an office, decorated with baroque *boiserie*, from which we had a magnificent view over the old city. He was somewhat peremptory in manner, but serious and

---

* The general stabilisation of the currencies was not achieved until 10 years later at Bretton Woods, to be abondoned in 1972. As for the creation of a Reserve European Fund, it still figures on the agendas of the E.E.C.

moderate, commenting sceptically on the projects of M. Hodza to which 'Germany and Italy will only agree under conditions which will be unacceptable to France and Great Britain.' Nevertheless, he was reassuring and self-confident. Maurice Frère concluded his report on Prague on a resolutely optimistic note, 'From all these conversations I obtained a feeling of strength, great activity and constructive dynamism.'[23]

At the end of June, while van Zeeland was making a spectacular tour of the United States, Maurice Frère visited Vienna, Budapest, Belgrade and Bucharest, where he saw Schuschnigg, Duranyi, Stoyadinovich and Tataresco, but without any concrete results. One fine morning, in July, we came in the newspapers upon the text of a letter from King Leopold to his Prime Minister. Referring to most of the great economic problems—customs barriers, raw materials, equilibrium between the industrialised and agricultural nations, it proposed the creation of a new organisation for international economic cooperation. The astounded Frère immediately took up the telephone and asked the Prime Minister how he was to reconcile his mission with the unexpected and, frankly, untimely initiative of the King. All that van Zeeland would say was that he had had no part in it. This was difficult to believe. But it was an assertion which evaded the responsibility of another blow at the League of Nations and its economic competence—to the great irritation of the democratic capitals.

During the summer, Frère gave up his holidays and settled down to editing a report for the French and British governments. Van Zeeland was a secretive man, difficult to fathom. Everything indicated however that he had lost faith in his mission. Without being prepared to admit it, his visit to the United States had been a disappointment. President Roosevelt had been very reticent about projects which, without a general settling of the European disputes would, he contended, only contribute a gratuitous aid to the German and Italian economies. Here he put his finger on the essential point—as incidentally had Vincent Auriol in April. The van Zeeland mission could perhaps have succeeded if it had been able to convince the Reich to moderate its political claims *present and future*. The only Franco-British attempt at economic 'appeasement', it failed because the warrior mentality of the Führer put territorial expansion well before economic expansion. The German Embassy in Brussels made this very clear by soon displaying a total lack of interest in our work.*

* A significant incident in Hitler's career, the failure of the van Zeeland Mission appears, curiously, to have escaped the attention of historians.

Simultaneously, the economic crisis, which had appeared to be receding, resumed with a new virulence. On three occasions, the report had to be redrafted to weaken the more interesting propositions. Van Zeeland was slowing down, floundering in a bog of Parliamentary intrigues; it became difficult to see him. On 15 October, Frère wrote him a brave letter advising him to terminate the mission by proposing a reserve monetary fund. Ten days later, Paul van Zeeland, unfairly implicated in financial irregularities, was forced to resign.

We still had two or three conversations at intervals with him, but he seemed to have lost all resilience. In January 1938, he finally drew up a report which suggested methods to reach 'a pact of international economic cooperation'. 'The governments', he wrote, 'have shown, on the one hand, evidence of goodwill and a marked desire to collaborate in a general action leading towards an extension of international commerce; but, on the other hand, a great reserve when it comes to practical steps to implement it.'[24] This was an understatement. Received with polite noises, the 'van Zeeland Report' was soon buried in the archives.

Three weeks later the Wehrmacht invaded Austria.

CHAPTER 12

The End of Austria

I shall not forget that cold, rainy morning in March 1938. The Austrian Minister had come to the Rue de la Loi requesting an audience of the King, to announce officially that his functions were over, as his country had ceased to exist. I had arrived early at the Rue de la Loi and found Monsieur Alexich in the ante-chamber sunk in an armchair. I took him into the *Chef de Cabinet's* room. Ties of friendship united the two men, reinforced by a common childhood shared in Vienna. Face to face they clasped hands, silent, their eyes filled with tears. I slipped quietly away.

After the assassination of Dollfuss and the failed *Putsch* of 1934, a precarious calm had settled on Austria for a while. Kurt von Schuschigg had been confirmed in the role of Federal Chancellor which he had assumed during the *Putsch*. He was not a great man, and unlikely to unite the Austrians. On the Right, the National Socialists continued their subterranean agitation. On the Left, the Social Democrats, excluded from the Federal Diet where they had 42 per cent of the seats, harassed and thrown into concentration camps in thousands, refused to give him the support for which he asked sporadically, while continuing to persecute them. Among his own followers, his authority was challenged by a rival, the redoubtable Vice-Chancellor, His Serene Highness Ernst Rudiger, Prince Starhemberg and a Prince of the Holy Roman Empire, the last descendant of a family which had been powerful for a thousand years, and the idol of a large section of the public.

Starhemberg, Vice-Chancellor, Minister of the Police, leader of the political militia the Heimwehr, fawned upon by the youth, enjoying the favour of Mussolini, could have supplanted the unimposing Chancellor and become the hero of Austrian patriotism. His downfall was due to the love of a woman as much as to his eccentricities. After a conventional marriage, he had become enamoured of a Burgtheater actress. He quarrelled with the episcopate when it refused to annul the marriage of one of the principal personalities of apostolic Austria. Deprived of the all-powerful support of the Church, hated by the Nazis, he also imprudently aroused the wrath of Paris and London when he sent a fulsome telegram to Mussolini congratulating him on his conquest of Ethiopia. With a serpent-like strike, Schuschnigg seized the opportunity. Starhemberg was forced to resign, discovering that the annulment of his marriage would reward his submission and that of his faithful militia. The bargain struck, exit Prince Charming.*

'The tortoise has beaten the hare', commented an English journalist. Henceforth, Kurt von Schuschnigg was master of Austria; the various opposing factions were prohibited or absorbed into his 'Patriotic Front', the private militias had to comply with his law. At the same time, the taciturn and lonely lawyer, a man entirely without effulgence and lacking the flamboyant personality which the Vice-Chancellor had brought to the regime, managed to alienate the moral forces of the nation—with the exception of the Church which was also, at the crucial moment, to abandon him. The Austrian Chancellor, full of old-fashioned values, aware too of the frailty of his regime, could see no other solution than to humour Nazi Germany. In July 1936 (while Belgium took refuge behind neutrality) he consented to a treaty with the Reich, recognising the Germanic character of Austria. In secret protocols, part of which were soon to become public knowledge, he also tolerated the Austrian National Socialist Party. It was a promise which no one in Vienna had taken seriously. A fatal step on an irreversible course.

★   ★   ★

Mussolini, when young, had helped to involve Italy in one of the most terrible wars, in order to destroy the Germanic empires which had threatened its frontiers for a thousand years. Mussolini, who had long disliked his emulator, was now giving up more and more to him. In September 1937, he accepted an invitation to make his first official visit to the Third Reich. Hitler had been waiting a year for his colleague, whom he regarded as essential to his plans. He had neglected nothing which might flatter and impress him. The Duce, clad in a new uniform made especially for the occasion (a Prussian-style peaked hat replacing his usual headgear), accompanied by a suite of a hundred

---

*In 1939 Starhemberg, true to his anti-Nazi stance, joined the French Foreign Legion air force. In 1940, serving under General de Gaulle, he and his squadron took part in the Battle of Britain. Later, he joined the Leclerc division in Africa, where he contracted the malaria from which he later died, in 1956.

persons, was welcomed at the Brenner by a crowd of high dignitaries, ministers, diplomats and generals in brilliant uniforms. The Führer greeted him in person at Munich station, outside which they inspected a double line of Roman emperors' busts erected in his honour. The visitor was presented with an edition of Nietzsche's works bound in a sea-green Moroccan leather, the colour of the glaciers from which Zarathrustra contemplated the universe.

In Berlin, a triumphal avenue several kilometres long had been laid out, Unter den Linden, bordered with giant flags and immense pylons bearing Nazi and Fascist emblems, the axe with the fasces and the eagle of the Reich. Standing up in a huge Mercedes, the Italian basked in the sensuous pleasure of the ovations. In the ensuing days, transported from one end of the Reich to the other, he beheld in the great factories the most modern machinery mass-producing artillery, tanks and bombers. In Mecklemburg, he was present at the greatest Gearman Army manoeuvres since 1918.

Mussolini was infatuated by uniforms, military music and martial pomp. He used to spend hours at the window of the Palazzo Venezia watching the changing of the guard, expressing displeasure when a 'present arms' or an 'about turn' lacked precision. The Germans flattered him with impressive march-pasts. During a gigantic popular gathering on the 'Field of May' in a Berlin suburb, the two heroes exchanged exalted compliments—unfortunately interrupted by a thunderstorm and a violent downpour. 'A genius', cried the German, 'one of those rare geniuses not created by history, but themselves creators of history.' To which the Italian shrieked in reply, 'I will march with you to the end of the road.' Later, invited to have tea with Göring, the great man was able to admire the miniature electric trains which delighted the leisure hours of the 'Dauphin' of the Reich. He returned to Italy fascinated by the grim spectacle of a Germany encased in steel, sure of the invincibility of its war machine; dominated by the superman proclaimed by Nietzsche, 'Bearer of a sword thirsting for blood'.*

★　　★　　★

French memorialists continue years after the event to reproach their governments, and in particular Alexis Leger, the influential Secretary-

---

* On returning from Germany, the Duce decided that the Italian army should adopt the Prussian parade march, the famous 'goose step', transformed in Italy into the *passo romano* (the Roman step). 'Geese', he said in all seriousness, 'are the Roman birds which saved the Capitol.'[1]

General of the Quai d'Orsay, for throwing Italy into the arms of Germany. It is difficult to follow their train of thought. If it is true that Paris allowed itself to be influenced by its repugnance for the 'Carnival Caesar', London spared no efforts in trying to separate him from the Germans and draw him into its own fold. What was the result? Humiliating rebuffs and public affronts.

Chamberlain, who accused Eden of 'anti-Fascism', and the Foreign Office of incompetence, had made his sister-in-law an unofficial agent in Rome, to rival the Embassy. A fervent admirer of the Fascists, she displayed this openly by wearing on her corsage a gold party insignia. One day the Prime Minister, wishing to please the Duce, rebuked his Foreign Secretary in the presence of the Italian Ambassador, who was as much astonished as he was delighted. He finally succeeded in bringing about Eden's resignation, to the great satisfaction of the Italians. Could he have done more? New agreements were, it is true, signed in April 1938, but they changed nothing. Italian troops were not withdrawn from the Iberian Peninsula. Mussolini was profuse in irascible threats about a devastating surprise attack that he would launch against the Royal Navy after the Spanish war was over. His Air Force intensified its bombardments of Barcelona, and renewed its attacks on merchant shipping in the Mediterranean. The Italian special services and the Bari radio undertook a violent campaign of incitement among the Arabs, who were harassing the British in Palestine.* It is true that, periodically, the Roman dictator did fear a head-on collision with the democracies; but he quickly forgot it to challenge their vital interests again and again. Only awe of London and Paris could have possibly sobered him up. But neither Daladier, nor even less Chamberlain, were of the stature to inspire it.

His mania to show off, to shine at any cost in the eyes of the world, in those of Hitler, in those of his young mistress, in his own eyes, was manifested in the most unexpected gestures. Ciano relates that his father-in-law, furious at learning from the secret police that the Belgian Ambassador had expressed doubts about the martial qualities of the Italians, sent him a propaganda book about the Ethiopian war, accompanied by an anonymous letter: 'You said the Italian people do not like fighting. However, they have waged four victorious wars in a quarter century.' The Ambassador of Great Britain also received anonymous letters full of insults, accompanied by photographs extolling the Italian armed forces.[2]

---

* Great Britain had to cope in Palestine with an Arab insurrection. Syria and Lebanon under French mandate were also unstable.

The great Duce submitted himself without demur to the domination of the ruler of the Third Reich in whom he saw a master to fawn upon and to equal. In September 1937, during their spectacular encounter in Germany, he had made him understand that he could have Austria in exchange for a free hand in the Mediterranean. On 6 November, when Ribbentrop (who was still Ambassador in London) visited him for the signature of the Anti-Comintern Pact, which had been signed a year before between Germany and Japan, Mussolini confirmed that he agreed to let events take 'their natural course' in Austria—which meant abandoning it to the Reich. On 11 December, with much ado, he stalked out of 'the pestilential hearth which is the Sanhedrin of Geneva', in other words the League of Nations. Significantly, he adopted anti-Semitism quite pointlessly (Hitler had not even asked for it). He had once condemned racism as senseless, and had even intervened in Berlin against it. He had promoted Jews such as Count Volpi and Guido Jung to the highest offices in the Fascist state, and had found in a Jewess, Margherita Sarfatti, one of the few women worthy of his lasting attention. Now he became convinced of the need to purge Italy of the accursed race which until then—all witnesses agree—had never troubled him. To the astonishment of his compatriots, most of whom were ignorant of a Jewish community in their midst, which numbered only 50,000 persons, he began an anti-Jewish drive. He pursued it with an eagerness which went beyond simply obliging Hitler and can only be explained by his desire to identify himself with him and to merit his strange respect.

The press now stressed that the Jews did not belong to the 'Italian race'. The Fascist Grand Council promulgated racist laws similar, although less severe, to those of the Reich. The background of the closest collaborators of the Duce, including his son-in-law Ciano, were scrutinised in detail for possible 'impure origins'. 'I am a Nordic', announced this son of the Romagna, 'My daughter has married an Etruscan, my son a Lombard.'[3] To quote once again the Nietzsche whom he so admired, he had become, 'the ape of his own ideal'.

★   ★   ★

On 5 November 1937, Hitler returned from one of his long retreats at Berchtesgaden, and summoned to the Chancellory his Minister for Foreign Affairs, von Neurath, and the military leaders—von Blomberg, Minister for War, Göring, Minister for Air, Raeder, Grand Admiral, and von Fritsch, Commander-in-Chief of the Army. Officially convened to take stock of the raw materials situation (iron and steel, in particular, were in short supply), the meeting gave the Dictator the opportunity to explain his programme of action—his political testament he told them melodramatically, in case of his premature death.

The minutes of this meeting which his ADC, Colonel Hossbach, drew up, is a revealing document. After having made his listeners swear a solemn oath of secrecy, the Führer harangued them for four hours, developing his favourite theories on the *Lebensraum* which was vital to the Reich to overcome its supply problems. Overseas colonies were not enough; it was towards Eastern Europe that Germany's ambitions must turn. The very existence of the nation depended on their rapid achievement, within five or six years. The annexation of Czechoslovakia, if circumstances permitted, by a surprise attack in 1938, and then of Austria, were to constitute the preliminary stages. The use of force could not be ruled out. If this meant taking risks, they were minor ones. France was weakened by her domestic quarrels. The British Empire was not unshakeable. In all probability, the French and English would resign themselves to the abandonment of Czechoslovakia. A discussion followed. Baron von Neurath, Field Marshal von Blomberg (who had just received his baton), and General von Fritsch raised objections. Their master told them to be silent. They obeyed. Five days later, to 400 selected journalists, Hitler announced with cynicism that his pacific protestations had always been for tactical reasons alone, and that the moment had come to prepare the German people for 'Thunder and Lightning'.[4]

Did the governments in Paris and London know about this? It is said that from the beginning of December, Churchill and Roosevelt had knowledge of the Hossbach document.[5] In fact, the designs of the Führer were common knowledge. In his speeches of 5 and 10 November, he only repeated what he had said many times since he wrote *Mein Kampf*; what he and his closest henchmen had announced to various foreign personalities; and what the Nazi Press proclaimed almost daily. Ribbentrop, on some unspecified date in 1937, had even spoken of this to Churchill, in the absurd hope of obtaining his agreement. On a map of the world, covering an entire wall, he had expatiated at length on the plans of his master. If Great Britain opposed them, 'War would be inevitable. Nothing will stop the Führer'. Churchill, of course, informed the Foreign Office, and very probably his French friends.[6]

Many other indications sounded the alarm. At the beginning of 1938, Berlin announced a radical reshuffle of the government. At the

Ministry of Foreign Affairs, Joachim von Ribbentrop (or Joachim Ribbentrop, as the particle of nobility with which he gilded his name was of doubtful authenticity) took over from the elderly Baron von Neurath. He was a Rhinelander, the son of an artillery officer who had retired to Switzerland. He had failed to distinguish himself at the school for commerce in Grenoble. After a spell in Great Britain, he had drifted to Canada in 1910 where he worked in a bank, on the railways, and as a journalist in New York. Mobilised in 1914 in a Hussar regiment, he fought well. After the Armistice he became a commercial traveller in spirits, and married the daughter of a rich sparkling-wine grower—a hypochondriacal and cantankerous Valkyrie intensely disliked by the diplomatic corps of Berlin. Having come later to National Socialism and from rather modest origins, he compensated for this by unbounded vanity and fierce fanaticism. Displaying the most abject submission before his master, he craved adulation, while behaving harshly and brutally to subordinates; he censured diplomats with glacial arrogance, frequently lashing out in demonstrations of rage at his secretaries and clerks. On the gilded epaulettes of the uniform which he had himself designed, he had embroidered a globe of the world surmounted by the Eagle of the Reich. One day, not so very far distant, to his astonishment, he was to mount the scaffold at Nuremberg.

At the head of the Ministry of the Economy was Dr Funk, an undistinguished Nazi journalist attached to the Ministry of Propaganda. He succeeded Dr Schacht, having been chosen at random by Hitler during an interval at the opera; but he was a favourite of Göring because, being a homosexual, the threat of blackmail rendered him docile. Generals von Blomberg and von Fritsch were retired on the pretext of sexual depravity.* The first was replaced by Hitler himself, assisted by a new body of supreme command, the *Oberkommando der Wehrmacht* (OKW), replacing the War Ministry; the second by General von Brauschitch, a more supple personality than the austere Fritsch. A number of other military commanders with the reputation of not being sufficiently bellicose or National Socialist were dismissed or retired prematurely. As the German press announced blatantly, the

---

* Blomberg had married the daughter of a masseuse—a typist thirty years his junior, whose past was not spotless. Fritsch had been unjustly accused by the Gestapo of a homosexual liaison. Brauschitz was also involved in deep extra-conjugal trouble. However, as his girlfriend was a committed Nazi, Hitler allowed a second marriage, paying off the first Frau Brauschitz with a considerable sum from public funds to persuade her to divorce.

reorganisation of the high command confirmed the authority of the Führer over the only organ of state which had not yet been entirely subjugated.

★   ★   ★

In Austria, the Nazis had resumed the war of attrition. Almost daily, bomb explosions shook the people of Vienna. In the country and small towns, processions and demonstrations, often accompanied by acts of violence, undermined the authority of a government torn between the preoccupation of not annoying Hitler and that of preserving what remained of its sovereignty. The economic situation had again deteriorated, with innumerable unemployed, creating a climate of profound unease. At the beginning of 1938, the Vienna police had got wind of a new plot to repeat the failed *Putsch* of 1934. However, Mussolini continued to promise that the Axis would not be 'a spit on which to roast Austria'.

In February 1938, Schuschnigg, summoned to Berchtesgaden for a meeting 'man to man', accepted in the vague hope of a lasting accommodation with his dangerous neighbour. The meeting at the Berghof with its scenes of cruel intimidation has often been described. The Austrian Chancellor, after resisting courageously finished by capitulating, having received from Hitler three days in which to declare a general amnesty for political prisoners, and to allow National Socialists to occupy the principal cabinet posts. The following weeks were a long agony for him. Abandoned by the great powers, intimidated by military demonstrations on the frontier, the Chancellor and the President of the Republic, with heavy hearts, were forced to yield. Guido Schmidt was promoted to Minister of Foreign Affairs. Seyss-Inquart, another National Socialist, a childhood friend of the Federal Chancellor, who placed confidence in him because he was 'a good Catholic', was nominated to the crucial post of Minister of the Interior and Police. Without waiting, the 'good Catholic' went to Germany for his orders. Photographs in the press showed him seated on the arm of an easy chair chatting familiarly with the Führer.*

At the Rue de la Loi, in spite of our neutrality, which distanced us from the crisis, we were much concerned and had no doubt that the destiny of Austria had been settled.[7] Nevertheless, Schuschnigg stood up to the young hooligans in *Lederhosen* and white stockings (sub-

---

* Seyss-Inquart was sentenced to death at Nuremberg and went to the scaffold for crimes committed during the war, when he was Governor of the Netherlands.

stituted for the forbidden uniforms) who had been released from prison, or had come from over the frontier to sow disorder on the Austrian streets. On Wednesday 9 March at Innsbrück, joyously acclaimed by 20,000 people, the lustreless David, popular for the first time, announced a plebiscite on behalf of 'an Austria free and Germanic, independent and social, Christian and united'. Foreign observers believed he would win it and defeat Goliath.

★   ★   ★

Those who admired the unbelievable success of the Führer spoke readily of his 'intuitive genius'. There is no doubt that to the boldness of the gambler was added—at least during his first years—an acute political flair. But it was less remarkable than it appeared. More often, Hitler *knew* exactly what lay ahead. On his arrival in power, Göring had set up an intelligence service under the title *Forschungsamt* (Research Office), whose control he jealously guarded when Minister of Air. Employing as many as 3,000 bureaucrats camouflaged as working for his Department, they specialised in the supervision of the postal services, telephones, telex, telegrams, concentrating their attention clandestinely on thousands of people (including Frau Göring) and naturally on foreign Embassies. A team of 240 cryptographers armed with the first computers decoded on an average 3,000 messages a month. Baron von Weizsächer, Secretary of State at the Ministry of Foreign Affairs, stated after the war that the *Forschungsamt* read at least a half of the despatches emanating from the Embassies and foreign legations in Berlin, including those of Great Britain, France, Japan, Turkey and Belgium. It broke the British codes (with the exception of the most secret), and decoded all the French telegrams, including those destined for eastern Europe, which passed through the telecommunication centres of Berlin and Vienna.[8]

In the case of the Anschluss, the *Forschungsamt* was probably superfluous. Well before the event, it had appeared clear to Hitler that there would be no opposition. Czechoslovakia, the most directly threatened, was not powerful enough to frighten him. Göring had given that country his 'word of honour' that it had nothing to fear. It appeared to trust him. What else could it do? To Mussolini who, in spite of his tacit acquiescence, still aroused some fear in Hitler (he thought him much more dangerous than he was), the Führer sent a letter of explication through the Prince of Hesse. The latter, bubbling over with enthusiasm, telephoned the Führer at the last moment, to tell him that the Duce had taken it very well (which was not strictly true), and that he sent him his best wishes!

There remained Paris and London, the capitals guaranteeing the international order instituted by the League of Nations. For some time, the first had not dared to act without the second. Baldwin's main concern had been not to be disturbed. Chamberlain was of another stamp, eager to cover himself at all costs with laurels, replacing the cult of Geneva with the shibboleth of détente (the word is not new; like that of 'appeasement', it was in current use). Its real meaning is still not known today but Chamberlain defined it by a negative, 'No division of the world into ideological blocs!' This is a well-known argument. It is meaningless in the case of tolerant societies; but it threatens the peaceful one when the other is aggressive.

The first stage was an invitation to the German Minister for Foreign Affairs to visit London. After having accepted, Baron von Neurath extricated himself in a somewhat cavalier manner. In November 1937, Lord Halifax—known as 'The Holy Fox' to his enemies—was sent to Germany (it was always the British who crossed the Rhine, not the other way round). The Lord President of the Council was not without ambition; but he mitigated it by his indolence, even later hesitating to accept the succession to Eden for fear of having to give up his fox-hunting. On that score he was reassured. Not above sharp practice if it bore political fruits, he nevertheless inherited from his father, a devoit Christian, a sincere and generous humanism. This could have been a high ideal, had it not been diminished by an aristocratic aloof-ness, a kind of scornful irony which made him accept men without judging them; that, he thought, was God's affair. Although he did not like the Dictators, he did not condemn them. He had not bothered to read *Mein Kampf* until, much later, he received a copy from the hands of the Queen.[9]

Using the pretext of an invitation from Göring to an international hunting exhibition, Chamberlain sent Halifax to Germany. Halifax accepted the long journey from Berlin to Berchtesgaden imposed on him by the Führer—incidentally in a special luxury train—without demur. On 19 November, a cold autumn day, he was conveyed in an SS motor-car from the little Bavarian station to the Berghof. With his customary skill, the author of *Mein Kampf* manoeuvred him into playing the role of plaintiff. It was therefore the British Minister who spoke first, suggesting a four-power understanding between Great Britain, France, Germany and Italy, to guarantee European peace. He would not oppose the restitution of Germany's ex-colonies, mentioned the return of the Reich to the League of Nations, and disarmament. He also brought up the subjects of Austria, Czechoslovakia and Danzig, assuring Hitler that the British Government was not opposed to gradual changes in the European order. Hitler was delighted, but careful not to give a definite answer, limiting himself to condemning the English press and protecting his peaceful intentions. This conversation took place just a few weeks after the Führer had expounded his plans of conquest to his generals and to journalists.

The next day, Halifax lunched in the ostentatious luxury of the Karinhall, Göring's country residence, served by lackeys in green and white livery. The man who had founded the Gestapo, who had organised the first concentration camps, and who had been the assassin of the 'Night of the Long Knives' in Berlin, was clad in a silk shirt, a green leather jerkin, a dagger in a red Morocco leather sheath at his belt. 'Frankly, attractive', was the judgement of the Yorkshire Lord of the Manor. Not insensible to the gulf which separated him from the Nazis, Halifax was to compare his visit to Germany with 'an expedition into a savage land'. He was astonished to find Hitler wearing silk socks and patent leather shoes: scarcely less surprised when he recommended him to shoot Gandhi and his principal followers. However, in spite of his reservations on the regimentation of the population, everything appeared to him 'absolutely fantastic'. Hitler was 'a Gandhi wearing Prussian boots': Göring, a big schoolboy full of vitality and proud of what he is doing; Goebbels, was 'more agreeable than I had thought before having tea with him'. These men were 'genuine haters' of Communism; and Anthony Eden was quite wrong to prefer Leon Blum to them. On his return to London, Halifax even tried to suppress the publication of the witty caricatures for which David Low and other humorists were famous, on the ground that they were unfairly cruel to the Führer.[10]

As his secretary Oliver Harvey wrote: 'He easily blinds himself to unpleasant facts and is ingenious and even Jesuitical in rounding awkward corners in his mind.' With his polished manners and the obliging imprecision of his language, Halifax had confirmed in Hitler's mind the notion that the British Government would react feebly when confronted with a *fait accompli* in Austria and Czechoslavakia. This heralded Munich, one year before it took place. Had he unconsciously deceived his colleagues?—Hardly! Chamberlain agreed with the report of his mission, concluding that it would be impossible to prevent German expansion in Eastern Europe, noting in his diary 'a great success'.[11]

Alone among the senior Ministers, Eden showed some dissatisfaction; but only because as Foreign Secretary he had been usurped by Halifax. He approved the results of Berchtesgaden as much as his colleagues. In December, he encouraged Ribbentrop (which was hardly necessary) by telling him that England recognised the legitimacy of 'a closer connection' between Germany and Austria. In January 1938, passing through Geneva, Eden stated to Spaak, 'Germany behaves much more reasonably than Italy'. A little later he wrote to Chamberlain, 'As you know, I am completely in agreement with you that we make every effort to get on with Germany'; he added, 'It is otherwise with Italy.' He even justified his opposition to a rapprochement with Italy on the ground that it might annoy Berlin.[12]

On his recommendation, the Cabinet adopted a document entitled, 'Further Steps Towards a General Settlement'. Its principal feature should have satisfied the colonial aspirations of the Reich, for it associated Germany with a vast African territory, most of it taken from the Belgian and Portuguese possessions; but cynically omitting any of the colonies acquired by Great Britain at Versailles. Sir Neville Henderson, the British Ambassador in Berlin, was instructed to inform the Führer personally of these proposals.* On 3 March 1938, after having been kept waiting several days, he was ushered into the Presence to find Hitler 'crouching in an armchair with the most ferocious scowl on his face'. In vain Henderson attempted to display to the Führer, on a globe of the world, the extent of the area offered to the Reich in a reorganised basin of the Congo. To this Hitler replied with a furious diatribe against the Press, the Bishops, and the British Ministers. The colonies, he said, were not an urgent question; central Europe was. He would tolerate no exterior intervention. If Great Britain wanted to oppose a just settlement, Germany would fight.[13]

★   ★   ★

This meeting took place three weeks after Schuschnigg's dramatic visit to Berchtesgaden, of which all the European Chancelleries were

---

* British diplomats stated in Brussels and Lisbon that there was no question of returning the colonies to Germany. In the House of Commons Eden declared in December 1937 that, 'publicly and categorically nothing could be further from the intentions of His Majesty's Government than to recommend and support any transaction at the expense of other colonial powers'. At the beginning of January, meeting Spaak in Geneva, he replied to a direct question from his Belgian colleague that London was studying the colonial question, but that nothing would be done without consulting Belgium.[14]

now fully informed. It was evident that Austria would shortly be seized, '*so oder so*', one way or the other, as Hitler put it. London decided on a policy of *laissez-faire*. 'Why all this agitation?', noted Sir Alexander Cadogan, the new Permanent Under-Secretary at the Foreign Office, on 15 February. 'It will not worry me if Austria does have to be *gleichgestaltet*.' London's action was limited to informing the Wilhelmstrasse politely that His Majesty's Government was much concerned. The step was taken independently from France to avoid giving the impression of collusion. As early as 2 March, in replying to a question from the opposition in the House of Commons, Chamberlain had declared that, 'Nothing makes me suppose that Austrian sovereignty is threatened.' Pressed with more questions, he refused any further comment. On Thursday 10 March, in possession for six days of the report from his Ambassador in Berlin, knowing therefore the intentions of the Führer, and while the European press was filled with dire news about Austria, Chamberlain limited himself to replying to Arthur Henderson, who again asked if he had any declaration to make, 'No Sir!'

Hitler had got the message. In any case, Ribbentrop had confirmed it to him. Having returned briefly to London on the pretext of 'closing his establishment' (as the diplomats say), Ribbentrop had telephoned his master on the Thursday evening to dispel any last minute uncertainties. Next day, as a guest at lunch, with his wife, in Downing Street, he was again talking about appeasement and détente with Chamberlain and Halifax, when a secretary came in with a telegram announcing the German ultimatum to Austria. Churchill, one of the guests, noted, 'This was the last time I saw Herr von Ribbentrop before he was hanged.'[15]

If London implicitly encouraged the Führer, Paris did nothing to restrain him. Nine months earlier, the exhausted Leon Blum had retired. The *Front Populaire* had survived, but its vital impulse was gone. Its new leader, the radical Camille Chautemps (the man in office at the time of the Stavisky scandal), was one of those cunning Parliamentary figures who come and go, and of whom it is impossible to discern the qualities which enable them to survive every setback. On 10 March 1938, the day after the Vienna referendum had been announced, Chautemps again resigned, without any clear reason, unless it was the fear of having to face a serious crisis.

Since Versailles, the integrity of Austria had been a fundamental part of French foreign policy. When the German threats increased, Alexis Leger had intensified his warnings to the Ministers—as General

Gamelin said, 'heartbroken by their apathy'. Even Gamelin was moved to suggest 'doing something'. But nothing was done, save a sounding in Rome, fruitless appeals to London, one or two vague diplomatic *démarches* in Berlin and a courageous speech by Yvon Delbos, which the *Chambre des Députés* approved almost unanimously—but in vain.

Delbos's speech was, in any case, disavowed by the reticences of many of the other Ministers. Chautemps did not hide his defeatism. Daladier told Bullit, the American Ambassador—who was not famed for his discretion—that 'nothing could be done to save Austria'. Franz von Papen, passing through Paris, was 'astounded to realise that Chautemps and Bonnet consider a reorientation of French policy in Central Europe wide open for discussion', that they had 'no objection to a marked extension of German influence in Austria by peaceable means, or in Czechoslavakia, through a regionalisation of nationalities'.[16] These remarks were hardly less clear than those of Chamberlain, Eden and Halifax.

★   ★   ★

The plebiscite announced by the Austrian Chancellor on 9 March infuriated Hitler. In a burning rage against the wretches who were thwarting his plans (but not without some final reservations) he decided to annihilate them. On the morning of 10 March 1938, he gave the order to prepare Operation Otto (the invasion of his native land); only, in the throes of hysterical excitement, to annul it almost immediately, before again confirming it. Inundated with contradictory orders, hasty decisions immediately postponed, by threats and fits of Hitler's uncontrollable temper, the generals undertook the enormous task of improvising in two days the mobilisation of an army of 100,000 men.

In Vienna, Thursday 10 March was calm. Schuschnigg, who had returned from Innsbruck, proceeded actively with the preparation of the plebiscite to be held the following Sunday. Bills were posted on the walls of public buildings, propaganda vehicles equipped with loudspeakers and covered with red-white-red flags toured the streets, applauded enthusiastically by the passers-by. Workers' organisations, although forbidden, responded favourably. The Cardinal Archbishop advised Catholics to vote 'Yes'. Everything seemed set fair.

On Friday the storm broke. Before dawn, Schuschnigg was woken by his bedside telephone with the voice of the chief of police announcing that road and railway communications were cut and the frontier closed on the German side. Shortly after, the Austrian Consul-General in Munich reported that the Bavarian Army Corps was in a state of general mobilisation. During the morning, a courier arrived by air from Berlin with an ultimatum. The plebiscite was to be cancelled, and Schuschnigg's government replaced immediately by a complete National Socialist Ministry. Otherwise. . . .

Hours passed in diplomatic discussions and anguished goings to and fro. The Palazzo Venezia when telephoned, stated that Mussolini could not be found; he was skiing somewhere in the mountains. Paris and London had no advice to offer. While young Nazis dominated the streets, the police, under the orders of Seyss-Inquart, looked on and did nothing. The Austrian Army, of some tens of thousands of men, was incapable of opposing the Wehrmacht. The situation appeared insoluble. During the afternoon the plebiscite was cancelled, and Schuschnigg, broken-hearted, was driven to resign.

Göring, who had recently succumbed again to the euphoric servitude of morphine, took charge of the operation, shrieking more and more strident threats down the telephone. However, this did not prevent him from presiding that evening over a musical evening in the sumptuous House of Aviation, built by the regime. He made his appearance in a splendid sky-blue uniform, encrusted with gold braid and studded with decorations, his fat fingers sparkling with rings, sweating profusely, mopping his brow nervously with a handkerchief which wafted clouds of scent. Moving among the guests in their dinner jackets and evening dresses (among them the Austrian Ambassador), he was seen to take Sir Nevile Henderson aside by the arm for a private conversation.[17]

At about the same time, Schuschnigg broadcast from his office in the Ballhausplatz in a sobbing voice that he was yielding to force, that the Army had received orders to lay down its arms, and that he was resigning. Descending the great marble staircase of the Chancellery, the valiant little lawyer refused to take flight; he collapsed into his car and returned to his residence at the Belvedere, where he was promptly arrested by Seyss-Inquart's men.*

'As I crossed the Graben, the brown flood was sweeping through

---

* Transferred shortly afterwards to the Gestapo Headquarters, Schuschnigg was to be imprisoned for months, submitted to the most degrading humiliations, forced to clean the wash-rooms and lavatories with the only towel which had been supplied him for his personal use. Thrown into concentration camps, he survived miraculously, and was freed by American troops in May 1945.

the streets' reported an English journalist. 'It was an indescribable witches' sabbath—storm-troopers, lots of them barely out of the schoolroom, with cartridge-belts and carbines, the only other evidence of their authority being a swastika brassard, were marching side by side with police turncoats, men and women shrieking or crying the name of their leader hysterically . . . motor lorries filled with storm-troopers clutching their long concealed weapons, hooting furiously, smoking torches . . . the air filled with a pandemonium of sound in which intermingled screams of: "Down with the Jews, Heil Hitler! Sieg Heil! Death to the Jews! Schuschnigg to the gallows! Heil Seyss-Inquart! Down with the Catholics! One people, one Reich, one Führer!"'[18]

The Chancellery, the public buildings, the radio premises and the railway station, where thousands of people were herded in the vain hope of flight, were occupied by armed members of the SA. The leading men of the old regime, including the Mayor of Vienna and President Miklas, were brutally arrested. At 5 a.m., that morning, Himmler arrived by air with his special Gestapo and SS teams to organise the brown terror. That day 70,000 militants, monarchists, nationalists and Catholics joined the Socialists and Communists whom Schuschnigg had incarcerated in the prisons and concentration camps. The persecution of the Jews began with a savagery and sadism hitherto unknown. The great Sigmund Freud, aged 82, was imprisoned before managing to find refuge in England. The writer Stefan Zweig also succeeded in escaping, just in time. The rich were incarcerated and ransomed. Baron Louis Rothschild was detained for several months and threatened with death, until he handed over his financial interests in a number of enterprises. The less rich had their shops and apartments sacked, emptied of their possessions, furniture, crockery, jewels and their motor-cars confiscated. Doctors, lawyers, merchants, men and women, young and old, were arrested in thousands 'to make an example'. The sinister Eichmann (a native of Austria) began the career which was to end on an Israeli gallows, by installing a 'Bureau for Jewish Immigration', which issued exit visas to those prepared to hand over all they had. In the streets and the public places, the SS in black uniforms, pistols in their belts, whips in their hands, forced Jews and anti-Nazi priests, together with some of the great names of the aristocracy, to wash the pavements and scrape off the walls the patriotic notices of the defunct regime; or to clean the street urinals with their bare hands. Night had fallen on the capital of Austria.

In spite of her many tribulations, Vienna had, for half a century, been one of the most shining centres of European civilisation: painting, music, philosophy and science scintillated.* For the intellectuals, Jewish or not, who had given this lustre, there was no place in the Hitlerian empire; almost all went into exile—never to return. While the Wehrmacht paraded the boulevards, greeted with enthusiasm by a part of the population, particularly by the 600,000 unemployed, who felt they had been delivered from their nightmare, the opposition went to ground. A 'Constitutional Law' promulgated simultaneously in Berlin and Vienna annexed Austria, to be called henceforth *Ostmark* (The March of the East). Seyss-Inquart, short-lived Chancellor, was reduced to provincial governor.

On Monday, 15 March, surrounded by SS in their black uniforms and by '*Schupos*' (civilian police) in their traditional green garb, Adolf Hitler (with his mistress Eva Braun concealed among his followers) made a triumphal entry into the capital of the Habsburgs, which he had left 25 years previously to escape his military duty. The jubilant city was bedecked with Nazi flags—even the churches, even the cathedral had hoisted the pagan emblem by the orders of Cardinal Innitzer.† From the balcony of the Imperial Hotel, the son of the customs officer addressed joyful crowds, remembering the days when he had been gazing for hours at the impressive building, to nourish his hatred of the rich and the powerful. He is said to have wept with happiness.

★   ★   ★

Among the perfidious coups by 'the madman who thinks he is God', as Schuschnigg called Hitler, this was his first attack on a foreign state, moreover, on an immediate neighbour state. The fact that Austria was of Germanic origin impressed only the 'realists'. For the Third Reich, it was a resounding success, rallying to the Nazi cause many Germans hitherto diffident or hostile to National Socialism.‡ Everywhere else,

---

* It was in Vienna that psychoanalysis, linguistic philosophy, 12-tone music, brilliant expressionist school, art nouveau, Austromarxism, and Sionism were born.

† Cardinal Innitzer, who had publicly professed loyalty to the new regime, was called back to rome, lectured by the Pope and directed to publish in the *Osservatore Romano*, the Vatican's newspaper, a *mise au point*.

‡ Operation Otto had been a disaster from a military point of view. The armoured units, badly prepared and badly led, had proved very difficult to manoeuvre. Without maps (Guderian had given Baedekers to his divisional commanders) and without guides, they also lost a number of tanks through breakdowns. However, the 'Austrian Campaign' was a most informative general rehearsal for the Wehrmacht High Command.

consternation reigned. Brussels was severely critical: 'Downfall of France. Mortal blow to the prestige of England'; but, at the same time, it was relieved to have taken refuge in neutrality—assuredly, the reflex of the ostrich. But had it not all been set in motion by the Great Powers? In all ears rang the brutally frank warnings of Chamberlain in the House of Commons debate on the resignation of Eden: the small countries had to give up all their illusions, there was no question of their being protected by the League of Nations against aggression.[19]

The unfortunate Austria had learned this bitter lesson. During its agony, the French ministerial crisis had followed its usual course. The President had asked Leon Blum to form a Ministry of National Unity including the Left, the Centre and the Right. The Socialist leader tried to do so; but his past, the inflexibility of his declared doctrinal beliefs— even if only verbal—the setback to his first government, made him personally unacceptable to the Conservatives. He had to be satisfied with the reticent collaboration of the Radicals and Communists. Inspired always by the loftiest principles, he presented himself to the *Chambre* by proclaiming France's attachment to peace and collective security—fine words, which no longer meant anything.

For peace and security were no longer possible without the firm determination of the great democracies to impose the rule of law— what the false wisdom of their governments called 'the mid-summer of madness'. The League of Nations had not even been informed. London and Paris confined themselves to notes of protest, which Berlin rejected disdainfully, on the grounds that they constituted interference in Germany's internal affairs. When, some days later, Moscow proposed, in the context of the League (or outside it), a conference of the peace-loving nations, with the aim of preventing further acts of aggression, Blum and Chamberlain declined to follow it up. The British Prime Minister stated in the Commons that the Soviet proposal referred to, 'an eventuality which does not exist', and was likely to 'encourage the formation of opposing groups of nations', which His Majesty's Government considered detrimental to the future of European peace. As for Paul-Boncour, the French Foreign Minister, he promised the Soviet Ambassador that the Kremlin suggestion would be seriously studied. Then he forgot it—to the extent of not even mentioning it in his three volumes of memoirs published after the war.

The watch-word was: 'No confrontation'.

★   ★   ★

In spite of its outstretched hand to the democratic nations, Moscow was still regarded as a hive of iniquity. The third series of its awesome political trials had taken place the very week of the Anschluss; the purges were in full swing. Even more, the Spanish war, in which Left faced Right and the USSR fought the Fascist powers, exacerbated the old dilemma: Moscow or Berlin? 'With cholera on my right, and the bubonic plague on my left, I prefer the middle way', said Sir Eric Phipps, the British Ambassador in Paris. A way which would no doubt have been chosen by most French, English and Belgians. The real question was—was it still practicable?

To a lady who became indignant at hearing the Soviet alliance extolled, Churchill, wreathed in clouds of cigar smoke, retorted, 'I believe in holding to the carnal, until the spiritual is free.' But his less intelligent rivals could not distinguish between ideology and strategy. It would be unfair to accuse them all of sympathising with Hitler. On the day of the Austrian invasion, Chamberlain noted, 'It is now clear that force is the only argument that Germany understands.' He was sometimes heard describing Hitler as a mad dog, and a lunatic dictator. However, he continued to adjure, 'No division of the world into ideological blocks!' Samuel Hoare went even further, hoping for 'a war in which Fascists and Communists will kill one another'; a hope which, in the last resort, is defensible if the two calamities present equal threats. That was not the case. Another of the leading Ministers, Lord Stanhope, disliked 'his country playing the role of unpaid policemen of the globe'.[20] Why indeed worry about Ethiopia, Spain, China, Austria, Czechoslovakia, the Belgian and Portuguese colonies? A magnificent egoism. But despising the ethics which had justified the British Empire, he adopted a kind of neutrality which, in the nature of things, could only encourage the more aggressive states.

I have often talked to people about those troubled years. How was it that the British élite, so conscious of moral values, should take refuge in such blindness?

'They are curiously bereft of imagination, a quality which, in any case, inspires in them some distrust', says an English friend who has an affection for, as well as a clear vision of, his fellow countrymen. 'Perhaps this is due to the educational system, to those stern boarding schools which, in isolated parts of the land, discipline flights of the imagination as much as unruly behaviour. It is bad form to get excited; self-control is necessary, as are understatement and pragmatism. Those who promise great things are as poorly regarded as those who announce disasters. Many of our celebrated reformers have not been English—Disraeli a Jew, MacDonald a Scot, Gladstone and Lloyd George Welsh. Chamberlain and his associates were of a different class. Deciding to live in the present, their sense of good manners was shocked by the more imaginative spirit of the Churchills or French politicians—too excitable to be gentlemen.'

Some of them, often near the top, were still quivering with the Great Fear and imagined naïvely that Hitlerism would protect them from revolution. Much has been said about Cliveden, Lord and Lady Astor's country estate near London, where at weekends, in the elegant drawing-rooms or on the manicured lawns, politicians, journalists and idlers gathered to hold forth on 'eternal values', while indulging in their favourite games, charades or musical chairs. Members of the government rubbed shoulders with notorious Germanophiles, such as the editor of *The Times*, Geoffrey Dawson, who wrote to a friend, 'I spend my nights in taking out anything which I think will hurt their susceptibilities and in dropping little things which are intended to soothe them.'[21]

Also among the company were bankers and leaders of industry, looking out for good business with Central Europe. Or Nazi and Fascist visitors to Great Britain who painted to their frightened table-companions the well-known image of 'Mongol ponies grazing in the ruins of civilisation'. The Cliveden Set was certainly a pressure group favourable to the Dictators. There were others, among them the active Anglo-German Fellowship. There were also, as in France and Belgium, a heterogeneous fauna who sang their praises, men and women, chiefly women hypnotised by the mysterious attraction of force, not very intelligent idealists and adventurers in search of easy profits. Or a *Jeunesse dorée* which, with cheap 'tourist marks', shared the pleasures of rich Nazis on the ski slopes of old Austria, in the bars of the Adlon hotel or the Munich brasseries; who accompanied them for rides in open-roof sports Mercedes, sparkling and chromium-plated, who envied the erotic appeal of their boots and leather belts, drinking to excess and fornicating day and night.

In actual fact, the number of those duped was decreasing day by day. The visit to Berchtesgaden in the summer of 1937 by the Duke of Windsor and his wife (paid by an organisation of the Nazi Party) and his Roman salute to the Führer had been severely condemned. The Anglo-German Fellowship which had numbered 1,000 members in 1936, had lost most of them by 1938. Ribbentrop, who had been warmly welcomed on his arrival in the British capital, left it detested in the drawing-rooms, despised by the politicians and literally booed on the streets; his unpleasant personality was not the only reason for this. Parliament, since the Ethiopian war, had been badly disposed towards Italy, and not much better disposed towards Germany. Baldwin himself, after having long regarded Hitler and Mussolini as champions of anti-Bolshevism, confided to the Commonwealth Prime Ministers that they were 'demons'. 'The British are slow to rouse', my friends tell me. But by the beginning of 1938, they were losing confidence in a government elected three years before to suppress international brigandage.

The rhetorical refusal of some Englishmen to take up arms, which had caused such a stir in 1933, was forgotten. Events had transformed a philosophical aversion to war into a horror of approaching disaster. Ahead lay a gigantic catastrophe, a nightmare of aerial bombardments and toxic gas which would annihilate western civilisation.* Nevertheless, it had to be faced. The best contemporary writers and most of the youth now accepted it, not without bitterness but with unshakeable courage. Even the red stars which, at the beginning of the decade, had been reflected in the dazzled eyes of many intellectuals had ceased to shine. Auden, the most famous of the young poets, became a Catholic. Stephen Spender and Isherwood left the Muscovite Church, and with Aldous Huxley, Priestley, Orwell, Graham Greene, and others, turned their energies to the defence of the dignity of man. Bernard Shaw remained an admirer of Stalin; 'You can't make an omelette without breaking eggs', he wrote airily. But the erratic political views of the controversial old fellow were not taken seriously. There was talk in vain of a Front Populaire. Mosley and the British Union of Fascists had come to naught.

For most people, a world dominated by totalitarian ideologies would abolish the values which gave human life its meaning, an alternative worse than the most frightful of wars.

> *O let them witness*
> *That my fate is the angel of their fate*
> *The angel of Europe*
> *And the spirit of Europe destroyed with my defeat.*

So mourned the hero of Stephen Spender in the *Trial of a Judge*. That spirit was the old tradition of the West.[22]

The public had become aware of everything which the government was trying to conceal from it, 'with a perfect deceit', wrote Harold Nicolson. They saw clearly that the more they were promised peace, the nearer appeared the sinister shadow of war. For the proletariat itself, class warfare lost its urgency before a more direct threat. In

---

* The first gas masks were distributed in 1937. The effects of aerial bombardments were much exaggerated. With extravagant theoretical calculations the British experts had forecast an aerial offensive of 60 days which would cause 600,000 deaths and 1,200,000 wounded. In fact, after nearly six years of war, British casualties from air raids totalled 60,000 dead and 250,000 wounded.

November 1937, in response to one of the first opinion polls operated by Gallup, 38 per cent of English males declared that if war came, they would join the Armed Forces—a minority admittedly, but an impressive minority, not far from the patriotic fervour of 1914. Parliament reflected these currents of opinion—even on the Labour benches, where anti-militarism was now silent. Attlee turned a half circle. Forgetting his earlier protestations, he made energetic speeches about the 'indivisibility of peace'—but without renouncing his opposition to military service. The Trade Unions, less concerned with the electors, demanded the acceleration of rearmament by a large majority. On 5 March 1938, *only a few days before the Anschluss*, in another poll, 58 per cent of the English disapproved of Chamberlain's foreign policy; only one in four (25 per cent) was in favour of it.

Anthony Eden, harassed by Sir John Simon and Sir Samuel Hoare (his predecessors at the Foreign Office) and hustled by Neville Chamberlain, became the unconscious standard bearer of the resistance. When he was forced to resign, his gesture was seen by the uninitiated as the solemn manifestation of a conscience in revolt. The opinion poll of 5 March condemning Chamberlain, approved massively (60 per cent) of him. When he left the Prime Minister late on the afternoon of 19 February 1938, having informed him of his scruples, he had been the object of an ovation from the crowd in Downing Street who cried, 'Down with Hitler! Down with Chamberlain!'[23]

Much more than Churchill—then far from being the uncontested leader he would be in the Second World War—'Eden was the most popular politician in the country', as Harold Macmillan was to recall. According to the words of his closest collaborator, he dreamed of leading 'a country which believed passionately in all in that he believed in himself (a country) that was anti-defeatist, pro-League, anti-dictator'.[24] He refused to heed the anti-Communist and anti-Soviet obsession of his older colleagues, for whom red ghosts made their flesh creep. Addressing himself indiscriminately to Conservatives, Liberals, Labourites, Trade Unions, old soldiers and youth, he extolled, as did Churchill, a 'Grand Alliance' which would unite under the sign of collective security, Great Britain and her Dominions, France, the Soviet Union and the small nations—democratic unanimity and international morality. Eden and his 'glamour boys', a score of rebel Conservatives (but by no means the least important) appeared to echo the great voices of Disraeli and Gladstone. The strength of character of the young Eden was not on a par with his insight. He made good speeches, the masses applauded him, Parliament listened to him. But indecisive and without lyricism, he avoided colliding with the men in power, hoping to resume the place in the cabinet that he had just left, being careful not to join Churchill and his friends. At the time of Munich, he distinguished himself by his caution. Chamberlain's hold on Parliament remained complete. Détente was still the watch-word.

In France, the first opinion polls were not taken until the end of 1938. Although less clear than in Great Britain, the situation was very similar. Amongst the intelligentsia there were few cases of dereliction among the great names. André Gide abandoned Communism. The aged Romain Rolland, after having objected to 'the land of Socialism', returned to it—but due to his dislike of the Nazis. Aragon and Eluard remained faithful to it. Malraux, who had commanded a bomber squadron in the Spanish Civil War (without having ever piloted one) continued to believe in the message of the Communist Party (without becoming a member of it), claiming that the Moscow trials 'do not affect it any more than the Inquisition diminished the teaching of Christ'.[25] Indeed, for most of these 'fellow travellers', Communism was no more than a further step on the road to Liberalism.

The extreme Right, it is true, indulged in paroxysms of fury. Charles Maurras repeated his appeals for the assassination of the political leaders ('haven't you somewhere an automatic pistol, a revolver or even a kitchen knife?')—a call which was to land him in gaol. Alphonse de Chateaubriant in the *Gerbe des Forces* found in National Socialism 'the renewal of the work of God'. Brasillach in *Je Suis Partout* surpassed himself:

> The fresh early morning when they take Blum to Vincennes (to shoot him) will be a festive day for French families, an occasion on which to drink champagne . . . the day is not far distant when the red Bishops will be hanged in their purple rags, and the democratic curés will be disembowelled with their choir boys at the font of overturned crosses, their pyxes polluted with excrement.[26]

Rebatet, Celine and others pronounced similar neurotic imprecations.* They were not without imitators; but what was their

---

* Robert Brassilach thought he had found in Fascism the only system which meant anything to him: Youth. Plump, wearing spectacles, attaching an unhealthy importance to his physical appearance, he was literally terrified of growing old. Ferdinand Celine, whose real name was Ferdinand Destouches, a doctor neurotically attracted to and haunted by death, poured out his hallucinations in his writings. He stated, without any evidence to support it, that his skull had been trepanned after a war wound. Alphonse de Chateaubriant was an unbalanced homosexual who fell in love with 'the warm nape' of Hitler's neck. Drieu la Rochelle, a Don Juan, obsessed by the fear of impotence, drank to excess and suffered from suicidal tendencies. After two abortive attempts, he killed himself in 1945.

real meaning? On the Right as on the Left, the most prominent members of the French intelligentsia remained solidly faithful to the cause of the dignity of man: Henri Bergson, Jacques Maritain, André Gide, Paul Valéry, Jules Romain, Roger Martin du Gard, Georges Duhamel, André Chamson, Paul Claudel, Romain Rolland and others. Even Mauriac and Bernanos, whose eyes had been opened by the abominable excesses in Spain, even perhaps Drieu la Rochelle and others of the same unusual breed, sunk in despair by an apparent collapse of the old European ideal.

Was it the same with the masses? The Communist Party boasted 300,000 members; 1,500,000 French people had voted for it. But the country had more than 10 million electors, and the PCF had only been successful by abandoning, at least superficially, many of its revolutionary themes, including anti-militarism. Among the Socialists some 'suicidal pacifists' had grouped around Marceau Pivert; excluded from the Party, they had been followed by a mere handful of militants, four or five thousand.[27] It should not be forgotten that since the about-turn of Stalin and the Komintern in 1935, the extreme Left had become intensely patriotic.

The popularity of the extreme Right, which had joined the camp of the defeatists, never a united force, is more difficult to evaluate. The *Parti Populaire Français* of Jacques Doriot, the only one of any importance to represent an authentic version of European Fascism, had boasted at the height of its power of having 250,000 members. No doubt it exaggerated. In any case, by 1939 its driving force was exhausted. As for the *Action Française*, with its elitist character, it had only 60,000 members, of whom only 6,000 were in Paris, most of them remaining Germanophobe. Moreover, it was forced into dissolution after the attempt on the life of Leon Blum, and the disavowal by the Pretender to the throne whom it claimed to serve. Condemned by the Pope and led by old men (Maurras and Daudet were aged 70), it had lost a great deal of its former prestige.

The *Parti Social Français*, born from the *Croix de Feu*, a patriotic association of veterans, with its 700,000 members, were the only movement of the new Right which had acquired a broad clientele. Its leader, Lieutenant Colonel François de la Roque, was an ambiguous character. A hero of the Great War, in which he had been badly wounded, he had no sympathy for Parliamentary democracy, and spent his time vigorously denouncing its weaknesses. The Left accused him of being a French Mussolini. This was an exaggeration; for the little colonel had none of Mussolini's explosive violence and his opinions—not always very clear—were remote from most of the totalitarian watch-words, including anti-Semitism, one of its central themes. He was also notable for his condemnation of all weakness in dealing with Berlin, describing appeasement as 'under-cover defeatism'.*

The other leagues hardly counted. Obscure conspirators subsidised by German and Italian money were to be found in secret societies such as the *Cagoule* (or CSAR, *Comité Secret pour l'Action Révolutionaire*). The Cagoulards infiltrated part of the officer corps and maintained relations, it appeared, with Laval. Terrorist assassination attempts, one of them probably instigated by Mussolini, gave them an unhealthy publicity. But they were no more than a handful of young hot-heads, double-agents and habitual criminals.

Oswald Mosley in Great Britain, and Léon Degrelle in Belgium saw their political careers wither in 1936 and 1937. In both cases, the improvement of the social climate had contributed to it. It was the same in France, where the storms raised by Maurras, Doriot, and others, were dissipated a little later. Had they, incidentally, been more tempestuous than those of Boulangism in 1887, or of the 'anti-Dreyfusards' around 1900? Have not French political passions been exaggerated, especially the spectacular but very limited influence of the far Right? Lucien Rebatet himself, one of its fire-brands, recognised bitterly in 1942 that the anti-Fascist propaganda 'put out by England' surpassed that of his political friends 'in all fields'.[28]

The blemishes of Parliamentary life remained ineradicable. They had been with the Third Republic since its origin; but they had not prevented it from acquiring a vast empire, nor terminating the Great War by a resounding victory. That victory should not obscure the pre-1914 uncertainties any more than the defeat of 1940 should exaggerate the unrest of the Thirties—desperate religious struggles, bitter revolutionary agitation, harsh opposition of the Right and the Left. In the north and the Parisian region, violent strikes were frequent, blood was often spilled. In 1907, in the south, the poverty brought 500,000 people together under the leadership of the Socialist mayor of Narbonne; after the sack and arson of the 'sous-prefecture', he was arrested. When the 17th Infantry Regiment was commanded to re-establish order, it mutinied.

---

* During the Second World War, after having at first supported Marshal Pétain, La Roque collaborated with the British Secret Service, and was thrown into a German concentration camp.

This was not an isolated incident. The Army was penetrated with an anti-military cancer which was absent in 1938–39. From 1908 on, the Trades Union movement had led a campaign for a general revolutionary strike in the event of war. Desertion and absenteeism were rampant—more than 75,000 men in 1911, the equivalent of two army corps. Military service, which was reduced to two years in 1905, gave France a permanent army of only 480,000 men, to face the Kaiser's 800,000. A Barthou government, in spite of international tension, had managed, with the greatest difficulty to have a 'law of three years' adopted in 1913, designed to establish a better equilibrium of forces.* It caused great unrest. When troops due to be discharged were kept with the colours, they demonstrated noisily; here and there more mutinies broke out. The 'Confédération Générale du Travail' and the Socialist party had increased their pacifist activities, organised many meetings, obtaining 700,000 signatures, among them many from non-Socialist intellectuals. The backwash corresponded to a considerable radicalisation of the electoral body. In the 1910 elections, the block of the Left had 414 seats in the *Chambre*, as against 175 of the Right—a greater majority than that of the *Front Populaire*. The elections of 1914 had returned more than 100 Socialist deputies violently opposed to national defence and passionately, religiously, pacifist. Governmental instability was endemic; between 1909 and 1914, ten different Ministeries succeeded one another in power.[29]

It would be quite erroneous to believe that the Parliament elected in 1936 was inferior to that of 1914. In spite of short-comings, it contained few dishonest men, and only a handful of Fascists. Debu-Bridel, a deputy of the Right, and ex-Camelot du Roi, not always an impartial witness, was probably right when he wrote, 'Anyone in the habit of visiting the corridors of the Palais Bourbon must be struck by the importance that everyone, even the most obscure Deputy, attaches to foreign policy. Anxiety increased, little was required to awaken patriotism. What was lacking was a Clémenceau to transform their goodwill into energetic action.' Many others share this view, including the austere observer Raymond Aron.[30]

This same Parliament voted the enormous military credits demanded by the government without demur, an event unknown in the annals of the Republic. In following Leon Blum it also showed

---

*In August 1914, the French Army aligned 80 divisions against 100 German divisions, 2,500 machine guns against 4,500, 3,800 75 mm guns against 6,000 77 mm guns and no heavy artillery. But Joffre was a better general than Molkte the Younger.

CHAPTER 13

Two Hapless Men: Daladier and Chamberlain

In the fifth act of classical tragedies, the different themes which so far have developed incoherently and uncertainly, now fall into place. From the ordering of separate events, each one imprinted with its own logic, there suddenly emerges the meaning (or the absurdity) of the story. The supporting cast fades into the background, and the illustrious personages, carried away by their passions, remain alone to face one another, and transport the spectators to the highest pitch of terror and pity.

The year 1936 saw the start of the great misfortunes which preceded the Second World War. By 1938 the last glimmers of hope had been extinguished on the world stage. The public was now aware only of Mussolini and Hitler, of Chamberlain and Daladier, sinister figures who were to drag mankind into chaos and death.

★ ★ ★

In July, when passing through Paris, I was taken by one of my colleagues at the Embassy to watch the march-past of French troops celebrating the National Day. The government had wanted that year to put on a particularly impressive display. From the last row of the diplomatic tribune, I could admire the regiments of the Republic marching from the Arc de Triomphe. Thirty thousand men trod with measured step down the Champs-Élysées headed by '*les Ecoles*', *Polytechnicians* in black uniforms and cocked hats, *St Cyriens* in blue, with shako plumes in their peaked caps; then marines, infantry, Alpine troops, African units, the dragoons and Spahis, their sabres unsheathed, trotting to the sound of trumpets. After the traditional army formations, rumbled the formidable mechanised units, armoured vehicles, gun-carriages and tanks. Under a hot sun, in a city decked with blue, red and white bunting, an enthusiastic crowd cheered them on with cries of, 'Vive la France! Vive l'Armée!', applauding the flags and standards. It would have been difficult to remain unimpressed.

A few yards away from me on the purple and gold draped presidential dais, the members of the government in black frock coats and top hats, headed by the President of the Republic and the President of the Council, received the sword salutes of the unit commanders. In front was Albert Lebrun, affecting with his narrow shoulders and drooping moustache a stiff solemnity. Edouard Daladier, in a suit which was too big for him, the trousers too long, showed anxiety on his commonplace face, despondency in his eyes. I found it difficult to avert my gaze from this little man who held the fate of millions in his hands, even perhaps the fate of civilisation. He appeared strangely listless and ill at ease, fatigued, occasionally making an effort to pull himself up and raise his heavy chin, only to sink again into lassitude. What depressing thoughts were passing through his mind?

Edouard Daladier was born in 1884, at Carpentras in Provence. He came from a long line of independent artisans, bushel makers, master masons, and, lastly bakers.[1] As his eldest brother would inherit the bakery, the young Edouard concentrated on his studies. Thanks to scholarships, he was able to ascend the rungs of the University hierarchy. The people of Carpentras admired him, and his friends encouraged him to become the mayor of the little town which was his birthplace. Quite naturally, he became the candidate of the Radical Party, which had wide support among the class from which he sprang—half-peasant, half-artisan, small independent proprietors, fiercely individualistic. They were at once conservative, in that they were attached to their modest properties, and at the same time reformers, in that they opposed the privileges of the rich and powerful; also anti-clerical because, in general, the Church supported the latter class. Easily elected mayor, Daladier failed for the Legislature in the elections of 1914. Owing to general mobilisation he had little time to regret this. As early as the second day of the war, he had joined his regiment and was sent to a Foreign Legion volunteer battalion. In October, he went into the line in Champagne. For four years, he endured hell, weeks of monotony spent in fear and misery, the murderous attacks, fiercely repulsed, often in hand-to-hand fighting, the useless and bloody offensives. A gallant soldier, he was promoted to 2nd Lieutenant in 1916, Lieutenant and then Captain, he was thrice mentioned in the despatches, was awarded the *Croix de Guerre* and the *Légion d'honneur*. No man can experience such horrors without being profoundly marked by them.[1]

The ensuing ten years brought all the satisfaction he could have dreamed of—re-elected mayor of Carpentras, professor at a Paris Lycée, and member of Parliament for the Vaucluse in 1919. He married the daughter of a Parisian doctor, 'a war godmother', whom he had met on leave in Paris during the war. She was to bear him two sons. In 1922 Daladier visited the Soviet Union with Herriot, with whom he was still friendly (although later to become rivals and to loath one another). The two Deputies met Trotsky, Chicherine, Stalin and Litvinov, but not Lenin, who was receiving hardly anyone. Herriot returned full of admiration. We do not know what his colleague Daladier thought, only that he was to be fiercely anti-Communist all his life. In 1924, after the success of the 'Cartel of the Left', he became Minister for the Colonies. From then on, he was to be one of the *'caciques'* of the most important political party in France. In 1927, he was elected to its presidency and became one of the leading figures in Parliament. Uncommunicative, serious-minded, not brilliant but solid, the Deputy for the Vaucluse had gained a strong electoral backing in his native province. In Parliament, in contrast with a number of eloquent and brilliant orators, his relatively rare and lustreless interventions were treated with respect. He did not seem ambitious enough to be dangerous; but he was also always available for any office. He was to receive them.

On 31 January 1933, already Minister of War (his principal interest), he was appointed President of the Council—on the same day that Hitler became Chancellor of Germany, and Roosevelt was preparing to enter the White House. France was feeling the first symptoms of the Great Depression. The former professor of history knew nothing about economics. 'Finance first', he announced, meaning a strictly balanced budget and deflation. At one stage he was attracted by 'floating money', a charlatan notion which had obtained some notoriety, but he quickly returned to orthodoxy. Neither Keynes nor the New Deal were to claim his attention.

He displayed the same short-sightedness on the international stage. If on the periphery of the Economic Conference in London, he revealed an inclination to support European cooperation, it was only by participating in the absurb *'bloc de l'or'*, a relic of the nineteenth century. Towards Hitlerian Germany he made a few ambiguous gestures. On the other hand, he agreed to the 'Pact of Four', France, Great Britain, Germany and Italy, a grave mistake which would have substituted the contradictory desires of a Directoire of the great powers for the regime of law ordained in Geneva. Less than ten months later, in October

1933 during a debate on 'Financial Recovery', the Daladier Ministry was overthrown; but, paradoxically, the stature of its leader was not diminished by its failure. In the words of a right-wing pamphleteer, 'The general state of stagnation in the country gave him an excellent excuse for not acting. It added to his legend that he was circumspect, which was equally false. For six months he gave the impression of energy by doing nothing.'[2]

Recalled in February 1934, his second term of office was both brief and dramatic; it also revealed his weaknesses more conspicuously. Although he dealt successfully with the riots after the Stavisky scandal, and was assured of the confidence of Parliament, Daladier, after long hours of anguished hesitation, succumbed and resigned. It was the only example in the history of the Third Republic of a head of government surrendering to the 'street'.

★   ★   ★

The real vocation of the 1914 sergeant was Minister of War. He was fascinated by military matters. Did he find a refuge from the torments of loneliness and uncertainty in army life? With its rough-hewn fraternity and strictly hierarchy perhaps—in spite of the horror of the trenches—it gave this uneasy man the sense of security which he seems so desperately to have lacked. From the very outset of his career, he concentrated on military problems, and his first intervention in Parliament concerned them. Minister responsible for the Army from 1932 to 1934, he was again at its head in 1936, to remain there till 1940.* President of the Council three times, he always kept the department of War or Defence in his own hands. On each occasion, he refused to leave the old 'hotel' in the Rue Saint Dominique, once the residence of Napoleon's mother, which was now the headquarters of the Services. He appreciated the peaceful atmosphere of the room in which Clémenceau had worked, its fine proportions, the walls hung with green silk, and the colourful portraits of past marshals.

During the six years spent there, Daladier proved himself an odd Minister, a devoted servant of the General Staff, much more so than his constitutional master. Added to a strange deference before the 'Syndicat des Généraux', the defects of his own character increased their authority. His relations with Weygand, self-willed and quick to

---

* In London, during those eight years, five Secretaries of State succeeded one another as War Minister (Hailsham, Halifax, Duff Cooper, Hore-Belisha and Stanley); and there were five First Sea Lords at the Admiralty.

take offence, were glacial, marked by a mutual antipathy, 'My father,' Jacques Weygand told me, 'despised Daladier's weak character, which led him to dissemble. Nor did he conceal his scorn from him.' With Gamelin, his relations were more ambiguous. Daladier was well aware of the true character of his subordinate. 'The papers Gamelin puts before me,' he complained to Weygand, 'are inconsistent, so much sand that runs through my fingers.' He was irritated by Gamelin's tergiversations and ambiguities and had no confidence in his judgement; he also considered him disobedient. But he never had the courage to use his authority. Exasperated by the frequent quarrels between Gamelin and his principal deputy, General Georges, the only action Daladier took was to threaten resignation: 'If you continue to undermine one another, I shall throw in my hand.'[3]

Ever since the Rhineland fiasco, General Gamelin's abilities were being increasingly questioned. Daladier, strangely enough, believed his own position was being threatened by Gamelin's detractors; far from removing Gamelin, he defended him tooth and nail, not hesitating to implicate the very existence of the government to protect him. There was no one, he contended, capable of taking Gamelin's place—which was inconceivable. Some powerful but elusive element in the philosopher General, perhaps his ability to please, zealous but at the same time remote, seemed to impress the ex-regimental officer. Gamelin for his part was not unaware of his Minister's reserve. In his memoirs, he expresses his displeasure and deplores the difficulty of being able to talk frankly with him. He had to request an audience several days ahead and almost always had to wait in the ante-chamber. When he was ushered into the ministerial office, the conversation was ceaselessly interrupted by the telephone, or by importuning visitors, and was seldom fruitful.[4] Sometimes absurd quarrels separated the two men for weeks, particularly during the summer of 1938 when the Czech crisis was at its height. On several occasions, General Gamelin spoke of resigning; but it was not in his nature, any more than in Daladier's, to create a furore. He consoled himself by attributing his chief's reserve to the natural prejudice of politicians against military men.

It was not that Edouard Daladier lacked the necessary political authority to make his presence felt. The practice of the parliamentary system tended, it is true, to limit the powers of the executive. Generally speaking, the position of the President of the French Council could not be equated with that of the British Prime Minister, who was the master of his government, as well as of a disciplined majority party.

However, in April 1938, Daladier was returned to power in exceptional circumstances. The *Chambre des Députés* from which he had requested 'a permanent mobilisation in the service of peace and the country', gave him a vote of confidence with a majority unknown before in the lifetime of the 3rd Republic. The French people followed suit. 'Extraordinary popularity, unlimited credit' stated a right-wing Deputy. For some time the President of the Council appeared to the public, and not only in France, as a great charismatic leader, at the head of a government bent on national salvation.[5]

But he was not the man of the legend. 'A reed encased in iron', Blum had said after the 1934 riots. Within the rough husk to which he owed his fame, was an uneasy, hesitant spirit, a feeble and unhappy character. He often appeared abrupt, haughty and intolerant; yet his aggressiveness depressed him, he regretted it and was haunted by doubts. His worries were assuaged by alcohol, as those of Baldwin were by the abuse of medicines, Herriot by eating to excess, and Mussolini by amorous pursuits.

Although, with time, the infernal logic of Hitlerism became abundantly clear to Daladier, his aversion for the Soviet Union obscured the conclusions he should have reached. He hated and feared the Muscovites who wanted to share wealth, '*les partageux*', almost as much as he feared the Nazi barbarians. 'The Cossacks will dominate Europe', he prophesied to Chamberlain. His thirst for power had driven him to join the *Front Populaire*. This occurred after the riots of February 1934, when all the doors of the Right were closed to him, and *L'Action Française* called him, 'that unspeakable scoundrel'; whilst, on the other hand, the Union of the Left offered him the hope of becoming President of the Council. Quite unexpectedly, it was Blum who had obtained the supreme office. When Daladier's hour came, he quickly formed a centre-oriented Ministry. At the Radical Congress of Marseilles in 1938, he made a violent attack on the Communists, which was greeted with thunderous applause. A year later, the complicity of Stalin with Hitler further fuelled his hatred of the Soviets. He was to outlaw the Communist party, and throw its members into gaol in hundreds; although not all of them were traitors.

Even after the declaration of war, Daladier was not sure that the Hitlerian Reich was the principal enemy. Those close to him often heard him express his doubts and predict the world revolution which its defeat would bring about. He was terrified by the '*Grand Soir*' (the 'Great Evening'), that is the general social upheaval to come. In November 1939, after the Wehrmacht's victory in Poland, he sent one of his close associates to neutral Belgium. Emile Roche, a former assistant of Joseph Caillaux who had been convicted in 1920 for intelligence with Germany. Roche suggested to Spaak that King Leopold should intervene as a mediator; France was tacitly prepared to recognise the Reich's Eastern European conquests. Spaak declined.[6] When the Red Army invaded Finland, Daladier, the champion of peace, came within a hair's breadth of bombing Baku, intervening militarily and thereby adding the Soviet Union to the list of France's enemies. Ironically he was only prevented by British lack of enthusiasm; and above all by the nonchalance of General Gamelin, who, for weeks, neglected to give the necessary commands. The German attack on Denmark and Norway put an end to these insane projects.[7]

In 1966 when I was appointed to Paris I called, as was the custom, on the President of the Council of the 3rd Republic, at the apartment where he had lived most of his life. It was near the Arc de Triomphe, in a street which was curiously provincial, with its small family businesses, barber, baker, butcher and tobacconist. He was still a Deputy, still a leading figure in the moribund Radical party and, in spite of his 83 years, still with a lively mind. He received me graciously but without any warmth in a dusty study cluttered with books, ugly furniture and windows hung with thick, dark curtains. He showed little desire to talk about the past, nor did the present seem to interest him. After fifteen minutes of exchanging amenities, perplexed and disappointed, I felt I must take my leave.

That interview confirmed the picture I already had of him, a small melancholy man, well meaning but weak, elevated more by the hazards of parliamentary life than by any outstanding qualities to the first place in one of the principal great powers of the planet. In ordinary circumstances, Edouard Daladier's name would have sunk into oblivion, like those of so many other heads of government, honest administrators of the public weal, devoted but colourless, ephemeral silhouettes on the great stage of history. But the circumstances were not ordinary; a fearful force dedicated to the overthrow of Western order had come into being. Encouraged, perhaps, by a Churchill, Daladier might have had the courage to stand up against it. But on the other side of the channel, it was Neville Chamberlain who wielded power.

★   ★   ★

The Chamberlain family was like a comet which appeared in the skies of the British Empire, emitting a brilliant light, only then to plunge it into darkness. He did not come like the Cecils, the Cadogans and the Stanleys, from one of those ancient and illustrious families who had by tradition been associated for centuries and as a matter of course with the government of the land. The Chamberlains were of rural origin, but they had moved to London where they practised as boot-makers for several generations. Respected by their equals, often syndics of their guilds, they prospered. Their background was similar to the Daladiers'. Like them, they felt ill at ease in the official Church and became Unitarians, an austere sect long ostracised as much by the law as by the social prejudice.

Joseph Chamberlain, the father of Neville, was the first to rise in the world. We must look at him in order to understand his son. Very tall and thin, elegant if somewhat exaggeratedly dressed, an orchid in his button-hole and wearing a monocle, he had built in the suburbs of Birmingham (his adopted city) an enormous house in neo-Gothic style; it had a vast reception room decorated with stained glass and furnished with reproduction antique furniture. Like the Forsytes or the Thibaults, a parvenu, he was inclined to view his success as proof of divine favour. He was also a man of wide interests, regarding himself as the founder of a dynasty which would raise the Empire to its apogee. At the start of his career he was a Radical, an emulator of John Stuart Mill. When he became Mayor of a large commercial city, he championed pretectionism. Later, as Colonial Secretary under Queen Victoria (who considered him a dangerous agitator), and under King Edward VII, he became aggressively imperialist. The last conqueror of Africa and inspirer of the Cairo-to-the-Cape policy, he clashed with the French at Fashoda in 1898. National passions rose to fever pitch and France and England were prepared to go to war over this little outpost on the upper Nile. But Paris withdrew and the settlement of the incident led to the *Entente Cordiale*. This was not thanks to Joseph Chamberlain. He looked towards Germany and the alliance he sought with that country—only failed because Berlin did not want it.

Three times married, twice widowed, his first two wives had given him Austen, Neville and four daughters. Austen, the eldest, obviously the most gifted and the favourite, had been prepared in the best schools for a political career in the steps of his father. Neville, who had lost his mother when he was six, while surrounded by a multitude of close relations—his brother, sisters and cousins— showed himself to be a taciturn and lonely boy. At his preparatory school and at Rugby, he remained uncommunicative, taking refuge in his love of nature, plants and birds. At twenty-one after a spell in a technical college and an apprenticeship in a firm of chartered accountants, he was sent to the Bahamas to earn a living as manager of a sisal plantation belonging to the family. There he was to spend seven years among native workers, hardly ever in contact with Europeans. But the plantation went bankrupt and had to be liquidated at a great loss. Back in Birmingham, Neville took over a small enterprise specialising in the manufacture of metallic berths for ships. He also joined the boards of several other companies. A bachelor and music lover, he read a great deal and participated actively in the work of local charities. On weekdays, he could be seen riding a bicycle on his way to his workshop or office. On Sunday, he would preach at the Church of the Messiah, a Unitarian centre of worship. And so the years went by in the dull, greyish atmosphere of his native town.

In 1906, the elections relegated old Joe Chamberlain to the Opposition; shortly after this he was struck down with apoplexy and had to retire from public life. It was now that Neville Chamberlain decided to enter the lists.[8] In 1910, he became a municipal councillor. In the same year, at the age of 42, he married Anne Vere Cole, who appears to have been the only woman in his life. In 1915 he became Mayor of Birmingham. Owing to the war, and thanks to family patronage, he was summoned to London to take over a Department of National Service which had just been inaugurated. There, for various reasons, he was again unsuccessful. Nevertheless, he was elected a Member of Parliament in 1919, becoming Postmaster-General in 1922 and Minister of Health—a position he held for several years. In 1932, Ramsay MacDonald appointed him Chancellor of the Exchequer in the second National Government.

One of his biographers points out that in spite of the many notebooks which he scrupulously kept, and the hundreds of letters, sometimes indiscreet, which he wrote, his personality is difficult to fathom. Macmillan in his portrait of Neville Chamberlain describes him as haughty and forbidding in manner, with a harsh, rasping voice, given to sarcasm. Lord Home, who was his close associate, recounts that 'to lure him into the smoking room in the House was like catching the wariest bird ... and he would escape at the first possible excuse'.[9] He attributes these traits to sensibility and acute shyness. But were they not also part of an egocentric and misanthropic character?

However the disdain Chamberlain showed to individuals (apart from his own family) was accompanied by a display of solicitude for the human race. While Mayor of Birmingham, and during his long term of office at the Ministry of Health, he displayed a reforming spirit well in advance of his time. Thanks to his intervention, several laws were passed which heralded the Welfare State. Was he conscious of the winds of change which were blowing through the Conservative party? So it has been said—but they were not strong enough to clear away the cobwebs from the old edifice. As Chancellor of the Exchequer under MacDonald, he remained a firm supporter of financial orthodoxy; like most of his peers, he was a convinced deflationist and deeply dedicated to 'economies'. He also believed that the only remedy for industrial stagnation and unemployment was a protective tariff combined with 'Empire preference'; a form of nationalism which excluded all European economic cooperation.* Was he inspired by the memory of his father, a social reformer as much as a convinced imperialist? One is tempted to believe this, because it is difficulty to discern in his character any quality of spontaneous generosity. In a letter to a friend, he referred to the first old age pensions introduced by the Liberal government; he considered them to be 'a scandalous attempt to catch votes . . . a direct discouragement of thrift (among the working class)'.[10]

In the early Thirties MacDonald had become senile, and Baldwin was weighed down by indecision and fatigue. In his letters, Chamberlain appears to have been obsessively driven to act, often writing that he could not bear to see people making a muddle of things without intervening himself. His inordinate ambition was nourished by his contempt for his colleagues (Baldwin included), and he was very soon to take a direct part in the elaboration of major strategic and diplomatic decisions.[11] There were as many contradictions in his handling of foreign policy as of domestic affairs. Initially a supporter of collective security, he even conceived a nebulous project for an international police-force—which would have limited Britain's need for rearmament. When the Ethiopian crisis broke on 6 July 1935, he remarked that, 'If Mussolini goes on, he will torpedo the League of Nations, and the small states will just race one another to Berlin'; during the Rhineland crisis, he sided with those who refused to invoke the Geneva pact, or that of Locarno—of which his brother Austen had been a principal author. Sanctions against Italy were, for him, in his own words, 'Midsummer madness'. Towards Germany, in concert with Eden, he championed what he called 'a general settlement'—the goal of his existence, nothing else mattered any more.

---

* The new imperial tariffs had been prepared in the very year Aristide Briand suggested the creation of a European Common Market (1930).

Appeasement soon identified itself with Chamberlain. He was not the only one to practise it; but no one else promoted it with such dogged determination and fanatical obstinacy. In principle, it was an admirable idea. There were many who thought that more pondered thinking in 1914 could have prevented the Great War; many who, revolted by the cost in human lives and loss of wealth, abhorred the idea of another holocaust. There is no doubt that Chamberlain was among them. He cannot therefore be reproached for having wanted to appease Europe, or to avoid war. But many of his means he employed to this end, exceeding all reason, finally rendering a conflict inevitable. Collective security, combined with adequate defence, would not have been incompatible with a hand outstretched to Germany— but with the eyes open. The capital fault was the policy of isolation and thrift pursued by the Prime Minister. He claimed that balanced budgets were 'the secret weapon of British power'. More than anyone else, he was responsible for defence expenditure decreasing in 1933 to its lowest level since the Armistice, much lower than in any other great power—even in the less affluent France and Germany.

Before the Great War, a 'Blue Water School' had already advocated the avoidance of any commitment on the Continent, by limiting the role of the British Army to a police force in the colonial possessions or to the defence of the island's shores, 'an imperial reserve'. In 1932, the military theorist Liddell Hart acquired a reputation for great wisdom by publishing a book rationalising the old instinct of insular defence, while at the same time taking into account technical progress.* A second book confirmed this in 1937. One of the survivors of the carnage in the trenches, Liddell Hart was inspired by the fundamental concern to save the youth of his country at any cost from undergoing a repetition of the horrifying ordeal of 1914–18. For him, salvation lay only in a return to the traditions of the past, those of Drake or Nelson, a maritime strategy leaving the great land battles to Britain's allies, and concentrating on the navy, to be backed up in future by a powerful bomber air-force. The blockade would be Britain's main contribution to an eventual war. A small professional, highly trained army composed of mechanised units would form the imperial reserve. Dictated by extreme national egoism, the doctrine of limited responsibility, although refusing to take into account the realities of Hitlerian strategy, was approved in a number of influential

---

* Basil Liddell Hart. *The British Way in Warfare* (London 1932); *Europe in Arms* (London 1937).

circles. In 1937, Liddell Hart became the unofficial but influential adviser to the Secretary of State for War.

For the Prime Minister, 'limited responsibility' was a fertile land where appeasement would flourish. That year, through his initiative, true enough, but under the growing pressure of the Conservative Party (which since 1932 had been voting motions in favour of rearmament every year) an important programme of naval and aerial construction began—subject albeit to frequent delays. But the Army still remained unprovided for. 'Great Britain's frontier is on the Rhine', Baldwin had said (only to forget the phrase immediately). For his successor, defence could only be envisaged in an imperial context. The historian A.J.P. Taylor has remarked that, 'the practical effect of rearmament was actually to increase Britain's isolation'. Was this due to the memory of his father's extolling 'splendid isolation'? Perhaps. In any case the Prime Minister continued to resist the pressure to form a field force capable of engaging in large-scale operations on the Continent. This he considered was the job of France's armies. To promise her reinforcements would lead to political commitments which he found unacceptable.* While often underestimating their real strength he seemed convinced, as did Hore-Belisha, the Secretary of State for War, that the French forces were adequate to face the situation alone. Nor did he depart from this view until the eve of war.[12]

In June 1937, Neville Chamberlain achieved the goal he had set himself—10 Downing Street. Power is an acid which transforms those who acquire it, or at least dissolves the veneer which conceals their personalities. Chamberlain gave free rein to the least agreeable aspects of his character, among them an unshakeable belief in his own infallibility, and a bitter aggressiveness. In the Cabinet, he exercised an autocratic authority, and did not hesitate to confront his colleagues with '*faits accomplis*', or to travesty the truth. In the House of Commons he became even more arrogant, replying only in a summary and disdainful manner to the questions put to him. Those, like Churchill, who ventured to criticise him were accused of being agents of the Soviet Union, or of sabotaging his efforts to prevent war. He treated members of the Labour Party like garbage; in the words of Ian Mcleod and Leo Amery, two of his Conservative colleagues, 'he delighted in making mince-meat of them'. Attlee was 'a cowardly cur', 'a cantankerous dog'. He displayed the same disdain towards the Liberals.

---

* As mentioned before, the bulk of the British Army was stationed in India or the Middle East.

Among them, Sinclair was one of his favourite *bêtes noires*; he spoke of his 'fatuous and imbecile propositions', of his 'hypocritical cant'. For Lloyd George, he felt his antipathy dwindling when he looked down 'at his red face and white hair', 'All my bitterness passed away . . . for I feel myself the better man.' Even Ministers close to him did not escape his bitter tongue. He rudely recommended Eden, who had 'flu and had deplored the slow pace of rearmament, to take an aspirin and go to bed. His misanthropy increased his xenophobia. If he felt nothing but disdain for the Italians, if he detested the Germans—although less than the French, whom he considered corrupt and decadent—he was nevertheless, according to Harold Nicolson, 'bitterly anti-Soviet and equally anti-American'. His letters to his sister confirm this, and he made no attempt to conceal it. 'If it could be said that any Englishman was anti-American, Chamberlain was that Anti-American Englishman', reported Ambassador Bullit to Roosevelt.[13]

It is true that the White House was indecisive, swayed by the changing moods of the American people, permeated with a horror of totalitarian despotism, but also with a strong antipathy towards the diplomatic amorality of the great democracies. The result was a jealously guarded isolationism, which had been reinforced by the Hoare–Laval agreements and the comedy of non-intervention in Spain. It led to the disastrous neutrality laws which were imposed on a President who hesitated to become involved in the European wasps' nest and who was reduced to lie in waiting for any opportunities he might find to arouse his compatriots. In July 1937, following the disappearance of a Japanese soldier in a Chinese brothel, the Marco Polo bridge near Peking was attacked with rifle fire. The Army of the Mikado resumed its march, capturing Nanking, Chiang Kai-shek's capital, where it indulged in an orgy of murder, rape and pillage. In October, counting on the American pro-Chinese sentiments, Roosevelt made his famous speech suggesting that those states which contravened international law should be 'put in quarantine'. It was a cautious appeal for collective security, but it simultaneously provoked the wrath of the isolationists, and the derision of Paris and London. His efforts came to nothing.

A short time after, a conference of the Nine Powers, guaranteeing Chinese integrity, took place in Brussels (Geneva had become a den of iniquity). The questions of sanctions against the aggressor and a common programme of aid to the victims was discussed. The delegations put out feelers to each other, but to no avail, isolationism had reached its nadir. When, on 17 December 1937, the American gunboat USS *Panay* was deliberately sunk on the Yangtse by Japanese aeroplanes, an opinion poll showed that 70 per cent of Americans favoured a complete withdrawal from the Far East—including missionary and medical establishments.[14]

Roosevelt did not discourage secret contacts between the American and British administrations. He started negotiations which were to lead in 1938 to the signature of an important commercial treaty with Great Britain, of which the political aspect was fully emphasised. He also suggested a broad scale international conference to resolve the main problems of the day; or, failing this, to reveal the bad faith of the Dictators. The suggestion was put to London. Chamberlain, without consulting Eden, who was on holiday in the south of France, immediately answered the White House in a telegram which had the effect of 'a douche of cold water'. Woolly rubbish', his closest collaborators would say. Perhaps; but in his note-books he wrote that the President's proposal would have appeared to the Dictators as an attempt to form a 'bloc of the Democracies ... It might cut across our own efforts.'[15] Shortly before, he had declined an invitation from Roosevelt to visit Washington. The attitude of the Prime Minister towards the Soviet Union confirmed his astonishing ignorance of global forces. To his sister Ida, he wrote in March 1938 of 'the Russians stealthily and cunningly pulling all the strings behind the scenes to get us involved in war with Germany (our secret service doesn't spend all the time looking out of the window)'. To the members of the government he expressed this outburst in more moderate terms. Curiously, his fear of the Soviets was accompanied by the conviction that they were militarily impotent—a further reason for keeping them at a distance! As with the Americans, he did not conceal his antipathy. Maisky, the brilliant Russian Ambassador wrote that, 'From the moment that Chamberlain became his own Foreign Minister, coldness towards us increased with rapid strides ... After 21 February 1938, the British government began a strange diplomatic boycott of the Soviet Union. My meetings with the Foreign Secretary became less frequent, irregular, and producing no concrete result.' The Russian drew a pitiless portrait of the Prime Minister: 'His drooping moustache hides a rather flabby mouth, his large eyes perpetually betray the anxiety of an adolescent caught in the act. His enormous eyebrows make one forget that he has a low forehead. To the many questions which I took some care to put to him, he answered with banalities and commonplaces.'[16]

The Kremlin had gradually become convinced (as Khrushchev was later to tell Western visitors, and relate in his memoirs) that, 'the English and French are rubbing their hands with glee at the thought of lying doggo while Hitler is let loose to absorb his share of our territory, our blood and riches'. In more sober language, Maisky in his despatches defined British policy as 'based on a four-power pact, in reality a two-power pact, because France and Italy cannot become confederates in a Europe divided between Great Britain and the Third Reich, the latter left with a free hand in central, eastern and south-eastern Europe—in exchange for some stabilisation of European security'. If we are to believe the American Ambassador Davies, it appears that Stalin had expressed the same fears to him.[17]

No British, French, German, or even Russian document available to historians reveals the existence of concrete plans foreseeing such an eventuality. The Foreign Office and the Quai d'Orsay, where such ideas would have been elaborated if necessary, were increasingly opposed to the policy of appeasement. Vansittart, the influential Permanent Under-Secretary at the Foreign Office until 1938, was fervently anti-German. The General Secretary at the Quai d'Orsay, Alexis Leger, saw only one threat to world peace, Berlin and Rome. If it is certainly untrue that London and Paris had prepared the policies suspected by the Soviets, it is difficult to believe that they had not played a part in the ulterior motives of many important civilian and military personalities. There can be little doubt that the Prime Minister shared the feelings and attitudes of these people, as seen in his letters.

Let us try to fathom something of this enigmatic man on the eve of Munich. Nearly 70 years of age, he had become bankrupt at the age of 28, dismissed from a high office when aged 47, then a minor industrialist and provincial politician until the age of 53. His life had been passed in the shadow of his austere father, the overwhelming figure of an Empire builder, and besides a brilliant brother ever ready to sermonise him. Nevertheless, he succeeded in surpassing his illustrious relations. Now, there he was, at the head of one of the greatest world powers of all times, controlling the destiny of 500 million people, surrounded by a dazzling panoply of an Empire at its zenith. It is clear that the renown of the father had profoundly marked the life of the son. In his innumerable letters to his sisters, he expresses endlessly his desire to continue his work, and to do better—the poignant obsession of wanting to be approved by his father's memory. He was conscious of it himself: 'It has been a great handicap to be the son of my father, and the brother of my brother.' Lord Beaverbrook who was one of his supporters stated, 'He lives on an inflated version of his Father's reputation, on a diluted measure of his Father's policy.'[18] Circumstances no longer permitted the great colonial conquests of the Victorian era. The British people were deeply attached to the maintenance of peace. It was in the role of pacifier of Europe that the third Chamberlain wished to take his place in history, as had Czar Alexander I after Waterloo, and President Wilson at Versailles. There is no reason to doubt his sincere horror of war. But more than a humanism which could have confronted the Nazi tide, it was probably due to an intense need for personal success, accompanied by that fear of change we have so often seen. Aggravated by the cult of the paternal image, it was to be transformed into a neurotic obsession.

In Chamberlain's behaviour after he entered Downing Street, we see such excessive bias and obstinacy that it is difficult to explain them rationally. For some people 'appeasement' was only the mask of fear or impotence. For Chamberlain it was a priesthood, as it had been for the Czar of the Holy Alliance, or for the founder of the League of Nations. Without wishing to draw too close parallels, are we not tempted to compare their lives? Alexander and Wilson had both suffered in their childhood from the oppression of an autocratic father before becoming messianic apostles—Alexander as we know, was implicated in the assassination of Paul I. In a curious biography of Woodrow Wilson, American psychiatrists establish a direct relation between the humiliation, the feeling of inferiority that the head of the family had instilled in him, and a passionate need to surpass him and to dominate. Only one step separates passion from mysticism. The young Woodrow, condemned by his complexes to a solitude from which he never escaped, paralysed by a timidity towards women even more acute than that towards men, compensated for his lack of self-confidence by flattering himself that he had a supernatural revelation. God, 'his only friend', had entrusted him with the mission of imposing the Law. Clemenceau stated in 1919, 'he thought he was the only man for 2,000 years capable of giving peace to the wrld'. It perhaps explains the haughty and aggressive intransigence, deprived of all sense of reality, with which President Wilson confronted the United States Senate after Versailles—to bring about his downfall. Characters such as his cannot, in fact, tolerate any contradiction. Their intention coincides with a great ideal; even more, it comes from a divine message. All forms of compromise are moral faults. To renounce is to sink into iniquity.[19]

In the case of the man of Munich, as much as in the man of Versailles, the conviction of being right led to personalising completely any divergence of views, and to seeing enemies to be struck down in those who disputed them. With Eden replaced by Halifax, Vansittart by Cadogan, the Foreign Office (which Chamberlain detested) was subjected to his law—with dire results. He consulted only these Ministers who shared his opinions, in particular Samuel Hoare and John Simon. He got rid of sceptics—Eden, Duff Cooper, Swinton, de la Warre and Hore-Belisha. Around him, he retained only collaborators who obeyed, or colourless people who gave him the approval and effective support that his uneasy nature required. The strange Sir Horace Wilson, a senior official at the Treasury, 'Principal Industrial Adviser to the Government', who had no diplomatic experience, or knowledge of Europe, was his confidant at all hours. Wilson's office was next to the Prime Minister's, to which he alone has access; a faithful shadow of his master and friend, to whom he seemed to play the same enigmatic role that Colonel House played to President Wilson, or the Baroness de Krüdener to Alexander I.

Like the Russian Czar and the American President, the British Prime Minister belonged to the race of prophets. 'Almost a form of maniacal obsession', said Harold Macmillan when referring to the policy of appeasement. For his part Ambassador Maisky wrote, 'The Prime Minister is penetrated with a semi-mystical conviction that he has been elected to bring peace to humanity. He considers he is entrusted with a divine mission to save the human species from war.'[20] A weird vision dazzled him, concealing from him the arguments of reason, and one which justified the most questionable measures; at the same time an unreal and inaccessible objective which left him unsated and which drew him, as was President Wilson in his time, to taking more and more problematical actions.*

In May 1940, engaged in the war which he had wished to avoid, but which he had made inevitable by his obstinate attempts to please the Third Reich, and his obstinate refusal to ally himself with France, humiliated by the first defeats, he was driven from power by the revolt in Parliament. The clash of arms wakened him to reality, and he was revealed as a despairing bankrupt old man, fallen from his high estate. The proud champion surrendered and submitted to the authority of Churchill, his detested rival. The great strength that had led him on seeped away, as water through a cracked vessel. His arrogance

---

* As we know, Czar Alexander finished by requesting the assistance of the Turkish infidel against his Greek co-religionists, to safeguard the authority of the Holy Alliance of Christian peoples.

CHAPTER 14

Munich

Without Mussolini's support, Hitler might, perhaps never have ventured on the greatest war of all times. Without Chamberlain's influence, Daladier, in spite of his failings, might, perhaps, have prevented the war. It was the meeting of these four heads of government, so different in character, who wielded so much authority which created the explosive mixture destined to blow up Europe.

The fuse of the conflagration, the Munich agreement, has been the subject of innumerable commentaries. They have described in detail the conference in the Führer Bau, the House of the Party, where, in 'an atmosphere of general goodwill', as a German witness said, the dismemberment of the ill-fated Czechoslovakia was sealed.[1] As we know, the status of the Sudetenland ethnic Germans was the pretext for the conference. Czechoslovakia had been restored in 1919 from the ancient realm of Bohemia conquered by the Habsburgs in the 16th century. Of its 14 million inhabitants, nearly 10 millions were Czechs and Slovaks. Of the others, more than a million were of Hungarian, Ruthenian and Polish origin; and more than 3 million of Germanic origin, living for the most part in the Sudeten and Carpathian frontier regions. All enjoyed democratic liberties. The Sudeten Germans had their own newspapers, schools, churches and even a University. Four political parties were assured freedom of voting. Two or three Ministers of Germanic origin were in the Czech government.

Everything was not completely fair. Far from it. But of the numerous Germanic minorities in central Europe, none benefited from better conditions than did the Sudetens; not those in Poland, more than a million;* nor those in Rumania, more than 700,000; nor those in

---

* Danzig not included (360,000 Germans). (The Soviet Union and the 'popular democracies' have put an end to the problems of minorities after 1945, either by expelling them in large numbers, or by reducing them to silence.)

Hungary and Yugoslavia, more than half a million in each country. Nor those of the South Tyrol, where 200,000 Austrians were subjected by Mussolini's brutal regime to forced Italianisation—without raising much outspoken protest. Until now, there had been little talk of the Sudeten ethnic Germans. But as a result of the successes of the Third Reich, and the economic crisis which had severely affected these highly industrialised regions, they had allowed themselves to be won over by Hitlerian propaganda. A political party inspired by National Socialism, the SDP (*Sudeten Deutsche Partei*) came into being, led by an ex-bank clerk Konrad Henlein. In 1938, 75 per cent of the Sudeten population supported it.

In spite of ethnic tensions, the country had prospered more than had most of the new Central European nations. Its steel works endowed it with an armament production capacity equal to that of Italy. Its army was well equipped and trained, supported by a powerful network of fortifications based on the natural obstacle of the famous Bohemian quadrilateral, its security was completed by a network of close alliances; with France, the corner-stone of its foreign policy since 1925; with Yugoslavia, Rumania and the USSR. It seemed clear that any attack on its integrity would mean war. The French Ministers had restated this in Parliament just before the invasion of Austria, and had obtained a massive majority (438 votes against 2, with 163 abstentations).

On 14 March, two days before the entry of the Wehrmacht into Vienna, the new Blum government confirmed, in a communiqué, that France would fulfil its obligations towards its ally. They asked London for support; but, in vain. Did Chamberlain hesitate before he refused, as some people said? It is true that he had asked for a fresh appraisal of the strategic situation from the Chiefs of Staff. On 28 March they had submitted an extremely pessimistic report ('of the most extreme melancholy nature', said Lord Halifax), rendered even more sombre by the tendentious nature of the questions put to them. But a letter of the Prime Minister to his sister Ida dated 17 March, *that is eleven days before he received the military report*, proved that his ideas had crystallised long before, and that they owed very little to military arguments. He rejected the 'Grand Alliance' (Great Britain, France and the USSR), 'which I had considered before Churchill did', he wrote, 'We could not help Czechoslovakia, she would simply be a pretext for going to war with Germany . . . I have therefore abandoned any idea of giving guarantees to Czechoslovakia, or the French in connection with their obligations to that country.'[2]

The next day, 18 March, the principal Ministers met in a foreign affairs committee. On the table they found an aide-memoire from the Foreign Office stating that the German government intended *to annex the Sudeten territories by all means, fair or foul*. It suggested three choices: one, the Grand Alliance suggested by Churchill; two, new guarantees in association with France; three, negotiations with Berlin. It was the third which Chamberlain unhesitatingly selected, with the immediate support of Halifax. Their colleagues followed suit, implicitly accepting from that moment the dismemberment of Czechoslovakia. Four days later, now in possession of an advance copy of the report from the military, the entire Cabinet ratified, not without reservations, the conclusions of their colleagues. 'Czechoslovakia is not worth the bones of a single British grenadier', was Lord Halifax's not very original comment. 'An invitation to Hitler to march', noted his secretary bitterly.[3]

Chamberlain's explanation to the House of Commons was more measured. In an ambiguous declaration, he renewed the pledge given at Locarno to come to the aid of France and Belgium, 'in case of unprovoked aggression', specifying at the same time that this hypothesis did not include a war in defence of Czechoslovakia. He added, however, that no one could foresee what would happen in the event of war. To these vague warnings, hardly calculated to deter an aggressor, Churchill replied in a prophetic warning, referring to the 'imprudence, lack of vision and courage . . . which will be paid in blood and tears'.

★ ★ ★

Chamberlain and Hitler were under the spell of their dreams. 'I know that I can save this country, and I do not believe that anyone else can', wrote Chamberlain to his sister. Hitler boasted, 'No German has ever been granted such unlimited confidence as I have. I alone am capable of making war.'[4]

Five days after Chamberlain's tame warning to the Commons on 29 March 1938, the Nazi Dictator gave a secret order to the OKW to prepare a plan for an attack on Czechoslovakia, *Operation Green*. At the same time, he received Henlein to whom he gave secret instructions: he was to negotiate with Prague, but imposing unacceptable conditions. This was what the Führer of the Sudeten Germans did on 24 April, in a resounding speech at Karlovy-Vary (Carlsbad). He demanded not only autonomy for the Sudeten land but their right to adopt the National Socialist ideology, that is to say to instal a totalitarian regime. In addition, the Czech government would have to repudiate all its alliances—which meant unconditional surrender.

Four days later Daladier and Bonnet, the successors of Blum and Boncour, were in London. It was a decisive meeting. To express his horror of war, Daladier recalled the fearful months he had spent in the trenches. But to capitulate once again, he said, would prepare the conflict which London and Paris so wished to avoid. 'If Germany is not confronted with a determined joint attitude by the English and French governments, she will assume hegemony over all Europe.' He was prepared to persuade Prague to make important concessions for its minorities; but he regarded the Franco-Czechoslovakian Alliance as vitally important and was resolved to fulfil France's obligations. Chamberlain, Halifax, Hoare and Simon reacted glacially; they were categorically opposed to extending the Locarno guarantees to a conflict brought about by France's obligations to the Czechoslovak Republic. Nor did they want to give a warning to Germany, a gesture which, in their opinion, would have meant the risk of war, 'even if the risk was one in a hundred'. Repeating what he had written to his sister, Chamberlain added, 'If Germany decides to destroy Czechoslovakia, I don't see how she can be prevented'.[5]

Disagreement was complete. The conversations lasted two days in an unpleasant, often bitter atmosphere, interrupted by a dinner at Windsor where the courtesy of the King and Queen hardly alleviated the arrogance of their Ministers. The British agreed, it is true, to reopen conversations between the two General Staffs, but on the modest military attaché level, 'so as not to disquiet the Germans unduly', and concerning only their air forces. The British had virtually no land forces, and were determined not to have any. Chamberlain was adamant: France could not expect to have any substantial military aid, perhaps two divisions, but even that was uncertain. Daladier now almost broke off negotiations. But he was not of the mental to confront men who took a hard line. He finished by resigning himself to an agreement which was devoid of substance.[6]

It was agreed that the Foreign Office, in exchange for energetic French pressure on Prague, would make a *démarche* in Berlin to emphasise the danger of 'France intervening' . . . in which His Majesty's Government cannot guarantee not to do the same'. Lord Halifax kept his word. However, at the same time, he summoned the German Chargé d'Affaires to express his deep desire for an alliance of the 'three kindred nations, Germany, Britain and the United States (which) could unite in a joint work for peace' and to assure him that no further military commitments had been made to the French. While taking the agreed steps at the Wilhelmstrasse, Ambassador Henderson let it be known that the British were on the side of Germany in this affair. 'A formula,' he was to write in his memoirs, 'which was to be employed in various warnings to the Reich government in the course of the next five months', adding naïvely that it had been 'warmly welcomed by the Führer' (*herzlich begrüsst*). But there was more. On 10 May, addressing a group of American and Canadian journalists lunching at Lady Astor's, Chamberlain spoke 'off the record' of a 4-Power Pact to preserve peace (Great Britain, France, Germany and Italy). He would not fight for the frontiers of Czechoslovakia; neither, he added, would France and the Soviet Union.[7] Three days later, the *New York Times* echoed his words. They must have been heavenly music to Hitler's ears.

In Paris, the climate was only a little better. General Gamelin drew up reports for the government as alarmist as those he had made at the time of the reoccupation of the Rhineland, adding all manner of imaginary diplomatic disasters, greatly exaggerating, as was his habit, the means at the disposal of the enemy.* However, neither he nor Chamberlain succeeded in breaking down the courage of the President of the Council, who repeated publicly and in good faith it seems, the 'sacred and inescapable engagements' of France towards Czechoslovakia. Curiously, it was he the ex-combatant who was most inclined to resist the Dictator, while his colleague in London, who had escaped trench warfare, was eager to give in. A paradoxical situation, not unusual among members of governments in which ex-combatants were few. Nevertheless, doubts persisted. Georges Bonnet, at the head of Foreign Affairs, was ambitious and fickle, one of the least attractive actors on the Parliamentary stage. Devoid of principles, his cynicism attributed to himself the gift of perceiving the reality of things through the fogs of pretence. Falsely attributing his own moral infirmity to French opinion, he hoped to supplant Daladier by flattering the 'appeasers'. With the agility of an acrobat, he proclaimed that France would remain faithful to her commitments, while whispering that Czechoslovakia was not a viable state. To the German Ambassador he confided that, 'France would consider herself released from her bond if the Czechs proved really unreasonable'.[9]

---

* In the autumn of 1937, a General Staff exercise presided over by General Gamelin had supposed a war caused by a German attack on Czechoslovakia. It assumed the number of divisions mobilised by the Reich to be three times the number actually available in 1938.[8]

★   ★   ★

The Belgian authorities followed events with mixed feelings, concerned for the morrow, but at the same time with a certain egotistical optimism. They had shut themselves in a double-locked 'policy of independence', distrustful of all the great powers. To the fortifications against Germany', the General Staff had added a line of defence facing south, 'to shelter Brussels against a sudden attack'—by the French.[10] This was in the logic of neutrality and, if the population was badly informed about it, the politicians did not object. Reassured by a belief in the invincibility of the Franco-British, they shut their eyes to the possibility of being manoeuvred into the camp of the Third Reich as a consequence of their policy.

At the Rue de la Loi, Le Ghait was almost alone in stating that neutrality was a serious blunder, that it would collapse at the first sound of the guns. To arguments based on Hitlerian psychology or strategic realities, he added that of Belgium's total dependence on abroad for raw materials or military supplies, such as explosives and fuel-oil. Van Langenhove, the General Secretary of the Department, although one of the artisans of the 'policy of independence', had emphasised in a memorandum as early as 1936 that Belgian industry produced only a twentieth of the explosives necessary for the Army, one-third of the infantry cartridges; and that the stocks of petrol for the air force would last for only four days of hostilities! Some munition and petrol dumps were formed; but as we did not know in this little country where to protect them from aerial bombardment, they were loaded onto barges and lighters![11]

Although Le Ghait gave us cause for concern, circumstances prevented his views from being entirely convincing. If it came to choosing allies, we would certainly choose the French and British. But, allies for achieving what? To resist Hitler, or to give in to him? In the latter event, which was becoming increasingly probable, there was no need for an alliance. For over a year, our Ambassadors in Paris and London had reported that Czechoslovakia or Poland would be sacrificed as Austria was to be. Without pronouncing categorically, and with the circumlocutions used by diplomats of the old school ('it comes back to my mind that . . . everything leads to the conclusion that . . . we are led to believe that . . .'), they were repeating the old warnings. We were naturally aware that the Daladier–Chamberlain meeting had ended in the decision not to decide anything—except to hustle the Czechs. We had also learned—the Press reported it—that Henlein had been cordially received in London by a number of prominent personalities. There could be little doubt that the British were using their vast authority to sacrifice Czechoslovakia.

The truth was that the agitation in the Rue de la Loi was not very great. Were we not neutral? So much the worse for Austria, Czechoslovakia, Poland and Rumania. The same resigned attitude was adopted towards the Spanish Republic, whose long sufferings had at last exhausted any capacity for strong feeling. In the Non-Intervention Committee in Geneva, the democracies covered themselves with ridicule, 'It is better to have a flawed dyke than no dyke at all', explained Eden in a Geneva speech. However, the flaw was a wide door. All the war planes in Spain were of foreign origin. Artillery and infantry arrived from Italy in entire divisions. From Mussolini, they received decorations and congratulatory telegrams, widely reported in the Roman press. In spite of some deliveries recently of French and Russian material in July, two-thirds of Spain was in the hands of Franco; and the zone controlled by Madrid was cut in half. The Spanish Republic was dying.

While London, deep in its appeasement, obstinately refused any collaboration with Paris ('no ideological bloc' was the slogan), Berlin and Rome extolled their common martial spirit. At the beginning of May, Hitler, accompanied by several hundred Ministers, Party dignitaries, generals, diplomats and journalists, all in uniform, returned in Rome Mussolini's visit to Berlin the previous autumn. The meeting did not pass off without hitches. Pope Pius XI ostentatiously retiring to Castel Gandolfo, deplored 'the Crosses in Rome which are not those of Christ'. Pius XI was no friend of the Third Reich where the Catholics had a hard time; in the previous year his encyclical *Mit brennender Sorge* had severely censured the un-Christian Nazi doctrines. From the moment of his arrival, the Führer had given offence to Victor Emmanuel by occupying the first place in the royal carriage. Hitler was irritated by the disdain with which he considered the dignitaries of the Court viewed him. He felt extremely ill-at-ease beside the Queen at the official banquet in the Quirinale. He could not hide his low opinion of a people whom he considered lacking in martial qualities. On the other hand, his annexation of Austria had re-awoken the deep fear of Germanism engraved in Italian minds. Mussolini, still hesitating to burn his boats, had just concluded new agreements with London, which displeased Berlin.

All these asperities evaporated in the warm sunlight of an Italian spring. Hours were passed in grandiose ceremonies. In Rome, there were military parades in which Italian troops marched past (somewhat raggedly) with the *passo romano*. In Naples, there were naval manoeuvres. Hitler was much impressed by the Italian squadron, in particular by the spectacle of 100 submarines diving simultaneously, to re-emerge with perfect precision some minutes later. In Florence, Mussolini felt obliged (for the first time in his life) to visit the museums, in the company of his guests. Some days later, he announced in a bitterly anti-French speech, that 'Stresa was dead and buried'.

★　　★　　★

As the Dictators were embracing one another, the Nazis in the Sudeten cantons were stirring up the unrest which had made them successful in Germany and Austria: march-pasts, martial music and swastika flags; vociferous meetings, sabotage, acts of brutality towards Communists, Socialists and all other opponents. With the approach of local elections, the clashes increased. The Reich press and radio, harbingers of bad news, were lavish with the most fearful descriptions of the alleged tortures inflicted on the Sudetens, promising the coming extermination of the Czechs, their wives and children. On Saturday 21 May 1938, the Prague Government, fearing the troop concentrations on its frontier, decreed a partial mobilisation. On the following day, two Germans, attempting to cross the frontier illegally, were killed by a Czech gendarme. Henlein seized on this as the pretext for breaking off negotiations.

The din was awful. Was this a new Sarajevo? However, the weekend passed off without any new crisis, and the agitation abated. Without any precise reason, the Western Press rejoiced, announcing that the Germans had withdrawn. Had they? We can now read a document dated Berlin 20 May, which contained relatively prudent instructions from the Führer excluding, 'military action in the immediate future, in the absence of provocation'. But, after the alert, his mood hardened To his military chiefs gathered at the Berghof on 28 May, he signified his 'unshakeable intention to destroy Czechoslovakia by military action in the near future'. He fixed the latest date as 1 October 1938.*

Paris, becoming increasingly resigned to leaving the initiative to the British, remained inert. London had reacted energetically and stepped up its approaches to Berlin. However, as the future General Stehlin

---

* On the same day, 28 May 1938, Hitler decided to recognise Manchukuo officially—a gesture in favour of Tokyo—in spite of the opinion of the Wehrmacht, which thought there was no help to be expected from Japan, whose army was seriously impaired by the war in China.

testified, 'in such a way that neither Great Britain nor France appeared to have decided to risk a war'.[12] For if anxiety, even panic, had stiffened the British Government's attitude, it was primarily in its attitude towards France. In the middle of the night of 21/22 May, it addressed a note to Paris, hastily drawn up and couched in the harshest terms. Bonnet was dragged from his bed half-asleep, to read that he was to have no 'illusions', and that Britain would not be on the side of France, if she intervened. The substance of the note, if not the text itself, must have been known in Berlin, as it was in Brussels. But London did not stop there. On 1 June, the Prime Minister repeated 'confidentially' to English journalists what he had confided to their American colleagues during the luncheon given by Lady Astor. Great Britain would not fight for Czechoslovakia. On 3 June *The Times* envisaged the secession of the Sudeten territories to the Reich—a claim that Hitler had not yet made. On 8 June, the German Ambassador in London could report to his masters that the British Government would not oppose this, if the operations took place without the recourse to force.

★   ★   ★

Hitler, ensconced in his eagle's nest above Berchtesgaden, was to spend most of the summer there. Dreaming before the Untersberg mountains—in which, according to an old German legend, reposed the body of the Emperor Barbarossa, awaiting rebirth to give back their lost glory to his people—he was going through the cyclothymic pangs which accompanied the formulation of his grave decisions, alternating between deep excitement and melancholic depression; then feeling himself once more the Elected One for whom everything was possible.

Could he have been stopped in his vertiginous course? Paris was inclined to think he could have been. But in London, Chamberlain refused even to consider it. In the Rue de la Loi, my masters were convinced, until the middle of the summer, that he could be—in particular Paul-Henri Spaak who, without being able to state it, wished with all his heart that the Western Powers would stand up to Hitler. Later, they began to hesitate, but now without noting the ruse of prudence which Hitler dissimulated in his stentorian vociferations. Indeed, it was only during Chamberlain's pilgrimage to Berchtesgaden that Hitler would demand *for the first time* annexation of the Sudeten cantons. Would he have been content up till then with an honest compromise? Erich Kordt, the anti-Nazi chief of Ribbentrop's cabinet, was inclined to this view. Others close to the Führer were too. But we shall never know for certain; perhaps Hitler did not know himself.[13]

The obstacles in his way were enormous, not least among them the opposition of the German generals. Since the Nuremberg trials, we know in detail of their erratic attempts to prevent the Second World War. Their responsibility before history remains great. Without them, Hitler would not have acceded to power. They did not disapprove when he established his dictatorship, violated international treaties and initiated the disastrous armaments race. In their defence, they pointed out that many other prominent personalities in Great Britain, France and Belgium or elsewhere, military and civil, were guilty, almost as guilty as they were, of excessive fidelity to codes which make the promotion of the most selfish national interests into a supreme law. The argument cannot be ignored.

First of the Generals was the head of the General Staff, Ludwig Beck, who had faithfully served the Führer, until he realised that the man would bring about disaster to the Reich and all Europe. When in the spring of 1938 it became clear that the German Army would have to attack Czechoslovakia, entailing the risk of war with France, the British Empire and the Soviet Union, he would not go on. In a number of increasingly unambiguous and critical memoranda, he denounced the grave risks of the adventure. On 18 August, aware of the ineffectiveness of his protests, he decided to abandon his functions. He can be criticised for being slow. Equally, he must be admired for revolting. His mind once made up, he was to remain consistent to the end—his fearful suicide in 1944, after the failure of the Stauffenberg plot. Having tried twice to shoot himself in the head, he was despatched, whilst unconscious, by an army sergeant.

Immediately after resigning, General Beck had become a prime mover in the resistance. Around him and General Halder (his successor) were grouped a number of senior officers and civil personalities determined to arrest the tyrant, to judge him and instal a military dictatorship, which would prepare the return to a conservative democracy. The horror of a European war, which was shared by a large section of the German people, justified in their consciences a gesture which was deeply alien to their nature; this alone could bring about the agreement of the masses, without which the plot could not succeed. The conspirators had therefore wished to liaise with the Western governments. Carl Goederler, the ex-mayor of Leipzig, an important personality in conservative circles, visited Paris, Brussels, London and the United States. Ewald von Kleist-Schmerzin, who had a number

of British friends, visited London on 18 August 1938 and informed
Vansittart that an attack on Czechoslovakia was planned for 28 September. Weizsäcker himself, the Secretary of State at the Foreign
Ministry—not exactly a pacifist liberal—sent a message recommending that the British should speak up unequivocally to Hitler,
through the go-between of a 'riding-whip General'. On 5 September
Theodore Kordt, Councillor at the German Embassy in London,
acting on behalf of Beck and Halder, and in agreement with Weizsäcker, approached Sir Horace Wilson to confirm the coming Wehrm-
act offensive. Two days later he returned to 10 Downing Street, slip-
ping in quietly through the garden gate, to suggest for the last time
that Britain should give a warning, 'which could not be clear and
solemn enough'.[14]

It is clearly useless to rewrite history from imaginary hypotheses.
But on the other hand, what must be emphasised is that there *was* a plot
against Hitler, and that the conspirators were serious men knowingly
risking their lives. Most of them were dead before the end of the war,
assassinated, hanged or beheaded. Among them were some of the
finest brains in Germany. It is true that their demands often appeared
excessively nationalistic. But far from discussing anything with them,
London, if not Paris, barely listened to their voice, regarding them
with disarming scorn for 'betraying' their Führer.*

★   ★   ★

Were the German strategists completely mistaken? Was the enormous military superiority that they saw in the French Army the product of their imagination? On both sides of the Channel, historians
have maintained this legend. But it does not stand up to examination.
'There could be absolutely no question of resisting 100 French divisions with a dozen German ones, of which five were regular and seven
reserve, behind a fortified wall which was a vast military work-yard',
said General Jodl at Nuremberg. The vice-head of the OKW and one
of the soldiers closest to Hitler, Jodl was hanged in 1946 for obeying
him unhesitatingly. General Halder, who, as we have seen, was a
convinced anti-Nazi, took the same line. Field Marshal Erich von
Manstein, perhaps the most brilliant of the military chiefs in the
Third Reich, a cautious man, who distanced himself from all political
engagements, also agreed.

---

* Daladier was to write in *Candide* of 19 September 1961 that he had been completely unaware in 1938 of the German Generals' conspiracy against Hitler.

In spite of his famous 'protection bulletins' during the first weeks of the crisis, General Gamelin appears to have appreciated the situation in much the same way. In London, with Daladier, just before Munich, he delivered, in the presence of the British generals, a written report evaluating the German forces in the West at eight divisions. General Laurent, the French military attaché in Brussels, talked with his Belgian colleagues of six German infantry divisions on the French frontier, three on the Belgian frontier, and two or three in reserve.[15] These figures corresponded more or less with Belgian estimates.* Gamelin could oppose them with 23 French divisions ready for an immediate offensive, apart from those (more than 60) available from the recall of reservists which had taken place in August. General mobilisation would have assembled 85 divisions on the eastern frontier, without counting those stationed in the Alps, North Africa and elsewhere—a total of 100 divisions, of unequal quality, but all formed from trained men and cadres. This was the total strength which would be mobilised in 1939.

What forces had the Reich at its disposal? The transformation in a short time of the 100,000 men authorised by the Treaty of Versailles into a mass army of several millions had proved a gigantic undertaking, with serious deficiencies. If the French forces suffered from the 'hollow classes' (those of conscripts born during the Great War), the Wehrmacht was affected in addition by 'white classes' (those of young Germans who, for fifteen years, had done no military service). Conscription, re-established in 1935, had produced three trained classes three years later, that is 55 divisions fit for combat (*Feldheer and Ersatzheer*), of whom 37 were to be concentrated against Czechoslovakia, the rest being deployed in a thin curtain on the eastern marches, or on the Franco-Belgian frontier. The Landwehr of some untrained divisions were almost unarmed and without cadres, and could not at the time be taken into consideration.†

The image of an invincible German army, completely mechanised and possessing an unlimited number of enormous tanks is utterly wrong; about 10 per cent only was motorised. In 1938—it would still be in 1939—it was basically an army of conscripts, marching to the

---

* As a consequence, the Belgian High Command had considered German aggression against its territory to be impossible; but it did not exclude the possibility that France might be tempted to cross it in order to help Czechoslovakia. 'The danger is in the South', wrote General von Overstraeten in a memorandum to the King.[16]

† In September 1939, the German Field Army numbered 103 divisions. Of these, 25 were stationed on the Western Front.[17]

battlefield from the railway heads and supplied by horse-drawn vehicles. An infantry division would muster about 5,000 beasts. The Supply Corps, the Medical Corps, divisional and regimental artillery were generally dependent on horses. On the 1 September 1939 the Wehrmacht would have 445,000 of them. The Panzer divisions, in spite of their impressive name, were not better than the DLM (*divisions légères mecaniques*) of the French. Their tanks, Mark I (6 tons) with 2 machine guns and Mark II (10 tons), with a small cannon of 20 mm, did not equal the French machines, slightly slower but equipped with stronger armour and cannons of 37 mm—and as numerous as the Germans.*

In spite of an immense expansion, German industry was not in a position to satisfy the growing demands of the Army, the Air Force and the Navy. A report by the High Command stated at the beginning of 1939 that only 34 infantry divisions were completely equipped, and that the reserve forces possessed only 10 per cent of the prescribed small arms. The supplies of munitions were sufficient for only fifteen days fighting.[19] The artillery, apart from anti-aircraft guns, was considerably less in number than that of the French—7,760 guns against 11,200. Half the heavy artillery in 1940 would come from the arsenals pillaged in Czechoslovakia.

The West Wall, the famous Siegfried Line for protecting the western frontier of the Reich, was far from complete. Started in 1936, it had entailed long preparatory work, and was built with much delay. At the beginning of 1938, it possessed barely 640 machine-gun emplacements over 500 kilometres. It was only in May, having decided to annhiliate Czechoslovakia, that the Führer gave personal instructions to speed up the work—accompanying this order with the noisiest publicity. Several hundreds of thousands of workers, he announced, would be employed in the construction of 17,000 armoured concrete strong-

---

*The French had also begun to produce the 'Somua', a fast tank of 20 tons, equipped with a 47 mm high velocity gun, and the 'Char B' of over 30 tons mounting two guns, a 75 mm in the hull and a 47 mm in the turret. The 'Char B' was the best tank of its time and would serve as the prototype for the American 'Grant'. The only German tanks ready in 1938 were the Mark I and II, both light machines, very lightly armed, which would be relegated to command and reconnaissance roles after the French campaign. The Mark III (50 mm gun) and the close support tank Mark IV (75 mm short gun), both of about 20 tons, together with a number of 10 ton Skodas, seized in Czechoslovakia, would be operational in small numbers in Poland and come into their own in France.[18] The Mark IV was to develop as the work-horse of the German Panzer forces after it had been up-gunned and up-armoured. By 1944 the Germans had 'Panther' (45 tons) and two marks of the giant 'Tiger' at 57 and 68 tons respectively.[18] The Italian tanks (Fiat L.3) were of 3.5 tons only.

points. In reality, these were largely infantry combat shelters, vulnerable to artillery, poorly situated owing to the speed with which they were planned, often no more than 'passive shelters', that is, without loop-holes or embrasures.[20]

At sea, Franco-British superiority was overwhelming, even taking into account the need to maintain powerful squadrons in the Far East—where the American fleet was also well represented. In the Mediterranean, the French fleet alone was strong enough to deal with Italy. The German Kriegsmarine was virtually powerless. Hitler, who had long been convinced of the benevolent neutrality of Great Britain, had delayed profiting from the clauses of the 1935 naval agreements. The German Navy had three so-called 'pocket'-battleships (compared with some 20 heavy British and French battleships), six light cruisers, seven torpedo boats, and 36 submarines of which only six high-sea ones were operational.* Had they ventured out, they would have been pulverised.

There remained the air force, whose role is more difficult to assess because the data concerning quality, type, speed, manoeuvrability, operational coefficient and armament, were inextricably interwoven with quantity. If the fledgling Luftwaffe surpassed the French and British air forces (which is contradicted by the most careful research), the overwhelming superiority which Germany announced with deafening publicity was certainly make-believe—as was that about the superiority of the Wehrmacht in assault tanks. As in France and Great Britain, the role of the air force in battle had been the subject of long and bitter contention. Relations between the German High Command (composed mostly of officers from the land army) and the engineers, had been ill-tempered, abounding in contradictory views. The types of planes, often unsuited for a kind of warfare which had not been defined clearly, had proliferated. There were as many as 40 types being constructed, of which many were never to fly. Göring and his brilliant deputy, Erhard Milch, had, it is true, succeeded in giving a strong stimulus to the aircraft industry in a short time. But the performance of the planes had suffered from the speed with which they were produced. Quickly out of date, they had had to be replaced by more modern models capable of equalling those produced abroad.

---

* In September 1939, the situation was more favourable to Germany: Three pocket battleships, two battle cruisers, two heavy cruisers, six light cruisers, 14 torpedo-boats and 24 high-sea submarines were in service.

In 1938, the Luftwaffe was being completely reorganised. Jealous of Milch's success, Göring had attached to him a director of armaments, Ernst Udet, an ex-fighter pilot selected on account of his clear inability to rival his chief. A dare-devil, the inventor of dive-bombing, before the Hitler era he had earned his living by aeronautical acrobatics. Udet drank to excess and was given to narcotics; he was to be found one morning in November 1941 with a bullet through the head, the walls of his office plastered with graffiti accusing his chiefs of being Jewish and traitors. As authoritarian as dissolute, he had under his command as many as 36 heads of departments. But he had been incapable of maintaining discipline among his various constructors who were in perpetual rivalry, each with his highly-placed protectors. Several of their machines had been disappointing, such as the Dornier 11 bomber, which had the unfortunate habit of losing its wings in flight. The Junker 88, a bi-motor bomber which went into service in June 1938, had responded to contradictory demands which doubled its weight and reduced its speed by half; it was said that 250,000 successive modifications had been applied to its prototype. The bi-motor fighter Messerschmidt 110 (which appeared only in 1939) was also to prove inadequate, too slow and difficult to manoeuvre.

The German fighter squadrons possessed the redoubtable Messerschmidt 109, equalled incidentally by the British Hurricane (the Spitfire was better, but it was not to be in general service until 1939), or by the French Dewoitine 520. It was not superior in numbers to the Franco-British. Among the best aeroplanes in service was the excellent bomber Heinkel 111, which was not to be operational until the end of 1939. Of the famous Stuka (Junker 87), the dive-bomber which was so frightening to inexperienced troops in 1940, there were only 159 machines in service, soon to be declared obsolete because slow and vulnerable.

It should also be emphasised that, whilst the Germans concentrated much attention upon tactical aviation, designed to operate with the Army, they neglected the strategic air forces which their enemies feared. Considered too demanding and too slow to construct, the Luftwaffe was deprived during the whole war of those long-range bombers which could have delivered fearful blows in the Atlantic, in Russia and elsewhere. If, after July 1940, it was able to bomb southern England, this was because its short-range machines could operate under the protection of fighters based near the Dutch, Belgian and French coasts. On the eve of Munich, the few available German bombers (nearly all were deployed in the east), were technically capable of delivering some heavy blows to the French urban and industrial centres. The English towns, factories and ports, protected in addition with the first radar installations, were sheltered from massive attack. 'With the means in our possession,' wrote the General in charge of the Western command of the Luftwaffe to Göring, 'a war of annihilation against England in 1938 is out of the question'. Air Marshal Kesselring was later to confirm, 'the Luftwaffe could engage in combat, but it was weak, barely capable of formation attacks, and in the process of being re-equipped'. He should have added that the lack of raw materials was beginning to slow down the production of fighter aircraft, and that the stocks of fuel were extremely low.[21]

It would also be wrong to think that the morale of the German army was flawless. By 1939 it was to need 25,000 regular officers, and 100,000 reserve officers; there had been only 3,400 of them in 1933, ancillary services not included. Selected hurriedly from amongst the NCOs, from the police forces or the Party organisations, hastily trained in improvised schools, many of them were poorly qualified for their tasks (less qualified than the French). In short, while the High Command was preparing a *coup d'état* against Hitler, senior officers were concerned about the value of an army which they considered unready for great trials. The subaltern cadres were also ill prepared, and the other ranks were often refractory, in spite of the intense activity of the 'propaganda companies'. General Halder noted in his diary, '. . . suspicious tracts . . . in certain units, talk of laying down arms . . . the same signs of lassitude as in 1917–18'. Another General referred to, 'worrying reports from unit commanders'. Another said again, 'the cadres are mediocre and utterly lethargic'.[22]

To add to this, the German High Command's planning was still far from the strategic conceptions which were to assure its victory in 1940. There has been much talk of *Blitzkrieg*. If the expression was to enrich the Nazi rhetoric, it had at the outset no precise military significance. It is true that General von Seeckt, the first head of the Reichswehr, who had to make do after Versailles with a regular army of 100,000 men, had wanted to build it into a high-quality instrument capable of moving at high speed. But he had to resign, and when rearmament began after 1932, he was no longer there. For a long time, the German generals remained convinced of the superiority of their adversaries. Fearing a European war begun with an Allied offensive, perhaps on two fronts, they were to remain faithful to plans which envisaged an essentially fixed defence front in the West on the line Rhine–Black Forest, against which the French attacks would crumble (Red Plan).

Until 1939–40, the Blitzkreig existed only in the imagination of a few innovators. Among them, Heinz Guderian foresaw the revolution which would be caused by the internal combustion engine and the armoured vehicle in the conduct of war. However, long years of stubborn effort and the fanaticism of an inventor, had been necessary before his ideas prevailed. He had no difficulty in convincing his superiors about the use of tanks and motor transport. In 1935, three 'panzer' divisions were formed. However, the use to which he proposed to put them, an autonomous striking force dominating the battlefield, was firmly opposed by the High Command and its chief. For them, armoured forces could only constitute (as was the view in France) auxiliary elements of the infantry and cavalry or, at the most, units to be employed in limited operations. General Beck was a patriotic soldier of the old school; the author of a doctrine of 'restraining defence' or 'defensive attack', he was not a conqueror. Guderian did not forgive him for this. In his memoirs he wrote, 'Beck was opposed to the revolutionary consequences for the art of war of technical progress, and he attempted to put a brake on it.' If, in Paris, the instructions for the deployment of tanks in mass formations prepared by the *Ecole des Chars* were 'forgotten' until February 1940, General Beck rejected similar directives drawn up by the future victor of Sedan. General Halder, his successor, showed no more inventive spirit. The Infantry Regulations published under his aegis in January 1940 still laid down, 'The Infantry is the principal arm. All others are subordinate to it.'[23]

The civil war in Spain had increased the conservatism of the military mind. The armoured vehicles of the German expeditionary corps had proved much too light, of little danger to the enemy, and very vulnerable. Daladier expressed the opinion of most European General Staffs when he stated in the *Chambre des Députés*, '. . . based on certain machines, the great hopes have not been fulfilled'. Even the Soviets thought as he did. In the history of the Spanish war published by the Soviet government we read, 'The limited and special character of the Spanish war was badly interpreted. One may conclude that the use of large tank units was an erroneous principle—although we were the first to apply that tactic.'[24]

When the Wehrmacht crushed Poland in 1939, it was by the most classical methods, those used by the Prussian General Staff since 1870: a battle of encirclement won by infantry attacking on foot, after having been conveyed by the railways. The six panzer divisions, still apportioned among several army corps, played only a contributory role, even if they delivered some devastating blows. As it was, the experience took a long time to sink in. Spread over the great spaces of the East, opposed by ill-equipped and badly led armies, could that experience have been repeated on the Western front? In General Halder's diary for 29 September 1939 we find the following, 'The technique for the Polish campaign is not a recipe for the West . . . impossible against a powerful army.' Ordered to attack France, the head of the German General Staff and his colleagues resumed their conspiracy to bring about Hitler's downfall. Then they gave way. Resigned to the offensive in the West which he demanded, they irresolutely drew up a number of 'Yellow' Plans more or less inspired by the Schlieffen Plan of 1914, which would have led to a vast battle of the traditional kind on Belgian territory. In his time, General von Schlieffen had thought (rightly) that it could not be won and it filled the German High Command of 1939 with dread. Incidentally, General Gamelin was to deploy his armies on the assumption of such an offensive. It was only on 24 February (unknown to Gamelin) that Berlin adopted a new *Aufmarchanweisung Gelb* suggested by a relatively junior staff officer, General von Manstein—to the great vexation of his superiors, who had tried vainly to silence him.* Assembling for the first time at a principal point, a huge armoured army, the *Sichelschnit* (the Sickle Cut), was to assure three months later the rupture of the Allied front at Sedan.

During the summer of 1938, the French and British intelligence services could not ignore the fact that the Czechoslovakian Army was a tough nut to crack—30–35 divisions based on a powerful system of fortification, along one of the most rugged frontiers of Europe.[26] It would be a campaign during which the Reich would have been virtually defenceless in the West, and which would have demanded a long period of reorganisation and re-equipment before the Wehrmacht could be fit for further operations.

Paris lacked the strength of character to draw obvious conclusions. London refused to recognise the facts, continuing to rely on analyses of the Chiefs of Staff, of which the least that can be said is that their lack of precision astonishes anyone reading them today. They took no account of the Czech forces, which they considered would be

---

* The strangest twist of destiny contributed to the abandonment of the mediocre plans of the autumn. In January 1940, they were discovered on board a courier aircraft of the Luftwaffe which lost its way in Belgian air space and was forced to land. Brussels communicated these plans secretly to Paris and London—which Hitler had suspected would happen. It was only then that he forced the German High Command to adopt the Manstein Plan which was to assure the victory of 1940.[25]

annihilated at the outset; they made no mention of the Soviet Union, which they regarded *a priori* as a neutral. Inexplicably, they evaluated the French forces at variable levels, oscillating between 40 and 70 divisions, a figure much inferior to the true one. On the other hand, they enormously exaggerated the number of enemy divisions (a common reflex of general staffs), while the civil power closed their ears to the experts who doubted the danger of mass aerial bombardments, the 'knock-out blow' of which the Luftwaffe was quite incapable.*

Certainly the Nazi propaganda, with remarkable effect, greatly exaggerated the true power of the Reich. Certainly Lindbergh, the hero of the Atlantic, whose views were then fashionable, contributed to the pessimism, by touring Europe describing the immense and invincible German air fleets. Nevertheless, it is impossible to understand how London could have allowed itself to be so gulled.[27] Harold Macmillan, with all the experience of long years at the head of affairs, asks what use had been made of the military attachés and intelligence services. The latter were dispersed in various departments and benefitted from great autonomy; their reports were only loosely coordinated. In the inner Cabinet, the Prime Minister and the Foreign Secretary alone had direct access to them. Chamberlain was very parsimonious about communicating these to his colleagues. Were they completely erroneous, or skilfully selected? It is an enigma which continues to blur the genesis of the Munich Agreement, in spite of the innumerable works on that subject.†

In France, it was principally General Vuillemin, chief of the Air Force, who played the role of Cassandra. On an official visit to Germany in August (a moment one would have supposed more appropriate for fraternal meetings between French and British airmen), he allowed himself to be duped. Received very warmly, he was present at Luftwaffe manoeuvres where thanks to clever presentation, its planes appeared to him much more dangerous, and above all more numerous, than they were. A modern version of the Potempkin village,

---

* A report by the Royal Air Force in 1937 (approved by the Cabinet Defence Committee) concluded that Great Britain had nothing to fear from the German Air Force so long as Germany did not occupy the southern coast of the Channel. The heads of the General Staff had not flatly contested this.

† Lord Hankey, the ex-Secretary to the Cabinet and as good a witness as any, stated on 23 March 1943 in the House of Lords, 'When the pre-war archives about the origins of the war are published, it will be seen that the Intelligence Services were numerous and precise, their opinions well founded, and their oft repeated warnings seldom heeded.' As is known, the Intelligence services archives are, unlike the Diplomatic archives, not open to historians.

the best German aircraft were shuffled about from base to base, showing themselves off several times with different markings. The fear of them, which the French General Staff felt, was not without its influence on Ministers.

The latter were in fact no better informed than their colleagues in Great Britain. The *Deuxième Bureau* of the General Staff with hundreds of officers and thousands of agents was, according to abundant literature, fully aware of everything to do with the armies of the Reich. Together with the ambassador's despatches it was the civil power's principal source of information. As we have seen, Gamelin did not hesitate to disguise the facts. At the same time, he took good care to preserve his own monopoly. The Foreign Minister complained, 'I know nothing about the state of the Army, even about staff agreements, I learn only what they are prepared to reveal to me.' Gamelin professed to distrust the loyalty of Georges Bonnet. However, he displayed the same unbelievable reserve towards Daladier, the Minister of National Defence and the President of the Council. When, on 12 September, at the height of the Czech crisis, Daladier wished to convene the Supreme Council of War (over which he presided by right), the future Generalissimo opposed it. To have even an approximate picture of the strategic situation, Daladier had to be content with what Gamelin was prepared to tell him, and with conversations with his two principal deputies, Generals Georges and Billotte.[28]

However, in the last resort, it was not military reasoning which would primarily dictate the line of conduct adopted by the French and British Prime Ministers. Chamberlain had set himself up as Prince of Peace (as Churchill said, expressing astonishment that his colleague should have been born in Birmingham, and not in Nazareth), not because he was frightened of losing the war, but because he dreamt of a new European peace of which Germany and England would be 'the twin pillars . . . and barriers against Communism'.[29]

As for Daladier, he was not to refuse to defend Czechoslovakia, against his better judgement, until the eve of Munich; only then did he give way to a series of pressures which his hesitating nature could not resist—among them those applied by Chamberlain being the determining factor.

★　★　★

In Germany, the risks involved in the *Green Plan* made the Generals hair stand on end. The attitude of the Soviet Union was partly responsible. Committed to coming to the aid of Czechoslovakia along with

France, as the treaties foresaw,* it proved resolute. The 'mystery' of Soviet policy has often been emphasised, as much as an excuse for Munich, as because the available Russian archives are incomplete and tendentious. However, the facts suggested clearly that the Soviet leaders, fearful of isolation, were looking for powerful allies—a simple assessment which appears not to have been altered by the passage of time. They made no ideological distinction between the non-Communist powers, totalitarian and democratic; they were both equally class enemies. 'The lot of them are shit', as Kruschev said to Spaak in 1964 with a friendly smile [*sic*].

But the Kremlin could distinguish between 'the carnal and the spiritual' just as well as Churchill. From 1934 onwards, with each of the nasty deeds of the Dictators, Litvinov, the Peoples Commissar for Foreign Affairs, bombarded them with criticism. He never ceased warning Foreign Ministers and Ambassadors of the German peril. He established close relations with Czechoslovakia, to the extreme displeasure of Berlin, who claimed his action constituted a threat. At the beginning of 1938, he spoke so harshly to the Reich Ambassador that the latter, deeply impressed by his words, reported that, although the Soviets would stand aside in event of war, they would furnish Prague with economic, technical and even military aid on a broad scale.[30]

The USSR had taken part with the other European powers in the armaments race. Its regular army, half a million men in 1934, had increased by 1937 to one and a half million, equipped with more tanks and aeroplanes than any other power in the world. We also know today that its scientists had explored the mysteries of the atom, and in 1939 possessed the theoretical knowledge necessary to construct nuclear devices.† Although prudent, it did not hesitate to use its weapons. The first undeclared war had broken out in 1936 with Japan

---

* At the request of Prague, but at the suggestion of Paris, which had seen that this was the best way to remain master of the situation.

† Besides Philby, Burgess and others, who were enrolled in the Soviet secret service, several scientists, including Rutherford, openly informed the Russians of their researches in nuclear physics. Thanks to them, and to the French Communists—Joliot-Curie, the Soviet Union had probably acquired the theoretical knowledge necessary for the fabrication of the atom bomb in 1939. But it had not the enormous resources available to the United States for making the bomb in 1945—more than 200,000 personnel and nearly three billion dollars. In Germany, too, the fission of the uranium atom was achieved in 1939, without its practical use being developed. Hitler saw in it, 'a baneful invention of Jewish science'. He did much to slow down research and to deprive the Reich of nuclear arms.[31]

on the border of Manchuria, Mongolia and Siberia. In July 1938, there was violent fighting again in the Far East. The Soviets gained the advantage. Simultaneously, they provided financial and military aid to the China of Chiang Kai-shek—without showing much concern of the lot of the Chinese Communists. Hundreds of Russian planes and pilots fought in the ranks of the Chinese army; thousands of 'advisers', tanks, guns and vehicles were put at its disposal—enough to equip 24 divisions.

Was not Czechoslovakia with its privileged geographical position, its vast natural resources, its army and powerful industry, as important for the security of the Soviet Union as Mongolia? At the beginning of the month of May, Litvinov took advantage of a meeting of the Council of the League of Nations to confer with his western colleagues. The great difficulty was, as has often been emphasised, that Czechoslovakia and the Soviet Union, separated by Poland and Rumania, had no common frontier. How could Soviet troops come to the aid of the Czechs? Bonnet, and later the British, had asked Litvinov about this, and had received only evasive replies. 'Nothing is impossible', he said, 'We will find a way. It is for France, the ally of Poland and Rumania, to do the necessary.' Somewhat insincerely, Bonnet asked the Russians if they intended to invade these countries without permission. To which Litvinov replied that the Soviet Union certainly did not intend to attack them. What other answer could he give? Nevertheless, on several occasions, he had shown himself ready to act—if France did the same. Indeed, it seems that a few Soviet bombers actually joined the Czech Air Force. It was possible to argue that *legally* by the Charter of Geneva, Poland and Rumania had to authorise the passage over their territory of troops coming to the aid of a state which was the victim of unprovoked aggression. Great Britain and France had taken certain steps in this direction in Warsaw and Bucharest; but their considerable authority—which was to be employed successfully to make Prague commit suicide, was not used to come to its aid. Poland, attracted by the prospect of obtaining a pound of flesh from the corpse of the victim (the coal basin of Teschen), had implied that it would oppose militarily the passage of Soviet troops.* Rumania on the other hand, was bound to Czechoslovakia and Yugoslavia by the Little Entente pact, the pillar of French eastern

---

* Colonel Beck, Poland's Germanophile Minister of Foreign Affairs, was nevertheless to recognise later that it would have been impossible for Poland to line up with the Reich.

alliances and showed herself more accommodating. In February 1936 King Carol II had promised Paul-Boncour that he would not oppose the Russians; in any case, he would have been quite incapable of doing so. In September 1937, General Gamelin, attending the Rumanian Army manoeuvres, had received the same assurances.[32] In 1938, the situation was less clear; Carol had become 'the Royal Dictator', and was sliding towards Fascism. Nevertheless, Bucharest agreed to close its eyes to the passage of Soviet aircraft crossing its airspace—a concession which Litvinov somewhat strangely rebuffed as insufficient. Would the government of Bucharest have gone further, if pressed?

What has not been stressed enough is that the Soviet Union, even without committing itself completely, could have given considerable aid to the Czechs, in aeroplanes, raw materials, munitions, credits, etc., which it was giving to the Chinese. This would have obliged the Reich to concentrate in its eastern provinces, and on the Baltic, large ground and naval forces, or which the Western frontier would be deprived. As his Generals had foreseen, Hitler would have found himself at a dead end.

But emotion took precedence over the calculations of *Realpolitik*. Chamberlain, a prisoner of his fixed ideas, spoke to those closest to him of the diabolical manoeuvres of the Soviets to foment war between Great Britain and Germany; the Führer was absolutely right, he said, to fear the Bolsheviks. The policy of appeasement meant to discard the Soviet Union, which implied the end of the pacts which united it with Czechoslovakia, and even with France. In Paris, the spirit was much the same. Bonnet considered denouncing France's treaties with the eastern European countries, Poland and the Soviet Union included; he was to claim later that his 'policy had been to make the Germans and Soviets fight one another'. The President of the Council did not go as far as this; but in his usual way he could not make up his mind. Ambassador Coulondre made the long journey from Moscow to Paris to entreat him to take part in the military discussions which the Russians desired. Daladier recognising his good sense, listened to his prediction that a German–Russian rapprochement would inevitably result from placing the Kremlin in quarantine. He allowed himself to be convinced, only to change his mind almost immediately, 'so as not to offend the susceptibilities of the English Conservatives', as he said to the Czechoslovak Minister in Paris. And this without even informing Coulondre.[33]

The Russians did not give up. As is known, Churchill published in his memoirs the text of a letter he sent to Lord Halifax on 3 September

1938, after having received the Soviet Ambassador. The latter handed him a proposition by Litvinov to the French Chargé d'Affaires envisaging the adoption of Article XI of the League of Nations, which foresaw 'the danger of war'. The Peoples' Commissar thought that Rumania would not oppose a process which, by invoking collective security, would permit the free transit of Russian troops and aeroplanes across its territory. Halifax replied to Churchill two days later that he did not consider the suggestion useful, but that he would think about it! The proposition was not followed up, either by London or Paris.[34]

On 21 September, the Assembly of the League of Nations heard Litvinov repeat emphatically that the Soviet Union would remain faithful to its obligations towards Czechoslovakia. Two days later, while Chamberlain was meeting Hitler at Bad Godesberg and Europe was mobilising, he confirmed it for the last time, publicly and privately, 'A shame', cried the 'realists', 'a propaganda dupery!' Perhaps. The shadowy universe of the Kremlin was certainly not calculated to inspire confidence. However, we may note that no Western Minister took the trouble to make the journey to Moscow. If they had wanted to sound the intentions of the Soviets, nothing would have been easier than to drive the latter into a corner by engaging in the military *pourparlers* they asked for.

★   ★   ★

'Word appeasement', promised the British Prime Minister in a speech in Birmingham. To attain his goal, according to an English historian, 'He had to soften up the Czechs, immobilise France, and restrain the Germans.' As Hitler was the most dangerous, it was towards the friendly powers that his main efforts had to be directed.[35] From the spring of 1938, London had been attempting, with increasing brusqueness, to put pressure on the Czechs to accept the German demands. In May, William Strang, a senior Foreign Office official, was despatched to the Continent. He duly reported that the Czechoslovak Republic was condemned to become a satellite of the Reich, and that it should cede the Sudeten territories—*a claim which Berlin had not yet formulated.* At the beginning of the summer Chamberlain, after consulting Berlin (but not Paris), imposed upon Czechoslovakia a 'mediator', stating untruthfully in the Commons that the Czechs had asked for one. Lord Runciman, a rich shipowner and former President of the Board of Trade, but a personality of mediocre stature, was instructed to find a common ground to relax tension between Prague and the Sudeten Germans.

Parliament being prorogued, the sessions of the ministerial committee on foreign policy, a principal cog in the governmental machine, were interrupted. During the crucial five weeks of July–August, the Prime Minister even arranged matters so that the Cabinet did not meet. Much activity took place outside official diplomacy unknown to the Ministers—except to Halifax, Hoare and Simon, who were completely submissive to their chief.* The Foreign Office continued its under-cover conversations with Henlein, the Sudeten leader. Other intrigues were hatching. In July, a certain Captain Wiedemann, the ADC and so-called confidant of the Führer, was warmly received in London by the highest personalities. Although supposed to be secret, his visit was soon known to the Press as having been arranged by Lady Astor and a Princess Hohenlohe-Schillingsfürst, an adventuress with whom the American police was later to have a bone to pick. The German agent, received at Halifax's private house in Eaton Square, 'made a good impression'. With some exaggeration, Chamberlain communicated to the Cabinet that the German brought with him 'the most binding assurance' that the Führer did not contemplate having recourse to force, perhaps for a year. A fine promise! There was also question of a visit by Marshal Göring to London. When escorting the German emissary to the door of his house, Halifax confided to him, his fervent hope that, before he died, 'he would see the Führer at the side of the King of England, driving to Buckingham Palace to the cheering of the crowds'.[36]

In Paris, the intriguer in the background was Georges Bonnet. Léon Noel, ex-French Minister to Prague, after an exploratory mission to Czechoslovakia concluded, as had Strang, that the country was about to disintegrate. (These were appreciations which the events of the last fifty years have hardly confirmed.) Other 'special missions' followed, invariably opposed to the Czechs and to an allied intervention (the missions of Brunet, Pozzi and Grandmaison).[37] On the initiative of the 'Franco-German Committee' suspicious persons, a fifth-column it was said, were hatching obscure plots in Germanophile salons and (unknown to senior officials) even in the anti-chambers of the Quai d'Orsay'.† Otto Abetz, the 'intellectual Nazi', and agent of

---

* Sir Samuel Hoare had returned to the government as First Lord of the Admiralty, shortly after his forced resignation from the Foreign Office.

† The Germans were talking to the French, almost as much as to the English, about the division of the world.[39]

Ribbentrop's, and Fernand de Brinon, a journalist close to Laval, Bonnet and even to Daladier, went from Left to Right, holding forth on the common Franco-German heritage, on the common struggle against the Jews and Bolsheviks. The Minister of Foreign Affairs, in person, indicated to a Czech representative in July that France would not go to war over the Sudeten question. And the German Ambassador telegraphed to Berlin that the Minister had promised to 'go to the extreme limits of compromise'. Even in Brussels, Bonnet's efforts had not gone unnoticed—a fact which sapped the energy of the last opponents of neutrality.[38]

★   ★   ★

To defend its independence, Prague fought back inch by inch. Edouard Beneš, President of the Republic, led the struggle. A recalcitrant victim, he was accused of the principal sins of Israel. 'He's pig-headed', said Henderson. 'An unscrupulous rascal', it was said in Whitehall. Chamberlain had taken a great dislike to him, on learning of the unflattering epithets Beneš bestowed on him when telephoning the Czech Legation in London.* Certain Parisian circles went so far as to accuse Beneš of complicity with Stalin to bring about a war. Bonnet and several other Ministers openly criticised his 'criminal attitude'. François Pietri, ex-Minister of the Navy, warned the Belgian Ambassador against recourse to the League of Nations which was under 'clever and cunning pressure exercised by international Jewry supported by the representatives of certain powerful material interests, and by Communists in starched collars'. Daladier, his mind under pressure from the great decisions he had to take, had recourse to private conversations as 'soldier to soldier' with the German Ambassador in which, while declaring his intention to defend Czechoslovakia, he referred to the 'Red Danger', the obstinacy of the Czechs and 'Jewish intrigues'.[39]

However, the 'pig-headed man' made great efforts to give satisfaction to the Franco-British—not without difficulty, for the Army, the political parties and the Czech people showed little inclination to allow itself to be destroyed. An unprecedented factor, he resigned himself to permitting Lord Runciman, a foreigner, to mediate between himself and his fellow citizens—a foreigner who showed him little respect, and who spent the weekends playing golf in the chateaux of

---

* These conversations, passing through the Berlin telephone centre, were intercepted by the *Forschungsamt*. The German Embassy found it a most agreeable duty to communicate them to Downing Street.

his pro-Nazi enemies. Beneš had endured the increasingly abrasive behaviour of the Franco-British. He had proposed several successive compromises to the Sudetens. On the 6 September, in a courageous throw of the dice, he agreed in a 'fourth plan' to almost all their demands.

Less than 24 hours later, during an altercation with the Czech police in Moravska Ostrova, a Nazi Sudenten Member of Parliament was slapped in the face—an incident greatly inflated by Nazi propaganda. It was also a pretext for Henlein to break with Prague and take refuge in Germany. On the same day, *The Times* published a new editorial suggesting the annexation of the Sudeten territories by the Reich. All the Chancelleries knew of the close ties between the famous London paper and the English Ministers. In spite of official disavowals no one—the Germans least of all—had doubted that *The Times* proposals had been inspired from high quarters.*

A little later the Nazi *Parteitag* opened. This was the annual congress at Nuremberg, held this year under the aegis of the 'Great German Empire'. A million worshippers gathered in the little city to indulge—for the last time in history—in their frenzied communion. Would this offer the occasion for the Führer to plunge into adventure? The Nazi chiefs appeared to think so. On 10 September Göring, in a speech whose violence exhausted him almost to the point of collapse, described the Czechs as 'a race of miserable pygmies coming from no one knows where—behind them, Moscow and the diabolical Jew'. The Nazi Press fell into step with him with torrents of abuse couched in language of unimaginable vulgarity.

The culminating point of the congress of the Great Empire was the closing speech by the Führer on 12 September 1938. On the eve of that day the Foreign Office had announced that Great Britain would not stand aside in event of a European conflict.† The peoples expected the worst.

---

* It was apparently an erroneous assertion, even though *The Times* had mentioned it before, and its editor could not ignore views privately expressed by Chamberlain. It is not wihout interest to point out that two days later, the German Chargé d'Affaires asked to meet Spaak, and told him, while protesting the pacific intentions of the Führer, with surprising reserve, 'I cannot specify our precise conditions, but the article in *The Times* corresponds certainly to our desires.'[40]

† In fact the Foreign Office communiqué had to be corrected on the next day by the embarrassed declarations of Chamberlain. The Cabinet, starting from the hypothesis that Hitler was 'possibly or even probably, mad', had given way to the objurgations of the Prime Minister to do nothing which might humiliate or provoke him. A letter from Halifax to Bonnet confirmed this, its object being to hold back Paris, it indicated that His Majesty's Government could not define its future attitude over 'circumstances which it could not at present foresee'.[41]

At the same time, like millions of other men and women throughout Europe and America, I listened to Hitler's harangue. Together with some colleagues in our room at the Rue de la Loi, we waited heavy-hearted, hypnotised by the mahogany box from which his roarings poured forth, and the baleful words which would plunge the world into the nameless horror of a new conflict. Deafened by the strident burst of sound, by his sadistic descriptions of the alleged tortures inflicted on the Sudetens, by the bestial invectives heaped on the heads of the Czechs and, almost as much, on the French and English, we were relieved that it was not to be war—today at least.

Calm had however, not been re-established. As in Austria some months before the Nazi militia, obeying the orders of their chiefs, occupied little towns and villages, hanging out the forbidden swastika, brutalising its adversaries, pulling up the frontier posts, taking police stations and city halls by assault. The newspapers described the Czech and Jewish shops sacked and pillaged in the Sudeten towns, the streets covered with debris, the Trades Union offices (German, but Social Democrat) riddled with revolver bullets. Prague reacted strongly, declaring martial law in the most disorderly zones. The police made use of their arms; there were 20 dead and many wounded. The insurrection crumbled, but the impasse was complete.

Europe seemed to be reliving the last days of July 1914. From all sides came the rattle of sabres. In Germany, the mobilisation of the Armed forces was virtually complete. As an extreme measure of war economy, the Reichsbank received the order for unlimited credits to be made available to the government.[42] In France, hundreds of thousands of reservists were recalled. In Czechoslovakia, the conscripts rejoined their regiments, the motorised divisions were put on the alert; but owing to the intervention of Paris and London, general mobilisation was delayed. Even the placid Dutch recalled two classes of militia, and in England, precautionary measures were adopted. However, these fell short of the mobilisation of the Fleet, which the Prime Minister refused. On 15 September, Konrad Henlein abandoned all pretence, crying, '*Wir wollen ins Reich*—we want to be Germans!' What was going to happen?

That very day Neville Chamberlain was at Berchtesgaden. Two days before in the evening, he had 'felt the moment had come', and he asked to meet the Führer—a project he had been nursing for some weeks, but which may perhaps have been suggested initially by Germany. 'Plan Z', as he called it with emphasis, filled him with intense exal-tation; he wished his meeting with the Führer to be a poignant scene, the triumph of his public life.* He had therefore confided in secret that he was ready to concede the Sudeten territories after a plebiscite; a magnificent present which even then had not been formally demanded. The Cabinet was only *informed* of 'Plan Z' on the eve of his departure. The project of a plebiscite, which implied the concept of auto-determination, overcame its scruples. In fact, it had not been truly *consulted*. Nor, of course, had Prague, nor Washington nor Moscow; nor even Daladier, who had telephoned in the evening suggesting a meeting of the three heads of government. Chamberlain wished to share with no one the heavy burden weighing on his shoulders. The world learned of this extraordinary step with amazement. Was this a last warning? Or, as it appeared, an act of submission? In the Berlin suburb, at General Halder's private house, General Beck and his fellow-conspirators, assembled in great secrecy, were putting the last touches to the *Putsch* which was to lead to the arrest of the Führer next day, and to prevent war. Chamberlain's initiative announced on the radio cut short their plans. On the eve of Munich, they abandoned them for the time.

Late that evening, I was with Edouard Le Ghait in his ill-lit, gloomy office preparing the next day's work, when I suddenly heard the teleprinter hidden behind a door start tapping. When, after glancing at the spool of paper emitted by the machine, I handed it to my chief, he stared at me for seconds, stunned. 'War within a year', he murmured with a choking voice. 'War under the worst conditions. Nothing will stop him any more.'† I felt he was near to despair. Although very anglophile. He had no doubt that the policy of the Conservative Party was leading straight to war. Was it true?

Hitler made Chamberlain, his senior by twenty years, come to him in his lair in Obersalzburg, a long and uncomfortable journey, four hours by air to Munich, then on by train and car. Chamberlain left Croydon at eight in the morning, and night was falling when the old man, accompanied by Horace Wilson and William Strang, walked up the steps of the Berghof in the wind and rain. His host had not taken the trouble to meet him at the station. But 'the Saint George with the umbrella' did not mind. On the contrary, he was overflowing with restrained joy, trembling beneath his rigid exterior with the bliss of

---

*Originally the Prime Minister had intended to appear suddenly in Berlin at the last moment *without announcing himself*, 'for a face to face meeting with the Führer, as Cleopatra with Caesar'. His advisers spoke of it as a Canossa, and had succeeded in dissuading him.[43]

† At Aldershot, at about the same time, the future Field Marshal Lord Alexander was speaking in the same vein to his officers.[44]

his apostolate. Without any documents or collaborators, he was going to beard the Dragon in the mountain, alone except for a German interpreter. It was his supreme hour. He was ready for any sacrifice, if it assured the success of his sacred mission. The sacrifice would be Czechoslovakia's. Almost immediately, he agreed to transfer to the Reich of the Sudeten region—for which, he confided to Hitler, he didn't care two hoots. There was not even a mention of a plebiscite.

Saturday 17 and Sunday 18 September. On Chamberlain's return to England, he reported to the Cabinet. He made it uneasy by referring to the possible hail of bombs on English towns. He justified the cession to the Reich of the Sudeten districts by the right of people to self-determination. The Ministers were doubtful, dissatisfied—but they resigned themselves to it. The French President of the Council and his Foreign Minister were again summoned to London. Daladier, in a secret agreement with Beneš, was disposed to a considerable rectification of the frontier in favour of the Reich. But it was the first time he had heard officially of the massive transfer of territory which would impair the strategic frontiers. He became indignant, predicting that the Reich, once it was master of Eastern Europe, would launch its armies against France and Great Britain. 'You exaggerate', said Chamberlain haughtily. 'I have confidence in the word of the Führer. His unique objective is the racial unity of the Germans and not the domination of Europe.' Daladier's reserves of energy were rapidly being sapped. On 18 September, after discussions which had often been acrimonious, he submitted as midnight was striking. Whether Czechoslovakia liked it or not, it would cede to the Reich its predominantly German territories. There was no talk of self-determination or plebiscite. For good measure, Czechoslovakia would abrogate her foreign alliances, so as not to constitute a threat to the Reich! However, Great Britain and France, who had refused to defend her when she was strong, would guarantee her when she was reduced to impotence—and they asked Germany, not without irony, to do the same.

Monday 19 September. Chamberlain made his colleagues endorse the 'Franco-British plan', blaming the French for the abandonment of the plebiscite.* The dejected Daladier took the aeroplane back to Paris in a sombre mood. In his turn, he made his divided and undecided government approve what he had consented to. The Franco-British

---

* Daladier feared that a plebiscite might lead to an explosion in the Balkans, by encouraging their many nationalities to follow suit.

plan was sent to Prague with, 'a request for immediate acceptance'. Would Beneš agree to it? Hourly, the German radio put out military marches and the frantic speeches of Sudeten agitators. There was much talk of a free-corps enrolled in Germany, and ready to cross the frontier. In the churches people prayed for peace. The Czechoslovak Minister was seen to leave the Quai d'Orsay after an interview with Bonnet, his eyes full of tears.[45]

Tuesday 20 September. Hours of anguish. The Press gave unedifying details about the Anglo-French manoeuvres to prevent the Czechs from completing their mobilisation, and to drive them to suicide. In spite of the most brutal and unfair threats by the British Legation, the Czechs did not flinch. At 8 o'clock after long deliberation, they demanded arbitration by the permanent Court of the Hague, laid down by the German-Czech treaty of 1926.

Wednesday 21 September. In the middle of the night, the French and British Ministers in Prague received fresh instructions. At 2 o'clock in the morning they went to the Hradcin Palace. To the President of the Republic, half awake and in his dressing-gown, they emphasised the 'realities'; their proposals offered the only chance of preventing an imminent German attack. If they were rejected, 'a situation would arise for which Paris and London could accept no responsibility'. In other words, the Czechs would be responsible for a conflict in which the Franco–British would take no part. On hearing the ultimatum delivered, not by his enemies but by friendly or allied governments, Beneš could not hold back his tears. In the early dawn, he gave in.

Thursday 22 and Friday 23 September. At two o'clock in the afternoon Chamberlain returned in triumph to Germany, this time to Bad Godesberg to give the present of the Sudetens to the Führer. Amazed, he found that the hasty bargain struck at Berchtesgaden was no longer valid. '*Es tut mir leid*', said the Nazi Dictator, 'I am sorry'. There were further strips of Czech territory he required for Germany, Hungary and Poland. The Sudeten Germans he said, were being massacred (which was untrue); he must occupy the regions they inhabited immediately. The Czech authorities, their army, police, customs officials and civil administration must evacuate the region before 28 September, in four days time. A plebiscite could be organised later. If he did not obtain satisfaction, the Wehrmacht would march. Unable to believe his ears, Chamberlain retired to the Petersberg Hotel on the other bank of the Rhine. He attempted to bargain; two days passed in conversations and exchanges of letters. He finished by giving way, flattering himself on a success, because Hitler had agreed to postpone the date of the expiration of his ultimatum—to 1 October, that is the day he had selected long before.

Saturday 24 September. On returning to London, the Prime Minister was received with rebuffs. The Conservative Party was shaken by what it heard. Several Ministers, including Halifax himself, were deeply worried. In Paris too, the attitude stiffened. Daladier, who was poorly informed about what had happened at Bad Godesberg, appeared decided to reject Hitler's new demands. In Prague, general mobilisation was declared without raising any more objections in western capitals. On the public buildings in the towns and villages of France appeared the fatal notices calling up several classes of the militia; 750,000 men rejoined their units, 'in a calm and orderly manner', reported the German Embassy in Paris.[46] The Kremlin warned the Poles, who clearly had their eyes on the Czech district of Teschen, against any unconsidered action.

Sunday 25 September. In London, new and stormy Franco-British conversations took place in the late evening. 'Painful in the extreme', Sir Samuel Hoare recalled. 'France is resolved to do her duty', announced Daladier, 'He who wishes to follow her can do so.' He painted an encouraging picture of the military situation. Without denying the aerial supremacy of Germany, he emphasised that 'in Spain, where since the beginning Franco has ruled the skies, and in spite of the destruction of towns and human lives, the air force has not proved effective enough to win the war'. He spoke of 'destructive offences on the soil of Germany'. Chamberlain displayed an arrogance and toughness quite different from the long patience he had shown at Bad Godesberg. Sir John Simon, with the aggressiveness of an examining magistrate, subjected the head of the French government to a close interrogation on the intentions and capabilities of his army. 'Awful!', noted Cadogan. The interview finished inconclusively, in a hostile atmosphere.[47]

Monday 21 September. General Gamelin, summoned to London, completed the information furnished the day before by the French Premier and Minister of National Defence. He reaffirmed his full confidence. It was now that he revealed that the German fortifications, the Siegfried Line, was barely outlined, and that the French Army had positioned 23 divisions on her eastern frontier against 8 enemy ones. While remaining vague as to his strategic objectives, he declared that, in spite of air inferiority, he could mount a large-scale offensive five days after the outbreak of hostilities. He also referred to a message received from Marshal Voroshilov, announcing that the Soviets had massed 30 infantry divisions, large forces of cavalry, many armoured divisions, and most of their air force on their western frontier.[47]

The Prime Minister listened to him distractedly, and soon sent him off to the British Generals. He told Daladier that he had decided during the night to send Sir Horace Wilson to Berlin with the mission of addressing a final appeal to the Führer—while warning him that Great Britain would be at the side of France in the event of any aggression against Czechoslovakia. When the French left by air, this was confirmed to the world by an official communiqué from the Foreign Office, authorised by Lord Halifax.* Shortly after, Wilson landed at the Tempelhof airport and was met by the British Ambassador. The two men were escorted to the Chancellery to be received immediately by Hitler, who launched himself into a scene probably unrivalled in the annals of modern diplomacy. Prancing with rage, foaming at the mouth, he shrieked his insults, as much at Chamberlain as at them—too foul and scurrilous, they said, to be included in an official report. He roared that he would do to Czechoslovakia what he had always intended, on 1 October. Intimidated and dumbfounded, Wilson and Henderson lost their nerve and withdrew, without having dared give him the warning which was the object of their journey— an unforgivable fault.

That evening in the *Sportspalast* in Berlin, in the most violent speech of his career, the Dictator proclaimed *for the first time* that he would seize the Sudeten territories—whatever might be the consequences. 'The snarling of a wild animal', said Leo Amery, an English former and future Conservative Minister. 'There was something terrifying and obscenely sinister in this outpouring of sheer hatred . . . in the culminating almost endless "Sieg Heils" that followed his outburst.' The American journalist William Shirer wrote, 'In a paroxysm of rage, in a state of over-excitement such as I have never seen before. It seemed he was no longer in control of himself . . . his eyes blazing with a fanatical flame . . . hungry and distraught . . .'.[48]

During the day, people were clearing for action all over Europe. From London, our Embassy telephoned that the distribution of gas-masks was being accelerated, and that the civil defence personnel were in a state of alert. Trenches were being dug in the gardens and public parks. The evacuation of schoolchildren and the hospital sick had started. In Paris, the railways stations were crowded with reservists. The city lights and private houses were blacked out. In Italy, the Fleet

---

* A communiqué which lost all value. Bonnet attempted to prevent its circulation in Paris, insinuating that it was false; and Chamberlain, once again, was to minimise its importance in public.

took to the high sea; there were troop movements in Sicily, Libya and opposite the Alps. In Czechoslovakia, a million men were under arms—as many as in Germany. Late that evening the Belgian government decided to put the army on a 'reinforced peace footing', a euphemism which meant the mobilisation of the first reserve regiments. I was in one of these, and I returned to my flat to prepare my uniform case, feeling miserable but ready for the worst.

Tuesday 27 September. Empty-handed, Wilson took the aeroplane back to London. Before leaving Berlin, he saw the Führer again, and thought fit to congratulate him on his success in the *Sportspalast*, marvelling at his 'magnificent human experience'. What could be more rewarding than the ovations which had glorified him? Prompted by a new message from Downing Street, the wretched special envoy, taking his courage in both hands, finally fulfilled his mission by telling Hitler that, in the event of war, Great Britain would take her stand beside France; but he weakened the warning with such a flood of apologies as to make it meaningless.[49] It in no way prevented further shrieking; 'I will annihilate the Czechs! . . . I will annihilate the Czechs! . . . come what may. . .'.

The mobilisation of the Royal Navy was announced; this time, it really took place. Late that morning having donned my uniform, I went to the 'Carabiniers' barracks to meet the thirty men of my troop. I led them, uniformed, tin-hatted, provided with their arms and gas-masks, to the cantonment which had been assigned to us in a suburban school centre. That evening, in a cafe, I listened with them on the radio to the tired and quavering voice of Chamberlain announcing his failure. 'How horrible, fantastic, incredible it is that here we should be digging trenches and trying on gas-masks . . . because of a quarrel in a far away country, between people of whom we know nothing!' Heavy-hearted, I recalled my visit to Prague the year before and Maurice Frère's conversation with Beneš in the beautiful setting of the Hradcin.[50]

The rest is well known. Before retiring for the night, Chamberlain received an unexpected letter from Hitler asking him to continue his efforts to bring the Czechs to reason. All his energy reawakened, the 'Prince of Peace' immediately replied promising the essentials of what he had demanded, 'without war, and without delay'. He suggested a five-power conference—Great Britain, France, Germany, Italy and Czechoslovakia. He made an appeal to Mussolini, who intervened in Berlin. On 28 September, during a dramatic sitting, he announced in the Commons, 'with an air of moral satisfaction . . . and the aura of personal triumph', that Hitler had agreed to a conference in Munich, in the company of Mussolini and Daladier.[51]

On 29 September, the four heads of government met in the Bavarian capital—without a representative of Czechoslovakia, whom Hitler had refused to see; and, it need hardly be added, without their Soviet allies, whose presence none of the four powers wanted. Hitler and Mussolini met to prepare the conference. Chamberlain and Daladier, arriving separately, had not considered it necessary to consult one another. In a few hours, an agreement was reached which did not even specify the exact limits of the transferred territories. With a week's delay, Hitler had obtained what he wanted, once again his 'last claim'. The Prague plenipotentiaries, relegated for ten hours to their hotel bedrooms, were not consulted. Admitted to the conference room after the departure of the dictators, they listened to the English and French—supreme indignity—read out the sentence of death on their country. They were not allowed to comment on it; they had three hours to accept. Daladier was particularly curt. Chamberlain yawned, feeling pleasantly tired.[51] The wretched Beneš abandoned by everyone, capitulated. He was soon to resign and take the road of exile, to escape the lot of Schuschnigg. When, while passing through Paris, he made a request to meet the President of the Council, it was turned down.

From the 1 October, the Wehrmacht began crossing the frontier and occupying the abandoned fortifications—not without some retrospective shock at discovering how powerful they were. Some 30,000 square kilometres of Czech territory had been amputated—the area of Belgium. Czechoslovakia had lost 60 per cent of its coal, 86 per cent of its chemical production, 80 per cent of its textiles and 70 per cent of its iron and steel, including its armaments industry. More than three million Sudetens became citizens of the Reich, most of them joyfully, some against their will. At the same time, so did almost 700,000 Czechs, a new ethnic minority for whom no-one evoked the right to self-determination. As in Austria, the security police and the Gestapo began immediately 'clearing up the liberated territory'. With savage cruelty, the hunt began for Czechs, Jews, liberals and social-democrats.

A few days later, in the House of Commons, the pacifier of the world was to state with the certitude of the visionary, 'To accuse us of betraying Czechoslovakia is quite absurd. What we have done is to save it from destruction and Europe from Armageddon.' Had he succeeded in convincing himself?

CHAPTER 15

Peace with Honour, Peace for Our Time

On their return from Munich the statesmen were given a tumultuous welcome. In London an enormous crowd, delirious with joy, thronged the streets, and threw bouquets of flowers at the Prime Minister. At Buckingham Palace the King escorted him onto the balcony, presenting him to the crowd. In Downing Street to the repeated cries of 'Good old Neville!', he appeared at the window of Number 10, his face radiant with happiness, brandishing a piece of paper, announcing, 'Peace with honour, peace for our time'.

The piece of paper was a curious, perhaps unprecedented, document, which the Prime Minister had caused William Strang to draw up at 7 a.m. in Munich, without consulting Paris or anyone else and which he had persuaded Hitler to sign during a brief interview at the latter's private residence—the same apartment in which Hitler's niece, Geli Raubal, had committed suicide in 1931, in a room which had since been sealed. Expressed in imprecise terms, it was a pact of friendship, allowing for mutual consultation. Did Chamberlain see in this the first outline for an alliance between Britain and Germany—in other times, one of his father's great conceptions?

For the public, the scourge of war had been lifted. The Prime Minister received thousands of congratulatory letters and telegrams. In spite of some discordant voices—the resignation of Duff Cooper, the First Lord of the Admiralty, Churchill's warnings, the abstention of about 40 Conservative M.P.s, and the opposition of Labour—the House of Commons renewed its confidence in him by a big majority. *The Times* summed up popular feeling: 'No conqueror returning from a victory on the battlefield had come adorned with nobler laurels.'

France was no less enthusiastic. When Daladier looked through the window of the aeroplane bringing him back to France, and saw the crowd that had invaded Le Bourget, he blanched, convinced that this was a demonstration against him. But when the engines stopped, he realised that he was being greeted not with boos and jeers, but with acclamations. 'Poor fools!' he whispered to his ADC. 'If they only knew what they are applauding!' However, to the journalists pressing him with questions he stated, after thanking Hitler and Mussolini warmly, that the Munich agreement would assure world peace. It was a promise which, as in London, delighted the 500,000 people massed between Le Bourget and the Rue St Dominique to acclaim the Prime Minister with patriotic songs, cries of joy, flowers and flags; he stood up in an open car, Bonnet at his side. It was a promise which caused the *Chambre* to give him a standing ovation, and to ratify the Munich agreement by 515 to 75 (73 of the latter being Communists). It was a promise applauded by the Press: the extreme Right like *Le Matin*, 'Peace has been gained against the crooks, traitors and madmen'; of the Centre like *La France Catholique*, 'The sky is blue again'; of the Socialist Left like *Le Populaire*, 'The world can breath again ... we can return to our work, and sleep again.'

Great relief was felt in all the Western capitals. Thanksgiving masses were said in the churches. President Roosevelt hurriedly sent a telegram to Chamberlain, 'Good man!' The President of the League of Nations said, 'The name of the British Prime Minister is blessed today by all the households of the world.' Mussolini, not without attributing to himself the most important role, exclaimed, 'What happened in Munich is quite simply colossal.' In Brussels, there was the same explosion of popular joy; nearly all circles echoed a phrase of Leon Blum's, 'The danger of war has been averted, we can enjoy the beauty of the autumn sun.' But when it bacame known that the Belgian Ambassador had been instructed to congratulate Hitler, people felt uneasy.

I do not believe that the deep sigh of relief heaved by Europe expressed, as has often been claimed, the exhaustion of the people's will. The British were to show later that they had lost none of their virile virtues. For the French, the unhappy fate of their arms in 1940 gave rise to the opinion that, old and tired, they had given up the will to defend themselves. However, losing a great battle has never in itself been a sign of decadence. How often have Great Britain, France and Germany given proof of this in the course of their glorious histories?

The horror of war had certainly not abated. No one wished light-heartedly to 'die for the Negus, for the Czechs, or for Dantzig', a formula composed by hot-headed publicists, or those in the pay of the Dictators. 'On the half corpse of a nation betrayed,' mocked Henri de Montherland, 'on the half skeleton of its honour, its dignity and its

security, millions of men danced the Saint Guy de la Paix dance.'
Yes; but they also realised they could no longer avoid having to take
up arms to save their heritage. The first opinion poll on the morrow
of the Munich conference gave 57 per cent of the French in its favour,
with 37 per cent against—the same majority which in Great Britain
was satisfied with Chamberlain. In any case, to a question put at the
same time, 'Do you think that in future France and England should
refuse any new demands made by Hitler?', 70 per cent answered Yes,
against 17 per cent No. A massive majority. The contradiction was
only too apparent. They had bowed before a *fait accompli*, while at
the same time being resolved not to tolerate its repetition. With their
eyes wide open; as they were asked, 'Do you think that a world war
would result in the destruction of civilisation?', 75 per cent said Yes,
and 20 per cent No.[2]

There is a good deal of evidence testifying to the healthy morale
and calm courage of France. If the German Ambassador had ques-
tioned, not without some anxiety, whether France would fight for
Czechoslovakia, his doubt was founded on the hesitancy of the French
Government, not on a lack of courage among the population. The
Belgian Ambassador viewed the situation in much the same light.
Bullitt the American Ambassador, although a firm believer in appeasement wrote on 13 June 1938 to President Roosevelt, 'As I have cabled,
public opinion in France has solidified to such an extent that if the
German Army should cross the Czech frontier, France would mobilise
at once and march against Germany.' He was to repeat this view right
up to the end of the crisis.[3]

The views of the British Ambassador, who was most closely in touch
with events, deserved special mention. Sir Eric Phipps belonged to the
appeasers. He was determined, often in an ungracious and hardly
diplomatic manner, to discourage the French Ministers, while at the
same time repeating to London that they were giving way. On 24
September, he made a resumé of the situation in a telegram to the
Foreign Office: 'All that is best in France is opposed to war, almost
at any price. The only ones in favour are small, noisy and corrupt
groups.' This incredible piece of information earned a curt request for
an explanation. Two days later the Ambassador, who had become
calmer, made known that 'opinion has undergone a complete change'.
He had consulted the Cardinal Archbishop of Paris, the Presidents of
the two Chambers of Parliament, and various personalities; they had
all declared that 'the people are resigned but resolute' . . . 'as was a
large majority in the Chamber of Deputies', added Herriot. The British

Consulates in the provinces confirmed almost unanimously that the French were resolute, and resigned to not giving in.[4] North and south of the Channel, high priests of appeasement found in their counterparts on the other side of the water a pretext to justify their stance.

In July the British King and Queen made an official visit to France, which gave the population the opportunity to show its true feelings. Lord Halifax's secretary relates how agreeably surprised he was to see along the road from Boulogne to Paris, in the fields and villages innumerable French people waving British flags, acclaiming the fast-moving Royal train. 'It was clear', he wrote, 'that all France had turned out to honour us.' The Sovereigns were received at the station of the Bois de Boulogne by the President of the Republic, with a children's chorus singing 'God save the King!' They and their suite descended the Champs-Élysées in brilliant sunshine, escorted by the Garde Republicaine, and acclaimed by an enthusiastic crowd. On the next day, in Versailles, there was a march-past of 40,000 infantry, cavalry, artillery, tanks, in perfect order, making a deep impression on the British. In the evening, after the traditional dinner at the Quai d'Orsay, King George and Queen Elizabeth had to come out twice on the balcony of the Salon de l'Horloge to acknowledge the acclamations of an estatic crowd. Not since the Armistice, stated a French witness, had such a dense crowd, unanimous in its fervour, been seen. An opinion poll taken in August confirmed that 78 per cent believed that, 'the Anglo-French *entente* will keep the peace in Europe'[5] by a common resistance to aggressors.

At the beginning of the summer of 1938, with the return of Daladier to power, the Parisian confusion of the previous years was resolved. Assisted by Paul Reynaud in the Finance Department, and by outstanding technocrats, Daladier restored social order by embarking on an imaginative economic strategy, abandoning both the traditional deflationary measures and the more untimely ones of the *Front Populaire*. 'I am the son of a workman, faithful to my origins, a son of France . . . uncouth maybe, but free, and intending to remain so!', he cried, a lock of hair falling over his brow, his shoulders squared on the tribune facing the attentive Deputies. By a massive majority, they confirmed their confidence in him. Stretching out his hand to Left as well as to Right, to the Socialists as to the Catholics, the head of the government united the parties and renewed the authority of the State.[6]

What was the situation in Great Britain? The defenders of Chamberlain's policy justified Munich by maintaining that the country was neither militarily nor psychologically prepared. This argument was specious. If the Army was not in a fit state, whose fault was it? The fault of the government which disposed of an enormous parliamentary majority favourable to rearmament, and which had for so long put a brake on it. A government which, far from alerting the nation, deliberately concealed the dangers ahead. Chamberlain was the first occupant of Downing Street to make full use of the media. Helped by Sir Samuel Hoare, he brought to bear all the pressures that his authority disposed of, on the newspapers, often through the intermediary of their owners, or on the BBC, through a barely disguised censorship. The London press, in particular, was subjected to a daily indoctrination. Alfred Duff Cooper, Harold Nicolson and others were later to complain of this. Harold Macmillan wrote in his memoirs of 'A fragile and insubstantial screen of complacency and self deception, skilfully designed to delude a whole people into a fictitious sense of security.'[7]

But public opinion was beginning to show increasing signs of exasperation. Already, before the *Anschluss*, opinion polls were indicating how much it disapproved of Chamberlain's policy. Already, before Munich, political parties were expressing anxiety. The Socialists and Liberals had shown themselves almost unanimously ready to stop Hitler, even at the risk of war. On 8 September, the Trade Unions had passed a motion with an imposing majority indicating that Great Britain should fight for Czechoslovakia. The National Council of Labour followed suit. Among leading Conservatives, the deep unease was exacerbated when they learned the full extent of the sacrifices demanded from the Czechs. Senior officials at the Foreign Office did not disguise their disapproval, if discreetly. Several Ministers talked of resigning. Many on the majority benches wished for much firmer policies, although not daring to say so. Dining in a Tory club, Harold Nicolson found his fellow members 'in despair over the government'.

Did the man in the street, the ordinary Englishman, think differently? Opinions are divided. However, much evidence leads to the belief that, as at the time of the Abyssinian war, his sympathies lay with the under-dog, with the victim, and that he was ready to defend him, Duff Cooper spoke of 'a massive majority'. And Harvey said, 'He is very worked up and anti-German.' Nicolson wrote in his diary when war appeared imminent, 'Everyone is calm, resolute and joyful.' Eden received great applause when he proclaimed, 'The British people know that the moment to resist has arrived.' In the schools, particularly Eton, and in the Universities, young people crowded to the recruiting centres. Eton, it is said, is for the sons of the rich. Perhaps—but the territorial regiments made up of volunteers from all classes of society were inundated with requests for enlistment. In London, there were street demonstrations. On his departure for Berchtesgaden, Chamberlain was greeted with voices demanding a firm line. If we are to believe the *Daily Herald*, 'On 22 September, while he was preparing at Godesberg to capitulate, a vast cortege of 10,000 people marched down Whitehall shouting, "Long live Czechoslovakia! Down with Chamberlain!"'[8]

Much has been said about the reticence of the Dominions, Australia, New Zealand, South Africa and Canada. It is true that after the First World War, they considered themselves independent states, no longer prepared to follow the United Kingdom blindly. It is also true that at the Imperial Conference of 1937, they supported the policy of appeasement—at the suggestion of London. During the Czech crisis, ill-informed and lulled by the purring noises of officialdom, they showed themselves little disposed to 'die for the Sudetens'. But, as in the case of the people, they had not been informed of the real stakes at issue. For many years, the Dominions had been the most fervent supporters of collective security; they had been vigorous in their support of sanctions against Italy. Would they have been more forceful in 1938, if they had realised that they were defending the interests of peace, and not those of the Czechoslovakia Republic? However, when the crisis was at its peak, the Secretary of State for the Dominions could inform the Cabinet that they would not abandon the mother country.[9]

If the creative genius of a country is a sign of its vitality, there is nothing to show that France and England were in decline in 1938. Science and arts shone as brightly as they had in previous years. In painting, the cosmopolitan École de Paris was in full flower; the French theatre more splendid than ever. Fine novels, characteristic of the inter-war period, continued to pour out of the publishing houses. In London, there were innumerable outstanding writers, the famous Bernard Shaw, poets like T. S. Eliot, Robert Graves, Lord Dunsany and Spender; philosophers like Toynbee and Russell; novelists like Huxley, Waugh, Priestley, Greene, Joyce, Orwell, Isherwood and Nicolson. As in Paris, nearly all of them were humanists, faithful to Western ideals. They presented a striking contrast to Berlin and Rome, where authority, taken to its extreme, revived a medieval way of thought which led to the sterilisation of ideas, arts and sciences. Indeed, it was not the people which failed, it was those who were leading them at the time. Churchill wrote:

> Delighted in smooth-sounding platitudes, refusal to face unpleasant facts, desire

for popularity and electoral success, irrespective of the vital interests of the State, genuine love of peace and pathetic belief that love can be its sole foundation, obvious lack of intellectual vigour ... marked ignorance of Europe and aversion from its problems ... fatuity and fecklesness ... (which) played a definite part in the unleasing upon the world of horrors and miseries which even so far as they have unfolded are already beyond comparison and human experience.[10]

★   ★   ★

The sheer physical pleasure of no longer facing imminent death had passed; the resounding words of Churchill in the House of Commons stirred hearts on both sides of the Channel 'Silent, mournful, abandoned, broken, Czechoslovakia recedes into darkness.'—Failing a great effort, a major disaster for Great Britain and France.

Circumstances would have allowed this great effort. The national unanimity, obtained in the totalitarian countries through the demagogy of Mussolini and Hitler, was now achieved in the liberal democracies, thanks to the perception of the external danger and to an improved social climate following a better economic situation. The governing classes were regaining the confidence they had lost at the beginning of the decade. London was gripped with rearmament fever. Conservative Members of Parliament rallied against inadequacy and delay in government programmes. The Labour Party and the Trade Unions, forgetting their traditional pacifism, demanded a military apparatus, 'adequate for the defence of the country, and its participation in collective security'. Even the pro-Munich newspapers joined in, including *The Times* and the *Daily Express*, which now supported compulsory military service. They reflected public opinion. A Gallup poll on October showed that 72 per cent of the public were in favour of an increase in armament expenditure; and 78 per cent to a national register preliminary to conscription.[11]

The British Prime Minister found himself henceforth almost alone in thinking otherwise. He had returned from his German visits on the brink of nervous depression; but even more persuaded than ever in the inordinate presumption of his infallibility. 'The Führer', he wrote, 'has been profoundly and favourably impressed by my personality ... he would not deliberately deceive a man he respected, and with whom he had negotiated ... he was extremely anxious to secure the friendship of Great Britain.' In short, there was every reason to have faith in his word.* In view of the innumerable lies, perfidies and crimes marking

* A surprising opinion to hold, because Hitler took a dislike to the solemn, stiff old Englishman, who imagined he pleased him by describing at length the joys of angling, his favourite sport.[12]

Hitler's lurid career, it was an extraordinary declaration of faith from a man who distrusted Roosevelt and Daladier, not to mention Stalin.

In October and November in a state of euphoria, Chamberlain summed up the situation with astonishing vanity, castigating those who doubted his success, comparing them to 'birds which foul their own nest'. Far from an expedient dictated by strategic imperatives, he saw in Munich a step towards the 'general settlement' of which he had spoken since 1937. He did not abandon hope of a treaty on arms limitations, and was distressed by the insistence in the country on rearmament, astonished that 'it should be the logical consequence of Munich'. Irresistible pressure had made him accept the acceleration, if not the increase, in programmes directly linked to the island's defence—for the Navy, anti-aircraft artillery and fighter planes. But he had opposed the construction of bombers, both because of their high cost, and because they were offensive weapons, which would have repudiated his policies. Also, as he confirmed in a Commons speech on 1 November, he continued to oppose compulsory military service. The regular army remained limited to a few divisions, of which only two or three were more or less fit for combat.* It was not on account of financial difficulties; the 1938 budget included a significant surplus.

Daladier was fully aware of what he himself described as 'the immense defeat of Munich'. With about 100 divisions, the French Army had reached the limit of its recruiting capacity. The ex-infantry officer of 1918 remembered that victory had been achieved only with the help of many allied divisions. Military and political circles insisted in their requests to Britain on what they called 'the blood tax'. At the end of November, when Daladier received Chamberlain and Halifax on their first official visit to Paris, he ventured to ask for a reinforcement of two mechanised divisions in the event of war. The British refused to grant this modest request, limiting their contribution with all sorts of reservations to two infantry divisions—while criticising severely the state of the French Air Force (justifiably). The meeting lacked warmth and proved sterile. Chamberlain was greeted on the streets with cries of, 'Down with Munich!'

★ ★ ★

---

*By the decision to insist on the increase in fighter planes (which also had the virtue of being cheaper), Chamberlain paradoxically contributed to the RAF's victory in the Battle of Britain in 1940. it was only in March–April 1939 that it was decided to mobilise a significant British Expeditionary Force.[13]

When, at Munich, Mussolini openly made himself Hitler's accomplice, his scorn for the French and British was increased by the flattery they bestowed upon him. Wildly acclaimed by the Italians on his return, greeted as 'the Angel of Peace', the cheers had only increased his phantasmal megalomania. He dreamed of military expeditions against France, in North Africa and the Balkans—although the Italian Army was exhausted by years of fighting in Ethiopia and Spain, and above all by the general slipshod nature of Fascism. The number of divisions had been increased by reducing the man-power in each. Ciano himself stated that they lacked munitions, were short of anti-tank and anti-aircraft guns, and that the artillery was out of date (in fact, it dated from the First World War). It was not known how many aircraft could be put into the air, so Ciano suggested that a census should be made by the local prefects.[14] Mussolini, although Minister of Defence, was quite unconcerned; problems of supply bored him to death.

In October, the Duce again eluded the advances of Ribbentrop, who came to Rome to discuss a military alliance. Mussolini had not entirely abandoned his earlier judgement of the Führer—'a dangerous idiot, a horrible sexual degenerate', he still sometimes muttered. But his desire to dazzle him was irresistible. 'It is a pathological case', said Attolico, the Italian Ambassador in Berlin. 'Like a rat mesmerised by a serpent.'[15] It was also the judgement of his Belgian colleague in Rome. Obsessed with the desire to appear virile and terrible, Mussolini declined one evening to dine at Hitler's table, for fear of letting him see that he suffered from gastric troubles and lived on porridge. He received André François-Poncet and Sir Percy Lorraine, the new French and British Ambassadors, with humiliating insolence. He again began to write anonymous letters containing 'carefully chosen insults' to diplomats who displeased him.[16] Proclaiming that to be respected it was necessary to be 'hard, implacable and hated', he closed his ears to all advice. He did not listen to his own Ambassadors, nor read their despatches. The same could be said of his Foreign Minister, who was too frivolous to devote time to such matters. Mussolini spoke increasingly of abolishing the monarchy and ridding Italy of the House of Savoy, which had made feeble attempts to retrain him. Anti-Semitic measures were intensified, in spite of general reprobation and protests from the King and the Pope.

Official propaganda railed against the democracies, and stepped up its demonstrations against France. In November, Mussolini spoke of razing her cities to the ground and sowing salt in their ruins. He wished to repatriate a million Italian workers who lived on the other side of the Alps, without considering how too employ them, or where to house them! In the Chamber of the Fasces and Corporations, during a carefully orchestrated sitting, and in the presence of the Foreign Minister and the French Ambassador, the 'Deputies' got up on the benches and bayed for Corsica, Nice, and Savoy, while chanting the Fascist hymn. On 14 January 1939, the *Tevere* published an editorial, 'I spit on France'; it was rumoured that Mussolini had written it himself. In his own words, he was trying to open an unbridgeable gulf between Italy and France.[17]

In Germany, as in Italy, there was of course no question of an opinion poll. But there were many signs indicating that the Germans were no less appalled at the prospect of war than were the other European nations. Several witnesses have described a military parade down Unter den Linden on Tuesday 27 September, when war seemed imminent. For three hours men, horses, tanks and guns on their way to the frontier, rumbled past the Chancellery balcony, to the accompaniment of fifes and drums, where Hitler took the salute. No applause arose from the stoney-faced crowd. 'It was almost like a hostile army passing; through a conquered city', noted the British Ambassador.[18] In contrast, Chamberlain and Daladier had been given ovations in the Bavarian capital, when the population believed they were the bearers of peace. On the morrow of Munich, Mussolini, in one of his curiously inspired moments—alas, too infrequent to enlighten his policies— remarked, 'As soon as Hitler saw Chamberlain, he realised he had won. The old man did not understand that presenting himself in the role of a peaceful bourgeois and British parliamentarian was tantamount to giving a wild beast the taste for blood.'[19]

Swigging champagne with the Nazi dignitaries and the generals, all reconciled by success, the German Führer solemnly announced that he had no more territorial demands. Yet even before the end of October, he had given the secret order to the Wehrmacht to prepare at any moment to reduce the remnant of the unfortunate Czechoslovakia to unconditional surrender. Perhaps with the vague idea of driving a wedge between London and Paris, the Führer now made a few aimable gestures towards the French, while giving free reign to a paradoxical rage against the British. 'The old idiot has spoilt my entry into Prague', he was heard to mutter about Chamberlain, adding, 'If ever that silly old man comes interfering here again with his umbrella, I'll kick him downstairs and jump on his stomach in front of the photographers.'[20] To a South African diplomat passing through

Berlin, he complained that no one treated him with more scorn than did the Aryan cousins on the other side of the Channel. All his hopes, which he had maintained all his life, stated in *Mein Kampf*, to associate the English with his grandiose plans, had foundered; the British had succumbed to the Jews and the plutocracies of the City. In a speech in January 1939, he promised the Germans the restitution of their colonies, 'if necessary by force'. By giving a green light to a vast programme of naval construction to counter the supremacy of the Royal Navy, he repeated the great mistake of the Kaiser, which he had so often criticised. The political analysts in London were aware of his moods; they emphasised that Munich appeared to him as a defeat, and that the warm welcome given to Chamberlain and Daladier by the German people had exasperated him. The anti-Jewish propaganda of the Reich, as in Italy, took a new turn when it attempted to incite the Arabs against the French and the British in their Middle East possessions, where they had to cope (in Palestine) with an insurrection or deep unrest. One particular report described the Nazi Dictator as 'barely sane, consumed by an insensate hatred of Great Britain, capable of ordering an immediate air attack on any European country, and of having his command instantly obeyed'.[21]

Henceforth, aversion to National Socialism was augmented by a series of disgraceful incidents. Cardinal Innitzer, Primate of Austria (who had hastened to greet Hitler when he entered Vienna) had fallen into disgrace. The Nazis, irritated by the Catholic clergy's tendency to independence, intimidated their leader—and would soon arrest and intern him. On the evening of 8 October, a group of young men in brown uniforms assembled in front of the Archbishopric in the Stephenplatz—shouting, 'Death to Innitzer! Give us the black dog! All of them to Dachau!' With the aid of a ladder, the most violent climbed into the palace, smashed the windows of the first floor, and hurled chairs, furniture, pictures and a large wooden sculpture of Christ onto the pavement. In the presence of an impassive police directing the traffic, they then set fire to them.

A short time after this event, I was awakened one morning by my bedside telephone. It was my mother, who in a distraught voice, read me the newspaper headings: 'Crystal Night in Germany ... The windows of hundreds of shops owned by Jews smashed, the pavements strewn with broken glass and burning, pillaged objects ... 20,000 to 30,000 Jews arrested and thrown into concentration camps (in order to protect them!). The Foreign Embassies thronged with Jews wanting to emigrate ... There were many suicides ... Two hundred synagogues burnt down.'

The pretext for this was a crime committed by a hothead. Herschel Grynszpan aged seventeen, a member of a family from the ghettos of Poland, exasperated by the sufferings of his relations, had fired a revolver at a Reich Embassy attaché in Paris, mortally wounding him. The murdered man, Ernst Von Rath, incidentally an anti-Nazi, died on 9 November. Shortly afterwards, in virtually all German cities, in the presence of disapproving but frightened and silent passers-by, and of police who had been ordered not to intervene, groups of Nazis in brown shirts or civilian clothes, attacked the Jews. Finally, when the police were allowed to restore order, a contribution of one billion marks was levied on the Jewish community—to compensate the insurance companies.

From time immemorial, anti-Semitism has been expressed in Eastern Europe by vexatious discrimination, and sometimes by barbarous pogroms. In Western Europe, this was the first time since the Middle Ages that they had reappeared. It was not that Hitler had broken his promise. From the outset, he had inveighed against the half million citizens of Jewish origin who had been integrated into German society for more than a hundred years. The Nuremberg Laws of 1935 relating to the 'purity of blood' had brutally imprisoned them in a suffocating moral ghetto. They were subject to sporadic violence; synogogues were burned down in Munich, Nuremberg and Dortmund; sadistic placards were erected depicting tortured Semites, hanged or decapitated; obscene inscriptions were scrawled on the facades of Jewish houses. It created for the Jews an atmosphere of perpetual fear. All this hardly enhanced the reputation of the Third Reich. Most decent people sympathised whole-heartedly with the sufferings of the 100,000 Israelites who had been forced to leave their native land and abandon their possessions; and with the cruel humiliations of those who had either not wished, or had been unable, to flee.

But the condemnation was not unanimous. To people believing fervently in 'the values of the past', the large numbers of Jews who were leading Bolsheviks, Trotsky in Russia, Bela Kun in Hungary, Eisner in Bavaria, Rosa Luxemburg in Berlin, for example, were evidence of a Zionist plot against civilisation. To the supporters of appeasement at any price, the Jews appeared as tiresome encumbrances, adding to the difficulties of maintaining relations with the Reich. For the lower middle class, badly hit by the Depression, for minor intellectuals worried by change in society, anti-Semitism was a derivative. It has been said that racism is the socialism of fools; it is also the heroism of cowards, It is undeniable that here and there it aroused sympathy for the Nazis. However it was one thing to see the Jews as an impediment to the policy of détente, or as detested economic rivals, but quite another to approve the transformation of xenophobia into a vast operation of ferocious brutality.

In the United States, the Press had given great headlines to the *Krystalnacht*. The opinion polls revealed a strong condemnation; President Roosevelt echoed these sentiments by publicly stigmatisiing the Nazi regime, and by recalling his Ambassador 'for consultations'. The French, Belgians and Scandinavians were shocked when they saw photographs in their newspapers of unfortunate Jews being beaten by hooligans in uniform, the wrecked shops and the synagogues in flames. The revulsion was greatest perhaps in Great Britain. On the Right as well as on the Left, even in circles inclined to a sort of social anti-Semitism, Germany appeared to be sinking into barbarism. The newspapers, including the notoriously Germanophile ones like *The Times*, suddenly started to publish the facts. Lord Halifax, already shaken by Munich, wondered, 'of what use will be any further negotiations with Germany?' Chamberlain, on the other hand, who did not like the Jews, saw in these pogroms only an obstacle to appeasement. To his sister Ida, he complained of 'some fatality about Anglo-German relations which invariably blocks every effort to improve them'.[22] But he went on, not doubting that he was saving the human race from Armageddon.

His colleague in Paris wished to remain close to his 'English governess'. Regardless of what the world, in particular Washington and the Soviet Union, might think they concluded a political agreement with the Reich, similar to the one made by the British Prime Minister in Munich. On 6 and 7 December 1938, Joachin von Ribbentrop came to Paris to sign it. In spite of the wish of this ex-champagne commercial traveller to be received with great pomp and ceremony equal, he demanded, to that accorded to the King of England, his visit took place in a disagreeable atmosphere. Hostile demonstrations by the Parisian public were feared. Madame Bonnet did not present a bouquet of flowers to Frau Ribbentrop on the station platform, but sent them more discreetly to her hotel.[23] The agreement once again granted to France the inviolability of her eastern frontier. In return, she gave an undertaking, at least so said Ribbentrop, that she would disengage herself from Eastern Europe, and give Germany a free hand there. Was this true? Bonnet was to deny it. It will probably never be known.

What is certain is that the meetings in December, with all their patter about détente, commercial exchanges and tourism, could only have made such a brutal character as Hitler's Foreign Minister more convinced than ever that France had lost her combative spirit.

At the end of January, at the celebration of the 6th anniversary of the Nazi assumption of power, in one of the regular sessions of the Reichstag, the Führer referred for the first time to the possibility of a world war provoked by 'International Jewish finance'. 'Once again I shall be a prophet,' he shrieked 'A world war will not result in the Bolshevisation of the world, and therefore of a Jewish victory. It will end in the annhiliation of the Jewish race.' In the words of the *Völkischer Beobachter*, 'One of the Führer's greatest speeches, a prophetic warning to the Jews.' It was indeed a most significant harangue, because it marked another step on his path, and revealed his true face, a warning of the 'Final Solution' to come.

The euphoria of the Munich aftermath had evaporated on both sides of the Channel. In the workshops and offices, in the pubs and drawing-rooms, there was ceaseless speculation about where the next blow from the man of Berchtesgaden would fall—on Poland, Rumania, the Ukraine or the Low Countries? Although war seemed imminent, people were not demoralised. On the contrary, the true weaknesses of the Wehrmacht were overstated, as also the shaky economy of the Reich. Italy gave little cause for concern. Daladier received tumultuous applause when he declared that France would not cede one acre of her land, nor any of her rights, even if it led to war. It was the same in January 1939 when he arrived in Corsica on the cruiser *Foch* (where he was photographed brandishing a dagger presented to him by the locals), and then went on to Algeria and Tunis, to reaffirm France's sovereignty.*

This did not prevent the British Prime Minister and his Foreign Secretary from taking up their pilgrim's staffs in the same month, and going to preach in Rome; after a brief stop in Paris, to calm the anxieties that their zeal for peace aroused. But there was no cause for alarm, because the Italians made it quite clear that cooperation with Germany remained the basis of their foreign policy. Chamberlain was not discouraged. He was satisfied with Mussolini's promise to repatriate 10,000 Italian volunteers from Spain—without considering

---

* Daladier's firm gesture lost all validity, because he simultaneously sent to Rome—unknown to the Quai d'Orsay—a secret envoy bearing an olive branch. A calculated leak from the Palazzo Chigi made this known immediately.

that they would be replaced by others. He presented the Duce with a signed photograph of himself. On his return to London he noted, 'Mussolini is straight and frank ... full of consideration for me ... he has a sense of humour which makes him likeable'. He might perhaps have been less happy, had he known that the 'sense of humour' was to be used at the expense of the English statesmen, 'whose intelligence is situated in the seat of their trousers'. 'How far we are from these people,' commented Ciano, 'they come from another world.' He telephoned Ribbentrop to assure him that the meeting with the British Ministers had been only 'lemonade'.[24] We know now that three weeks later, the Duce told the Fascist Grand Council that he would take Corsica and Tunisia, Suez, Cyprus, Malta and Gibraltar.

★　　★　　★

Neville Chamberlain, his hand in the hand of God, saw no reason to deviate from his course. All through the winter, secret German emissaries, among them Goerdeler, representing conservative groups and some of the principal generals, had tried to interest him in their conspiracy against Hitler—only to be dismissed. Although the Secret Service had received detailed information from a German staff officer on 3 March 1939 of an imminent invasion of Czechoslovakia, Chamberlain still encouraged Sir Samuel Hoare to make a speech on 10 March predicting a 'Golden Age of peace and prosperity, the end of the armaments race, and future cooperation between nations'.[25] Chamberlain himself spoke to Parliamentary journalists of a 'period of tranquillity', and promised a conference on disarmament before the end of the year. In one of his innumerable private letters, we can see to what extent he deluded himself: 'Far from plotting against us, Hitler and Ribbentrop are hoping to approach us without a rebuff.' To his Birmingham administrators, he declared that the risk of war was receding 'all the more now that the world had seen that Mr Chamberlain is a nice, kind, old gentleman who would not ever want to treat Germans roughly and unfairly'.[26] The most surprising naïvety!

For weeks, paid agitators had stirred up the Czechs. The Nazi press had renewed its attacks against them, accusing them of not disarming, being in the pay of the Jews, and of maintaining close relations with Moscow. All these accusations were without foundation. Beneš was in exile, and had been replaced by an ex-judge Dr Hacha, an old man lacking in experience and character, a pathetic figure who thought he could trust German generosity.

A few days after Sir Samuel Hoare's speech, in the cold, grey dawn

of 15 March 1939, columns of the Wehrmacht advanced through snow
storms on icy roads to occupy what remained of Czechoslovakia,
without a shot being fired. At the same time, a brigade of parachutists
landed in Prague. The day before, early in the morning a local political
prelate, Monsignor Tiso, had persuaded the provincial authorities in
Bratislava to proclaim an independent Republic of Slovakia. Whereupon Hacha and his Foreign Minister, Chalkovsky, hurried to Berlin
to ask for advice and assistance, unaware that the German Army was
even now preparing to invade their country. Arriving at 11 p.m. at the
Anhalt station, they were received with the usual ceremonial accorded
to heads of state—bands and an SS guard of honour presenting arms.
The President's daughter was presented with a bouquet of flowers,
and on arrival at the Hotel Adlon the Czechs found boxes of chocolates
in their bedrooms. They had one hour to which to rest, after which they
were driven to the Chancellery where Hitler, Göring and Ribbentrop,
surrounded by generals in uniform, received them.

After a few brief preliminaries, the Führer made Hacha sit beside
him on a sofa and listened, not without impatience, to the latter's
protestations of friendship. He soon interrupted him, and launched
into a ferocious diatribe, levelling all manner of accusations. Carried
away by his wrath, gesticulating and screaming, he got up, compelling
the Czechs to do the same. Hacha started to cry, and confessed his
faults. Chalkovsky, who suffered from arthritis in his knee, bent his
leg from time to time to alleviate the pain.[27] Threats soon followed.
The Wehrmacht was ready to march, the planes were ready to take
off and bomb Prague. Hacha, who suffered from cardiac troubles,
fainted and was revived by the bizarre injections of Dr Morel, Hitler's
private physician, who had been summoned urgently. He again
attempted to bargain, but at 4 o'clock in the morning, exhausted and
broken, the old man finally collapsed. He signed a document put by
the Germans into his hand, recognising that Bohemia-Moravia was
henceforth a *protectorate* of the Reich. A telegram despatched by
Monsignor Tiso, but drawn up in Berlin, simultaneously placed the
new Slovakian Republic in the German orbit. Ruthenia (also coveted
by Rumania) was given to Hungary.

That same evening, 15 March 1939, the Führer, travelling by road
in a military convoy escorted by the SS, made a discreet entry into
snow-bound Prague. He mounted to the Hradcin, where he ordered the
swastika flag to be hoisted to celebrate the renaissance of the Great
Germanic Empire. After an improvised candle-lit supper in the magnificent banqueting hall of the Kings of Bohemia, hung with coats of

arms and antique paintings, he was seen to leave the table to stand in front of the window, looking down on the conquered city silent under its blanket of snow. No doubt he was dreaming of the medieval Emperors, of those Hohenstaufens with whom he liked to identify himself, 'Always august, never defeated', Vicars of the Almighty, his equals of Popes masters of the earth. Thus a year after Austria, Ccechoslovakia was erased from the map of Europe.

'Peace with honour', Chamberlain had promised. 'An imperial withdrawal', suggested the 'Municheers' in Paris. Both were expressions of utter egoism. Of the Franco-British supremacy, the liberties and system of law associated with it, nothing remained. Except for France, Great Britain, the small North Sea monarchies and Switzerland, all Europe from the Atlantic to the Urals was subjected, willingly or by force, to the Dictators. With the return to the law of the jungle, the Greater Reich and its might terrorised the smaller powers. Eighty million Germans under one sole authority. Furthermore, one of the most powerful steel and armament conglomerates in Europe had now been added to the far from negligible Austrian industry. All this, together with an immense arsenal of modern weapons which the Reich lacked, representing the equipment for more than 30 divisions and thereby increasing the Wehrmacht's potential by 30–40 per cent.* So it was that economic and military tools of which neither Bismarck nor William II could have dreamed had been put into Hitler's hands. 'The most beautiful day of my life', he exulted, bursting into his secretaries' office after extracting Hacha's surrender. 'I shall go down to history as the greatest of the Germans.'

---

* Hitler announced to the Reichstag that he had seized in Czechoslovakia 1,500 planes (500 of them front-line), 469 tanks, 500 anti-aircraft guns, 43,000 machine-guns, a million rifles, an enormous quantity of munitions, in addition to 60 millions in gold and foreign currencies.

CHAPTER 16

Mane, Thecel, Phares

The rules of law being no longer recognised, and the policemen having retired, the wrong-doers, big and small, could no longer be restrained. The day after Hitler's entry into Prague, the Hungarians and the Rumanians (the latter unsuccessfully) were quick to take part in the division of the spoils, as were the Poles. Less than a week later, on 23 March 1939, Ribbentrop demanded the annexation of the free city of Dantzig, and extra-territorial communications across the 'Polish Corridor'.* The same day a German flotilla led by the battle-cruiser *Deutschland* penetrated the roadsteads of Memel, which had been ceded at gun-point the day before by the Lithuanians. Here Hitler, barely recovered from acute sea-sickness, disembarked at the head of a detachment of marines. On 1 April, a nationalist army marched into Madrid to celebrate the victory of the Caudillo over the Spanish Republic. On 3 April, the Führer gave the secret order for the preparation of a *White Plan*, a 'definitive settlement' with Poland. On 7 April, Good Friday, it was Mussolini's turn to pull off a resounding coup. He invaded Albania, forcing King Zog to flee, together with his newborn son, his Queen Geraldine, his sisters, his parrots, and his country's gold. Following the example of Berlin, Rome made the little kingdom an Italian 'protectorate', of which Victor Emannuel III assumed the crown.

As at the time of the Ethiopian war, a wave of irresistible disgust and anger swept through the free peoples. The cabinets of London

---

* Since the 15th century, Dantzig had been a 'Free City' under Polish sovereignty. After the first partition of Poland, it had been incorporated into Prussia, and had so remained until 1914. By the Treaty of Versailles, it again became a 'Free City', administered by a Senate elected by its 400,000 inhabitants, of which 96 per cent were of German origin. Linked to Poland by a customs union, it was 'protected' by the League of Nations, which was represented by a High Commissioner. The corridor linking it with Poland isolated East Prussia from the rest of Germany.

and Paris had to yield before the evidence: appeasement was finished. Yet, in spite of the guarantees given at Munich, to the mutilated Czechoslovakia, they once again began to accept the *fait accompli*. On 15 March, Chamberlain, in an address to a deeply worried House of Commons, made his habitual adjurations, 'not to let us be defeated from our course'. As for the guarantee to the Czechs, there was no cause for concern; Sir John Simon, a brilliant lawyer, undertook to explain that legally it was null and void, because its object had disintegrated! The following day, in a plaintive note of protestation to Berlin (which treated it with disdain), London insisted that 'His Majesty's Government does not wish to intervene unduly in the affairs of Eastern Europe.'[1]

Then, on 17 March, came a complete *volte-face*. In a speech in the Birmingham Guildhall, Chamberlain was loudly applauded when he promised to oppose any attempts 'at world domination'. It had taken Lord Halifax many hours, and all his eloquence, to persuade him that unless he spoke up, the anger of Parliament would put the very existence of his government at stake. On 31st of the same month, the Prime Minister, 'looking gaunt and ill, the skin above his high cheek bones parchment yellow', astounded the Commons by announcing that His Majesty's government would come to the aid of Poland 'by every means', in the event of her independence being threatened.* He said he was authorised to make the same declaration in the name of France (which was not true). However, Paris was allied to Warsaw by time-honoured treaties. For London, as Lord Halifax stated in the House of Lords, this was a 'capital innovation'. The pledge was made as a result of false and unverified information about an imminent invasion of Rumania! It was done without asking any surety from Warsaw, and against the advice of the Chiefs of Staff, who were no less timid than the year before.[2]

Guarantees of the same kind were hastily given to Rumania, Greece and Turkey. Simultaneously, dispositions were taken for industrial mobilisation and compulsory enlistment.† These measures being demanded by Parliament, the government resigned itself to them, while hoping they might dissuade the Dictators from embarking on fresh adventures. They might have impressed them, had their credi-

---

* Although he spoke of Poland's independence, he did not mention her *territorial integrity*, a reservation whose significance was rapidly to become apparent.

† Labour, while protesting against appeasement, persisted in opposing conscription.

bility not been undermined by persistent displays of weakness. For example, London had been prepared to hand over to the Reich the gold of the National Bank of Czechoslovakia which had been placed for safe keeping in the City vaults. On the other hand, not a penny or a gun was offered to the new ally Poland, in spite of its urgent requests for help. The Foreign Office was civil enough to assure the *Auswärtigesamt* that the imminent introduction of conscription in Britain was in no way a threat to Germany.[3] This was very close to the truth, for it was limited to six months, and it applied only to 20 year olds. It would be a long time before it could have any effect on the field army.

In Paris the situation had definitely improved. Daladier admitted at a secret session of the Senate Commission of Foreign Affairs that the Munich agreements were in ruins, and that without a last minute exertion of will, France would again be invaded and threatened with destruction.[4] This effort he supported. The economic crisis which had plagued France for five years was over. Inflation was under control, industrial production had risen by 20 per cent and salaries in real terms had improved. The strikes of the previous year had ended. Capital which had left the country was returning; the gold reserves, 'the war treasure', had risen from 55 to 92 milliards of francs. Vast supplementary credits were put at the disposal of the Armed Forces, the duration of military service was increased to three years. The output of war planes was accelerated; imports from the United States made up for any delay in national production. Heavy armoured forces were built up, although their precise tactical use was not yet defined. By a substantial majority, Parliament gave the head of the government new powers—truly a Republican dictatorship. The British Press wrote of a spectacular recovery in France, *The Times* in May 1939 referring to the 'French miracle'. A group of historians was to sum it up in 1975: 'He incarnated the collective will of France to resist Hitler'— stating that the ex-mayor of Carpentras was then at the height of his success, that his authority and the extent of his power in Parliament was complete—greater than that of Chamberlain, who was hated by Labour.[5]

It is true that the lobbies of the extreme Right continued their invective against those whom they called 'war mongers'. Robert Brasillach, who had referred to Beneš as 'human excrement', rejoiced at the collapse of Czechoslovakia. The ex-Socialist Marcel Deat, in a celebrated article 'To die for Dantzig', was violent in his condemnation of the guarantees to Poland. They were not the only ones; Laval,

Flandin and Bonnet furthered their ambitions by professing to 'defend peace'. Otto Abetz pursued his undermining efforts by generous distributions of Ribbentrop's secret funds to the Left and Right. With increasingly hackneyed phrases, he encouraged his coteries, and a handful of impoverished and misguided journalists. But the credit of the 'fifth column', as much as that of the Cliveden set and the pro-Nazi groups in Great Britain, was almost exhausted.

The French Government had no longer anything to fear from the Left wing. The Communists, on the orders of Moscow, were violently anti-German, and were to remain so until the beginning of September. Among the Socialists, the old pre-1914 pacifist views survived, but they were controlled by the now much firmer Léon Blum, and had much less influence than on the eve of the Great War.[6]

It was only now that, after so many years of misunderstanding and frivolous rivalry, the two great Democracies came together. At the end of March, the President of the Republic and Madame Lebrun were warmly greeted in London with cries of 'Vive la France!', when they returned the state visit made by the British King and Queen to the French capital. The month before, the two governments had appeared to be allied for the first time since 1919, by announcing that they would in common defend, 'the liberty and independence of all nations'. For the first time also, Chamberlain agreed, very much against his wishes, to drop the idea of 'limited liability' and to raise an Expeditionary corps. Although the Army was still a tiny force (four infantry divisions, one mobile division, four Territorial divisions), it gave a semblance of reality to the Franco-British entente.* The general staffs now really began to exchange information; for they had known almost nothing of each others armed forces, and their respective commitments. However, there was little real confidence, and no common military body was created; Gamelin had not wanted it. None of the great strategic, economic or financial choices which make for a real alliance were prepared. And no mutual sympathy drew Chamberlain and Daladier together—very much to the contrary.

United, firm and decided, the two greatest Empires with their enormous riches, their genius, industrial power, raw materials, gold, their mastery of the world's maritime routes, together with material supplies from the gigantic American arsenal, could probably have saved every-

---

* The goal was to be 32 divisions (26 of them Territorials). When war broke out, only 4 divisions were ready for combat—9 or 10 in May 1940. The money spent on defence in Great Britain (including a loan of 90 million pounds) only amounted, as it did in France, to 37 per cent of the budget (against 74 per cent in Germany).

thing, peace included. Japan, a 70 per cent agricultural country, with limited industries and lacking raw materials (almost all of its petroleum products were imported from America), would not have dreamed of attacking their vital interests; it was only after the great Axis victories that it took the risk to do it. Italy, poor and badly armed, was a fundamentally pacific country governed by an exhausted *condottiere*. Germany, apart from a fanatical minority, did not aspire, more than did any other European country, to martial glory; above all, it lacked the raw materials which were indispensable for prolonged military operations.* However, the time lost by the convenient illusion of 'détente' would have had to be retrieved by collaborating with the only non-committed great European power, the USSR.

The Soviet Union appeared not to have renounced the idea of participating in what the journalists called 'The Peace Front'. Stalin, it is true, during the 18th Communist Party Congress of the USSR at the beginning of March 1939, attacked with equal severity 'the aggressive states' and the 'non-aggressive states', stating that he, 'would not pull the chestnuts out of the fire for the sake of the Western bourgeoisie'. Nevertheless, on 18 March, the day after the occupation of Prague, the Kremlin repeated its proposition (which had already been made after the *Anschluss*), of convening a conference (Great Britain, France, Poland, Rumania, Turkey and the Soviet Union) to oppose the aggressor countries. Paris saw in this an opportunity to reinforce the Franco-Russian treaty of 1935; but London remained aloof. 'No Minister of the Crown', said Lord Halifax to the Soviet Ambassador, 'can spare the time to take part in a conference.'[7] Due principally to pressure from Parliament, talks were started, but they quickly foundered in an atmosphere of deep distrust. At the Foreign Office, William Strang, the official in charge, noted that, 'the Soviets would be delighted to see France, Great Britain and Germany destroy one another mutually'. And the Soviet Ambassador, Maisky, reported that Chamberlain had not changed his policy; his new gestures were the result only of pressure by public opinion, to which he had sub-

---

* In spite of its national self-sufficiency policies and its accumulation of vast stocks, the Reich still depended on foreign imports for certain essential raw materials: Tin 99 per cent, nickel 95 per cent, copper 70 per cent, rubber 80 per cent, bauxite 99 per cent, and petroleum products 65 per cent. In the spring of 1939 some reserves of copper, tin and rubber were almost exhausted. Wool, cotton and strategic food supplies were running out, and the problem of the balance of payments appeared insoluble. Without the powerful economic support of the Soviet Union, and later of the conquered countries, the Allied blockade would soon have had a devastating effect.

mitted against his will. He was waiting for the moment when he could return to the policy of appeasement.[8]

'One must want the consequences of what one wants', Spaak often said. A study of the *pourparlers* which should have led to a Grand Alliance to prevent war, or at the worst to assure an easy victory, is clear on one point: France and England, particularly England, never, at any time, knew exactly what they wanted. In London, a common declaration, signed by Great Britain, France, Poland and the Soviet Union, had been envisaged. Then, following objections from Warsaw, guarantees to Poland and the other Eastern European states were to be enforced only on the express demand of the guaranteed states themselves. This proposition was obviously unacceptable to the Russians, who saw in it no safeguard for themselves. Paris was prepared to go further, but not if London objected. Four months of confused negotiations with endless quibbling ensued.

On 18 April, Litvinov proposed an Anglo-Franco-Soviet defence alliance, to last 5–10 years, coupled with a military convention, and guarantees to all Eastern European countries from the Baltic to the Black Sea which had common frontiers with the Soviet Union. 'An unhoped-for proposition!' exclaimed Robert Coulondre joyfully, the ex-French Ambassador in Moscow, who had since been transferred to Berlin. 'Mischievious and embarrassing', was the Foreign Office view. Chamberlain continued to grumble about, 'the division of Europe into ideological blocks'.[9] Weeks went by.

On 3 May 1939, the Chancelleries were shaken by sensational news. Maxim Litvinov was discharged from his functions, and replaced by Vyacheslav Molotov, President of the Council of Commissars of the People, and Stalin's closest collaborator. For some time, diplomats and the secret services had already had wind of a rapprochement between Moscow and Berlin. On the day after Munich, Vladimir Potemkine, the Deputy Commissar of the Foreign Office, complained to Robert Coulondre, 'My poor friend, what have you done? I can only see one issue—a fourth partition of Poland.' The French diplomat had heard of similar warnings given to various colleagues by a number of Soviet diplomats. When Coulondre was transferred to Berlin, his fears were confirmed. On 30 April General Bodenschatz, a confidant of Göring, sent for Captain Stehlin, his favourite contact at the French Embassy and, for two hours, gave him a lecture on grand strategy, in which he referred to an entente between Germany and Russia. Stehlin was sceptical. Bodenschatz became heated, insisting that negotiations were taking place. 'There have already been three partitions of Poland,' he said, 'and, believe me, you will see a fourth one.' On 7 May, Coulondre confirmed 'the orientation of Germany towards Russia'.*

The information disclosed in America, by a high ranking Russian defector, General Krivitsky, was attracting a lot of attention and was confirmed in London by the Services. The British Ambassadors in Moscow and Berlin referred to it in their despatches. Marshal Göring boasted to Henderson, 'Germany and Russia will not always be enemies.' Foreign diplomats, among them the Belgian Davignon in Berlin, and the Americans Bullitt and Davies, who had served in Moscow, warned their French and English colleagues. Anti-Nazis close to the Reich central government sounded the alarm. Erich Kordt, Ribbentrop's *chef de cabinet*, returned to Britain at the risk of his life, on the pretext of an invitation to fish in Scotland, in order to inform the English that Hitler intended to 'neutralise' the Soviet Union.[11] Suddenly, the prophetic writing on the wall appeared: *Mane, Thecel, Phares*. The least obtuse realised the extent of the disaster, should the Kremlin go over to the enemy camp. Suddenly, Chamberlain found himself almost alone in ignoring the Prophet's warning; but he still believed that the Lord communicated directly with him. In spite of increasingly clear warnings, he persisted in denying the possibility of a rapprochement between Berlin and Moscow. When the Chiefs of Staff, not without reticence, outlined the great strategic importance of the Soviet Union, he became very annoyed. In May, he announced that he would resign rather than sign a treaty of alliance with Russia.[12]

In June an opinion poll held by Gallup showed that in England 84 per cent (as against 9 per cent) were supporters of the Grand Alliance. The Germany sympathisers, still 15 per cent in 1937, were now only 3 per cent.† It is doubtful whether the Cabinet knew of this; but it could not have been unaware of the deep currents of opinion which it reflected. Even Sir Samuel Hoare, who was closest to the Prime Minister, began to have his doubts. Even Lord Halifax stated that it was, 'vital to close the door on any agreement between Moscow and Berlin'. He also realised the grave consequences which would ensue if the Soviet Union remained neutral in a Europe devastated by war.[14] Internal pressures could no longer be resisted. It was the same in Paris,

* Coulondre was deeply impressed by the news, and he immediately sent Stehlin to Paris, to inform Bonnet of his conversation with Bodenschatz. The Minister could not find the time to receive him.[10]

† However, all through winter and spring the British remained 'satisfied' by Chamberlain—in April 55 per cent against 45 per cent.[13]

where Daladier and even Bonnet, in spite of their prejudices, now tried
to reconstitute the 'force from beyond' which had saved France in
1914. Chamberlain, after weeks of stubborn resistance, had to give in.
The diplomats returned laboriously to their Penelope's web.

★   ★   ★

Once the shock of Litvinov's dismissal had passed, nothing much
seemed to have changed in Moscow. The authorities emphatically
confirmed it, and the newspapers continued their routine attacks
against the Reich. However, the new Soviet negotiator soon lived up
to the pseudonym he had chosen, 'Molotov, the Hammer'. His real
name was Scriabine. I was to have the opportunity in 1956 during an
official visit to Moscow to have a brief face to face meeting with
this son of a well-to-do bourgeois family, a cousin of the celebrated
composer Scriabine, trained as civil engineer at the St Peterburg Poly-
technic and Kazan University. He had been associated from the beginning with Stalin's worst crimes, and had shared a flat with him in
Petrograd in the first months of the revolution. With his eternal pince-
nez, always correct, always glacial, he seemed now as much at ease
among the advocates of peaceful coexistence as he had been among
the Cold War warriors. Although we did not know it, his authority
was exhausted. Soon after, he was appointed Ambassador to Outer
Mongolia, to finish in 1964 with the supreme indignity of being
expelled from the Communist Party, to whose creation he had contributed, and which he had served for nearly sixty years.*

When he replaced Litvinov, the future 'Mr Niet' had received the
French and British envoys in the sort of dentist's waiting room where
he worked in the Kremlin. Installed behind a large table, raised on a
dais,—beside him, his deputy Potemkine—he made them sit in a semi-
circle facing him with their notebooks on their knees, like children
before a school-master. They realised that a new era had begun. He
took no notes himself, but appeared to manipulate the buttons of a
magnetophone hidden in a drawer. The diplomats became accustomed
to him frequently interrupting the interview by leaving them, and
retreating through a half-open door, which gave onto a neighbouring
room, where Stalin himself was apparently waiting.

On 27 May 1939, 'The Hammer' listened without interrupting
Potemkine, who translated the text of the new proposals brought by
the Western ambassadors. When his deputy had finished, he rapped
out, 'These are calculated to produce the maximum of chatter, and the

* Reinstated within the Party in 1984, he died in November 1986 at the age of 96.

minimum of results'.[15] He then indicated brutally all the ambiguities in the Franco-British project. A few days later, in a speech to the Supreme Soviet, he censured the British and French, letting it be known that the possibility of an 'economic' rapprochement with Germany was no longer ruled out.

★　★　★

Any signs of opposition to his quest for expansion, however erratic they were, enraged Hitler. Pouring ridicule on the last sophists of détente, who made a distinction between his 'moderation' and the frenzy of his supporters, he celebrated his fiftieth birthday on 20 April 1939 with a military parade. For five hours, interminable columns of infantry marched through Berlin, together with motorised units, tanks and gun carriages. On 28 April, in a significant speech to the Reichstag, he openly claimed Dantzig, repudiated the 1934 treaty of non-aggression with Poland and the celebrated naval treaty with Great Britain.

A large part of his $2\frac{1}{2}$ hour diatribe was a reply to a somewhat naïve message by President Roosevelt, requesting the Dictators not to attack some thirty countries, designated by name. With ferocious sarcasm he made the docile members of the Reichstag laugh obediently. Hitler always displayed a boundless scorn for the United States, based upon the most complete ignorance and absurd prejudice. It was unlikely that he would learn better: He only very occasionally received American diplomats in Berlin, and paid little attention to his own representatives in Washington. In Jefferson's and Lincoln's ideals of liberty and justice, he saw only trickery, cowardice and Jewish internationalism. He considered the Americans devoid of martial virtues, subservient to the Jews of Wall Street, governed by other Jews, in short, 'a heap of Jewish filth'. 'My feelings for half Jewish, half negro America,' he said, 'where everything is based on the dollar, are of hatred and repugnance.' Roosevelt was one of 'the greatest enemies of modern civilisation . . . a crooked Jew and a haggler . . . his wife with her negroid features is clearly a half-caste'. When Roosevelt died on 12 April 1945, the Führer was overjoyed, seeing in it an act of Providence which would enable him at the last moment to triumph like Frederick II after the sudden death of the Czarina Elizabeth. He would now be able to end the war—which he had declared with incredible folly on the United States the day after Pearl Harbor.[15] Roosevelt's death took place eighteen days before the Führer, in the Berlin bunker, pulled the trigger of the pistol he held pointed at his head.

★   ★   ★

A principal factor in the general underestimation of the significance and potential of the United States was the way in which it had withdrawn into itself. The quarrel over the war debts had led to a law being passed in 1934 forbidding new credits to any defaulting state— a law which affected most of Europe. After so many dreadful events, the rape of Czechoslovakia had provoked a storm of indignation— directed, perhaps, as much at Great Britain and France as at Germany and Italy. The neutrality laws prevented the sale of war materials to all belligerents, the victim states as well as the aggressors. Imposed on an unwilling President by an almost unanimous Congress, their pacifism clearly reflected public opinion; 10 per cent only of the Americans declared themselves ready to fight overseas.*

Only Roosevelt and his entourage understood that there was no added security in isolation; Cordell Hull, the Secretary of State, dedicated an entire chapter of his memoirs to the 'alarming penetration of the Axis powers' in Latin America.[17] The President lost no opportunity in alerting his country. At Lima in 1938, he persuaded the South Americans to endorse a resolution severely condemning racist doctrines. The same year, he opened large credits to China at war with Japan. His annual message to Congress in 1939 was a strong indictment against the Dictators. But he was also a cautious politician. He stopped short of challenging the powerful isolationist lobbies and the religious or political organisations professing pacifism; or Senators like Bora and Vandenberg who had taken an oath that no American soldier would die in foreign lands.

Even if Roosevelt's hands had not been shackled, they were poorly armed. In 1938 he had succeeded in getting a vast programme through Congress to build a 'two oceans fleet'. But Capitol Hill was basically opposed to rearmament. On the eve of World War II, the American Air Force would have been unable to rival the number of Czechoslovakian aircraft. As for the land forces, 227,000 men, they were half of those Belgium would mobilise—with much better equipment.

Nothing at first sight revealed the vocation of a great power in the United States. Or, if it was, there was a tendency, here and there, particularly in London, to see it as a dangerous rival—the possibility of a transatlantic war had not been completely ruled out at times.

---

* An opinion poll in March 1982 showed that 56 per cent of the Americans were favourable to the use of their forces to protect Western Europe against a Russian attack.[16]

Very few indeed were the statesmen capable of foreseeing the immense role that America was to play in the very near future.

★   ★   ★

After his speech in the Reichstag, Hitler, in the company of Eva Braun, his ADCs and secretaries, retired to his lair in Obersalzburg. It was now an ostentatious residence which Albert Speer described ironically as, 'packet-steamer style with rustic touches'.[18] His intentions towards Poland could no longer be in doubt. Frontier incidents increased, the German Press and radio blared out that the Polish Army was preparing to invade German territory. It was the same story as in Austria and Czechoslovakia. 'Germans in Poland are a prey to sanguinary terror . . . women and children attacked . . . appalling blood-baths . . .', and so on. 'Tourists' thronged into Dantzig, where the Nazis were ostentatiously holding military exercises, snapping their fingers at the High Commissioner of the League of Nations. Rumours of a *coup de main* on the Free City spread through the Chancelleries. How would Warsaw react?

The Polish Government differed considerably from those with which Hitler had dealt with in Vienna and Prague. A military dictatorship inspired by Marshal Smigly-Rydz, it was by nature little inclined to compromise, even less to capitulate without a fight. Colonel Beck, who directed its foreign policy, displayed some eminent qualities. He was totally unscrupulous, possessed of a blind national egoism and the elementary chauvinism made fashionable by the leading figures of the extreme Right. Less intelligent than he imagined he was, lazy and frivolous, he passed much of his time in libertinage, absorbing vast quantities of whiskey and champagne. 'An ancient Pistol,' wrote the wife of Duff Cooper, 'and a weak, tipsy Pistol at that. He repeated himself with the persistence of a cuckoo and moved his tail with peacock vanity.'[19] The treatment of the cancer from which he was to die prematurely, caused him much suffering and did not contribute to his equanimity.

Beck saw himself at the head of a great nation in full expansion, capable of profiting from the disorder of the age for its aggrandisement by playing off his powerful neighbours one against the other. But vanity blinded him to the military limitations of his country, and therefore of his *Realpolitik*. He lacked the iron firmness required to hold the equal balance between the two wild beasts which stalked him. Even if he made a few attempts to avoid burning the bridges between Poland and Stalin, he did not disguise his preference for Hitler. In

1938, he had openly sided with him in the dismemberment of Czecho-slovakia. At the beginning of 1939, he took part in secret negotiations with Germany envisaging the conquest and partitioning of the Soviet Ukraine. They failed only because he refused to pay the price— Dantzig and the corridor.

When Colonel Beck obtained the guarantee without conditions from the French and British, his high self-esteem still increased. Without bothering about Paris and London, but fortified by their support, the 'super-Machiavelli' thought he could influence and trust Hitler. On the first two days of April 1939, after Chamberlain had promised to defend Poland, Radio Warsaw and the PAT, the official Polish press agency, had the effrontery to announce, 'Nothing has changed in Poland's independent foreign policy.' Beck admitted to his Rumanian colleague Gafencu, 'Our alliance with Great Britain and France is a reassurance . . . but it is in the agreement with the Reich that our security lies.'[20]

★   ★   ★

It was in May and June 1939 that Hitler put his last pawns on the chessboard. He offered a pact of non-aggression to Norway, Finland, Holland and Switzerland, all of whom wisely declined the honour; also to Denmark, Lithuania and Estonia, who accepted it. From the imprecisely phrased anti-Comintern pact, he hoped to forge a real alliance of super races. Ever since Munich, he had tried to influence the Italians and Japanese in this direction. The latter were elevated to the status of 'Honorary Aryans', not without some laughs about the twist to his racial doctrine; but Tokyo remained unmoved by the compliment. As for the Duce, after having said *No*, he said *Yes* (in January, after his meeting with Chamberlain), and then limited himself to *Perhaps*. The affair dragged on. Göring, who visited Rome in April 1939, returned empty handed. Then when in May, Ribbentrop and Ciano met again in Milan, the Duce, giving way to one of his customary impulses, and without further reflexion, ordered his son-in-law on the telephone to go ahead. Shortly after, he accepted a text drawn up in Berlin without any amendments.

The Pact of Steel—(its authors declined, at the last moment, to call it The Pact of Blood) was a defensive and offensive treaty unreservedly uniting the two powers, Germany and Italy. It was signed on 22 May 1939 in the new Chancellery in Berlin, an enormous, recently inaugurated marble palace with bronze doors. It was the scene of sumptuous festivities during which Joachim von Ribbentrop was invested with the Necklace of the Annunciata, which made him a 'cousin' of the King of Italy.* On the evening of the banquet at the Italian Embassy, the petulant ill humour of Marshal Göring made itself felt. Offended because he thought that he had not been treated with the consideration that was his due, he surreptitiously slipped into the dining room before the banquet, and changed the name places at the table. When Ribbentrop, his mortal enemy, appeared resplendent in his gold and diamond necklace, the Commander-in-Chief of the Luftwaffe could not restrain his tears. Only a promise from Ciano that he would receive the same decoration succeeded in calming him and persuading him not to leave the Embassy.[21]

On the next day, May 23, came another rousing speech from Hitler to his generals. The real problem, he said, was not Dantzig, but the economic situation of the Reich, which needed urgently to expand its *Lebensraum*. The moment had come to attack Poland. While formally promising that the Wehrmacht would not have to fight on two fronts he vowed, not without some contradiction, to take up, if need be, the challenge of Britain and France, and to crush them after having seized Holland and Belgium. As for the Soviet Union, the generals need not worry on that score—'It will not show any interest in Poland.'

★   ★   ★

A few months earlier Hitler surprised Berlin by talking amicably to the Russian Ambassador at a New Year reception—an unprecedented occurrence. On 30 January 1939, at an audience for the diplomatic corps at the Kremlin, it was Stalin who caused astonishment by taking the German military attaché aside for a conversation. We do not know what they said; but the vengeful invectives exchanged since 1933 ceased. The Soviet Embassy in Berlin began to talk to the Wilhelmstrasse of, 'new relations which can increasingly improve'. On 20 May 1939 Count von der Schulenburg, the Reich Ambassador in Moscow, having been instructed to offer commercial negotiations to Molotov, was clearly told that they could be undertaken only if 'appropriate political bases' had been created.[22] An obvious signal which was not lost on Berlin. On 30 May, the Ambassador was authorised, 'contrary to the previous political plans . . . to establish a certain degree of contact with the Soviet Union'. This was enough to encourage a diplomat who sincerely wished for an improvement in

---

*The bombed out halls were demolished after the war; their marble and stone furnished the material for the War Memorial erected by the Russians in East Berlin.

German–Russian relations; and enough to convince the Kremlin that its advances would not be rebuffed. Then, at the end of June, came the *vote-face*. A telegram to Schulenburg brought everything to a standstill.

The month had been eventful. In the Far East, the Japanese had again begun to harass the Soviets. The fighting of the previous years recommenced with several armoured divisions and numerous aircraft engaged—50,000 men on each side. Owing to the lack of reliable evidence, it is difficult to know how seriously the Kremlin viewed this. Nevertheless, the prominent place given to the fighting in the rare published archives, as well as common sense, would indicate that the Soviets were gravely concerned. The Kremlin could not have forgotten the Russian–Japanese war of 1905, whose reverses nearly caused the fall of the Czarist regime. Among others, the English historian Alexander Werth, the *Sunday Times* correspondent in Moscow, noted a 'deep anxiety', which the leaders tried vainly to conceal.[23]

By one means or another, the Soviets had to find a way out of their giddy isolation. Without discouraging Berlin, they continued to negotiate with Paris and London. On 2 June 1939, they suggested a new project of alliance, to operate automatically in the event of aggression against Belgium, Greece, Turkey, Rumania, Poland, Latvia, Estonia and Finland; it would be accompanied by a military convention. Once again, laborious negotiations were undertaken. As the British Ambassador was in bed with flu, and could not travel to London to receive instructions, the Foreign Office sent William Strang out to him. It was a routine journey which would have passed unnoticed, had it not coincided with a project for a visit by Lord Halifax to Moscow. Ambassador Maisky, who was reported to be a supporter of the Grand Alliance, wrote in his memoirs, 'When I spoke of an official invitation, Lord Halifax assumed a hard and impenetrable expression. He gazed at the ceiling and rubbed the bridge of his nose declaring in a solemn tone, "I must think it over". A week later there was still no answer.' Maisky added that the offence given to the Kremlin contributed largely to the reversal of its policy.[24] He may have over-dramatised this; but the fact remains that an offer by Litvinov to come to London was not followed up. A proposition for Eden to visit Moscow in June in Lord Halifax's place was vetoed by Chamberlain, who declared, in the House of Commons, that no invitation had been received from Russia (which was untrue). No French Minister had gone to the Soviet Union since 1935. There was a striking contrast between the despatch of a subordinate Foreign Official to Moscow, and the many visits to Germany by Simon, Eden, Halifax and Chamberlain himself.

More than questions of protocol, the persistent policy of 'appeasement' could not fail to alarm the Soviets. The term 'appeasement' in official language had been banned by Chamberlain. But no one believed that Downing Street had relinquished the policy; not even the Foreign Office, where Oliver Harvey noted angrily on 3 May that 'appeasement' was raising its 'ugly head' again.[25] Was Harvey unduly worried—as Halifax told him? The situation was far from clear. In May, *The Times* published an editorial under the headline, 'Is Dantzig worth a war?', the echo of a similar one published in *L'Oeuvre* of Paris. On 8 June, Halifax declared, in the House of Lords, with the usual rhetoric condemning the use of force, that all the German demands could be the subject of discussions around a table. In June and July, a close collaborator of Göring, Helmut Wohltat, who had come to London for an international conference on whale fishing, met Robert Hudson, the Minister for Overseas Trade. The latter was a conceited man, avid for publicity; he boasted to the newspapers that he had dangled in front of the German the prospect of credits worth a billion pounds sterling, an enormous sum.

More significant was Wohltat's meeting with Sir Horace Wilson ('Père Joseph' as the diplomats called him) who was said to have handed his visitor a memorandum envisaging a real treaty of alliance and disarmament. The document is missing in the British archives, and Wilson was later to state that it existed only in Wohltat's imagination. However, the Reich Ambassador reported to the Wilhelmstrasse propositions similar to those which Wilson was said to have made, adding that His Majesty's Government would forget its guarantees to the eastern countries in the event of an entente with Germany.[26]

Hitler, although not rebuffing these advances, showed ostentatiously that he thought little of them, as he did of those by other unofficial emissaries, or those of the British Ambassador. The latter, Sir Nevile Henderson, a vain, limited and unstable man, was also ill, suffering from cancer of the throat from which, in spite of an operation after the Munich conference, he was later to die. Hitler was irritated by Henderson's sartorial elegance, the eternal red carnation in his buttonhole, his affected manner, and had no respect for him. But Henderson had exceptional influence over the British Prime Minister, whose dreams he shared. Although the Foreign Office had become aware of his extremes and planned to replace him, this did not put a stop to his imprudent behaviour. During the entire summer, consciously or unconsciously, Henderson gave those he saw the impression (as did Wilson in London) that Whitehall would abandon all negotiations with Moscow in exchange for closer Anglo-German relations.[27] 'It is not necessary to be intelligent to be an Ambassador,' said Spaak, 'but it helps.'

Nothing remains secret for very long in diplomatic circles; familiarity, vanity and calculation naturally lead to gossip. The Kremlin had active Ambassadors in London and Paris, and well placed spies such as Burgess and McLean, and others who remain unknown. There can be no doubt that after the manner of Berlin and Rome (and to a lesser degree of London and Paris), the Kremlin was in a position to decipher many of the coded telegrams. The essence of the conversations between the Western Powers and Berlin must have been known to the Russians—as they were, more or less, to other European governments—just as the contacts between Berlin and Moscow were known in London.

The real stumbling-block to the talks was the fate of Poland, Rumania and the Baltic states. Lithuania, Lativa and Estonia on the Baltic Sea had, from time immemorial, been the natural ground for confrontations between Slavs and Teutons. Leningrad, the capital of Czarist Russia, the second city of the Soviet Union, was within artillery range of Estonia, and of Finland, where German influence was strong. During the very hours in which Molotov was conferring with the French and British Ambassadors, General Halder, the Chief of Staff of the Reich, was being received with great pomp by the Finnish and Esthonian governments, whose armed forces he reviewed. Tallinn and Vilna drew up treaties of friendship with Berlin.

Towards Poland itself, which had seized vast territories from Russia in 1921, and whose rulers did not conceal their Germanophilia, the Kremlin showed anything but cordiality. It was evident that the Soviets would lose no opportunity to take back the provinces conquered by Peter the Great and Catharine II and lost by the Bolsheviks. Paris was prepared to pay this price—London was not. It was this sudden surge of British political morality which the Soviets found themselves unable to understand. Why refuse us the Baltic States (which otherwise, in view of the situation, implied abandoning them to the Reich), after having sacrificed Manchuria, Ethiopia, Austria and Czechoslovakia, and after having renounced collective security? We can well believe that Molotov's angry outburst to the Western Ambassadors was deeply felt. 'You treat us as simpletons and fools.'[28] At the end of June a rupture appeared inevitable between the West and Moscow—resulting in the telegram from Berlin instructing Schulenburg to discontinue his soundings.

I am alone and despondent', complained Chamberlain, while

attempting by stubborn rearguard actions, to prevent the hated alliance. 'A provocation', he called it, 'which would unify Germany around its leader.' To Hugh Dalton, the Socialist leader, who was concerned about a failure of negotiations with the Soviet Union, he retorted with secret satisfaction, 'It would not be the end of the world.'[29] The obstinate old man was, it is true, becoming increasingly disregarded by his Minister. But which among them would have risked a ministerial crisis? After all, the elections were not far off.* Encouraged by the admonitions of Paris, they only tried to moderate his resistence; step by step, with ill grace, grinding his teeth, he had had, once again, to give ground.

The difficulties connected with the Baltic states had been resolved by a secret protocol which would guarantee them without their knowledge. Only one problem remained unresolved, that of 'indirect aggression'. Austria and Czechoslovakia, conquered by Germany with the nominal agreement of their governments, had shown that the danger was very real. However, to foresee the event in a treaty would have conferred on Moscow a virtually unlimited right of intervention in its neighbours' affairs. Even on this point, London and Paris had been near to giving in.

On 17 July, Molotov informed the Western Ambassadors that the time had come to start military conversations; staff agreements and the political treaty should be linked. Lord Halifax, after a new outburst of indignation—which is difficult to understand, but which reveals the persistent reticence of Whitehall—rallied the Cabinet with the curious argument that, 'as long as the military conversations last, Russia cannot join the German camp'.[30]

★   ★   ★

It remains impossible to determine the precise moment when the Dictators of Berlin and Moscow tied their knot of complicity. No doubt after Munich, they both gave it consideration. Hitler had, at all costs, to prevent an agreement between the principal powers which would shut the door to the East in his face—a door opened after the dismemberment of Czechoslovakia. In spite of his deep-seated repulsion for rapprochement, even a temporary one, with the triple abomination,

---

* The House of Commons, elected in 1935, was due to be renewed, at the latest, in the Spring of 1940.

Communism, Slavism and Judaism. He could not ignore that it was a *sine qua non*, if he was to reach his goal and rally the Wehrmacht.*

Was Stalin any freer? Although many diplomats accredited to Moscow in 1939 doubted both the integrity of the Soviet leadership and the value of the Red Army, nearly all were aware of a hostility towards the Germans which was greater than towards the West. The insults which had been exchanged for years between Moscow and Berlin had left their mark. The heaps of filth poured on Moscow's head by Hitler could not be swept away overnight. And then there was the question of the Jews. Ostracised in the time of the Czars, there were now many in the hierarchy of the Communist Party. Some were liquidated by Stalin's anti-Semitism during the great purge—but not all. Among the survivors was Lazar Kaganovich, one of the principle pundits of the Politburo; his sister Rosa, who was the companion (or second wife) of Stalin, after being Molotov's mistress; even the latter's wife, Polina, and others.† They could have felt only profound aversion for Hitlerism. They were not the only ones. Kruschev in his memoirs recognised that, 'It was very unpleasant to accept the notion of joining forces with Germany. If for us it was hard enough to admit the paradox, it would have been impossible to explain it to the man in the street'.[32] Some uneasiness about the Soviet–Hitlerian collusion is seen by the very limited space Kruschev devotes to the episode. Nevertheless, although pitiless about his predecessor, he was of the opinion that the circumstances in this case left Stalin no choice, and that his decision was 'historically inevitable'. A substantial majority of the party considered the signature of the Molotov–Ribbentrop treaty tactically wise, although no one could express it publicly'.[39] Nothing has come to light to contradict this evidence.

Did Stalin always incline towards Berlin deep down in his being? The enigmatic defector, known under the name of General Walter Krivitsky, who had occupied important posts in the intelligence services of the Red Army, and who took refuge in France (where the NKVD killers narrowly missed him) in 1938, and then in the United States, affirmed in sensational revelations that the master of the Kremlin had always maintained secret relations with Hitler. Krivitsky's

---

* It has been said that Hitler gave orders to his 'racial experts' to study photographs of Stalin, to determine whether his physiognomy was of Semitic or Ayran origin. The experts concluded that it was Aryan.

† Polina Molotov was to be thrown into the Gulag in 1948, by virtue of a warrant signed, it was said, by her husband. However, freed after the death of Stalin, she was to resume her life with her husband.[31]

corpse was discovered in 1941 in a Washington hotel room with a bullet in the head; whether suicide or assassination, it made his assertions all the more dramatic. Many things remain mysterious, but some indications seem to confirm that the Marxist Czar had never quite abandoned the German option. Among these, are the covert but persistent overtures found in the Reich archives from a man named Kotsia Kandelaki, who was the Soviet 'commercial' attaché in Berlin, and had been one of Stalin's accomplices in the Georgian conspiracies at the beginning of the century.[33]

The Soviet Union in 1939 cannot be judged in the light of its 1985 global ambitions. Far from being a super-power, striving to impose its law on the world, it was then a relatively underdeveloped and unstable country, suffering from the paranoic mentality of the besieged, convinced (as it probably still is) that the entire capatalist world was dedicated to its destruction. If we in Brussels, where so much united us with London and Paris, trembled at the prospect of the principle democracies capitulating before Hitler, it is easy to imagine the fears of the Marxist pariah walled up in the Kremlin. The Soviet Ambassador to France might well report enthusiasm in French political and military circles for the Grand Alliance; but his colleague in London, where the principal decisions were taken, found no such encouragement. In a despatch to his government, he described a lunch with Lloyd George on 14 July, dilating bitterly on the manoeuvres of the Chamberlain clique to gain time, 'in order to try once again to come to terms with the aggressors, or at least greatly to delay the signing of a treaty with the Soviet Government'. On 17 July, Molotov, in a telegram imparting information to his Ambassadors, echoed this pessimism: 'Our partners have recourse to every form of trickery and unworthy subterfuge,' he wrote. 'These cheats and swindlers, what are they aiming at? It seems that nothing will come out of these interminable negotiations'.[31] After the affronts of Munich and the snubs, one can hardly be surprised at his words.

★   ★   ★

The chronology of the decisions is most revealing, because it shows clearly that Hitler decided to overcome his aversion for the 'Judeo-Marxists', only when he believed that they were about to come to an understanding with the West. It also reveals the haste with which Stalin replied to him. Interminable comments on the Soviet–France–British negotiations appeared in the newspaper, although their accuracy could naturally not be vouched for. The German Ambassador in

London, Herbert von Dirksen had, however, no cause for concern; he benefited from the service of a particularly well-placed spy in the Foreign Office or Downing Street (who has never been identified).[35] The German archives published after the war reveal that he was able to follow step by step the evolution of the conversations, their vicissitudes and the improbability of their success. Then at the end of June, when a rupture seemed possible, Berlin cut short its first contacts with Moscow.

Three weeks later everything changed again. It was on 21 July 1939 that London and Paris, after having resigned themselves to the political demands of the Soviets, took the decision to accept military exchanges. Suddenly, the Grand Alliance appeared a redoubtable probability. *That very day*, Dirksen informed Berlin of it by cable.* *The following day* came Ribbentrop's telegram to Ambassador von der Schulenburg annulling the prohibition imposed at the end of June, and authorising him anew to 'set a bait'. Four days later Georgi Astakhov, the austere Russian Chargé d'Affaires in Berlin, was invited to dinner by a high ranking official of the German Foreign Office, Dr Schnurre, in a quiet restaurant in a Berlin suburb. During a lengthy meal, washed down with plenty of wine, the Russian and the German reached agreement on the common vital interests of their countries, and 'their common opposition to the capitalist Democracies'. On 2 August, Ribbentrop summoned Astakhov and went straight to the point, defining the spheres of influence for both countries from the Baltic to the Black Sea. The next day, Schulenburg was instructed to repeat these same propositions to Molotov. He was received cordially in the Kremlin but the Russian, he reported in his telegram, renewed his habitual complaints about Berlin and gave him the impression of still being inclined to negotiate a pact with the Franco-British—provided they agreed to all the Soviet demands. However, he was 'exceptionally open', added the Ambassador. 'Undoubtedly he was swallowing the bait.'

---

* On 25 July, a new telegram from Dirksen confirmed that the Western Powers were disposed to enter into military conversations with the USSR, *before* the conclusion of political negotiations. The German Ambassador in Paris transmitted the same information to Berlin by telegram on 28 July.[36]

CHAPTER 17

The Jaws of Darkness

Late in the evening of 9 August 1939 the *City of Exeter*, a small merchant steamer flying the British flag, after crossing the North Sea, passed Kronstadt, where it was saluted by the picket-boats of the Soviet Navy. Shortly after, it moored on the quayside of the inner port of Leningrad. Its passengers, twenty-five officers of a Franco-British military mission, gathered along the bulwark in evening-dress looking curiously out into the clear night of the northern summer at the quays littered with cranes, the broken down little hut which served as the harbour office, and the few shabbily dressed strollers.[1] The next morning, after sleeping on board, the French and British officers took the Red Arrow, the Moscow night express, which arrived in the capital on the morning of 11 August. There they were welcomed by numerous civil and military dignitaries. It was the end of a long journey. General Joseph Doumenc of the French Army, and Admiral Sir Reginald Plunkett-Ernle-Drax of the Royal Navy, had left London on 5 August with their twenty-three-man staff, and spent a quiet time on board the *City of Exeter*, an antiquated vessel requisitioned for the occasion, whose engines were in poor condition, being unable to cruise at more than 12–13 knots. Almost three weeks had elapsed between the planning of their mission and its arrival in Moscow.

Contrary to what has been said, the two heads of mission were officers of great distinction. After a brilliant career, Army General Doumenc, a *Polytechnician*, ex-Deputy Chief of Weygand's staff, and one of the few specialists in motorisation and armoured vehicles, was still a young man. Admiral Drax whom Captain (later General) Beaufre described as 'a portrait of Rodney lacking only the wig', was much more than an old sea-dog. The younger brother of the distinguished poet Lord Dunsany, and ex-Commandant of the Royal Naval Staff College, an opponent of appeasement, since Munich he had been in charge of the Admiralty Service of Strategic Studies. His

relatives recall the sarcasm with which he spoke of this futile journey
to Moscow—almost a joke, he said, but not a funny one. The mission
could not have travelled more slowly. There was no question of taking
the train and crossing Germany with a team of 25 officers and NCOs.
No question of an aeroplane, for the Russian airports did not, it
was thought, possess fuel suitable for English aircraft. There was no
question of a destroyer or a fast cruiser; for the presence of an Allied
warship in the Baltic might have been interpreted by the Germans as
a provocation. Someone had suggested bicycles, but the idea had not
been pursued.[2]

The two officers got on well together. Both knew that the chances
of success were slim: indeed, they did not know exactly what they had
been sent to achieve—except some sort of vague military understanding, as Doumenc reveals in his *Souvenirs*. Before leaving Paris,
he had been received by Daladier who told him to reach an agreement
in Russia 'at all costs'. Bonnet advised him to make promises, 'any
promise you consider useful'. However the instructions from his
immediate superior, General Gamelin (instructions of which Daladier
and Bonnet were unaware) were, according to Beaufre, 'vague on
essentials, and completely negative on all points which were to prove
crucial'.[3] The instructions to Admiral Drax were no better. The British
authorities recognised 'the vital nature' of Russian aid to Poland and
Rumania; at the same time, they advised him to proceed with the
utmost caution. The mission should extract the maximum information
from the Soviets, giving them a strict minimum in return. He was
instructed to drag out the negotiations until the rains and snows of
autumn would make a German offensive impossible. If they could
manage to hold out for a month, the threatened war would not break
out in 1939. As for 1940, that could be dealt with later. Chamberlain
in person told Drax what he expected of him. He remarked that the
House had 'pushed him further than he had intended' ... 'A worried
and uneasy man' the Admiral wrote.[4]

The Allied officers were received most cordially on the day of their
arrival by Molotov and by Voroshilov, the People's Defence Commissar. It was an encouraging sign. In the evening, they were invited to a
palace in the Spiridonov street, the old and sumptuous residence of a
Czarist merchant, to a banquet for fifty, with the military leaders all
in full uniform, with gold braid, studded with decorations; the Russians in white, the English in blue or scarlet, only the French in khaki.
After a meal served off plate embossed with the Imperial arms, washed
down with vodka and Crimean champagne, and punctuated by

innumerable toasts to the unbreakable entente of the three countries, the guests were escorted to a panelled ballroom for a musical entertainment. 'The Soviets seemed very pleased to welcome us', wrote Beaufre,[5] 'We could legitimately hope that agreement would be easier to achieve than we had expected.'

On the following day, the 12 August, a stifling Moscovite summer day, the delegates met in the salon in the Spiridonov street, seated informally around a huge table. The first two days were spent in an exchange of information. Beaufre wrote, 'We had to appear sincere, to give the impression of revealing secrets, when in reality the details we were to give were misleading.' Admiral Drax confirmed, 'We could only tell the Russians what we knew was known to the Germans.'[6] These were open secrets, which nevertheless made clear the disequilibrium of forces. The British, without admitting the whole truth, said they could mobilise only 5 infantry and 1 motorised division. The French had to admit the weakness of their air force. The Russians, on the other hand, professed to be able to put in the field 136 divisions, 9–10,000 tanks and 5,000 aeroplanes, 90 per cent of them modern.

Marshal Voroshilov rejected outright the suggestion of a convention in general terms, which the Franco-British had prepared on the *City of Exeter* as 'a meaningless declaration'. He almost immediately came to the crucial point of the negotiations. Emphasising that the Germans could invade Poland at any moment, and that the Soviet Union had no common frontier with the Reich, would the Soviet army be allowed on Polish territory—or, if need be, on Rumanian territory, to face the enemy forces? To this precise question, this *axiomatic* question, he wanted a precise answer.

On 14 August 1939, the crisis came to a head. Drax and Doumenc tried to persuade the Marshal that his concern was without foundation, that Poland and Rumania, as soon as they were attacked, would request Soviet aid. Doumenc suggested disingenuously that the Soviet Army should go ahead with concentrations on its own, so that it could intervene as soon as requested. This advice, which was as impractical as humiliating, was rejected heatedly and indignantly by Voroshilov. In the absence of a clear, unequivocal reply to his question of the day before, he saw no reason to continue the conversations.

Forty-eight hours after the opening of the negotiations, the Allied delegations found themselves with their backs to the wall, taken short by a question of whose fundamental importance they were well aware, but which both of their delegations had orders to avoid. Short of arguments, they asked for a suspension of the session. Taking refuge in the gardens of the Spiridonov palace to escape from indiscreet microphones, distressed and annoyed they realised that, in the absence of fresh instructions, their mission was doomed. Their anxious telegrams to Paris and London on the night of 14/15 August suddenly awoke the Western ministers. In spite of the Czechoslovak tragedy, in spite of Munich, they had made no attempt to define a strategy; no more than they had dreamed of doing so while offering or renewing their alliance with Poland. Certainly the idea of collaborating with the Russia of the Soviets was repugnant to them. But without it, British and French promises were so much hot air; Poland was lost, 'the Second Front' a mirage.

For some time the British Chiefs of Staff had been insisting that this was so in vain.[7] In Paris, there was the same alarming complacency. Particularly inconsistent was the all-powerful general Gamelin. In May 1939, he had initialled a military agreement with Warsaw which, although technically imprecise, bound France in event of aggression against Poland, 'to react immediately and to launch an offensive with the bulk of its forces 15 days after the outbreak of hostilities'.* Was this a hollow promise? Judging by his disclosures to the British, it was not; he considered a French offensive essential in the shortest possible time.[8] Moreover, the despatches of the French Ambassador in Warsaw confirmed this for him. Like all the foreign observers in the Polish capital (with the sole exception of his own military attaché), the French Ambassador had no illusions about the value of the Polish armed forces, some 39 regular divisions and 13 in reserve—undoubtedly brave soldiers, but weak in aeroplanes and artillery, almost entirely without armoured forces, or the heavy industry required to construct them. In spite of this the 'designated Generalissimo' did not hesitate to inform his Ministers that Poland could hold out, and that French troops would not have to go into battle until the spring, when they would have the support of several British divisions. Much prejudiced against the Soviets ('these people should be put beyond the pale of humanity', he told his officers), he did not want them to come to the aid of Poland—except with equipment, aviation support and perhaps some tanks.[9]

The civil power had been content with this convenient chiaroscuro. Now, with its back to the wall, it started for the first time urgent, almost frantic, démarches. The Polish Ambassadors were called to the

* The military agreement was subject to a political protocol, which was not signed until 4 September 1939—after the beginning of the war.

Quai d'Orsay and the Foreign Office; those of France and England were despatched to Colonel Beck and the President of the Polish Republic; their military attachés harassed the Polish General Staff. General Doumenc sent the young Captain Beaufre from Moscow to Warsaw (Paris had forbidden him to send his senior Adjutant, General Valin, 'because of the publicity which would result from it'). In vain. To the British Ambassador Colonel Beck retorted, 'If we agreed to cooperate with the Soviet Union, Hitler would see red, and would not hesitate to declare war.' To the French Ambassador he declared haughtily, 'I will not allow anyone to discuss the use of a part of our territory by foreign troops. In any case, the Russians are militarily valueless.'[10]

★ ★ ★

Shakespeare relates that King Lear, having lost his reason, felt he was 'bound on a wheel of fire', a medieval symbol for Hell. Were these the same flames which consumed Hitler, to atone for the sins of the Aryans, and give them the eimpre of the earth? 'I will make war', he had announced many years before. 'I will decide the propitious moment for the attack ... It is my mission. If I achieve it, I will have earned the right to send youth to its death.'[11]

His wait was over. A mysterious alchemy bore the Saviour of the Aryans to ebullition. Weizsäcker, the frigid Secretary of State at the German Foreign Office, noted on 13 August 1939 in his diary, 'For a week, his desire for war has become much more pronounced.' So blood must flow; was it not 'the cement of civilisation'? 'What governed his thinking,' said Field Marshal von Manstein, 'was the dreamed-of image of multitudes of enemy soldiers bleeding to death.'[12] If this statement is valid—and who can doubt it?—had he not always seen himself in terms of conquests?—it invalidates the thesis of the so-called revisionist historians; wishing to show that Hitler did not knowingly cause the Second World War; they condemn all the world on the pretext of judging no individual.

Birger Dahlerus, an obscure Swedish merchant who had gained Göring's confidence, has left a revealing account of an interview with the Nazi dictator towards the end of August 1939:

> Extremely excited, he leapt to his feet . . . pacing nervously up and down he declared, as if talking to himself, that Germany was invincible ... Suddenly he stopped in the middle of the room, staring into the void. His words became more and more incoherent, the phrases tumbling over one another. 'If war breaks out, I shall construct submarines, and submarines, and submarines, and submarines,

and submarines.' His language, increasingly indistinct, became unintelligible. Then he mastered himself, raised his voice as if addressing a vast assembly and shouted, 'I will construct aeroplanes, and aeroplanes, and aeroplanes ... I shall destroy my enemies.' At this moment, he appeared more like a phantom from a story book than a real person.[13]

One might be tempted to class this account with popular fiction, much in fashion at the time, readily representing the Führer as a raving lunatic; it would be a crude simplification. However, another witness, this time irrefutable, tends to confirm the words of Dahlerus. The Swiss Carl Burckhardt, the League of Nations High Commissioner in Dantzig, a precise and reliable university professor, went secretly on 11 August 1939 to visit Hitler in his mountain lair, in the hope of extracting a pacific solution to the problem of the Free City. He found Hitler much aged, giving the impression of being afraid, speaking excitedly, soon trembling with rage, rapping the table with his fists, shouting in a voice vibrating with fury, 'At the smallest incident, I shall crush the Poles without warning ... not a trace will remain. I will strike them like lightning, with all the force of a mechanised army, of which they have not the least notion. You hear me?' he shrieked at the top of his voice.

'Yes Chancellor. And that will mean war, general war.'

'Well, if I have to I shall not hesitate. I prefer to have it today and not tomorrow. I shall not be like William II ... I shall fight implacably right to the end.'

He then pulled himself together. Looking out at the Alps through the huge window, he assured Burckhardt that he was not frightened of France and England; but he remained disposed for an agreement with them—if they would leave his hands free in the east. All that he was doing, he added at the end of the interview, was directed against the Russians. If the Western Powers revealed themselves too stupid to understand him, he would be obliged to annihilate them, before turning on the Soviet Union.[14]

Perhaps there was a shade of comedy in this extraordinary scene— which Hitler knew would be repeated in London and Paris; if so, it in no way altered his intentions. When Mussolini sent Ciano to him on 12/13 August to explain that Italy was not ready for a general war, and to suggest a new 'Munich' the German Dictator did not conceal the fact that he was resolved to subdue Poland in its entirety, and that before the end of the month.* The Duce had no reason to be worried.

* The guest of Ribbentrop, Ciano spent the night at the Schloss Fuschl near Salzburg. It had been the property of an Austrian whom Ribbentrop had caused to be arrested and executed by the Gestapo after the Anschluss, in order to take possession of the castle himself.

There would be no European war. France and England would confine themselves to theatrical gestures; they would not take up arms. He was completely certain of this; 'through his psychological knowledge', Ribbentrop added. It would be a good occasion for Italy to take possession of Slovakia and Croatia. The Duce's son-in-law returned empty-handed to Rome. On this occasion, he was seized by panic, instead of his usual carefree cynicism, and he secretly reported the interview to London. In his diary he noted, 'The Germans are possessed by the demon of destruction.'[15]

The following day, the Führer summoned the C-in-Cs of the three Services to Berchtesgaden to confirm the White Plan, and to fix provisionally 25 August as *Day Y*, for the attack on Poland. He again gave the most categorical assurances that the French and British would not intervene, any more than they had in the previous year. His only fear was to be, 'embarrassed at the last moment by some compromise proposal from Chamberlain'. Whether he believed this or not, we shall never know. Perhaps a half of it, probably no more than that. On the other hand, he saw clearly that he was lost if the Soviet Union became allied to France and England.

★ ★ ★

As early as the month of August, alone with the Führer in the huge lift which, through the rock, connected the Eagle's Nest above the Berghof with the Kehlstein, Albert Speer heard him whispering, in a kind of enigmatic reverie, that something extraordinary was about to happen—and very soon. 'Even if I have to send Göring ... even if I have to go myself ... I will play all to gain all.'[16] His Ambassador in Moscow had just let it be known that the Russians seemed well disposed and the Molotov was 'swallowing the bait'.

Although a rapprochement between the Russians and the Germans had been a distinct possibility since Munich, only the United States was precisely informed about it. One of their attaches in Moscow, 'Chip' Bohlen, relates in his memoirs how he made friends with a Second Secretary at the German Embassy, 'Johnny' von Herwarth, in 1939. The personal assistant of Graf von der Schulenburg, von Herwarth was one of those highly civilised German aristocrats who were to become the heroes of the German resistance to Hitler—all the braver in that, having a Jewish grandmother, the Nazis had no confidence in him. Indeed, he only precariously escaped racist 'purification' by getting himself forgotten in Moscow.* Convinced that what was being hatched was a European war, he undertook, at his peril, to inform the West through the intermediary of Bohlen. The two young men met one another when hacking in the Muscovite countryside, a plausible pretext for frequent contact—thus protected from the NKVD and the Gestapo spies.

After some hesitation, the American appreciated the exceptional gravity of what he had been told, and managed to convince his superiors. His telegrams were placed before Cordell Hull and Roosevelt; due to an exaggerated sense of security, they were only communicated to the western allies by veiled allusions. These were ignored. Prophetically, the President put Stalin on his guard against collusion with the Führer, 'It will allow him to destroy France. But as sure as night follows day, he will then turn on the USSR.'[18] If the message reached its destination, which is not certain, it was not replied to and it came to nothing.

On 14 August 1939 (three days after the arrival in Moscow of the Franco-British and at about the same time that Voroshilov demanded their 'Yes' or 'No'), Hitler had felt that the moment had come to take the decisive step and, according to his own expression, to conclude 'a pact with Satan, in order to drive out the Devil'. Late that evening, he sent the historic telegram proposing a visit by Ribbentrop to Moscow. On the next day, 15 August, the Schulenburgs were giving a ball. But the Ambassador was not there to receive his guests, he was in the Kremlin with Molotov. He appeared at about 11.30. 'He was the urbane, smiling host and gave no indication that he had just pulled off one of the greatest coups in modern diplomatic history.' Bohlen would relate. A little later, in a corner of the ballroom, Herwarth, holding a glass of champagne, told his friend that Molotov had given Schulenburg reason to believe that the whole matter was settled. Washington was immediately informed and, this time, considered it urgent to inform the French and British Ambassadors fully. Owing to fatal carelessness, or, perhaps, to sabotage by a Communist agent, the coded telegram to the Foreign Office of 17 August was not deciphered and read until the 22 August.[19] Too late.

Forty years, and more have passed without any revelation of how

---

* Ambassador von der Schulenburg and von Herwarth were both implicated in the Stauffenberg plot of 1944. Schulenburg was tortured and executed. Herwarth escaped hanging thanks to a series of extraordinary circumstances. After the war, he again became a diplomat, and, in London and Rome, was one of the most respected Ambassadors of the Federal Republic. He has just published his memoirs.[17]

the Soviets reached their decision. At the most, we know that while Admiral Drax and General Doumenc, heavy-hearted, were made to cool their heels, the Politburo was in almost permanent session, instead of dispersing as was its habit for the summer holiday. It is thought that one of their meetings was held on the evening of 14 August 1939, immediately after the decisive confrontation of Voroshilov with the Franco-British delegation. Stalin is said to have announced that they had proof that the Russians had nothing to hope for from the Western Powers.[20] However, it was not until 19 August that the Red Czar, returning from his datcha at Kuntsevo on the outskirts of Moscow, is believed to have presided over the Politburo in the afternoon, and made his fatal decision. In any case, it was on this day that Schulenburg, summoned twice to the Kremlin, was informed by Molotov that Ribbentrop would be welcome in the Soviet capital on 26 and 27 August.

This was too late for the Führer. Only a week remained before the weather would make a campaign in Poland hazardous, He was also haunted by the fear of an agreement at the last minute between the Soviets and the Franco-British. On Sunday evening 20 August, after hours of hesitation, he sent a telegram to his mortal enemy, couched in almost supplicatory terms, signing it with his own name. In it he said that as a crisis might develop 'at any moment', he entreated Stalin to receive Ribbentrop on 22 or 23 August. By now, his fate depended on the Kremlin reply. If positive, it would mean the war which was necessary for Hitler to accomplish his Mission. If negative, it would mean a peace which would place him in an inextricable position. His closest associates have described the hours of growing tension in the Berghof, the Führer in a state of extreme agitation, incapable of sleep, pacing up and down the big room in the middle of the night. He even woke up the grumbling Göring to pour out his complaints and anxieties. At three o'clock in the morning, he was informed that the telegram to Stalin had gone astray; it had not arrived in Moscow. A little later, it was retrieved.

During the 21 August he was still agitated and in a nervous state. Near to exhaustion, he was still pacing up and down like a caged animal, in the presence of silent and frightened secretaries and ADCs. The vast Reich war machine, set in motion in the spring, was completing its preparations. Mobilisation was in its last stages. Innumerable trains loaded with men and material were rolling towards the front; regiments were assembled at their action stations, munitions being distributed. From Moscow there was still no reply.

In the course of a gloomy dinner, an SS NCO came unobtrusively into the dining-room and handed a note to the master of the house. Albert Speer recounts that Hitler ran his eyes over it quickly, 'stared in front of himself for a moment, his face reddening, rapped on the table causing the glasses to clink, and cried in a falsetto voice, "I have them! I have them!" It was the eagerly awaited reply. Later, on the terrace of the Berghof, the successor of the German emperors and his courtiers saw rising in the darkened sky an aurora borealis, flooding the mountains of the Untersberg with bright red light. 'One could not', said Speer, 'have dreamed of a more impressive *mise en scene* for the last act of the Twilight of the Gods.' He heard Hitler mutter to his neighbour, 'This means blood. This time, we shall not come out of it without violence.' He then gave the order for a full peal of all the church bells in Germany.[21]

The following day, some fifty of the principal military leaders were at the Berghof, summoned in civilian clothes 'so as not to attract attention'. Göring, interpreting the order in his own way, appeared in his favourite costume, a jerkin of green leather over a white silk shirt, grey silk breeches, grey stockings, a golden dagger dangling from his belt. Hitler, all his self-confidence regained, launched into a monologue lasting several hours. Briefly interrupted by a buffet lunch, he again announced his gigantic projects, and repeated his unshakeable resolve to make war. Circumstances, he said, demanded immediate action. No one could tell how much longer he or the Duce would live. Poland would be 'annihilated'. Daladier and Chamberlain were only 'earth worms'; they had revealed it at Munich. They would brandish their sabres, perhaps declare war; but they would not fight. Germany's treaty with Stalin would hold them back. It also disposed of all danger of an effective blockade. As for Stalin, he was critically sick. After his death, we will crush the Soviet Union. Then the domination of the Reich on the Earth will dawn. There was only one set-back to fear—a mediation proposed at the last minute by some 'dirty dog' (*Schweinhund*). In a burning peroration, Hitler's voice took on a tragic note, speaking of 'closing the heart to all pity', of 'an iron will', and a 'struggle to the bitter end'. The Wehrmacht must be ready to march at any moment; the order for attack would be confirmed later. Reduced to silence by the unexpected success of the preceding year, lulled into confidence by Russian neutrality, not one of the generals raised any objections. When Marshal Göring gave the signal, they warmly applauded their Supreme Commander. A few days later, London was informed of the meeting in a secret report.[22]

★   ★   ★

At the very moment when the jubilant Führer learnt that Stalin was ready to meet the Reich's Foreign Minister, the French Embassy in Moscow received a telegram with the instructions it had asked for more than a week before—squirming around, without actually settling, the 'axiomatic' questions brought up by Voroshilov. Doumenc had again seen the Soviet Marshal on the afternoon of 22 August in the presence of a solitary secretary-interpreter. It was an unreal interview because the die was already cast, and the aeroplane bringing Ribbentrop was flying to Königsberg, on its way to Moscow. The stenographic record which remains of the interview is a poignant document through which, after so many years, still blows the terrible wind of history. Doumenc clung desperately to the wisp of straw in the pitiable telegram. Courageously, extolling his brief, he declared he was empowered to sign a 'military convention' in which an authorisation would be stipulated for the passage of Soviet troops at points which they would choose themselves.[23]

The Russian, evidently informed by his Embassy and his secret services of the inflexibility of 'The Colonels' of Warsaw, would not be duped. Had they really decided? If 'Yes' why did the Poles not hurry to Moscow to take part in the negotiations? Without their agreement, what value had the French pledge? To the flood of questions with which he was inundated, Doumenc could only give evasive replies: 'I don't know . . . I think so . . . probably . . .' Voroshilov, not without some humanity, wanted to justify himself by lamenting the insanity of the Poles: 'Must we go on bended knees to implore them to accept our aid?' Absolute clarity was required if negotiations were to be resumed, '*if nothing happens from now on from the political point of view*,'* he finished mysteriously. The mystery was to be short-lived. Returning to the French Embassy, General Doumenc read in the evening edition of *Pravda* that Ribbentrop was expected shortly in the Soviet capital.

The following day, 23 August, at about 1 p.m. in brilliant sunshine, two large aeroplanes landed at the airport of Khodynka, near Moscow, which was decorated with red flags, the Hammer and Sickle flying joyously beside the Swastika. Ribbentrop and his suite were greeted most cordially by Potemkine, the Vice-Commissar for Foreign Affairs

---

* The following day the government of Warsaw was to declare that 'it did not exclude' a common Polish–Soviet action in event of German aggression—a tardy and inadequate decision.

Peace for Our Time

(Molotov had not bothered to come). After listening to the *Deutschland über alles*, and inspecting an Air Force guard of honour, Hitler's envoy was driven to the old Austrian Legation, which had been confiscated by the Germans after the Anschluss. At 3.30 p.m., walking into a conference room of the Kremlin with its unstylish furniture and its lugubrious portraits of Marx, Lenin and Engels, the Germans were much surprised to find Stalin in person—who, after a year in Moscow, Schulenburg had not been able to approach.

Three hours later, the brigands had reached virtual agreement on a 10 year non-aggression pact and, much more significant, on a secret protocol which divided up all Eastern Europe, from the Black Sea to the Baltic in 'two zones of vital influence'. After a break in the session at the end of the afternoon, they met again at 10 p.m. A little after midnight it was all settled.* The Georgian Tiger, full of joviality, circulated among the guests, helping personally to fill their glasses. He drank a toast to the health of the Führer, a *molodetz*, a good fellow, 'so greatly loved by the German people'. Strangely frivolous words were exchanged about France, Japan and the 'perfidious Albion'. Ribbentrop did not conceal the imminence of an attack on Poland. The photographers were then called to record Molotov and Ribbentrop signing, under the benevolent eye of 'the Father of the People', the cursed instruments which would allow Hitler to unleash all the beasts of the Apocalypse.

The world learned through the press agencies *Tass* and *DNB* of the unbelievable collusion of the two enemy ideologies—a Communism claiming to be libertarian and the worst form of tyranny known to the modern world. While the Nazis were overjoyed—as, with more reserve, were the Soviets—the free peoples of the world were stunned. With the exception of a few diehards, they had been prepared to forget their repulsion for the crimes of Marxism-Leninism and the Stalin purges, to see, in a grand alliance, the last means of preventing war. Now, as in a nightmare, the ground gave way under their feet. The alternative was fearful: either to submit to a 'Polish Munich', then to another, then to another, in accommodating themselves to the iron regime of a Nazi Europe; or to take up the challenge, and accept a

---

* The next morning, Herwarth invited Bohlen to the German Embassy to convey to him the terms of the agreement signed in the night. 'Johnny was depressed by the pact,' Bohlen wrote. 'Seated in his dark panelled office, he saw clearly they were preparing war against Poland. He told me he was returning to Germany to rejoin his regiment.' Ribbentrop, tired out by the long evening, was sleeping on the floor above.[24]

second world war which would mean, everyone believed, the death of civilisation.

★ ★ ★

The Belgians were making great efforts to pretend they were not concerned. Were not the faults committed by the 'Great Powers' the cause of this mess? Let them get out of it as best they could. In any case, Brussels thought there was a good chance of escaping the fire. 'Even on our own, we can hold out for three weeks,' officers of our General Staff told me, 'enough to make the Wehrmacht think twice'.

It was clear where the real threat lay. The April 1939 elections, a rout of Rexism, had shown that the fleeting popularity of the extreme Right had collapsed. The German Ambassador in Brussels was not deceived; he cabled to the Wilhemstrasse that 90 per cent of the Belgians were resolutely hostile to the Third Reich.[25] A Liberal-Catholic Ministry (that is, without Spaak) 'had carried on the policy of independence'. What else could it do? Adopt the policy of Czechoslovakia? However nothing forced it to the unbending Calvinism which advisers, diplomats and the military brought to it—to the growing butterness of Paris and London. In January–February 1939, amid rumours of an imminent invasion of Holland, the Rue de la Loi, in its blindness, replied to the questions of the Foreign Office that this did not concern Belgium. 'Our interest is to remain outside the conflict, and do all we can to avoid it,' recommended an aide-memoire by the sagacious Baron van Zuylen.[26] In 1937 and 1938, the French and British military attachés had been allowed, unofficially, all facilities for observing the Belgian defence works and the movement of troops. The Chief of the General Staff himself had offered to keep them informed—in secret. This was on the level of information rather than concerted action; but it was better than nothing. Now, in spite of the pressing demands of Paris and London, in spite of the wishes expressed by the Commission of Foreign Affairs in the Belgian Senate, the taps were turned off, contacts with the Allies became more and more difficult. In May, a senior officer of the British War Office, who had come to Brussels *at the invitation of M. Pierlot* the Prime Minister, had to return empty-handed, without having been able to meet either the Minister for Defence or the Chief of the General Staff.*

---

*Switzerland, no less neutral but more realistic, maintained relations with the French General Staff, which ended in secret agreements for cooperation between the two armies.[27–28]

The hours ticked by in this strange dreamlike state, a sort of suspended terror which invariably seems to precede great human disasters. Nothing in the normal routine of existence was changed, its pains, pleasures and loves; and yet we felt close to the end of the world. Around 15 August, I spent a few days of leave in Switzerland with my parents at Vevey. We went for long walks on the shores of Lake Leman, or in the woods and romantic dales of Mount Pélerin. Calm and idle hours they were, but darkened by the anticipation of approaching war: the fearful clash of arms on the battlefield, cities destroyed, millions of maimed bodies, a war which would open the door to the Dark Ages. From the terrace of the hotel, surrounded by summer visitors indulging their pleasures, elegant young women, carefree children, I contemplated, with a sort of avidity, the tranquil waters of the lake, spangled with little sailing boats, and the majestic Dents du Midi, draped in a light mist which on hot mornings softens their severe contours. One of the most beautiful landscapes in the world, it made me feel acutely the folly of those who by evil or stupidity were about to let loose hell on earth. So many things were to perish, so many hopes, so many young lives, loves, ambitions—a whole civilisation, the most beautiful and the most humane that had been conceived by the genius of the centuries. It was for this that death had to be faced—more than for our native lands, whose values no longer seemed so evident.

Moments of bitter sweetness, I will never forget them. On August 20, a telegram called me back urgently to Brussels. The direct train through Basle and Luxerburg, along the German border, was no longer running regularly. I went by Paris, seizing the occasion to meet a childhood friend, already in uniform. The city had lost none of the liveliness of its summer evenings. We had dinner on the terrace of a small restaurant facing Notre Dame to chat late into the night about the future. My friend had no doubt, the French were determined to put a stop to a chain of events which turned their life upside down every six months. They would fight the Germans without hatred, but they would fight hard for an idea of the world which gave meaning to their existence. I returned to Brussels persuaded, as much as were those close to me, that a hideous war would be less hideous than a Europe subjugated by Hitler. It was still 23 August, the date of the Ribbentrop–Stalin meeting. The same day, after long and mysterious comings and goings of a secret emissary, acting on the initiative of King Leopold, a conference of seven small countries, known as the

Oslo group* was held in Brussels, with the declared object of creating 'a moral force ... to stop the slide towards war'.

The 'war of nerves' was at its zenith. Beyond the Rhine, the Press and radio thundered, the Nazi leaders redoubled their imprecations, a cacophony which perturbed the most lucid minds. In Dantzig, where the 'Gauleiter' had proclaimed himself 'Chief of State', his henchmen indulged in the worst excesses. The Reich had virtually completed its mobilisation. France had followed suit. Pope Pius XII and President Roosevelt were uttering vain appeals for peace. The Rue de la Loi had received information from the Quai d'Orsay, the Foreign Office and even the Palazzo Chigi, all pointing to an attack on Poland during the weekend 25–26 August. On 21 August M. Pierlot had summoned his cabinet to an extraordinary session to announce that 'Hitler appeared decided to end it all'.[29] Would the governments of London and Paris intervene this time? It seemed possible, but not certain. However the decision of the gods had been cast.

★   ★   ★

Along the road to power, tragedy always lurks. Those who engage in it without mature reflection are fascinated by the distant mirage of power with which they create their enchanted garden. But the popular passions which they stir to serve their ambitions, without discerning their hidden, murky forces, can at any moment escape from their mastery, and carry them away like wisps of straw. In August, Chamberlain lamented in a heart-felt cry to his sister Hilda, 'Nothing can make me forget that the ultimate decision, the Yes or No which may decide the fate not only of all this generation but of the British Empire itself rests with me.' The American Ambassador in London wrote of him, 'A man profoundly depressed, haunted by the spectre of catastrophe.' As for Daladier, his colleagues saw him, 'bent and limping, morose and withdrawn, almost as inaccessible as before Munich'.[30] It is difficult not to feel compassion for these men, who without evil intent, had arrogated to themselves exceptional power on the pretext of saving the world, to finish by letting themselves be enmeshed powerless in the agony of a fearful dilemma. But this is not enough to absolve them from the enormous mistakes for which their presumption and weakness were responsible.

---

* The Group consisted of Belgium, the Netherlands, Luxemburg, Norway, Sweden, Denmark and Finland.

When after several hours of bewilderment the Molotov–Ribbentrop pact appeared in all its terrible reality, their first reactions were irreproachable. Chamberlain, who was salmon fishing in Scotland, returned to Downing Street to preside over the Cabinet. On the evening of 23 August, a communiqué read over the BBC announced that the Moscow pact would change nothing in the British guarantee to Poland. In Whitehall, street processions sang 'God save the King', and 'Rule Britannia'. The next day, the Prime Minister asked the House of Commons to pass an Emergency Powers bill. He obtained an almost unanimous vote of confidence—much greater than after Munich.

Equally, Daladier gave the impression of firmness. On the same dramatic 23 August, he presided at an unofficial session of the *Comité permanent de la Défense Nationale*. In an hour and a half, after encouraging reports from General Gamelin and Admiral Darlan (the Air Minister was more reserved but not discouraging), the committee concluded unanimously that 'France has no other choice . . . the only solution to envisage is to maintain our commitment to Poland.' On 23 August came partial mobilisation (in fact, it had been going on for several weeks). The following day, the President of the Council addressed the nation on the radio: 'The German–Soviet pact increases the chances of aggression against the friends of France, and against France herself. She is resolved to support Poland, if that country is attacked. Everyone must be prepared to do his duty.'

The French were prepared. During that summer, the 150th anniversary of the storming of the Bastille had been the occasion for enthusiastic celebrations. The traditional march-past on 14 July—in which units of the British Brigade of Guards took part—gave rise to demonstrations of fervent patriotism. 'National opinion is almost unanimous', said Georges Bonnet, who was by no means one of the more resolute. The journalist and politician Arthur Cante wrote of, 'A profound national unity. If we are far from the delirious atmosphere of 1914, there is no feeling of a country hesitant and confused.' Ambassador Bullitt expressed his admiration for the French people, '(Their) self control and quiet courage has been so far beyond the usual standard of the human race.' Well known American journalists like Mowrer and Gunther thought likewise.[31] The Belgian Embassy in Paris reported that the Molotov–Ribbentrop Pact had caused a curious reconciliation between the French Right and Left (with the exception of the Communists). General Weygand expressed it: 'All the swine are now on the same side.' An opinion poll in July had incontestably revealed the determination of the French; 76 per cent of them were of the opinion that, 'if Germany attempts to take the free city of Dantzig, it must be prevented, if necessary by force'.*

'The troops at this time were worth more than their leaders,' said Jean Chauvel, the future Secretary-General at the Quai d'Orsay.[32] Even at this late hour the good apostles in the democratic capitals, skilled in selfish policies, sometimes greedy but timorous and indecisive, could oppose the furies of Hitler only with insistant grovelling, or sometimes with the distant thunder of abortive storms. We may recall Gibbon's words:

> The good genius in the demon of Socrates affords a memorable instance of how a wise man may deceive himself; how a good man may deceive others, how the conscience may slumber in a mixed and middle state between self-illusion and voluntary fraud.

From Paris, secret emissaries, among them the dubious Fernand de Brinon, again took the road to Berlin. The usual clique continued to manoeuvre for what it called 'a conference which can, as at Munich save the peace'. At its head was Georges Bonnet, *'George le Désossé'*. On 27 August, he summoned the Ambassadors of Spain and Belgium. To the first he suggested a truce of 10 days, to be proposed by General Franco. To the second, he asked for an intervention in Rome by King Leopold—on the Belgian initiative—by which he would let it be known that 'Italy will not regret her pacifying mission ... she will reap the benefits of it by settling her differences with France'.[34] All these were initiatives which Daladier felt he need not veto.

On the other side of the Channel, the same weakness was evident. The British wished to avoid the disastrous silence which in 1914 had permitted Berlin to believe in the complacency of the British Empire; at the same time they were not prepared to abandon détente. Dangerous ambivalence. To all the unpleasant experiences suffered since 1933, were added once more the passionate warnings of the German resistance: war was imminent, they said, because Hitler was assuming that the French and the British would not fight. Although they were risking their life, although they had been turned down many times, the Kordt brothers, a Colonel von Schwerin, a lawyer van Schlabrendorff, a diplomat von Trott zu Solz again had taken the road

---

* It is not without interest to note the astonishing similarity of views (as in 1938) in French and British opinion. 77 per cent of the English were to reply negatively to the question asked by Gallup, 'Would you, or would you not, support a British government which now opened up peace conversations with Germany?'[33]

to London.* But in vain. Sir Nevile Henderson was instructed to hand
Hitler a letter from the Prime Minister emphasising the resolution
of Great Britain to defend Poland; but which also promised pacific
satisfaction of German claims. The Führer received the diplomat at
the Berghof on 23 August, the day of the Ribbentrop–Stalin meeting.
No longer having to handle Henderson with care, Hitler permitted
himself the pleasure of provoking him. He had, he said, no longer any
confidence in Chamberlain. England was poisoning the atmosphere
with her guarantee to Poland; she alone made a peaceful settlement
impossible. He gradually worked himself up, giving free rein to his
fury, making the mountain residence resound to his shouting. Far
from standing up to the maniac, Henderson was profuse in almost
servile explications. He thought it right to show his horror of the
Soviets, and he adopted the old plea in favour of close ties with the
Reich. The Führer must know that the Prime Minister shared these
views; had he not proved it by refusing to take the enemies of Germany
like Mr Churchill into his government? The unrest in England was
due to the Jews and a few anti-Nazis; it in no way represented the
feelings of the people.[35]

These honied words did not appear to sweeten Hitler's temper. But
the doors had barely closed behind the British diplomat when he burst
out laughing. To Weizsäcker, the silent witness of this interview, he
cheerfully foretold a ministerial crisis in London. After which, he
withdrew for lunch in the company of one of his English admirers, the
young and silly Miss Unity Mitford. In the afternoon, calmer, if no
more accommodating, he again saw Henderson briefly, to hand over
his written reply.

Prepared for an ultimatum, Chamberlain was waiting for Henderson's message with his wife in the penumbra of his drawing room
in Downing Street 'unable to read, unable to talk, just sitting with
folded hands and a gnawing pain in the stomach'.[36] When the Führer's
letter arrived, less brutal than he had feared, he revived. Sir Horace
Wilson, recently allured by a certain Fritz Hesse, a personal agent of
Ribbentrop's *en poste* in London, was once again employed (at least,
if one is to believe the German) to parade the brilliant prospect of a
treaty of alliance, a redistribution of colonies, vast credits—provided
that Berlin abstained from any act of aggression.[37] Lord Halifax also
persevered in the strangest of ways. To a proposal of Göring's to come

---

* Von Trott had even managed to be received by Chamberlain and Halifax. Like
almost all of his companions, he was to be executed in 1944.

over to England to parley with him, he readily agreed. Fantastic arrangements were made for the landing of a German aircraft on an unused airfield in the neighbourhood of Chequers, the Prime Minister's country house. The only telephone (in the butler's pantry) was to be disconnected, the domestic staff to be sent on leave, and replaced by secret agents to enable Chamberlain and Halifax to meet the Führer's Dauphin in great secrecy—this on that same 23 August when so much happened. Without discouraging the idea, Göring simply failed to turn up. The same day, Halifax again asked Ciano to intervene in Berlin, promising to 'create the conditions for a negotiation between the Germans and Poles'—which necessarily implied the sacrifice of the latter. Two days later, on 25 August, while signing the treaty guaranteeing Poland, Halifax was still speaking of a settlement—even after the outbreak of hostilities, now clearly imminent.[38] At the same time he handed over to Göring's Swedish friend Dahlerus a letter to the Führer, overflowing with protestations of peace and goodwill. As Bonnet had done, he criticized the Poles for 'pacific modification' of the Dantzig statute. He even asked the White House to bring pressure on Warsaw—which President Roosevelt refused to do.[39]

Without being completely informed of these steps, the European Chancelleries were not entirely unaware of them. They had observed— as Henderson had emphasised to Hitler—that Chamberlain was resisting all pressure to include in his government the opponents of appeasement; and that Daladier retained in his, men as ambiguous as Georges Bonnet or Anatole de Monzie. These were scruples which did honour to their theological virtues, but not to their political sense. In the light of the memories of Munich, their solemn promises to fly to the help of their allies were deprived of all plausibility. True or not, Stalin was later to confide to Churchill that he would not have come to terms with the Reich unless he had been convinced that France and Great Britain would not stand up to Hitler. All things considered, Mussolini and Ciano thought exactly the same. In Paris itself, the 'hard' Ministers, Reynaud, Mandel and Zay, had been much concerned by the gloomy mysteries with which Daladier surrounded himself. The 'soft' Minister, Anatole de Monzie, had judged that the preparations for war were only a feint, and that 'France would go no further than mobilisation'.[40] Winston Churchill himself, close to power as he was, feared a new capitulation until the last day—a fear shared by several members of the government and by almost all the House of Commons. Until the last minute Brussels kept wondering about the true intentions of the Allies.

How could the German diplomats have escaped these perplexities? With the prudence of their profession, they drew up circumstantial reports analysing the pros and cons, inclining however to believe that the patience of Paris and London was at an end. Ribbentrop, the great expert on international affairs, brushed aside their advice. The crumbling old Empire, as he put it, would do nothing and, as a result, France would once again give in. In any case Hitler, the absolute master, was not the man to pay much attention to the analyses of his diplomats or to listen to his Ministers. Like Mussolini, he boasted that he took note only of 'the facts which did not hinder the formation of his intuitions'. To all whom he met, he proclaimed that the Reich had nothing to fear from the great democracies. He was to continue repeating this until the first cannon shot—and even afterwards.

Did he still believe this? It is unimportant, for he had clearly passed the point of no return. To Göring, who begged him not to break the bank, he retorted, 'It's the only game I know'. A repetition of Munich which the Franco-British ostensibly offered him, and which would have given him at least Dantzig and the corridor, he no longer wanted. The stake was too small. 'I wager everything for everything,' he told Speer at the beginning of the month. He was aware himself sometimes of the obscure forces which drew him on, and which he could not, or would not, resist. To another of his closest associates, he confided in a kind of despair, 'I am like a traveller who must walk across an abyss on the edge of a razor' [sic] 'But I must do it, quite simply, I must do it.'[41]

★   ★   ★

While all good people were concerned with the getting in of the harvest—the traditional moment for the outbreak of wars—the governments were completing their final preparations. Paris had reassumed its wartime appearance. Long queues formed outside the recruiting centres, thronged with French and foreign volunteers. At night, the street lighting was dimmed and the windows were blacked out, the streets gloomy and deserted. Censorship was reimposed, the Communist newspapers forbidden. Soon, the Communist Party was to be declared illegal.

Long ago, Hitler had set *Day Y* for 26 August 1939. On the 24 August, returning from Berchtesgaden on a cloudless day, he drove in his open Mercedes through a cheerless Berlin. In place of the usual crowds, were only one or two morose looking passers by. On 25 August after a restless night, he awoke in an intensely nervous state.

The troops massed in their assault positions were awaiting the order to attack; he knew that he must give it before 2 p.m. Yet something inexpressible held him back, Everything was ready. The generals had left the War Ministry in the Bendlerstrasse to join their field headquarters. The submarines of the *Kriegsmarine* had gone to sea, lying in wait outside the French and English ports. The two battle-cruisers, *Graf Spee* and *Deutschland* were in the Atlantic. The merchant navy on the Seven Seas had received urgent orders to make for Geman bases, or to take refuge in neutral ports—all precautions which indicated that the hypothesis of war with France and Great Britain had not been excluded. Private communications, radio, telephone and telegraph with foreign countries were cut. Most of the French and Britons living in Germany had left the country.

The weather was stormy, heavy and clammy. In the vast rooms of the Chancellery the tension mounted. The Führer dictated a letter to be telephoned to Rome by special line, to keep the Duce informed (somewhat tardily) of the latest developments. Flanked by Ribbentrop, Himmler, Goebbels, Bormann and liaison officers of the three Services, he went from one to the other, walking in circles around them, unable to make up his mind. A little after midday, he warned the General Staff to be prepared for a delay in operational orders. When he was seated at table lunching with his acolytes, in a sudden fit of inspiration he had the British Ambassador summoned. When the latter arrived, announced by the drum-beats of the guard, Hitler made him an extraordinary offer—as Sir Nevile Henderson reported with his usual perspicacity, 'Calm and normal, speaking with great earnestness and apparent sincerity'. (Could Henderson still believe in his sincerity?) He proposed a treaty of alliance, by which Germany would guarantee the integrity of the British Empire, would recognise as definitive its frontiers, and would agree to a reasonable limitation of armaments. *All this, after the settlement of the German–Polish conflict!* Putting at the disposal of the Ambassador his personal aeroplane, he asked him to fly immediately to London to transmit the offer to His Majesty's Government, 'A most serious but final offer,' he said; 'if rejected, it would mean war'.

How can we understand the obscure thoughts in the Führer's mind? What could he hope for from this strange, absurd proposal, a new version of his old idea of the division of the world? *He did not even give it time to mature.* After having dismissed Henderson and swallowed his vegetables, he went off alone with Ribbentrop for some minutes. At 3.02 p.m. he strode into the great hall where his courtiers

were standing around. 'Pale but composed'— said a witness—he gave
the order to the ADCs for the attack at dawn the following day, after
which, he resumed his aimless waiting attitude, 'motionless at the
table, plunged in gloomy thought'. Towards 6 p.m. after a not very
convincing call to the French Ambassador, something seemed to
explode within him. He came out of his lethargy, calling loudly for
the astonished Generals Brauschitsch, Keitel and Halder (the latter
not to be found), and ordered a stop to everything. The great war
machine was brought to a standstill, the headquarters making strenu-
ous efforts to countermand the orders which were already on their
way to the command posts. The interior debate which had agitated
the Führer was provisionally resolved. But why, how? We do not
know.

Two pieces of bad news received during the afternoon may have
contributed to it—the signature of the Anglo-Polish treaty, which had
long been in gestation, and a letter from Mussolini announcing, in
embarrassed terms, that Italy was not yet ready for war. All the same,
the treaty only confirmed a guarantee which was several months old;
and the anxieties of the Duce had been known to him for some
weeks.* To the bewildered Generals and Göring he limited himself to
explaining that he needed several days 'to eliminate British intervention'. This did not convince them, for they asked what could a
delay of a few days alter? In fact, nothing; nor did Hitler long conceal
it from them. It was not Dantzig and the Corridor which were in
question, but all Poland, which he intended to annihilate, and share
'its rich black lands' with the Soviet Union. On Sunday 27 August, he
summoned the principal dignitaries into the huge Hall of the Ambassadors in the new Chancellery. Uncomposed, his features drawn, his
gaze wandering—witnesses related—he announced in a rambling
speech that he intended, like Frederick the Great, to stake everything
on one throw. 'The war will be hard, perhaps hopeless ... I shall wage
it fiercely ... as long as I live, there will be no talk of capitulation.'[42]

In London, there reigned a certain optimism. Although Chamberlain and his advisers deprecated the 'impudent proposals' brought
back by Sir Nevile Henderson, they could not resist the temptation to
see in them a gesture of goodwill, perhaps even a sign of panic. In

---

* What, on the contrary, Hitler did not know was that a secret protocol extended
the British guarantee to the statute of the Free City of Dantzig. Why was this
concealed from the Germans, instead of being emphasised to them? Doubtless, the
old fear of not 'provoking' them.

concert with the French, they would redouble their efforts to establish direct discussion between Berlin and Warsaw, imagining—one wonders why—that this might lead to a solution. But to what solution? Once again, on 27 August, Lord Halifax's secretary expressed his anxiety in his diary: 'A new Munich on the back of the Poles'.[43] The conduct of the English and French governments was so confused that it is difficult to follow their sinuosities. Probably without fully admitting it, they were thinking of a new retreat without war. 'They are more concerned with making the Poles give in rather than the Germans', stated Joseph Kennedy, the American Ambassador to Britain, father of the future President, and a strong believer in appeasement. In spite of the commitments which Halifax had just contracted, he again pressed the Duce to intervene in Berlin—without informing Paris, even less Warsaw; for 'differences confined to Dantzig and the Corridor can be settled without war'.[44] Daladier sent a letter couched in passionate terms to Hitler. It reaffirmed, it is true, the ties between France and Poland, but at the same time implored 'a last attempt at a peaceful arrangement with Warsaw'.

On Monday 28 August, the order was given to the General Staff of th Reich to tighten belts, in anticipation of *Day Y*, now definitely fixed for 1 September. Simultaneously, the rationing of food and essential products was introduced—soap, clothes, petrol, coal. It was a rude shock for the population, particularly for the older people among them, who had not forgotten the sufferings of 1918. At the end of the afternoon, the French Ambassador was summoned to the Chancellery, It was his last interview with Hitler who, distracted and clearly in a hurry, rapidly read out a letter for Daladier which barred the way to any further hopes. The worthy Coulondre was not to be shown the door in this way. Aware of the solemnity of the occasion, drawing himself up to the full height of his short figure, he put all his feeling into a last exhortation for peace. The Dictator listened to him impatiently. He was moved by it perhaps, so thought the diplomat; but he was certainly not deterred.

When, later in the evening, Henderson, who had returned from London, went in turn to the Chancellery through the darkened streets, he found Hitler in a better mood, courteous and attentive to what he had to say. Yes, said Sir Nevile reading his instructions, Great Britain was still ardently desirous of preserving the friendship of the two countries; but it was conceivable only in terms of peace. Why not negotiate directly with the Poles? The stubborn diplomat, incapable of containing himself, thought it right to add—without being authorised—that an alliance between Germany and his country still seemed possible.[45] A little after midnight, the interview was over. Hitler had promised to think about it, and to see him again the following day.

29 August went by. Henderson had regained his confidence. Summoned to the Chancellery at 7 p.m., he went cheerfully, believing almost that he had saved peace, if not Poland. He was to be disenchanted. The Führer was in a foul temper, and the interview degenerated into an altercation. Nevertheless, Hitler consented grudgingly to direct negotiations with Warsaw, but he demanded the arrival in Berlin of a Polish representative *armed with full powers, within 24 hours.* Although he denied it, this was a veritable ultimatum concerning the cession of Dantzig, the corridor and a part of Silesia—of which latter territory there had never been question until now. As for the modalities, they would be communicated later.

Because there were exorbitant demands, not different from those extorted from Austria and Czechoslovakia, London transmitted them, but without haste, to Warsaw. Paris pressed Colonel Beck to leave immediately for Germany. This would have been a leap into the abyss with which the latter, haunted by the spectres of Schuschnigg and Hacha, would have nothing to do. The Poles remained calm. Displaying a courage not without its elegance, although composed of a good dose of irresponsibility, they managed to believe that Berlin was bluffing and that they could impress it by counter-bluffing.

On the avenues of Warsaw, the *Szwolczeny*, regiments of Light Horse, trotted away, applauded by the populace, chanting patriotic songs. Nothing was done to prepare the defence of the city or to protect it against bombing. Only the foreign diplomats were sure that war was imminent. But Marshall Smigly-Rydz was not worried; he *knew* that if war broke out he would win—his astrologer had predicted it.[46] Colonel Beck, who had retired to bed late after an amorous *tête-à-tête* in his private suite at the Hotel Europeyskí, rose late, having attempted to drown in debauchery the cancer that was devouring him. Not without panache, he now threw on the poker table a new card; ignoring the protestations of the French and British Ambassadors, he ordered general mobilisation—as it was, too late, because the deployment of the Polish Army would not have been completed when the Wehrmacht struck.

★   ★   ★

At midnight on 30 August, the delay fixed by Hitler expired. Summoned for 11 p.m., Sir Nevile Henderson went to the *Auswärtigesamt* an hour later, believing that he would be handed the proposals Hitler had mentioned the day before. Ribbentrop, on the other hand, imagined that he was to receive the surrender of the Poles. A furious row broke out between the two men, both roaring at each other. They leapt about in their chairs, stood up face to face bawling, trembling with rage, breathless, almost coming to blows. When they had managed to calm themselves, the minister of Foreign Affairs took from his pocket a piece of paper on which were written the conditions demanded from Poland, ennumerated in sixteen points, which he recited in German. Still trembling, Henderson did not entirely understand the terms, although he thought he saw a gleam of hope. He asked for a copy of the text, which Ribbentrop arrogantly refused. It was useless he snarled, the points were now null and void, because the Polish plenipotentiaries had not arrived on time. As Hitler later recognised, they were indeed null and void; they had only been, he said 'an alibi primarily for the German people, to show that I had done everything to save the peace'.[47]

Henderson, never a model of self-control, lost all his *sang-froid*. On the evening before, he had already challenged his colleagues Coulondre, Attolico and Lipski, crudely demanding that they should intervene in favour of the despatch of a Polish plenipotentiary to Berlin. After his stormy interview with Ribbentrop, Henderson summoned Lipski in the middle of the night, and told him to ask for an immediate interview with Ribbentrop—'in the sharpest terms' commented the Pole, not without irritation. Although the latter did not obey, he telegraphed to Warsaw the little that Henderson had gathered from Ribbentrop's explanations. It was 2 a.m., and dawn was approaching.

The day broke on Thursday 31 August, warm and sunny, the last day of peace. Even before breakfast, Henderson was again on the telephone to Lipski who, exasperated, sent him one of his subordinates. The meeting was futile, the Englishman having no more to say. In fact, he had come to detest the Poles as much as the Czechs the year before. In his communications, official and private, he attacked them bitterly, demanding that they should capitulate. Were they not the spoil-sports, who were thwarting all his efforts? To London, he cabled that Hitler's proposals were 'very moderate' (without really knowing what they were). 'Warsaw wants to humiliate Germany.'[48]

At 10 a.m., he sent his principal assistant to Lipski, accompanied by Dahlerus. The latter brandished the sixteen points written on a loose sheet of paper which Göring had just given him. Why to this

Swede, who had no official capacity? The two men found the Polish Ambassador's house cluttered with bags and packing cases; they were clearly preparing to leave. Lipski pale and exhausted, on the verge of a nervous breakdown (he was to succumb to it later) listened to them angrily extolling the supposed moderation of the German demands. He disposed of Dahlerus by sending him off to dictate the sixteen points to a secretary in a neighbouring room. He did not conceal his disapproval of Sir Nevile's manner—most unusual and disrespectful of the sovereignity of a friendly country and, to boot, inconsiderate. What result could be expected anyway from the presence of Beck in Berlin, unless it was a repetition of the visit of Schuschnigg and Hacha?

Henderson, grey-faced with fatigue, having hardly slept, was stubborn in his contradictions. He had learned from a source that the German offensive would be launched during the day (he was proved wrong only by a few hours). In his memoirs, he writes that he had no doubt that Poland was condemned; 'she must crawl or get her whipping'.[49] It was the least of his worries. In the afternoon, he visited Göring at Karinhall, and entreated him for two hours to communicate to him *officially* the mythical sixteen points, whose bright prospects German diplomacy had held out. He continued to bombard the Foreign Office with wild telegrams recommending that Warsaw should be instantly brought to surrender—messages which were immediately decyphered by the *Forschungsamt*. He telephoned the Nuncio, the French Ambassador and other colleagues, pressing them to intervene in Warsaw, complaining angrily of obstruction by the Poles who, for 'a point of procedure', were endangering the peace of the world— conversations which were also intercepted by the German special services. In the evening, in a lively telephone discussion, he opposed Coulondre, who had taken the liberty of remarking that Warsaw still had not received any official communication of the 'sixteen points'. According to the *Forschungsamt*, the conversation finished with an exchange of the grossest insults.[50]

The last days of peace ended with the powerless spectators, Pope Pius XII, President Roosevelt, the King of the Belgians, the Queen of the Netherlands making fresh appeals, which were not listened to.* In Moscow, Molotov had the German–Soviet pact ratified by the Supreme Soviet. He delivered violent attacks against the French and British, while celebrating the lasting friendship between the Soviet Union and the Third Reich. The armies took up their final positions;

---

*Pope Pius XI, who died in February 1939, had been succeeded by Pius XII, Cardinal Pacelli, the former Nuncio in Munich and Berlin (1927–1930).

the peoples of Europe bowed their heads, while waiting for the bombs to fall from the sky.

★   ★   ★

However, all was not over. Since the beginning of the summer, the Duce had found himself at bay. He did not know which side to join. Like a weather-cock he followed the wind, changing his opinion from hour to hour; in the morning, terrified at having to fight with 'an army lacking shirts and guns, shoes and shells'; in the evening, horrified at betraying his honour and duty, or appearing a coward. Sometimes, he was convinced that the democracies would capitulate, and he feared to miss sharing the booty; he also feared the wrath of the Führer, and perhaps a German attack on Italy. He felt that events were overtaking him. Deprived of real advisers, he found comfort only in his mistress, the faithful little Petacci, with whom his relations for three years had acquired an almost conjugal nature. In reality, he was ill, gravely ill. Those nearest to him attributed his troubles to a return of his old illness; 'He should submit to an intensive anti-syphilis cure', recommended the Chief of the secret police to Ciano. His stomach ulcer made him suffer cruelly. One of his Ministers discovered him one evening in the grandiose surroundings of the Palazzo Venezia, lying on the floor writhing with pain, clenching his fists to avoid shrieking. It was said that he had recourse to morphine to assuage his sufferings. Sumner Welles, the American Under Secretary of State, described him in February 1940 as 'fifteen years older than his actual age of fifty-six.' He was ponderous and static rather than vital. He moved with an elephantine motion; every step appeared an effort.[51]

When on 31 August, the Duce was informed by his Ambassador in Germany that everything was about to explode, he threw caution to the wind, hoping to repeat the role of mediator, which he had assumed so successsfully at Munich. For several days, he had been besieged by the French and British Ambassadors entreating him (in secret, and independently) either to remain neutral, or to persuade Hitler to content with Dantzig and the Corridor. Now he instructed Ciano to propose a four-power conference at San Remo for 5 September, to 'revise the clauses of Versailles, which are at the origin at the present troubles'.

Chamberlain and Daladier were in no better form. After an interview with his colleague, Daladier said, 'He seemed broken . . . a man, who had passed from middle age into decrepitude'. He himself was worn-out, indecisive, badly supported by drink. The Italian proposal, although the logical sequence of their approaches to Rome, left them perplexed. At 3.30 p.m., Daladier told the British Ambassador that he would resign rather than accept it. However, at a Council of Ministers summoned for 6 p.m. at the Elysée, although he had a furious argument with Georges Bonnet, he made little attempt to impose his will. 'He turned his back on him for the first moment. His face wore a sulky look of scorn and disgust', stated one of his Ministers. During the session, Daladier read out a letter he had just received from Coulondre describing Hitler as ready to withdraw, and recommending the greatest firmness, Although the Ministers appeared impressed, he ended the meeting without any clear desision being taken.[52]

In fact the initiative lay with Berlin. At almost the same time Ribbentrop, his jaw set, his chin protruding, was facing the Polish Ambassador. Without offering him a seat, he listened to Lipski telling him that 'the Polish government was favourably examining the opening of direct discussions with the Reich'. He would answer no questions, not a word about the sixteen points. Almost immediately afterwards, he rudely showed the Pole the door, on the pretext that he did not have 'full powers'. Lipski returned to his Embassy to find his telephone cut; he could no longer communicate with his government.

The die was cast. Several hours before, the Führer, beaming, all his liveliness returned, signed the 'Directive No: 1 for the Conduct of the War', specifying the next day for the attack on Poland. A special scenario was put on by SS to stimulate German patriotism. At Gleiwitz, a large village on German territory near the frontier, a German detachment wearing false Polish uniforms took possession of a small radio station; they seized the microphone to shriek anti-Nazi insults, before disappearing into the night. For good measure, some German corpses were left lying on the ground—the bodies of prisoners put to death in the Sachsenhausen concentration camp. In Dantzig, the 'Gauleiter' proclaimed the return of the Free City to the Reich. Throughout Germany, the radio interrupted its programmes dramatically to announce 'the odious aggression of which the Reich is a victim'. It broadcasted the Führer's alleged 'proposals of peace'—the same that Ribbentrop had declared null and void to Henderson, and which he then finally communicated officially to the Western Ambassadors—but too late for them to be taken into consideration.

On 1 September 1939 at 4.45 a.m., as planned in April, 'Operation White' was on. Without a declaration of war, the *Feldgrau* columns began the assault across the frontier. At 6 a.m., the Luftwaffe let all hell loose on the Polish airfields, and soon on the Polish towns. In General Halder's diary is this entry for this day, 'The Führer is calm . . . he has slept well'.[53]

★   ★   ★

On arriving in the Rue de la Loi that morning, just after 9 a.m., I again found the feverish agitation which went with serious crises: visits of Ambassadors, comings and goings in the corridors, doors opening and slamming, telephones ringing—it was chaos. Although still not precise, the radio left no room for doubt; in Poland it was war. However, no one yet knew what the French and British would do. Would they once again capitulate to blackmail? Or would they at last stand up to the aggression?

All day, the tocsin of general mobilisation had sounded from the bell-towers of France. In Great Britain, too, the Fleet, the Air Force and the Army were openly preparing for war. The *casus foederis* was only too clear, the two great Democracies were bound by their promises and treaties to declare war *immediately* on Germany. But by midnight everything was still unclear. The Duce, reneging on the Pact of Steel, proclaimed himself 'non-belligerent'. This was comforting news; but not enough to give Paris and London the courage to reject the proposal for a conference to which Hitler, for his part, had said neither Yes nor No.

In the morning, the French Foreign Minister received the Polish Ambassador, and told him rather offhandedly that his government could not act without Parliament—it had been convened without haste for the next day. Bonnet persisted in demanding a conference, which a new Council of Ministers had not formally rejected. In London, Halifax, although more courteous, had been no less vague with the Polish envoy. But his freedom of action was more limited. Recalled from its vacation, the House of Commons displayed emotion and anger. Sharing the same exasperation, the Ministers were no longer in the mood to be gulled. In a sitting at the end of the morning, they had decided that there would be no more talks, so long as German troops remained on Polish soil. Chamberlain and Halifax had to agree. During the afternoon they persuaded Daladier, and even Bonnet, to notify the Reich that, failing an evacuation of Poland, a general war could not be avoided. However, it was emphasised that this was not an ultimatum, only a *warning*.

In Berlin, the Reichstag had assembled at 10 a.m. in the Kroll Opera

House, for one of those spectacular sittings which had marked the six years of the Hitler regime. The Ambassadors were in the diplomatic box to honour the Head of State. Those of France and Great Britain were absent; but strangely enough, they had felt obliged to send a deputy at the death ceremony of their ally. The Führer wearing the Feldgrau uniform of a simple soldier, substituted for the first time for his usual brown jacket, mounted the rostrum to announce, without any more ado, to an auditorium less excited than usual, that he had, 'been forced to take up arms to assure the defence of the Reich'. Alluding to his uniform, 'which is to me the dearest and most sacred thing', he ended with the prophetic words, 'I shall not take it off until the final victory—or when I shall be no more'.

The session was soon over and the Nazi dignitaries emerged into the street. To be received by a heavy silence among a scattered public, noted the diplomats, observing along the boulevards the interminable flow of troops moving eastward, on foot or in a variety of vehicles, military cars, delivery vans and all kinds of requisitioned trucks. This time, as in Paris, no flowers embellished the rifles—'In the streets along which I deliberately went on foot,' wrote Robert Coulondre, 'none of the patriotic fervour, the bellicose enthusiasm of the 1914 war . . . from all the information I have obtained, the events have surprised the population and caused anxiety, even consternation'. His Belgian colleague, Vicomte Davignon, also mentioned, 'the extraordinarily defeatist talk heard by my colleagues and myself'. Nevertheless, he added that, although the German people wanted only peace, they had discipline in their blood, and would fight courageously.[54]

Returning from the Kroll Opera House to the Chancellery, Hitler was very irritated at the absence of enthusiasm among the crowds. He was joined by Göring and Dahlerus, who insisted on taking the latest development in London seriously. By so doing they triggered off one of those strange crises of hysterical fury, which Hitler increasingly proved unable too control. Besides himself, frantically waving his arms—said Dahlerus—he roared that he would make war on the English and would annihilate them, whether it took one year, two years, three years, ten years. Brandishing his fists in the gesture of crushing them, his burlesque mimicry caused his body to crouch down almost to floor level.[55] In the afternoon, his calm restored, he caused the train which has to take him to the *Führer–hauptquartier* in Pomerania, to wait until he had received Attolico; he did not appear in the least affected by a message from the Duce confirming that Italy would, provisionally, remain outside the conflict. He lingered in the Chancellery, holding forth before his courtiers, railing against the diplomats, maintaining that the French and English would abandon Poland without fighting. He also signed a document ordering 'merciful death' for incurables in hospitals—the first step in a great carnage.*

In the democratic countries, resigned to their destiny, the joyless but firm public opinion brought pressure on the still timid governments. In London sand-bags were piled against the façades of the principal monuments. Captive barrage balloons floated in the clear sky. Citizens went about their business carrying gasmasks. In Paris, horses and requisitioned vehicles passed along the streets driven by soldiers. Around the Gare de l'Est thronged men recalled to the colours, haversacks swinging from their shoulders, calm and resigned, accompanied by their parents and fiancées. They took their places in trains with windows painted in blue, which carried them off to the frontiers. In Brussels on the other hand, few signs in the streets foretold the tragedy which lay ahead.

There was vaguely question of mediation by General Ironside, the future Chief of the British Imperial General Staff. Apart from official diplomacy, Dahlerus kept on crossing the Channel back and forth, carrying at the highest level, conciliatory and vague messages. Hitler, playing for time as the Wehrmacht penetrated deeper in Poland, did not stop it. It seems that he had ordered Fritz Hesse to promise Sir Horace Wilson that he would evacuate Polish territory and pay for the damage, in exchange for Dantzig and a road through the Corridor. It was such an improbable suggestion, that even the credulous 'Père Joseph' did not take it seriously. When night fell on a Berlin at war, Ribbentrop received, without apparent emotion, the Ambassadors of France and Great Britain, who came to hand over the 'warning' of their governments which, they indicated politely according to their instructions, was not an ultimatum.

In Warsaw, panic succeeded self-confidence. The first clashes revealed a German military potential of which the Poles had never dreamed. In a few hours, the Luftwaffe had established complete mastery of the air. Flooding in from East Prussia, Pomerania, Silesia and Slovakia, German divisions, emerging from the autumnal mist, spread out across the country, and battered the Polish troops massed foolheartedly on the frontiers. In the Brühl Palace, the splendid marble Ministry of Foreign Affairs, Colonel Beck, dragged from his bed,

---

*A note of April 1939 of the Gestapo also mentions that more than 300,000 political opponents were in prison—Jews not included.[56]

discovered in a moment the full extent of his impotence. Interrupted continuously by air alerts, and the explosion of German bombs falling on the periphery of the city, he summoned the friendly Ambassadors, who could only raise their arms in desperation. No strategic plan coordinating operations with the Allies existed. No organised liaison had been planned with the Western capitals. The distances were too great for normal radio communication. Telephone and telegram communications, which passed normally through Berlin, was cut; all that operated still very indistinctly were a few lines relayed through Bucharest or the Scandinavian cities. The Polish governmental machine had come to a full stop. Foreign diplomats accredited to Warsaw have not forgotten the fearful hours during which, beside the suddenly disillusioned Poles, they felt quite alone, almost without instructions, cut off from the civilised world, in a universe which was crashing down about them.[57]

On Saturday 2 September, the fighting continued on the plain of the Vistula. Cracow, Poznan, Kattowice, Warsaw were crushed under bombs, while the Allied capitals floundered. The Polish Ambassador in Paris returned to the Quai d'Orsay, but left it in despair, furious at being unceremoniously shown the door by Georges Bonnet. The latter, although unprincipled, was not unintelligent. To the American Ambassador, he declared that, unlike at Munich, he did not believe in, 'the least chance of peace'.[58] However, he continued to demand a Conference, and promised Ciano on the telephone that France would abstain from any act of war until Sunday—while awaiting an agreement with Hitler. What was he plotting? We do not know. For nothing indicated the least good will on the part of Berlin. On the other hand, Colonel Beck who had to be invited, let it be known that he would not come. Meanwhile, in London, Lord Halifax said he could no longer negotiate; public opinion would not allow it, except in the most unlikely case of a complete withdrawal of German troops from Poland.

This was an explicit condition of the 'warning' the day before. Who could be deceived? At the beginning of the afternoon, Daladier confirmed it emphatically at the Parliamentary tribune. One of the best speeches of his career, it was approved with a rousing ovation, without a debate and almost unanimously, including the extreme Right and the Communists, Thorez at their head. He obtained great support 'to face the obligations of the international situation'. It was an unequivocal authorisation to engage in hostilities. In the *Chambre* only one Deputy, the radical Gaston Bergery, and in the Senate only Pierre Laval, had vainly attempted to oppose it. A superb example of patriotism, it was regrettable that it did not go as far as a formal declaration of war. But such was Parliamentary tradition; although in conformity with the Constitution, it did not lack a certain grandeur.*

'A reed painted to look like iron,' it was said of Daladier. The paint had peeled off, and the reed was swaying. Three hours later, he astounded another meeting of the Cabinet by taking the side of the supporters of a conference, promising however that it must not take place before the withdrawal of the German troops. But what withdrawal? Had he forgotten the 'warning' of the day before, which demanded the prompt evacuation *from Polish territory*, a demand repeated in his parliamentary speech? Or was he so ingenuous as to believe that Hitler would agree to it? For his Minister of Foreign Affairs, a cease-fire *on the positions occupied* (the Italian proposal) would have been enough. Telephoning at the beginning of the afternoon to Ciano and Bonnet, Halifax left them under no illusions. He did not see how 'one could resuscitate a corpse with holy water'.[59] This was strong language, dictated to him by the state of mind of the Cabinet. Assembled for the second time that day at 4.30 p.m., his exasperated colleagues demanded a categorical and immediate ultimatum to Berlin. Halifax and Chamberlain, with the knife at their backs, had to agree, obtaining only with great difficulty a certain flexibility in a delay, to enable them to concert their action with Paris. Nevertheless, no less than the French Ministers, they had not entirely abandoned hope of appeasing the ogre of Berlin.

During the last hours of the day excitement reached its peak. Ambassadors rushed to and fro, international telephones rang, telegrams flew back and forth. Lord Halifax appealed yet again to Ciano to persuade the Führer to withdraw the German troops to their original positions; the dialogue with Warsaw could then be reopened with the mediation of the British. But Mussolini's son-in-law refused to transmit a proposal which he clearly saw had not the least chance of being accepted. 'Do your best,' Halifax recommended him politely, before hanging up the receiver.[60] Halifax did not mind these contradictions. At about the same time, he spoke to his French counterpart (and Chamberlain after him) to suggest the despatch of a final ultimatum to Berlin by the two powers during the night. But what a surprise! At the exact moment when for the first time London wanted

---

* The procedure conformed however to usage. No more than the Chamber of Deputies, the British Parliament in 1914 as in 1939 was not called upon to vote a declaration of war. This was the prerogative of the Executive.

to act, Paris jibbed. Although Mussolini himself had realised, while this was going on, that any conference was impossible, Bonnet stuck to it. Daladier did not react. Was he terrified by the extent of his responsibilities? Or embittered with the British, who would not be able to give substantial military aid for a long time? It is not clear. But procrastination was in his character. He had discovered a good pretext; General Gamelin demanded that general mobilisation must be completed before engaging in hostilities, alleging the danger of aerial bombardment—a non-existent threat, because almost all the enemy airforce was in Poland.

Chamberlain and Halifax now felt hemmed in. Uncertain of what was happening in Paris, they had the awful fear that Great Britain might find herself alone, without an army, fighting a war against the Reich. But they could not draw back. Already, the day before, the House of Commons had shown itself distrustful and impatient. The Prime Minister had had to promise that he would explain himself. Assembled that same 2 September 1939 at 3 p.m., the narrow benches were crowded to the full. The House was nervous, prey to an intolerable suspense, waiting impatiently for the tardy arrival of Chamberlain. The weather was sultry, the vast windows were streaked at intervals by the lambent flashes of a storm outside which would not break. Through the windows of the corridors opening onto the Thames, the M.P.s could see the barrage balloons protecting the city, which had been lowered on account of the bad weather.

The news was not reassuring. The communiqués from the belligerents, picked up partially by the BBC, presented an alarming picture, Polish road and railway networks had been cut by aerial bombardment. Their communications gone, the Polish armies fought heroically, but they could not stand up to the Wehrmacht. The Corridor had fallen. German advance-guards had occupied Upper Silesia. The rare radio reports from Warsaw told of a torrent of bombs and innumerable civilian casualties. For 48 hours, the Polish Ambassador and his assistants ran from right to left, calling on the politicians, imploring them to respect their pledges, emphasising that it was essential to take military action to relieve the Polish forces, until the arrival of the autumn rains. In the corridors of Westminster, the rumour went round that the French Government had refused to intervene. Was the Prime Minister about to find another pretext for giving in? Where was he anyway? What was he up to?

Towards 7.45 p.m., Chamberlain at last appeared on the front bench. The good Lord had deserted the old man. Worn out by a terrible day, carried away by events which submerged him, encouraged in his irresolution, as much as embarrassed by the indecisiveness of Paris, in a toneless voice he launched into an ambiguous explication. The House became exasperated when he spoke of fresh proposals in the event of retreat by the German troops, and when he referred in unclear terms to a conference proposed by Mussolini. 'We expected one of his dramatic surprises', wrote Harold Nicolson. 'But none came, it was evident when he sat down, that no decision had been arrived at.' For a moment the House remained stunned. Was it all going to finish with another Munich? When the spokesman for the opposition, the Socialist Arthur Greenwood, got up to call on the government, for the sake of national honour, to act immediately, he was greeted from all the benches, the Right as well as the Left, with applause and cries of approval. If a vote had been taken that night, the government would have fallen.[61]

More extraordinary was the pugnacity suddenly adopted by the principal Ministers. Shortly after Greenwood's speech they assembled in the office of Sir John Simon. The archpriest of the 'appeasers' had gone over in a matter of minutes to lead the resisters. Considering themselves duped, they announced that they would not leave Westminster until war had been declared; a real 'sit-in strike'. After a painful interview with the Prime Minister, they handed him a letter demanding in the most imperative terms an immediate ultimatum—with or without France—expiring at the latest the next day Sunday, at noon.

At the Quai d'Orsay and the Foreign Office, in the Rue Saint Dominique and Downing Street, the lights burned all night behind the thick curtains which blacked-out the windows. Anguished messages were exchanged between the two capitals. The British Ministers became more and more nervous; those in Paris braced themselves desperately to postpone by a few hours the plunge into Hades. Bonnet had never renounced, so he claimed, his wish 'to save the peace'. Later in the evening, he let it be known in Rome that *symbolic withdrawal* of German troops would permit the mythical conference of San Remo to take place. 'A suggestion,' wrote Ciano in his diary, 'that I put in the waste-paper basket, without even consulting the Duce'.[62]

Chamberlain, confused by the unexpected revolt of Ministers who had never failed for years to obey him blindly, felt the earth crumbling beneath his feet. Lord Halifax was unaware of the crisis which had developed in the Commons, In dinner jacket, he was preparing to join friends with his wife, when he was summoned urgently to Downing

Street. Informed of events, he realised that the government was condemned if it did not declare war with the shortest possible delay. Chamberlain could hold out no longer. At 11.30 p.m. the Ministers were summoned to Downing Street. The 'strikers', sitting it out in the House of Commons, set out for No. 10 on foot, soaked by the torrential rain which had begun to pour. After having listened to his almost unanimous colleagues the Prime Minister, in appearance 'calm and even icy cold' concluded, 'Right, Gentlemen, this means war'. To complete the tragic *mise en scène*, the storm which had been rumbling since the afternoon suddenly burst in full fury. 'The most enormous clap of thunder,' recounted a member of the Cabinet, 'the whole room was lit up by a blinding flash of lightning. It was the most deafening thunder-clap I've every heard in my life. It really shook the building'.[63]

Telephone conversations with Paris went on until a late hour. In the middle of the night, Daladier yielded to the exhortations of London. General Gamelin supported him; consulted again, he discovered that general mobilisation was sufficiently advanced to allow him to face the enemy. The two governments finally agreed to proclaim a state of war with Germany on Sunday 3 September 1939—London at 11 a.m., Paris, for no very clear reason, perhaps to display independence, at 5 p.m. The Ambassadors carried out their dramatic gestures; following ancient usage, they went to 'ask for their passports', not without doing it separately, the Englishman at 9 a.m., the Frenchman at midday.

When, in the bright morning sunshine, Dr Schmidt, who had come from the nearby Wilhelmstrasse, brought to the Chancellor the ultimatum which Sir Nevile Henderson had just handed him and which he slowly read out in German, a deathly silence fell in the huge study. 'The Führer', recounted Schmidt, 'remained seated at his table as if petrified, his gaze fixed, without saying a word, without making a gesture. After a moment, which seemed an eternity, he turned to Ribbentrop, who was standing immobile in a window recess. "And now?" he hissed between his teeth, a flash of fury in his eyes.'[64]

Sources

The general perspective of the book and many of its sources are due to the author's experience during the late Thirties in the private office of Belgium's Foreign Minister; Brussels, located at the strategic cross-roads of Europe, was at the time a central observation post. They are supplemented by the documents published by the governments involved in the events and by oral and written testimonies. The principal official sources used are listed below:

British Foreign Policy 1919 to 1939. Her Majesty's Stationery Office, London.

Belgian Diplomatic Documents 1920–1940. Academie Royal de Belgique, Brussels 1964 & 1965.

Documents on German Foreign Policy 1918–1945 Series C & D. US Department of State, Washington 1957–1966.

French Diplomatic Documents 1932–1939. First and Second Series 1932–35/1936–39, Paris 1963–67.

Foreign Relations of the United States. US Department of State, Washington.

SOURCE NOTES BY CHAPTERS

Chapter 1   *The War in China and the Great Depression*

1. Lord d'Abernon, *Diary*, London 1929, Vol. II, p. 24.
2. M. Gilbert, *The Roots of Appeasement*, London 1966, p. 232. *Also*: F. Seydoux, *Mémoires d'Outre-Rhin*, Paris 1975, p. 35.
3. A. J. P. Taylor, *English History 1914–1945*, London, Penguin Books, p. 501. *Also*: H. Nicolson, *Diaries and Letters 1930–1964*, London 1980, p. 34.
4. K. Middlemas & J. Barnes, *Baldwin*, London 1969, p. 211. *Also*: Lord Baldwin, *My Father, The True Story*, London 1955; H. Montgomery Hyde, *Baldwin, The Unexpected Prime Minister*, London 1973; H. L'Etang, *Fit to Lead*, London 1980; H. Macmillan, *The Past Masters*, London 1975, p. 108.

5. A. L. Rowse, *The End of an Epoch*, London 1947, pp. 74–89.

6. A. J. P. Taylor, Op. cit., p. 467.

7. C. L. R. Attlee, *The Labour Party in Perspective*, London 1937, p. 227.

8. J. Néré, *The Foreign Policy of France from 1914 to 1945*, London 1975, p. 158.

9. P. O. Lapie, *Herriot*, Paris 1967, pp. 239, 255. *Also*: A. Guerin, *La Vie quotidienne au Palais, Bourbon á la Fin de la Ire Republique*, Paris 1978, p. 51.

10. E. Herriot, *Jadis*, Paris 1948, Vol. I, pp. 120, 234.

11. A. Hudson, *The Far East in World Politics*, London 1937, p. 180.

12. Lord Vansittart, *The Mist Procession*, London 1958, pp. 437, 523. *Also*: C. Barnett, *The Collapse of British Power*, London 1972, p. 302.

13. A. C. Temperley, *The Whispering Gallery of Europe*, London 1938, p. 182.

14. J. Stevenson & Ch. Cook, *The Slump*, London 1977, p. 2. *Also*: C. L. Mowat, *Britain between the Wars 1918–1939*, London 1968, p. 483; B. S. Rowntree, *Poverty and Progress*, London 1941, pp. 103, 104.

15. H. Macmillan, *Winds of Change*, London 1966, pp. 284–294.

16. Ch. Fohlen, *The Fontana Economic History of Europe: France 1920–1970*, London 1973, p. 19 and following. *Also*: Y. Trotignon, *La France au XXe Siècle*, Paris 1968, p. 90 and following.

17. W. Guttmann & P. Meehan, *The Great Inflation*, Westmeath 1975. *Also*: M. Baumont, *La Faillité de la Paix 1918–19*, Paris 1967, p. 339; E. Weill-Raynal, *Les Réparations allemandes et France*, Paris 1946.

18. J. W. Wheeler-Bennett, *Knaves, Fools and Heroes*, London 1974, p. 46.

19. W. Laqueur, *Weimar, A Cultural History*, New York 1974, p. 254 and following.

20. R. Martin du Gard, *Les Thibault, La Mort du Père*, Paris 1934, pp. 180, 183.

21. H. Brüning, *Mémoires (1918–1934)*, Paris 1970, p. 202. *Also*: D. R. McCoy, *Coming of Age*, London 1973, p. 205.

22. D. Marquand, Op. cit., p. 551.

23. Diana Cooper, Conversations with the Author. *Also*: Duc de Brissac, *En d'autres Temps 1900–1939*, Paris 1972, p. 202.

24. Drieu La Rochelle, *Gilles*, Paris, Livre de Poche, p. 437.

Chapter 2   *Totalitarian Bewilderment*

1. Ch. Maurras, *Le Mont de Saturne*, Paris 1950, p. 187.

2. J. McCearney, *Maurras et son Temps*, Paris 1974, pp. 24–141.

3. P. Monelli, *Mussolini: An Intimate Life*, London 1953, p. 272. *Also*: E. Ludwig, *Entretiens avec Mussolini*, Paris 1932, pp. 50–52.

4. A. Balabanov, *My Life as a Rebel*, London 1938, p. 57 and following. *Also*: C. Hibbert, *Benito Mussolini*, Penguin Books 1975, p. 52.

5. C. Hibbert, Op. cit., p. 26. *Also*: P. Monelli, Op. cit., p. 32; G. Ciano, *Diary 1939–1943*, London 1947, p. 189; I. Kirkpatrick, *Mussolini—Study of a Demagogue*, London 1964, p. 64 and following.

6. D. M. Smith, *Mussolini's Roman Empire*, New York 1976, p. 2.

7. E. Ludwig, Op. cit., p. 96.

8. P. Guichonnet, *Mussolini et le Fascisme*, Paris 1966, p. 32. *Also*: A. Balabanov, Op. cit., p. 61, pp. 116–117, pp. 123–124; Ch. Hibbert, Op. cit., pp. 127–128, p. 134.

9. E. Ludwig, Op. cit., p. 240.

10. Dr W. C. Langer, *Psychoanalyse de Adolf Hitler*, Paris 1972, pp. 105 and 108. *Also*: E. Haufstaengl, *The Missing Years*, London 1957.

11. H. Hoffman, *Hitler was my Friend*, London 1955, p. 145. *Also*: E. Haufstaengl,

Op. cit., p. 162 and following; R. G. L. Waite, *The Psychopathic God Adolf Hitler*, New York 1977, p. 233 and following; W. Moser, *Hitler*, New York 1973, p. 194.

12. J. P. Stern, *Hitler*, London 1976, p. 36. *Also*: J. Fest, *Hitler*, Paris 1973, Vol. I, p. 387; J. Amsler, *Hitler*, Paris 1960, p. 58; R. G. L. Waite, Op. cit., p. 28.

13. R. G. L. Waite, Op. cit., pp. 77 and 83. *Also*: H. Rauschning, *Hitler m'a dit*, Paris 1939, p. 21.

14. H. R. Trevor-Roper, *The Last Days of Hitler*, London 1947, pp. 4 and 5. *Also*: R. G. L. Waite, Op. cit., p. 391 and following; J. P. Stern, Op. cit., p. 198 and following.

15. H. Rauschning, Op. cit., p. 251; W. Maser, Op. cit., pp. 170 and 174; R. G. L. Waite, Op. cit., p. 27.

16. A. Hitler, *Mein Kampf*, Trans. J. Murphy, London 1939, p. 273. *Also*: A. Bullock, *Hitler*, London 1952, p. 34.

17. A. Speer, *L'Empire SS*, Paris 1982. *Also*: K. Hillebrand, *The Foreign Policy of the Third Reich*, Los Angeles 1973, p. 118; S. Haffner, *The Meaning of Hitler*, London 1979.

Chapter 3   *The Great Fear of the Decent People*

1. P. Fleming, *The Fate of Admiral Kolchak*, London 1963, p. 124.
2. P. Drieu La Rochelle, *Le Jeune Européen*, Paris 1978, pp. 24, 203.
3. S. Hynes, *The Auden Generation*, London 1976. *Also*: A. Hamilton, *L'Illusion Fasciste*, Paris 1971, p. 248; R. Griffiths, *Fellow-Travellers of the Right*, London 1980.
4. Ch. Plisnier, *Faux Passeports*, Paris 1946, p. 29. *Also*: D. Desanti, *Drieu La Rochelle ou le Séducteur mystifié*, Paris 1978, p. 300; A. Gide, *Journal 1889–1939*, Paris, p. 1116.
5. F. Andreu, *Le Rouge et le Blanc*, Paris 1977, p. 93.
6. L. Rebatet, *Les Décombres*, Paris 1942, p. 30.

Chapter 4   *Hitler's First Successes*

1. A. Fontaine, *Histoire de la Guerre Froide*, Paris 1965, Vol. I, p. 91. *Also*: Ph. Robrieux, *Maurice Thorez*, Paris 1975, p. 174.
2. E. Weber, *L'Action Française*, Paris 1962, p. 315.
3. J. W. Wheeler-Bennett, *Munich, Prologue to Tragedy*, London 1948, p. 243 and following.
4. D. Marquand, *Ramsay MacDonald*, London 1977, pp. 749, 796. *Also*: M. Mac-Donald, *Titan and Others*, London 1972, p. 47.
5. J. W. Wheeler-Bennet, Op. cit., p. 243 and following. *Also*: M. Gilbert, *The Wilderness Years*, London 1981, pp. 125–126.
6. E. Weber, Op. cit., p. 315.
7. M. Cowling, *The Impact of Hitler*, Cambridge 1975, p. 147. *Also*: H. Montgomery Hyde, *Baldwin*, London 1973, p. 357; J. L. Garvin, *Observer*, London 15 March 1936.
8. J. W. Wheeler-Bennett, *Nemesis of Power*, London 1967. *Also*: J. Fest, *Hitler*, Paris 1973, Vol. II, p. 12; W. Deist, *The Wehrmacht and German Rearmament*, London 1981, p. 30.
9. H. Rauschning, *Hitler m'a dit*, Paris 1969, p. 127.
10. A. Bérard, *Un Ambassadeur se souvient*, Paris 1975, p. 223.
11. D. Carlton, *Anthony Eden*, London 1981, p. 45.

12. S. Baldwin, *Discours à la Chambre des Communes*, 12 November 1936.
13. P. Hymans, *Mémoires*, Bruxelles 1958, p. 674.
14. Fr. Wagner, *The Royal Family of Bayreuth*, London 1948, p. 99,
15. O. Mosley, *My Life*, London 1968, p. 359.
16. Fr. von Papen, *Memoirs*, London 1952, p. 246. *Also*: E. Starhemberg, *Between Hitler and Mussolini*, London 1942, pp. 168, 171; J. Gunther, *Inside Europe*, London 1940, p. 411; G. E. R. Gedye, *Fallen Bastions*, London 1939.

Chapter 5　*Roosevelt and the New Deal*

1. D. R. McCoy, *Coming of Age*, Penguin Books 1973, p. 116. *Also*: G. Saule, *Prosperity Decade: from War to Depression 1917–1929*, New York 1947 J. Reston, *Prelude to Victory*, New York 1942.
2. D. R. McCoy, Op. cit., p. 149.
3. K. Galbraith, *The Great Crash*, Boston 1961, p. 180 and following. *Also*: The Economist, *Dollar at the Summit*, London 1981, p. 13.
4. W. Manchester, *The Glory and the Dream*, New York 1975, p. 23.
5. W. A. Harriman, *Special Envoy*, London 1976, p. 54.
6. J. Gunther, *Roosevelt in Retrospect*, London 1950, pp. 121, 126. *Also*: W. A. Harriman, Op. cit., p. 19; C. Morgan, *F.D.R.*, London 1986, p. 399.
7. Earl of Avon, *The Eden Memoirs—The Reckoning*, London 1965, p. 373.
8. J. Gunther, Op. cit., p. 135. *Also*: R. Lacour-Gayet, *Histoire des Etats-Unis*, Paris 1974, Vol. II, p. 238; Fr. Perkins, *The Roosevelt I Knew*, New York 1946; A. O'Hare McCormick, *New York Times*, 15 August 1937; R. T. McTire, *Twenty Years with Roosevelt*, London 1948.
9. E. Lacour-Gayet, Op. cit., Vol. I, p. 232 and following.

Chapter 6　*The Brief Halt at Stresa*

1. P. Daye, *Mémoires—Le Dossier du Mois*, Brussels, December 1963, p. 7. *Also*: M. de Wilde, *L'Ordre Nouveau*, Brussels 1984, p. 25 and following.
2. A. J. P. Taylor, *English History 1914–1945*, Penguin Books 1973, p. 502 and following; Ch. L. Mowat, *Britain Between the Wars*, London 1968, pp. 571, 628; J. Hobécourt, *Une Histoire Politique de l'Armée*, Paris 1967, p. 210; H. Rosinski, *The German Army*, New York 1966; W. Carr, *Arms, Autarchy and Aggression*, New York 1973.
3. J. B. Duroselle, *Histoire diplomatique de 1919 à nos Jours*, Paris 1974, p. 180. *Also*: A. François-Poncet, *Souvenirs d'une Ambassade à Berlin*, Paris 1946, p. 232.
4. P. Schmidt, Hitler's Interpreter, London 1951, p. 18. *Also*: Earl of Avon, *The Eden Memoirs—Facing the Dictators*, London 1962, p. 132 and following.
5. Earl of Avon, Op. cit., p. 139.
6. W. K. Wark, *The Ultimate Enemy*, London 1985.
7. F. Donaldson, *Edward VIII*, London 1974, p. 194.
8. C. M. Young, *Stanley Baldwin*, London 1952, p. 63. *Also*: K. Middlemas & J. Barnes, *Baldwin*, London 1965, p. 793; T. Jones, *A Diary with Letters 1931–1950*, London 1969, p. 241.
9. F. W. Winterbotham, *The Nazi Connection*, London 1978, p. 51 and following; p. 83, Conversations with the Author.
10. J. Fest, *Hitler*, Paris 1973. *Also*: K. Middlemas & J. Barnes, Op. cit., p. 947; W. K. Wark, Op. cit., p. 144.
11. M. Privat, *Pierre Laval, Cet Inconnu*, Paris 1948. *Also*: G. Bechtel, *Laval, Vingt*

Ans Après, Paris 1963, p. 300 and following; J. Clermont, *L'Homme qu'il fallait tuer*, Paris 1949.
12. J. Clermont, Op. cit., p. 221. *Also*: G. Bechtel, Op. cit., pp. 110–111, 141.
13. L. Noël, *Les Illusions de Stresa*, Paris 1975, pp. 34, 31, 50. *Also*: J. Colville, *The Fringes of Power*, London 1985, p. 74.
14. A. François-Poncet, Op. cit., p. 235.

Chapter 7   *The Ethiopian War*

1. J. Morris, *Farewell the Trumpets*, London 1978, p. 115. *Also*: *Pax Britannica*, London 1968, p. 122.
2. H. Arendt, *Le Système Totalitaire*, Paris 1912.
3. J. A. Cross, *Sir Samuel Hoare*, London, pp. 198, 202.
4. I. Kirkpatrick, *Mussolini. Study of a Demagogue*, London 1964, p. 291.
5. Lord Vansittart, *The Mist Procession*, London 1958, p. 516.
6. Lord Vansittart, Op. cit., p. 531.
7. Earl of Avon, *The Eden Memoires: Facing the Dictators*, London 1962, p. 225. *Also*: R. R. James, *Anthony Eden*, London 1986; R. Guariglia, *Ricordi 1922–1946*, Naples 1949.
8. P. Aloisi, *Journal*, Paris 1957, p. 294. *Also*: F. Suvich, Conversations with the Author.
9. Lord Templewood, *Nine Troubled Years*, London 1954, pp. 164–165. *Also*: M. Cowling, *The Impact of Hitler*, Cambridge 1975, p. 109; K. Middlemas & J. Barnes, *Baldwin*, London 1967, pp. 188, 258, 469, 500, 929, 996; H. L'Etang, *Fit to Lead*, London 1980.
10. F. Hardie, *The Abyssinian Crisis*, London, p. 135. *Also*: K. Middlemas & J. Barnes, Op. cit., p. 852; J. A. Cross, Op. cit., p. 61; Lord Vansittart, Op. cit., p. 532.
11. Lord Templewood, Op. cit., pp. 166, 167.
12. C. Barnett, *The Collapse of British Power*, London, 1972, p. 366.
13. A. Speer, *Au Coeur du Troisième Reich*, Paris 1971, p. 103.
14. H. Macmillan, *Winds of Change*, London, p. 438.
15. D. M. Smith, *Mussolini's Roman Empire*, New York 1976, pp. 66–72. *Also*: J. P. Garnier, *Excellences et Plumes Blanches*, Paris 1961, p. 208.
16. S. de Madariaga, *Morning without Noon*, London 1973, p. 348.
17. E. Herriot, *Jadis*, Paris 1952, Tome II, p. 606.
18. L. Broad, *Sir Anthony Eden*, London 1955, p. 63. *Also*: J. A. Cross, Op. cit., p. 223; S. de Madariaga, Op. cit., p. 384; M. Cowling, Op. cit., p. 91; Lord Vansittart, Op. cit., p. 532.
19. R. Capelle, *Dix-huit Ans auprès du Roi Léopold*, Paris 1970, p. 66 and following.
20. M. Cowling, Op. cit., pp. 91, 98–99. *Also*: H. Montgomery Hyde, *Baldwin, The Unexpected Prime Minister*, London 1973, p. 404.
21. J. Debu-Bridel, *L'Agonie de la Troisième République*, Paris 1948, p. 328.
22. E. Herriot, Op. cit., Tome II, p. 628.
23. M. Cowling, Op. cit., p. 98.
24. F. Van Langenhove, *L'Elaboration de la Politique Etrangère de la Belgique Entre les Deux Guerres Mondiales*, Brussels 1980, p. 133.

Chapter 8   *The Bankruptcy of the League of Nations*

1. *Belgian Diplomatic Documents Vol. IV*, Brussels 1965, p. 67; Ibid., p. 71; Ibid., p. 85 and following.
2. Ibid., p. 75 and following.

3. Ibid., p. 102.
4. H. Greene, *Dear Mamma—Berlin 1936*. *Spectator*, London 7 June 1986. *Also*: W. L. Shirer, *Le Troisième Reich des Origines à la Chute*, Paris 1961, Vol. I, p. 319; P. E. Flandin, *Politique Française*, Paris 1947, p. 198.
5. A. Goutard, *1940—La Guerre des Occasions Perdues*, Paris 1956, pp. 78, 79.
6. G. Monnet, Conversations with the Author. *Also*: G. Loustaunau-Lacau, *Mémoires d'un Français Rebelle*, Paris 1968, p. 90.
7. J. Gunther, *Inside Europe*, London 1940, p. 197. *Also*: P. Le Goyet, *Le Mystère Gamelin*, Paris 1975, p. 15.
8. P. Le Goyet, Op. cit., p. 56.
9. P. Le Goyet, Op. cit., p. 67.
10. Général Beaufre, *Mémoires*, Paris 1965, p. 62. *Also*: J. Weygand, *Weygand, mon Père*, Paris 1970, p. 262.
11. H. Michel, *Il y a Quarante Ans, la Défaite*, Paris, 'Le Monde', 9, 10 May 1980. *Also*: Conseil Supreme Interallie, *La Strategie Secrete de la Drole de Guerre*, C.N.R.S. Paris 1979, p. 574.
12. P. de Villelume, *Journal d'une défaite*, Paris 1979, p. 279.
13. P. Rentschnick & P. Accoce, *Ces Malades qui nous gouvernent*, Paris 1976, p. 133 and following. *Also*: Author's correspondence with P. Accoce; H. Michel, *Le 2ème Guerre mondiale commence*, Paris 1980, p. 151; Chr. Ockrent and Comte de Marenches, *Dans le Secret des Princes*, Paris 1986, p. 2.
14. M. Gilbert, *The Wilderness Years*, London 1981, p. 149.
15. Saint John Perse, *Oeuvres Complètes*, Paris, La Pléiade, p. XXII.
16. J. Nobecourt, *Une Histoire Politique de l'Armée 1919–1942*, Paris 1967, p. 265.
17. *Belgian Diplomatic Documents*, Op. cit., p. 139. *Also*: F. Van Langenhove, *L'Elaboration de la Politique étrangère de la Belgique entre les Deux Guerres Mondiales*, Bruxelles 1980, p. 179.
18. M. Cowling, *The Impact of Hitler*, Cambridge 1975, p. 106; *Also*: J. Fest, *Hitler*, Volume II, Paris 1973, p. 148.
19. P. Schmidt, *Hitler's Interpreter*, London 1951, p. 40.
20. General Beaufre, Op. cit., p. 69.
21. J. Nobécourt, Op. cit., p. 197. *Also*: General van Overstraeten, *Albert Ier— Léopold III*, Brussels pp. 173, 174; P. Le Goyet, Op. cit., 125.
22. F. Van Langenhove, Op. cit., p. 179.
23. M. Baumont, *Les Origines de la Deuxième Guerre Mondiale*, Paris 1969, p. 216–217, 224.
24. *Belgian Diplomatic Documents*, Op. cit., p. 110. *Also*: J. Davignon, *Souvenirs d'une Mission*, Brussels 1951, p. 24.
25. Robert Aron, *Léopold III ou le Choix impossible*, Paris 1977, p. 113.
26. M. H. Jaspar, *Souvenirs sans Retouche*, Paris 1968, p. 112.
27. R. Capelle, *Dix-Huit Ans auprès du Roi Léopold*, Paris 1970, p. 46.
28. G. d'Aspremont-Lynden, *Revue Générale Bruxelles*.
29. R. Capelle, Op. cit., p. 84.
30. G. V. Gallup, *The Gallup International Opinion Polls—Great Britain 1937–1975*, New York Vol. 1, p. 1/2.
31. A. Fabre-Luce, Léon Blum en mars 1936, *Revue de Deux Mondes, Paris, April 1978, p. 79*. *Also*: Earl of Avon, *The Eden Memoirs—Facing the Dictators*, London 1962, p. 346.
32. J. B. Duroselle, Mentioned in *L'Idée d'Europe dans l'Histoire*, Paris 1965, p. 121.
33. Ch. Hibbert, *Benito Mussolini*, Penguin Books, p. 88. *Also*: J. Harvey, *The Diplomatic Papers of Oliver Harvey 1937–1940*, London 1970; Earl of Birkenhead, *Halifax*, London 1965, p. 361.
34. Général Beaufre, Op. cit., p. 68. *Also*: E. Weber, *L'Action Française*, Paris 1962, p. 323 and following.

35. O. H. Bullitt, *For the President, Personal and Secret*, London 1973, p. 247. *Also*: A. J. P. Taylor, *English History 1914–1945*, London 1965, p. 481; M. Cowling, Op. cit., p. 67; B. Bond, *British Military Policy Between The Two World Wars*, Oxford 1980, p. 197.
36. *About Anthony Eden*: S. Aster, *Anthony Eden*, London 1976; L. Broad, *Sir Anthony Eden*, London 1955; R. S. Churchill, *Rise and Fall of Anthony Eden*, London 1959; T. Eden, *Tribulations of a Baronet*, London 1933; A. Eden, *Another World*, London 1976; J. Colville, *The Churchillians*, London 1981; D. Carlton, *Anthony Eden*, London 1981; R. R. James, *Anthony Eden*, London 1986; E. Shuckburgh, *Descent to Suez*, London 1986.
37. R. Rothschild, Information collected by the Author.
38. Earl of Avon, Op. cit., p. 153. *Also*: Ch. Booker, *Spectator*, London, 18 February 1978.
39. M. Cowling, Op. cit., pp. 104, 105, 68.

Chapter 9   *Berlin and Moscow*

1. D. Hart Davis, *Hitler's Games*, London 1986.
2. W. Moser, *Hitler, Legend, Myth and Reality*, New York 1974, p. 209. *Also*: H. R. Trevor Roper, *The Last Days of Hitler*, London 1947, p. 35 and following; R. G. L. Waite, *The Psychopathic God*, New York 1977, p. 77.
3. A. de Jonge, *Stalin and the Shaping of the Soviet Union*, London 1986, p. 303.
4. *Report of the Trotskyite–Zinovievite Terrorist Centre*, Moscow 1936, p. 68. *Also*: Report of the Antisoviet Trotskyite Center, Moscow 1937, p. 111; J. Carmichael, *Stalin's Masterpiece*, London 1976, pp. 183–184.
5. J. Carmichael, Op. cit., pp. 184–185.
6. A. Orlov, *The Secret History of Stalin's Crimes*, London 1954.
7. Le Monde Dimanche, *Aragon joue Aragon*, M. La Bardonnie, 21 September 1979.
8. Ph. Robrieux, *Maurice Thorez*, Paris 1975, p. 124.
9. Ph. Robrieux, Op. cit., pp. 161, 177, 32. *Also*: G. Ceretti, *A l'Ombre des Deux T*, Paris 1973, p. 186 and following.
10. R. Rothschild, *La Chute de Chiang Kai shek*, Paris 1972, p. 35 and following.

Chapter 10   *The Popular Fronts*

1. *About Léon Blum*: Collection of the Fondation Nationale des Sciences Politiques: *Léon Blum et son Gouvernement*, Paris 1967. P. O. Lapie, *De Léon Blum à de Gaulle*, Paris 1971; A. Kriegel, *Les Communistes français*, Paris 1967; J. Moch, *Rencontres avec Léon Blum*, Paris 1970; J. Lacouture, *Léon Blum*, Paris 1977; J. Colton, *Léon Blum*, Paris 1968.
2. M. Martin du Gard, *Les Mémorables*, Paris 1978, p. 43.
3. A. Gide, *Journal*, Paris 1948, p. 15.
4. J. P. Azema & M. Winoch, *La Troisième République*, Paris 1970, p. 233. *Also*: Y. Tratignon, *La France au XXe Siècle*, Paris 1968, p. 146; B. de Jouvenel, *Marianne*, Paris, 17 June 1936; A. Prost, *Les Grèves de Juin 1936*, Collection Léon Blum, Paris, pp. 69–87.
5. A. Sauvy, *Histoire Economique de la France entre les Deux Guerres*, Paris, Vol. II, p. 198.
6. Ch. Roy, *Que lisait-on en 1936?*, Nouvel Observateur, 28 June 1976. *Also*: M.

Duverger, *L'autre Côte des Choses*, Paris 1977, p. 67; Ch. de Gaulle, *Mémoires de Guerre*, Paris 1954, Vol. I, p. 18.

7. H. Thomas, *The Spanish Civil War*, London 1961, pp. 168, 169, 170.
8. D. M. Smith, *Mussolini's Roman Empire*, New York 1976, p. 85. *Also*: I. Kirkpatrick, *Mussolini—Study of a Demagogue*, London 1964, p. 323.
9. D. M. Smith, Op. cit., p. 105. *Also*: D. W. Pike, *Les Français et la Guerre d'Espagne*, Paris 1975.
10. P. Monolli, *Mussolini, petit bourgeois*, Paris 1955, p. 167 and following.
11. Archives of the Belgian Ministry of Foreign Affairs, Report by the Belgian Ambassador in Paris, 30 October 1936 (not published).
12. J. Gunther, *Inside Europe*, London 1940, p. 254. *Also*: G. Ciano, 1947, p. 88; R. Guariglia, *Ricordi 1922–1946*, Naples 1949, p. 357.
13. G. H. Gallup, *The Gallup International Public Opinion Polls. Great Britain 1937–1975*, January 1937, New York, Vol. I, p. 1.
14. J. Zay, *Souvenirs et Solitude*, Paris 1941, p. 114. *Also*: H. Dalton, *The Fateful Years*, Memoirs 1931–1945, London 1957, pp. 95–96.
15. D. M. Smith, Op. cit., p. 92.

Chapter 11 *Belgium Returns to Neutrality*

1. J. Davignon, *Berlin 1936–1940*, Brussels 1951, p. 50. *Also*: R. Rothschild, Personal notes.
2. P. H. Spaak, *Combats Macherés*, Paris 1969, Tome I, p. 45. *Also*: A. Drion, *Evolution de la Politique extérieure de la Belgique, à l'égard la France depuis la Réoccupation de la Rhénanie en 1936 jusqu' à l'invasion du 10 Mai 1940*, Université Libre de Bruxelles 1968, 1969, p. 61 (not published).
3. L. Blum, *L'Oeuvre de Léon Blum*, Tome V, p. 89. *Also*: French Diplomatic Documents, Series II, III, No. 47.
4. D. O. Kieft, *Belgium's Return to Neutrality*, Oxford 1972, p. 140 and following.
5. *Belgian Diplomatic Documents Tome IV*, Brussels 1965, p. 349. *Also*: Archives of the Belgian Ministry of Foreign Affairs . . . Report of the Belgian Ambassador to London, 30 November 1936 (unpublished); B. Bond, *British Military Policy Between Two World Wars*, Oxford 1980, pp. 232, 233; *Belgian Diplomatic Documents*, Op. cit., pp. 238–239, No. 135; *New York Times*, 22 October 1936, p. 6; *Annals of the Chambre des Representants*, Brussels 28 October 1936, p. 376.
6. Belgian Diplomatic Documents, Op. cit., No. 130. *Also*: French Diplomatic Documents, Series II, III, No. 359.
7. P. H. Spaak, Conversations with the Author. *Also*: L. Blum, *L'Oeuvre de L. Blum*, Paris 1955, Vol. V, pp. 9, 10; J. Colton, *Leon Blum*, Paris 1966, p. 217.
8. B. Bond, *France and Belgium 1939–1940*, Oxford, pp. 25, 61. *Also*: R. Keyes, *Outrageous Fortune*, London 1984, p. 67; O. Harvey, *The Diplomatic Diaries of Oliver Harvey 1939–1940*, London 1970, pp. 15, 16.
9. General Van Overstraeten, *Albert Ier—Leopold III*, p. 232. *Also*: R. Capelle, Op. cit., p. 132.
10. P. van Zuylen, *Les Mains Libres*, Bruxelles, 1950. *Also*: General van Overstraeten, *Dans l'Etau*, Paris 1960, p. 63; R. Capelle, *Dix-huit ans aupres du Roi Leopold*, Paris 1970, pp. 30, 44, 46, 84, 89, 117; Robert Aron, *Leopold III ou le Choix Impossible*, Paris 1977.
11. *Belgian Diplomatic Documents*, Op. cit., p. 349.
12. L. E. Ellis, *The War in France and Flanders—The Official History*, London 1953. *Also*: B. Bond, *British Military Policy Between The Two World Wars*, Oxford 1980, p. 233; I. Colvin, *The Chamberlain Cabinet*, London 1971, p. 62; P. de

Villelume, *Journal d'une Défaite*, Paris 1976, p. 49; P. Le Goyet, *Le Mystère Gamelin*, Paris, pp. 90, 159; B. H. Liddell Hart, Foreword to *Panzer Leader—H. Guderian*, London 1957, p. 11.

13. J. Stengers, Foreword to a study by M. F. Vanlangenhove: *L'Elaboration de la Politique Étrangère de la Belgique entre les Deux Guerres Mondiales*, Academie Royale de Belgique, Bulletin de la Classe de Lettres 5e Serie, Tome LXVII, 1983–3, p. 171; R. Rothschild, Personal recollection.

14. R. Keyes, Op. cit., p. 49. *Also*: D. O. Kieft, *Belgium's Return to Neutrality*, Oxford 1972, pp. 74, 22 and following; P. van Zuylen, *Les Mains libres*, Bruxelles 1950, p. 308 and following; B. Bond, Op. cit., p. 232.

15. O. H. Bullitt, *For the President, Personal and Secret*, London 1973, p. 212.

16. Archives of the Belgian Ministry of Foreign Affairs, Report by the Belgian Ambassador to London 17/8/36 (unpublished). *Also*: R. Keyes, Op. cit., p. 71.

17. K. Hildebrand, *Vom Reich zum Weltreich, NSDA und Kolonial Frage 1919–1945*, Munich 1969. *Also*: A. François-Poncet, *Souvenirs d'une Ambassade à Berlin*, Paris 1946, p. 282; H. Schacht, *My First Seventy-six Years. The Autobiography of Hjalmar Schacht*, London 1955, pp. 378–381; Archives of the Belgian Ministry of Foreign Affairs, Report by the Belgian Ambassador to Paris, 24/6/37 (unpublished); *Documents on German Foreign Policy*, Vol. III, pp. 180, 181, Government Printing Office, Washington, 1948.

18. M. Frère, Letter to M. van Zeeland, 24 April 1937 (unpublished).

19. M. Frère, Letter to M. van Zeeland, 7 May 1937 (unpublished).

20. M. Frère, Ibid. *Also*: F. Van Langenhove, *L'Elaboration de la Politique Etrangère de la Belgique entre les deux Guerres*, Brussels 1980, p. 267.

21. M. Frère, Letter to M. van Zeeland, 22 May 1937 (unpublished).

22. M. Frère, Letter to M. van Zeeland, 10 June 1937 (unpublished).

23. M. Frère, Letter to M. van Zeeland, 10 June 1937 (unpublished).

24. P. van Zeeland, *Rapport sur les Possibilités d'obtenir une réduction générale des Obstacles au Commerce International*, Brussels, 26 January 1938.

Chapter 12 *The End of Austria*

1. P. Monelli, *Mussolini, Petit Bourgeois*, Paris 1955, p. 178. *Also*: I. Kirkpatrick, *Mussolini*, London 1964, pp. 335 & 385.

2. G. Ciano, *Diary 1937–1938*, London 1952. *Also*: G. Ciano, Ibid., 12 November 1938 and 16 December 1938.

3. P. Monelli, Op. cit., p. 182.

4. H. Vogt, *The Burden of Guilt*, New York 1964, p. 185. *Also*: F. Knipping, *Perception de la Puissance dans le Führer-staat*, from *La Puissance en Europe*, Paris 1984, p. 279; J. Fest, *Hitler*, Vol. II, Paris 1973, p. 195.

5. W. Stevenson, *A Man called Intrepid*, London 1976, p. 41.

6. W. S. Churchill, *The Second World War*, London 1948, Vol. I, p. 174.

7. F. Van Langenhove, *L'Elaboration de la Politique Étrangère de la Belgique entre les deux Guerres Mondiales*, Brussels 1980, p. 281.

8. D. Irving, *The War Path*, London 1978, pp. 25, 26. *Also*: L. Mosley, Op. cit., p. 187; M. Baumont, *Les Origines de la Deuxième Guerre Mondiale*, Paris 1969, p. 250; D. Irving, *Breach of Security*, London 1968; E. von Weizsäcker, *Memoirs*, Chicago 1951.

9. A. L. Rowse, *A Man of The Thirties*, London 1979, p. 175.

10. M. Gilbert & R. Gott, *The Appeasers*, London 1963, pp. 83–84. *Also*: Earl of Birkenhead, *Halifax*, London, p. 367 and following; M. Cowling, *The Impact of Hitler*, Cambridge 1975, pp. 272–274; The Earl of Halifax, *Fullness of Days*,

London, 1957, p. 184 and following; A. Adamthwaite, *Le Gouvernement Britannique et l'Opinion Publique 1937–1938*, in *La Puissance en Europe*, Paris 1984, p. 357.

11. J. Harvey, *The Diplomatic Diaries of Oliver Harvey 1937–1940*, London 1970, p. 124. *Also*: K. Feiling, *The Life of Neville Chamberlain*, London 1946, p. 332.

12. A. J. P. Taylor, *The Origins of the Second World War*, Penguin Books 1977, p. 175. *Also: Belgian Diplomatic Documents*, Vol. V, p. 48, Brussels 1966; R. Douglas, *In the Year of Munich*, London 1977, p. 11.

13. N. Henderson, *Failure of a Mission*, London 1940, p. 114 and following; J. Harvey, p. 114 and following p. 108.

14. *Belgian Diplomatic Documents*, Op. cit., p. 48. *Also*: M. Gilbert & R. Gott, Op. cit., p. 106.

15. D. Dilks, *The Diaries of Sir Alexander Cadogan—1938–1945*, London 1971. *Also*: W. S. Churchill, *The Second World War*, London 1948, Vol. I, p. 212.

16. F. von Papen, Quoted by A. J. P. Taylor, Op. cit., pp. 175, 176.

17. L. Mosley, *The Reich Marshal*, London 1974, p. 212 and following.

18. G. E. R. Gedye, *Fallen Bastions*, London 1942, p. 295.

19. F. Van Langenhove, Op. cit., p. 283. *Also*: K. Feiling, Op. cit., p. 325.

20. K. Feiling, Op. cit., p. 341. *Also*: M. Cowling, Op. cit., pp. 152, 165, 178; K. Middlemas & J. Barnes, *Baldwin*, London 1969, p. 961.

21. M. Gilbert, *The Roots of Appeasement*, London 1966, pp. 143–144.

22. S. Hynes, *The Auden Generation*, London 1976, Chapters VIII and IX.

23. G. Y. Gallup, *The Gallup International Public Opinion Polls, Great Britain 1937–1975*, New York, Vol. I, p. 3.

24. H. Macmillan, *Winds of Change*, London 1966, Vol. I, p. 520. *Also*: J. Harvey, Op. cit., p. 86.

25. D. Desanti, *Drieu La Rochelle ou le Séducteur Mystifié*, Paris 1978, p. 329.

26. R. Brasillach, *Je Suis Partout*, 8 August 1936.

27. J. Lacouture, *Léon Blum*, Paris 1977, pp. 433–434.

28. L. Rebatat, *Les Décombres*, Paris 1976, p. 35.

29. J. Rabaut, *L'Antimilitarisme en France*, Paris 1975, p. 78 and following. *Also*: G. Bonnefous, *Histoire Politique de la Troisième Republique*, Paris 1965, Vol. I, p. 72 and following; H. Bergasse, *Histoire de l'Assemblée*, Paris 1961, p. 278 and following.

30. J. Debu-Bridel, *L'Agonie de la Troisième République*, Paris 1948, pp. 412–413. *Also*: Raymond Aron, *Mémoires*, Paris 1983.

Chapter 13   *Two Hapless Men: Daladier and Chamberlain*

1. R. Renaud & J. Bourdin, *Edouard Daladier, Chef de Gouvernement*, Paris 1977. *Also*: J. P. Maxence, *Histoire de Dix Ans*, Paris 1939; Y. Lapaquellerie, *Edouard Daladier*, Paris 1939.

2. G. Suarez, *Les Heures Héroiques du Cartel*. Paris 1934, pp. 140–141.

3. J. Weygand, *Weygand, Mon Père*, Paris 1970, p. 265. *Also*: General Gamelin, *Servir*, Paris 1946, p. 92.

4. J. Debut-Bridel, *L'Agonie de la Troisième République*, Paris 1948, p. 436.

5. A. Germain, *Guerre Civile*, Paris 1934, p. 39. *Also*: O. H. Bullitt, *For the President, Personal and Secret*, London 1973, p. 293; R. Renaud and J. Bourdin, Op cit., p. 293.

6. P. de Villelume, *Journal d'une Défaite*, Paris 1976, p. 65. *Also*: J. Willequet, *Paul-Henri Spaak*, 1975, p. 93.

7. P. de Villelume, Op. cit., pp. 191, 196, 255. *Also*: H. Daridan, *Le Chemin de la Défaite*, Paris 1980, p. 180.

8. K. Feiling, *The Life of Neville Chamberlain*, London 1946, p. 7 and following. *Also*: J. Macleod, *Neville Chamberlain*, London 1961; L. W. Fuchser, *Neville Chamberlain and Appeasement*, New York/London 1982, p. 43; H. Macmillan, *The Past Masters*, London 1975, pp. 132–133.
9. Lord Home, *The Way the Wind Blows*, London 1976, p. 60.
10. K. Feiling, Op. cit., p. 48.
11. K. Feiling, Op. cit., p. 119. *Also*: T. Taylor, *Munich, the Price of Peace*, London 1979, p. 553.
12. M. Cowling, *The Impact of Hitler*, Cambridge 1975, pp. 152, 153. *Also*: B. Bond, *British Military Policy Between The Two World Wars*, Oxford 1980, pp. 192, 200, 205, 238; P. Fraser, *Lord Esher*, London 1973; M. Howard, *The Causes of War*, London 1983, p. 244.
13. The Earl of Birkenhead, *Halifax*, London 1965, p. 362. *Also*: M. Cowling, Op. cit., p. 304; H. Nicolson, *Diaries and Letters 1930–1939*, entry for March 1938, London 1966; O. H. Bullitt, *For the President. Personal and Secret*, London 1973.
14. W. Manchester, *The Glory and the Dream*, New York 1975, p. 174.
15. I. Colvin, Op. cit., pp. 84, 86. *Also*: J. Harvey, Op. cit., p. 67 and following; Sumner Welles, *The Time for Decision*, London 1947, p. 66; J. Macleod, Op. cit., p. 212; S. Roskill, *Hankey, Man of Secrets—1931–1963*, London 1974, p. 298 and following.
16. J. Macleod, Op. cit., p. 226. *Also*: G. Aster, *1939 The Making of the Second World War*, London 1973, p. 89; The Soviet Ministry of Foreign Affairs, *The USSR in the Struggle for Peace on the Eve of the Second World War 1938–1939*, Moscow 1976.
17. J. E. Davies, *Mission to Moscow*, New York 1947, p. 345.
18. A. J. P. Taylor, *Beaverbrook*, London 1974, p. 475. *Also*: K. Feiling, Op. cit., p. 92; C. Barnett, Op. cit., p. 459.
19. A. & J. George, *Woodrow Wilson and Colonel House—A Personality Study*, New York 1964. *Also*: S. D. Spector, *Rumania at the Paris Peace Conference*, New York 1962, p. 280.
20. H. Macmillan, Op. cit., p. 132. *Also*: The Soviet Ministry of Foreign Affairs, Op. cit., p. 146.

Chapter 14 *Munich*

1. P. Schmidt, *Hitler's Interpreter*, London 1951, p. 109.
2. K. Feiling, *The Life of Neville Chamberlain*, London 1946, pp. 347, 348.
3. I. Colvin, *The Chamberlain Cabinet*, London 1971, p. 103 and following. *Also*: T. Taylor, *Munich*, London 1979, p. 628; J. Harvey, *The Diplomatic Diaries of Oliver Harvey 1937–1940*, London 1970, p. 122.
4. M. Cowling, *The Impact of Hitler*, Cambridge 1975, p. 294; J. Fest, *Hitler—Le Führer*, Paris 1973, p. 505.
5. A. J. P. Taylor, *The Origins of the Second World War*, Penguin, p. 200. *Also*: I. Colvin, Op. cit., pp. 123, 124, 125; *Documents of British Foreign Policy*, H. M. Stationery Office, London, Third Series, Vol. I, pp. 198–223.
6. Lord Templewood, *Nine Troubled Years*, London 1954, p. 297.
7. A. J. P. Taylor, Op. cit., p. 203. *Also*: N. Henderson, *Failure of a Mission*, London, p. 132; H. Gilbert & R. Gott, *The Appeasers*, London 1967, p. 123; *Documents on German Foreign Policy*, Washington Government Printing Office, Vol. II, pp. 246–47.
8. J. Delmas, Les Exercices du Conseil Supérieur de la Guerre 1936–1937 et 1937–1938. *Revue Historique des Armées*, Paris 1974, no. 4, p. 31 and following.
9. *Documents on German Foreign Policy*, Op. cit., Vol. II, pp. 547–9.

10. *Belgian Diplomatic Documents*, Vol. V, Brussels 1965, 6 June 1936.
11. General Crahay, *L'Armée Belge Entre les Deux Guerres*, Brussels 1978, p. 221 and following.
12. P. Stehlin, *Témoignage pour l'Histoire*, Paris 1964, p. 81.
13. E. Kordt, *Nicht aus den Akten*, Stuttgart 1950, pp. 282–283.
14. J. Fest, Op. cit., p. 223. *Also*: I. Colvin, Op. cit., p. 147.
15. I. Colvin, Op. cit., p. 165. *Also*: J. Fest, Op. cit., p. 230; F. von Schlabrendorff, *Secret War against Hitler*, London 1966, p. 88.
16. General van Overstraeten, *Albert Ier—Léopold III*, Brussels, p. 302; *Dans l'Etau*, Paris 1960, p. 82.
17. F. M. Erich von Manstein, *Lost Victories*, London 1958. *Also*: W. Deist, *The Wehrmacht—German Rearmament*, London 1981, p. 86 and following; M. Cooper, *The German Army*, London 1978, pp. 154, 162 and following; A. Gautard, *1940. La Guerre des Occasions Perdues*, Paris 1956, p. 77 and following; B. H. Liddell Hart, *History of the Second World War*, London, Pan Books 1977, p. 19.
18. A. Goutard, Op. cit., p. 78 and following. *Also*: M. Cooper, Op. cit., p. 154 and following; K. Macksey, *Guderian—Panzer General*, London 1975, pp. 66, 100; General G. Raton, *La Course aux Armements 1933–1939*, Paris 1947; P. Le Goyet, *Le Mystère Gamelin*, Paris 1976, p. 82 and following.
19. W. Deist, Op. cit., p. 88. *Also*: J. Kimche, *The Unfought War*, London 1968, p. 55 and following.
20. D. Irving, Op. cit., p. 118. *Also*: A. Goutard, Op. cit., pp. 71–72; J. Kimche, Op. cit., p. 94.
21. W. Deist, Op. cit., p. 54 and following. *Also*: A. Goutard, Op. cit., p. 69 and following; C. Webster & N. Frankland, *The Strategic Air Offensive Against Hitler*, London 1961, Vol. I, p. 97; M. Hastings, *Bomber Command*, New York 1979, pp. 56, 57, 58; A. Horne, *To Lose a Battle*, London 1969, pp. 136, 137; A. Kesselring, *Memoirs*, London 1953; W. K. Wark, *The Ultimate Enemy*, London 1985.
22. General A. Heusinger, *Hitler et l'O.K.H.*, Paris 1952, p. 46. *Also*: A. Goutard, Op. cit., p. 108 and following.
23. P. Le Goyet, *Le Mystère Gamelin*, Paris 1975, p. 86. *Also*: K. Machsey, Op. cit., p. 97 and following; General H. Guderian, *Panzer Leader*, London 1952, pp. 90–91; W. Deist, Op. cit., pp. 42, 86 and following.
24. A. Werth, *La Russie en Guerre*, Paris 1964, Tome I, p. 117.
25. The Belgian Ministry of Foreign Affairs, *Belgium, the Official Account of What Happened 1939–1940*, London 1941. *Also*: B. Bond, *France and Belgium 1939–1940*, London 1975, p. 63; K. Macksey, Op. cit., p. 97 and following; M. Cooper, Op. cit., p. 197 and following; J. Fest, *Hitler*, Paris 1973 (Vol. II), p. 300 and following; J. Vanwelkenhuyzen, Le Plan Allemand du 24 Février 1940, *Revue historique de l'Armée*, Paris, November 1956; *Neutralité Armée*, Brussels 1979, p. 79.
26. General Gamelin, *Servir*, Paris 1946 (Vol. II), p. 352 and following. *Also*: B. Bond, *British Military Policy Between The Two World Wars*, Oxford 1980, p. 281; M. Hanner, Czechoslovakia as a Military Factor in British Consideration of 1938, *Journal of Strategic Studies*, No. 1, No. 2, September 1978, pp. 194–222.
27. H. Macmillan, *Winds of Change 1914–1939*, London 1966, Vol. I, p. 544. *Also*: I. Colvin, *The Chamberlain Cabinet*, London 1971, pp. 167, 268.
28. J. Nobecourt, *Une Histoire Politique de l'Armée*, Paris 1967, Vol. I, 1919–1942, p. 272. *Also*: P. Le Goyet, *Le Mystère Gamelin*, Paris 1976, p. 68.
29. Lord Ismay, *Memoirs*, London 1960, p. 92. *Also*: M. Cowling, Op. cit., pp. 79, 186; B. Bond, Op. cit., pp. 279, 280.

30. *Documents on German Foreign Policy 1918–1945*. Washington Printing Office, Vol. II, pp. 267, 629.
31. A. Sinclair, *The Red and the Blue*, London 1986.
32. Général Gamelin, Op. cit., Vol. II, p. 279 and following. *Also*: J. Paul-Boncour, Op. cit., Vol. III, p. 58.
33. M. Cowling, Op. cit., pp. 265–266. *Also*: I. Colvin, Op. cit., p. 38; G. Bonnet, *Le Quay d'Orsay Sous Trois Républiques*, Paris 1961, p. 244; R. Coulondre, *De Staline à Hitler*, Paris 1950, pp. 152–153.
34. W. S. Churchill, *The Second World War*, London 1948, Tome I, p. 229.
35. Ch. L. Mowat, Op. cit., p. 606.
36. I. Colvin, Op. cit., p. 135. *Also*: K. Feiling, Op. cit., p. 356; M. Cowling, Op. cit., p. 182; D. Irving, Op. cit., pp. 121–122.
37. L. Noel, *L'Agression Allemande Contre la Pologne*, 1946, p. 198 and following. *Also*: A. Mares, *La Faillité des Relations Franco-tchécoslovaques dans l'Histoire de la Deuxième Guerre Mondiale*, Paris, 11 July 1978, p. 65.
38. *Documents on German Foreign Policy 1918–1945*, Washington Printing Office, Vol. II, pp. 267, 629. *Also*: R. Rothschild, Personal notes.
39. N. Rose, *Vansittart*, London 1978, p. 224. *Also*: *Belgian Diplomatic Documents*, Op. cit., Vol. V, p. 111; A. Duff-Cooper, *Old Men Forget*, London 1954, p. 221; T. Taylor, Op. cit., p. 685.
40. *Belgian Diplomatic Documents*, Op. cit., p. 91. *Also*: E. Beneš, *Munich*, Paris 1969; L. Noël, *La Guerre de 39 a Commencé Quatre Ans Plus Tôt*, Paris 1979.
41. J. W. Wheeler-Bennett, *Munich—Prologue to Tragedy*, London 1948, p. 97. *Also*: The Earl of Birkenhead, *Halifax*, London 1965, p. 392.
42. H. Vogt, *The Burden of Guilt*, New York/Oxford 1964, p. 151.
43. K. Feiling, Op. cit., p. 363. *Also*: I. Colvin, Op. cit., pp. 146, 185–186, 265, 268; M. Cowling, Op. cit., pp. 185–186; M. Gilbert, *The Wilderness Years*, London 1981, p. 228; R. Douglas, *In the Year of Munich*, London 1977, p. 49; D. Dilks, *The Diaries of Sir Alexander Cadogan*, London 1971, p. 92; *Documents on German Foreign Policy*, Op. cit., Vol. II, p. 754.
44. General Crookenden, Conversations with the author.
45. J. de Pange, *Journal 1937–1939*, Paris 1975, p. 254.
46. Lord Templewood, *Nine Troubled Years*, London 1954, p. 312. *Also*: R. Girault, *Sous Edouard Daladier, Chef de Gouvernement*, Paris 1977, p. 218; D. Dilks, *The Diaries of Sir Alexander Cadogan*, London 1971.
47. I. Colvin, Op. cit., p. 165. *Also*: Général Gamelin, *Servir*, Paris 1946–49, Vol. II, pp. 248–350, 357, 352; R. Douglas, Op. cit., p. 64; E. Daladier, Articles in *Candide*, Paris 7–14 September 1961.
48. L. Amery, *My Political Life*, London 1955, Vol. III, p. 278. *Also*: W. L. Shirer, *Le Troisième Reich des Origines à la Chute*, Paris 1961, Tome I, p. 431.
49. The Earl of Birkenhead, *Halifax*, London 1965, p. 404.
50. H. Nicolson, *Diaries and Letters 1930–1939*. (Entry for 28 September 1938), London 1966.
51. A. J. P. Taylor, *English History 1914–1945*, Pelican Books 1973, p. 526. *Also*: J. W. Wheeler-Bennett, Op. cit., p. 174.

Chapter 15 *Peace with Honour, Peace For Our Time*

1. H. de Montherlant, *Equinoxe de Septembre*, Paris 1938.
2. P. Henry, *Sondages*, Paris, June 1939, pp. 7–8.
3. O. H. Bullitt, *For the President. Personal and Secret*, London 1973, p. 267.

4. A. J. P. Taylor, *The Origins of the Second World War*, Penguin, p. 977. *Also*: Lord Strang, *At Home and Abroad*, London 1964, p. 135; J. Harvey, *The Diplomatic Diaries of Oliver Harvey 1937–1940*, London 1970, p. 200; *Documents of British Foreign Policy*, H.M. Stationery Office, London, Vol. II, Doc. 1122, pp. 546–47; O. H. Bullitt, Op. cit., p. 291.

5. J. Harvey, Op. cit., p. 164 and following. *Also*: J. Debu-Bridel, *L'Agonie de la Troisième République*, Paris 1948, p. 449; P. Ory, *L'Opinion Publique et la Puissance Française vers 1938*, in *La Puissance en Europe*, Paris 1984, p. 345.

6. R. Renaud & J. Bourdin, *Edouard Daladier, Chef de Gouvernement*, Paris 1977.

7. J. Margach, *The Abuse of Power*, London 1978, p. 50. *Also*: A. Adamthwaite, *Le Gouvernement Britannique et l'Opinion Publique 1937–1938*, in *La Puissance en Europe*, Paris 1984, p. 349 and following; H. Macmillan, *Winds of Change*, London 1966, Vol. I, pp. 549, 550, 562.

8. J. Harvey, Op. cit., p. 178. *Also*: C. L. Mowat, *Britain Between The Two Wars*, London 1968, p. 613; H. Nicolson, *Diaries and Letters 1930–1939*, September 27 1938, London 1966; R. Douglas, *In the Years of Munich*, London 1977, pp. 44, 45, 56; Ch. Madge & T. Harrison, *Britain by Mass Observation*, Penguin 1939.

9. C. L. Mowat, Op. cit., p. 592. *Also*: J. W. Wheeler-Bennett, *Munich: Prologue to Tragedy*, London 1948, p. 184; R. Douglas, Op. cit., pp. 64–65.

10. W. S. Churchill, *The Second World War*, London 1948, Vol. I, p. 288.

11. G. H. Gallup, *The Gallup International Public Opinion Polls—Great Britain 1937–1974*, New York, Vol. I, p. 10.

12. M. Cowling, *The Impact of Hitler*, Cambridge 1975, p. 197. *Also*: I. Colvin, *The Chamberlain Cabinet*, London 1971; Op. cit., pp. 156, 162, 163; L. W. Fuchser, *Neville Chamberlain and Appeasement*, New York/London 1982, p. 174; R. Douglas, Op. cit., p. 83.

13. R. Douglas, Op. cit., p. 81. *Also*: C. L. Mowat, Op. cit., p. 625; I. Colvin, Op. cit., pp. 174, 218; B. Bond, *British Military Police Between the Two World Wars*, Oxford 1980; M. Howard, *The Causes of War*, London 1983.

14. G. Ciano, *Diary 1937–1938*, London, p. XIX.

15. D. M. Smith, *Mussolini's Roman Empire*, New York 1976, p. 143. *Also*: L. Simoni, *Berlin, Ambassade d'Italie*, Paris 1950, p. 106.

16. G. Ciano, *Ciano's Diary 1939–1943*, London 1947, pp. 79–81, 133, 155. *Also*: G. Waterfield, *Professional Diplomat—Sir Percy Loraine*, London 1973, p. 228.

17. A. François-Poncet, *Au Palais Farnèse*, Paris 1961, p. 39. *Also*: D. M. Smith, Op. cit., p. 134 and following.

18. N. Henderson, *Failure of a Mission*, London 1940, p. 161.

19. G. Waterfield, Op. cit., p. 225; *Also*: D. M. Smith, Op. cit., p. 138; I. Kirkpatrick, *Mussolini*, London 1964, p. 359.

20. I. Kirkpatrick, *The Inner Circle*, London 1959, p. 135. *Also*: J. Fest, *Hitler*, Paris 1973, Tome II, pp. 232, 245–246.

21. S. Aster, *1939 The Making of the Second World War*, London 1973, p. 47.

22. R. Douglas, Op. cit., p. 84.

23. J. Daridan, *Le Chemin de la Défaite*, Paris 1980, p. 100.

24. Chr. Hibbert, *Benito Mussolini*, Penguin Books 1975, p. 124.

25. N. West, *MI6—British Secret Intelligence Service Operations 1909–1945*, London 1983, p. 56.

26. M. Cowling, Op. cit., p. 205. *Also*: K. Feiling, Op. cit., pp. 394–395.

27. L. Mosley, *On Borrowed Time*, New York 1969, pp. 163–164. *Also*: J. Davignon, *Berlin 1936–1940*, Paris 1951, p. 102.

Chapter 16   *Mane, Thecel, Phares*

1. I. Colvin, *The Chamberlain Cabinet*, London 1971, p. 186.

2. A. J. P. Taylor, *The Origins of the Second World War*, Penguin, p. 327. *Also*: B. Bond, *British Military Policy Between The Two World Wars*, London 1980, p. 307.
3. A. J. P. Taylor, *English History 1914–1945*, Pelican Books 1973, p. 542. *Also*: D. Irving, *The War Path*, London 1978, p. 205.
4. Général Gamelin, *Servir*, Paris 1946, Vol. II, pp. 371–373.
5. J. Bouvier & R. Frank, *Sur la Perception de la Puissance Économique en France Pendant les Années 1930*, in *La Puissance en Europe*, Paris 1984, pp. 177, 180; A. Sauvy, *Le Figaro*, Paris 8 August 1983.
6. R. Remano and J. Bourdin, *Edouard Daladier, Chef de Gouvernement*, Paris 1979, p. 20. *Also*: H. P. Azema, *De Munich à la Libération 1938–1944*, Paris 1979, pp. 29–30.
7. R. Boothby, *I Fight to Live*, London 1947, p. 189.
8. S. Aster, *The Making of the Second World War*, London 1973, p. 158. *Also*: The Soviet Ministry of Foreign Affairs, *The USSR in the Struggle for Peace on the Eve of the Second World War 1938–1939*, Moscow 1976.
9. R. Coulondre, *De Staline à Hitler*, Paris 1950, p. 264. *Also*: S. Aster, Op. cit., pp. 157–163; A. J. P. Taylor, *The Origins of the Second World War*, Penguin Books 1977, p. 237.
10. P. Stehlin, *Témoignage pour l'Histoire*, Paris 1964, p. 148.
11. S. Aster, Op. cit., p. 274. *Also*: N. Rose, *Vansittart—Study of a Diplomat*, London 1978, p. 234; J. Davignon, *Berlin 1936–1940*, Paris 1951, p. 134.
12. M. Cowling, *The Impact of Hitler*, Cambridge 1975, p. 300. *Also*: I. Colvin, *The Chamberlain Cabinet*, London 1971; Op. cit., pp. 228–229; T. Taylor, *Munich, the Price of Peace*, London 1979, p. 976; D. Dilks, *The Diaries of Sir Alexander Cadogan*, London 1971, pp. 180–187.
13. G. H. Gallup, *The Gallup International Public Opinion Polls*, Great Britain 1937–1975, January 1937, New York, Vol. I, p. 20. *Also*: R. Lamb, *The Ghosts of Peace*, London 1987, p. 47.
14. H. Montgomery Hyde, *Stalin*, New York 1971, p. 234. *Also*: I. Colvin, Op. cit., p. 228.
15. The Soviet Ministry of Foreign Affairs, Op. cit., pp. 334, 363–368.
16. W. Manchester, *The Glory and the Dream*, Bonham Books, New York 1975, p. 201. *Also*: Daily Telegraph, London 9 March 1982, p. 7; J. V. Compton, *The Swastika and the Eagle*, London 1968, pp. 17–18, 23.
17. Cordell Hull, *Memoirs*, London 1948, p. 493 and following.
18. A. Speer, *Au Coeur du Troisième Reich*, Paris 1969, p. 120.
19. Diana Cooper, *The Light of Common Day*, London 1959, p. 227.
20. G. Gafenco, *Les Derniers Jours de l'Europe*, Paris 1947, pp. 62–63, 74.
21. Ch. Hibbert, *Benito Mussolini*, Penguin Books 1975, p. 131.
22. A. Fontaine, *Histoire de la Guerre Froide*, Vol. I, p. 117, Paris 1965. *Also*: J. B. Duroselle, *La Décadence*, Paris 1979.
23. A. Werth, *La Russie en Guerre*, Paris 1964, Tome I, p. 29.
24. I. Maisky, *Who Helped Hitler?* London 1964.
25. J. Harvey, *The Diplomatic Diaries of Oliver Harvey 1937–1940*, London 1970, p. 286.
26. A. Fontaine, Op. cit., Tome I, p. 192. *Also*: *Documents on German Foreign Policy*, Washington Government Printing Office, Vol. VI, p. 977; J. Kimche, *The Unfought Battle*, London 1968, pp. 78, 79.
27. S. Aster, Op. cit., pp. 247, 257.
28. S. Aster, Op. cit., p. 268.
29. M. Cowling, *The Impact of Hitler*, Cambridge 1975, pp. 300, 304. *Also*: H. Dalton, *Memoirs. The Fateful Years 1931–1945*, London 1957; C. Barnett, *The Collapse of British Power*, London 1972, p. 566.

30. I. Colvin, Op. cit., pp. 228–229. *Also*: S. Aster, Op. cit., pp. 271–273, 274.
31. H. Montgomery-Hyde, Op. cit., p. 260.
32. N. S. Krushchev, *Souvenirs*, Paris 1970, p. 134.
33. W. G. Krivitsky, *J'Étais un Agent de Staline*, Paris 1979, p. 218.
34. A. Fontaine, *Histoire de la Guerre Froide*, Paris 1965, Vol. I, pp. 92, 112. *Also*: Soviet Ministry of Foreign Affairs, Op. cit., pp. 364, 368.
35. A. J. P. Taylor, Op. cit., pp. 283–284. *Also*: D. Dilks, *The Diaries of Sir Alexander Cadogan—1938–1945*, London 1971, p. 249.
36. S. Aster, Op. cit., pp. 288, 289.

Chapter 17   *The Jaws of Darkness*

1. Général Beaufre, *Mémoires*, Paris 1965, p. 121.
2. S. Aster, *The Making of the Second World War*, London 1975, p. 296. *Also*: Mary Rothschild-Drax, Conversations with the Author.
3. Général Beaufre, Op. cit., pp. 120–122. *Also*: Général Doumenc, *Souvenirs*, Paris 1947; Général Gamelin, *Servir*, Paris 1946–1947; G. Bonnet, *De Munich à la Guerre*, Paris 1967, p. 561.
4. Admiral Plunkett-Drax, *Mission to Moscow*—The Naval Review (Part I), p. 253. *Also*: *Documents of British Foreign Policy*, H.M. Stationery Office, London, Third Series, pp. 558, 614.
5. Général Beaufre, Op. cit., p. 125.
6. Général Beaufre, Op. cit., p. 129. *Also*: Admiral Plunkett-Drax, Op. cit.
7. S. Aster, Op. cit., p. 306. *Also*: B. Bond, *British Military Policy Between The Two World Wars*, London 1980, p. 314.
8. B. Bond, Ibid., p. 314. *Also*: R. Douglas, *The Advent of War*, 1978, p. 67.
9. J. B. Duroselle, *La Décadence*, Paris 1979, p. 458 and following. *Also*: L. Noël, *La Guerre de 39 a Commencé Quatre Ans Plus Tôt*, Paris 1979, pp. 164, 165; P. Le Goyet, Op. cit., pp. 206–213.
10. L. Noël, Op. cit., p. 130. *Also*: S. Aster, Op. cit., p. 307.
11. H. Vogt, *The Burden of Guilt*, New York 1964, p. 184.
12. R. G. L. Waite, *The Psychopathic God—Adolf Hitler*, New York 1977, p. 23. *Also*: J. P. Stern, *Hitler*, Fontana Books, London 1976, p. 223; Field Marshal Erich von Manstein, *Lost Victories*, Chicago 1958.
13. B. Dahlerus, *The Last Attempt*, London 1948, pp 55–74.
14. C. J. Burckhardt, *Ma Mission à Dantzig*, Paris 1961, pp. 378–388.
15. G. Ciano, *Diary 1937–1938*, London 1952, p. 152.
16. A. Speer, *Au Coeur du Troisième Reich*, Paris 1971, p. 230.
17. J. von Herwarth, *Against Two Evils*, London 1981.
18. J. E. Davies, *Mission to Moscow*, London 1942, p. 287.
19. Ch. E. Bohlen, *Witness to History 1929–1969*, London 1973, pp. 78–79. *Also*: S. Aster, Op. cit., p. 316.
20. *Documents on German Foreign Policy*, Washington Government Printing Office, Vol. VI. *Also*: Département d'État, *La Verité sur les Rapports Germano-Soviétiques de 1939 à 1941*, Paris 1948; J. Ellenstein, *Histoire de l'URSS*, Paris 1974, Vol. III. *British Foreign Policy 1919 to 1939*, H.M. Stationery Office, London, Vol. VII, pp. 41–42; *Foreign Relations of the United States*, U.S. Department of State, Washington.
21. A Speer, Op. cit., pp. 230–231.
22. D. Irving, *The War Path*, London 1978, p. 241. *Also*: R. Lamb, *The Ghosts of Peace*, London 1987, p. 108.
23. General Beaufre, Op. cit., p. 154.

24. Ch. E. Bohlen, Op. cit., pp. 82, 83. For the description of the supper, see *Documents on German Foreign Policy*, Op. cit., Tome VII, pp. 225–229.
25. H. Michel, *La 2ème Guerre Mondiale Commence*, Paris 1980, p. 80.
26. *Belgian Diplomatic Documents*, Vol. V, p. 152 and following. *Also*: F. Van Langenhove, *L'Elaboration de la Politique Etrangère de la Belgique Entre les Deux Guerres Mondiales*, Brussels 1980, p. 309.
27. J. Harvey, *The Diplomatic Diaries of Oliver Harvey*, 1970, p. 292.
28. J. B. Duroselle, *La Decadence*, Paris 1979, p. 467.
29. M. H. Jaspar, *Souvenirs sans Retouche*, Paris 1968, p. 267. *Also*: R. Rothschild, Personal notes.
30. R. Douglas, Op. cit., p. 1. *Also*: G. Suarez & G. Labarde, *Agonie de la Paix*, Paris 1942, p. 224; A. de Monzie, *Ci-devant*, Paris 1941; J. Zay, *Souvenirs et Solitude*, Paris 1946.
31. G. Bonnet, *De Munich à la Guerre*, Paris 1967, pp. 17, 572. *Also*: A. Conte, *Le Figaro*, Paris 24 August 1979; O. H. Bullitt, *For the President. Personal and Secret*, London 1973, pp. 379, 369.
32. J. Chauvel, *Commentaires*, Paris 1971, pp. 59, 60.
33. P. Henry, *Sondages*, Paris August 1939. *Also*: G. H. Gallup, *The Gallup International Public Opinion Polls Great Britain 1937–1975*, New York, Vol. I, p. 23.
34. G. Bonnet, Op. cit., p. 474. *Also*: *Belgian Diplomatic Documents*, Brussels 1966, Vol. V, pp. 308–309.
35. N. Henderson, *Failure of a Mission*, London 1940, p. 259. *Also*: S. Aster, Op. cit., p. 333; *Documents of British Foreign Policy*, H.M. Stationery Office, London, Vol. VII, No. 200.
36. H. Cowling, Op. cit., p. 307.
37. A. Hesse, *Hitler and the English*, London 1954, pp 71–74. *Also*: S. Aster, Op. cit., pp. 258, 259; J. Tolland, *Adolf Hitler*, New York 1976, p. 537; D. Irving, Op. cit., p. 243.
38. H. Gilbert & R. Gott, *The Appeasers*, London 1963, p. 265.
39. S. Mosley, *The Reich Marshal*, London 1974, p. 230. *Also*: Cordell Hull, *Memoirs*, London 1948, p. 662.
40. P. de Monzie, Op. cit., p. 151.
41. A. Speer, Op. cit., pp. 234, 236, 237. *Also*: R. G. L. Waite, Op. cit., p. 393.
42. J. Fest, *Hitler*, Paris 1973, Tome II, p. 269. *Also*: D. Irving, Op. cit., p. 254.
43. J. Harvey, Op. cit., pp. 307–308.
44. M. Gilbert & R. Gott, Op. cit., pp. 271–272. *Also*: A. Ciano, *Diary 1939–1943*, London 1947, p. 138.
45. S. Aster, Op. cit., p. 351.
46. J. Chastenet, *Le Drame Final 1938–1940*, Paris 1963, p. 85.
47. P. Schmidt, *Hitler's Interpreter*, London 1951, pp. 150–155.
48. M. Gilbert & R. Gott, Op. cit., pp. 194, 296. *Also*: S. Aster, Op. cit., p. 363.
49. N. Henderson, *Failure of a Mission*, London 1940, p. 274.
50. D. Irving, *Breach of Security*, London 1968, pp. 115–116.
51. I. Monelli, *Mussolini*, London 1953, p. 181. *Also*: Sumner Welles, *The Time for Decision*, London 1947, pp. 84–85.
52. A. de Monzie, Op. cit., p. 146. *Also*: J. B. Duroselle, Op. cit., p. 481.
53. W. L. Shirer, *Le Troisième Reich*, Paris 1961, Vol. I, p. 635.
54. R. Coulondre, *De Staline à Hitler*, Paris 1949, p. 310. *Also*: *Documents diplomatiques belges*, Vol. V, p. 152; J. Davignon, *Berlin 1936–1940*, Paris 1951.
55. B. Dahlerus, Op. cit., pp. 119–120.
56. J. Fest, Op. cit., p. 283. *Also*: H. Bernard, *Esprit de la Résistance Européenne*, Brussels 1980, p. 15.
57. Baron Gevers & A. Hupperts, Conversations with the Author.

58. Cordell Hull, Op. cit., p. 661.
59. J. B. Duroselle, *La Décadence*, Paris 1979, p. 485.
60. M. Gilbert & R. Gott, Op. cit., p. 314.
61. H. Nicolson, *Diaries and Letters 1930–1939*, London 1966, p. 159. *Also*: L. Amery, *My Political Life*, London 1955, Vol. III, p. 324.
62. G. Ciano, *Ciano's Diary 1939–1943*, London 1947, p. 143.
63. The Earl of Birkenhead, *Halifax*, London 1965, p. 447.
64. P. Schmidt, Op. cit., pp. 450–451.

Index

Abetz, Otto 259, 290
Action Française 28, 52, 53, 213
Airships 98
Albert, Prince 54
Alexander I, Czar 232–3
Alexander, King of Yugoslavia 84
Alexich 190
Alliluyeva, Nadya 149
Aloisi, Baron 104
Amery, Leo 267
Anglo-German Fellowship 51, 209
Anti-Comintern Pact 194
Anti-semitism 26, 40–1, 281, 304
Antonov-Ovseenko, Vladimir 168
Appeasement 301
ARBED 4
Aron, Raymond 215
Assisses de la Paix et de la Liberté 152
Astakhov, Georgi 306
Astor, Lord and Lady 209
Attlee, Clement 59
Auriol, Vincent 184
Austria 190–216
Autarchy 183

Badoglio, General 109
Balabanoff, Angelica 30, 34
Baldwin, Stanley 7–9, 17, 60, 63, 88, 89, 105, 106, 114, 138
Barratt, Air Marshal 121
Barthou 69, 84
Beauchamp, Lord 105
Beaufre, General 126, 135, 307, 309, 311
Beaverbrook, Lord 60, 231
Beck, General Ludwig 244, 251, 297, 298, 311, 330

Belgium 128–32, 170–89, 319
Beneš, President 147, 187, 260
Bergery, Gaston 338
Berzin, Ian Antonovich 166
Black, General 182
Blitzkrieg 250–1
Blue Water School 227
Blum, Léon 59, 122, 141, 150, 151, 153–60, 162, 168–9, 175, 176, 200, 202, 207, 213, 215, 271, 290
Bodenschatz, General 292
Bolsheviks 46, 86, 141, 146, 257
Boncour, Paul 207
Bonnet, Georges 254, 259, 282, 293, 308, 323, 334, 335, 338
Brasillach, Robert 53, 212
Braun, Eva 206
Briand, Aristide 3, 9, 14, 15, 20
Brinon, Fernand de
British Union of Fascists 51
Brüning, Chancellor 14, 15, 20, 22, 64, 86, 95
Brussels World's Fair 96
Bukharin 146
Bullitt, Ambassador 322
Burckhardt, Carl 312

Cachin, Marcel 31
Cadogan, Sir Alexander 202
Cagoule 214
Camelots du Roi 53
Candide 53
Carol II, King 257
Cecil, Lord 95
Central Service of Economic Information 23
Cercle du Grand Pavois 53

Chalkovsky 285
Chamberlain, H. S. 28
Chamberlain, Joseph 224, 225
Chamberlain, Neville ix, 17, 137, 181, 193, 199, 201, 207, 208, 211, 223–34, 237, 257, 262–70, 282, 284, 286, 288, 290, 303, 316, 321–2, 340, 341, 342
Chamberlain, Sir Austen 3, 114, 137
Chautemps, Camille 54, 202–3
Chauvel, Jean 323
Chiang Kai-shek 13, 38, 48, 256
China 256
  see also Manchurian affair
Chinese Communist Party 152
Churchill, Winston 195, 202, 208, 211, 212, 257, 275, 325
Ciano, Edda 104
Ciano, Galleazzo 165, 166, 186, 193, 278, 284, 312–13
City of Exeter 307
Cliveden Set 209
Collective security 2, 10, 104, 116, 133, 172
Comité France-Allemagne 53
Common Market 5
Coudenhove-Kalergi, Count 4
Coughlin, Father Charles 77
Coulondre, Robert 292
Crédit Municipal de Bayonne 54
Croix de Feu 53, 213
Cuno, Chancellor 3, 19
Czechoslovakia 150, 151, 195, 198, 203, 235–69, 274, 275, 276, 279, 284, 285, 286

Dahlerus, Birger 311
Daladier, Edouard 54, 55, 59, 122, 135, 137, 215, 218–23, 238, 239, 245, 251, 254, 260, 264, 266, 270, 273, 283, 289, 293, 308, 316, 322, 334, 339, 342
Dalton, Hugh 168, 303
Dantzig 287, 295, 297, 298, 301, 312, 326, 328–30, 334
Darlan, Admiral 322
d'Aspremont-Lynden, Count Geoffrey (Jean de Failon) 130
Daudet, Léon 83
Dawson, Geoffrey 209
De Bono, General 102, 109
de Brinon, Ferdinand 59, 260
de Broqueville, Comte 64, 129
de Chambrun, Comte 186

de Chateaubriant, Alphonse 212
de Gaulle, Charles 2, 122, 158, 159
de Gobineau, Count 28
de Guise, Duc 55
de Kerchove de Denterghem, Count 118–19, 165
de la Rocque, Coloniel François 53, 55 213
de Llano, General Queipo 161
de Madariaga, Salvador 110
de Montherlant, Henri 271
de Revel, Count Thaon 186
de Villelume, Colonel 123
Declaration of war 342
Degrelle, Léon 83, 5, 179, 214
Delbos, Yvon 175, 176, 203
Disarmament Conference 62, 111
Dollfuss, Engelbert 67–9, 190
Domville, Sir Barry 51
Doriot, Jacques 213
Douglas, Lewis 24
Douhet, General 98
Doumec, General Joseph 307–11, 315, 317
Doumergue, Gaston 55
Drax, Admiral see Plunkett-Ernle-Drax

Ebbutt, Norman 61
Economic sanctions 6
Eden, Anthony 63, 86–9, 94, 107, 114, 124, 125, 137–40, 193, 200, 201, 207, 211, 241
Eichmann, Adolf 205
Ernst, Karl 66
Esprit 52
Ethiopian War 100–16

Fanjol, General 161
Fasci Italiani di Combattimento 32
First World War 182
Flandin, Pierre-Etienne 20, 114, 119, 120, 125
Foch, Marshal 121
Fontanges, Magda 186
Forschungsamt 198
Four Power Pact 15
Franco, General 161, 163, 166
Franco-Soviet pact 152

François-Poncet, André   87, 118, 182, 278
French Communist Party   151
Frère, Maurice   184, 185, 188
Freud, Sigmund   27, 205
Fried, Eugen (or Desider)   151
Front Populaire   141, 150, 153, 156, 159, 168, 184, 202, 222, 273
Funk, Dr   196

Gamelin, General   120–3, 125, 158, 203, 239, 246, 252, 254, 257, 266, 308, 322, 340, 342
Gandhi   200
Guariglia, Ambassador   165
Geneva Protocol   3
George V, King   112
German Air Force   248–9
German Communist Party   2
German Navy   248
Gestapo   58
Gide, André   156
Giral, Jose   161
Goebbels   27, 142, 200
Goederler, Carl   244
Göring, Marshal   36, 58, 66, 142, 145, 185, 198, 200, 204, 259, 261, 299, 316, 324–5, 326
Gorki   146
Grand Alliance   236, 237, 293, 305
Grand Siècle   28
Grandi, Dino   103
Great Crisis   18, 40, 44
Great Depression   16–18, 74, 97, 182
Great Purge   148, 149
Great Revolution   46
Great War   1, 12, 23, 26, 32, 36, 38, 49, 68, 71, 89, 137
Greenwood, Arthur   341
Gringoire   53
Grynszpan, Herschel   281
Guderian, Colonel   98
Guesde, Jules   155

Hacha, Dr.   284–5
Haile Selassie I   100
Halder, General   244, 245, 250, 252
Halifax, Lord   199, 200, 201, 259, 282, 288, 300, 303, 324, 339, 340, 341
Hankey, Lord   136, 253

Harriman, Averell   78
Harvey, Oliver   200
Henderson, Arthur   14
Henderson, Sir Nevile   201, 204, 239, 301, 324, 327, 328, 329, 330, 332
Henlein, Konrad   262
Herr, Lucien   155
Herriot, Edouard   3, 10, 15
Hervé, Gustav   60
Hess, Rudolph   42, 142
Himmler   66, 205
Hindenburg, President   22, 66, 67, 69
Hitler, Adolf   2, 15, 29, 34–45, 164, 191, 194–5, 198–9, 200, 201, 202, 206, 237, 315–16, 324, 331
Hitler, Angela   36
Hoare, Sir Samuel   31, 94, 104, 105, 106, 111, 112, 113, 114, 172, 208, 259, 274, 284
Hodza, M.   187, 188
Hoover, President   12, 21, 72, 74
Hossbach, Colonel   195
Hudson, Robert   301
Hymans, Paul   64, 129

Imperial Fascist League   51
Innitzer, Cardinal   206, 280
Institut de la Conjoncture   23
Itagaki, Colonel Seishiro   1

Jakir, General   149
Japan   *see* Manchurian affair
Jaures, Jean   155
Jefferson, Thomas   80
Jeune Droite   52
Jews   40–1, 194, 205, 280, 281, 295, 304
   see also Anti-semitism
Jodl, General   245
Joffre, General   121

Kamenev   146
Kandelaki, Kotsia   305
Kellogg-Briand Pact   5
Kennedy, Joseph   329
Kepler, Alexis   149
Kesselring, Air Marshal   250
Keynes, John Maynard   17, 43, 79
Khruschev   149
Kirov, Serge   146, 150
Klausener, Erich   66

Koestler, Arthur 46
Kordt, Erich 243, 293
Kordt, Theodore 245
Krivitsky, General Walter 293, 304
Krystalnacht 282
Kun, Bela 47
Kuomintang 13

L'Action Francaise 54, 222
L'Agence Inter-France 53
Laissez-faire 182, 183, 202
Lansbury, George 59
La Rochelle, Drieu 49, 50
La Solidarité Française 53
Laval, Pierre 9, 18, 20, 89–94, 103, 104,
　107, 108, 110, 111, 112, 114, 135,
　136, 138, 152, 182, 338
League of Nations 2–15, 62, 84–5, 93,
　101, 107, 108, 112, 116–40, 150, 188,
　194, 199, 200, 207, 258
League of Nations Union 95
Leger, Alexis 124, 127, 192
Le Ghait, Edouard 240, 263
Leith-Ross, Sir Frederick 187
Lenin 47
Leopold III, King 96, 112, 129, 131,
　132, 174, 175, 176, 323
Levin, Dr 148
L'Humanité 155
Liddell Hart, Basil 227–8
Liebknecht, Karl 47
Lighter-than-air dirigibles 98
Link 51
Lipski 331, 332
Litvinov 14, 255, 256, 257, 258, 292,
　294, 300
Lloyd George 47, 49, 63, 111, 117, 135,
　145, 229
Locarno Agreements 4, 118, 119, 130
Long, Senator Huey P. 77
Lorraine, Sir Percy 278
Ludwig, Emil 30, 32, 34, 145
Luftwaffe 85, 248, 250, 253, 299
Lundberg, Erik 76
Luxemburg, Rosa 47
Lygon, Lady Maud 105
Lytton, Lord 6

MacDonald, Ramsey 7, 15–17, 59, 60,
　93, 136, 154, 183, 226

Macmillan, Harold 18, 109, 114, 233,
　274
Mafalda of Hesse, Princess 87
Maffey Report 103
Maffey, Sir John 103
Maginot Line 130
Maisky, Ambassador 233, 300
Manchurian affair 1–16, 50
Mandchukuo 6
Mandel, Georges 59
Martin du Gard, Roger 23
Martinez, Miguel 168
Martin du Gard, Maurice, 155
Marx, Karl 38, 56
Maurin, General 120
Maurras, Charles 28, 29, 56, 83, 212
Mayrisch, Emile 4
Mein Kampf 39, 40, 43, 44, 60, 61, 66,
　195, 199, 280
Mercier, Cardinal 55
Miaja, General 168
Miklas, President 205
Milch, General Erhard 182, 248
Mill, John Stuart 23
Miller, General 147
Molotov, Polina 304
Molotov, the Hammer 294, 299, 303,
　308, 313
Monnet, George 121
Monte de Pieté 54
Morell, Dr 144
Mosley, Sir Oswald 51, 68, 214
Munich Agreement ix, 235–69
Mussolini, Benito 29, 30–4, 38, 68, 92–
　3, 100–16, 135, 141, 163–4, 165, 166,
　191–94, 204, 214, 242, 278, 279, 284,
　312–13, 333, 335, 340, 341

N.S.D.A.P. (*National-sozialistische
　Deutsche Arbeiterpartei*) 37
National Government 7, 17, 18, 59
National Socialist League 51
National Union for Social Justice 77
National Workers' Party 51
Nazism 58, 61
New Deal 71–82, 94, 159, 171
New York Stock Exchange 5, 72
Nicolson, Harold 7, 210, 229, 274, 341
Night of the Long Knives 65, 200
Nikolaev plot 146
Nine Powers Treaty 5
NKVD 146, 147, 148

Noel, Léon 91, 259
Nuremberg Congress 144

Oberkommando der Wehrmacht (OKW) 196
Olympic Games 141, 142
Open Door doctrine 11
Operation Green 237
Operation Otto 203, 206
Ordre Nouveau 52
Ostmark 206

Pact of Paris 4
Pact of Steel 298, 335
Parti Populaire Français 213
Parti Social Français 213
Parti Socialiste Français 156
Partito Nazionale Fascisto 32
Party Day 143
Peace Ballot 95, 104, 109, 133
Pearl Harbor 78, 295
Péguy, Charles 216
Petacci, Clara 164
Pétain, Marshal 10, 55, 63, 121, 181, 214
Phipps, Sir Eric 127, 208, 272
Pierlot, M. 321
Pietri, Francois 260
Pilsudski, Marshal 61
Plisnier, Charles 52, 56
Plunkett-Ernle-Drax, Admiral Sir Reginald 307–11, 315
Poincaré, Raymond 2, 11, 135
Poland 240, 251, 288, 289, 292, 295, 297, 298, 302, 310, 313, 315, 316, 321, 324, 328, 330–1, 334, 337, 338, 340
Pope Pius XI 241
Pope Pius XII 321, 332
Potemkine, Vladimir 292

Quadragesimo Anno 53

Raubel, Geli 144, 270
Rauschning 62
Rebatet, Lucien 53, 214
Reichstag fire 58, 65
Rentchnick, Pierre 123
Rexism 83

Ribbentrop, Joachim 89, 95, 142, 185, 194, 195, 196, 202, 209, 278, 282, 298, 306, 313, 317–18, 331
Riefenstahl, Leni 142, 143
Rintelen, Anton 67
Röhm, Major 36, 65, 66
Rokossovski, Marshal 168
Rome-Berlin Axis 141, 166
Ronin, Colonel (later General) Georges 89
Roosevelt, President 71–82, 94, 115, 154, 171, 188, 271, 272, 295, 296, 321
Rosenberg, Alfred 40, 88
Rothermere, Lord 61
Rothschild, Baron Louis 205
ROUS 147
Rudiger, Erns 190–1
Ruhr evacuation 3
Ruhr occupation 2, 19
Runciman, Lord 258

SA 65–7, 85, 143, 205
Sarfatti, Margherita 194
Schacht, Dr. 196
Schill, Major 22
Schmidt, General Wilhelm 67
Schmidt, Guido 197, 342
SDP (*Sudeten Deutsche Partei*) 236
Second World War 34, 41, 96, 147, 171, 214
Seyss-Inquart 197, 204, 206
Shaw, Bernard 59
Shirer, William 120, 267
Siegfried Line 130, 247
Simon, Sir John 9, 12, 13, 86–9, 94, 103, 288, 341
Skobline, General N. V. 147
Smigly-Rydz, Marshal 297
Snowdon, Philip 24
Sorel, George 28
Soviet Secret Services 50
Soviet Union 141–53, 166, 255, 257, 258, 291–306, 312, 313
Spaak, Paul-Henri 170, 171, 173, 243, 302
Spain 160–2, 166–9, 241, 266
Spanish Civil War 160–9
Speer, Albert 297, 313, 316
Spender, Stephen 210
Spengler, Oswald 38
SS 85, 143, 205, 206

Stalin, Joseph 48, 94, 139, 141, 145, 146, 148, 149, 213, 304, 316, 317
Stanhope, Lord 208
Starhemberg, Prince 68, 190–1
Stehlin, Captain 292
Steinbeck, John 73
Stempfle, Father 66
Strang, William 258, 270, 300
Stresa Conference 103
Stresa Front 94, 95
Stresemann, Gustav 3
Stresemann, Wolfgang 63
Sudetenland 235, 265
Suez Canal 107
Suvich, Flavio 93

Tardieu, André 11, 14, 15, 20, 121
Taylor, A. J. P. 228
Thibaudet, Albert 91
Thorez, Maurice 59, 150, 152
Trade Union 211, 215, 262, 274
Treaty of Locarno 119, 172
Treaty of Rapallo 64
Treaty of the Nine Powers 5
Treaty of Versailles 1, 12, 26, 85, 86, 118, 177, 246
Trotsky 47, 48, 147
Tukhachevskii, Field Marshal 147, 149

Ual-Ual incident 102
Udet, Ernst 249
United States 282, 295, 296
   New Deal 71–82, 94
USSR *see* Soviet Union

van Overstraeten, Colonel Raoul 126, 174, 178
van Langenhove Fernand 171
Vansittart, Sir Robert (later Lord) 13, 112, 231
van Zeeland, Paul 106, 111, 112, 115, 125, 129–32, 172, 173, 174, 175, 179, 182, 184, 188, 189
van Zuylen, Pierre 170, 171, 177, 182
Victor-Emmanuel III, King 32–3, 112, 115
Voluntaires Nationaux, L'Association de Jeunes Patriotes 53
von Rath, Ernst 281

von Blomberg, General 67, 120, 127, 196
von Brauschitch, General 196
von Bredow, General 66
von der Schulenburg, Count 299, 306, 313–15
von Dirksen, Herbert 306
von Fritsch, General Werner 120, 196
von Hammerstein, General 61
von Herwarth, Johnny 313, 314
von Hoesch 88
von Kahr, Gustav 66
von Kleist-Schmerzin, Ewald 244
von Manstein, Field Marshal Erich 245, 311
von Neurath, Baron 61, 196, 199
von Papen, Franz 15, 22, 66, 68
von Reichenau, General 88
von Ribbentrop, Joachim *see* Ribbentrop, Joachim
von Schleicher, General 15, 22, 66
von Schlieffen, General 252
von Schuschnigg, Kurt 190–1, 197, 203–6
Voroshilov, Marshal 167, 266, 308, 309, 317
Voyage au Bout de la Nuit 49
Vuillemin, General 253

Wagner, Friedeling 67–8
Weimar Republic 18, 21, 44, 64, 69, 117
Weizsäcker 245, 311
Welles, Orson 78
Wells, H. G. 145
Werth, Alexander 300
Weygand, General 63, 121, 322
Wiedmann, Captain 259
Wilson, President 9, 232
Wilson, Sir Horace 245, 267, 301, 324
Winterbotham, Wing-Commander 88
Wohltat, Helmut 301

Yagoda, Jenrihk 148
Yeshov, Nikolai 148

Zay, Jean 168
Zeppelin 98
Zweig, Stefan 205